WEIRD, WILD AND WONDERFUL

WEIRD, WILD AND WONDERFUL

A Naturally Autistic Tale

Stuart Nicklen

Book Guild Publishing
Sussex, England

First published in Great Britain in 2009 by
The Book Guild Ltd
Pavilion View
19 New Road
Brighton, BN1 1UF

Typesetting in Times by
SetSystems Ltd, Saffron Walden, Essex

Printed in Great Britain by
Athenaeum Press Ltd, Gateshead

A catalogue record for this book is
available from the British Library

ISBN 978 1 84624 284 7

Contents

APPENDIXES

PART 1

1

Our Beaming Baby

'Do you want to watch?' the nurse asked with a polite smile.

I was appalled at the idea of watching a loved one being cut open, so I declined and she led me into a big room adjacent to the operating theatre.

In the middle of the room was a large metal table with a clear Perspex cot on top of it. To my right were large swing doors that led into the operating theatre. I noticed a chair among all the medical equipment stored here and flopped down. I was way beyond pacing up and down.

I looked up at the electric clock on the wall; it was now 11.45, nearly midnight and over twenty hours since Ana had awoken me to let me know that our child had decided that it was time.

There were still three weeks to go, but she had been rumbling like a stirring volcano for some time. I could tell from her voice that this was not a false alarm. The roads were empty at that time in the morning, so we were in the Gloucester Royal Hospital within a couple of minutes. The maternity unit was modern and the staff were very pleasant; on the surface it didn't feel like a hospital. We were the first customers of the day, the place was empty and Ana had a choice of what style birthing room to have.

The rest of the day was spent huffing and puffing, then epidurals and gas followed by more huffing and puffing, all to no avail as our child had changed its mind. The midwife confidently predicted that it was going to be a boy.

'Boys are lazy and he's happy where he is. He'll come when he's ready,' she said knowingly.

As the afternoon wore on the birthing room started looking increasingly like a hospital and it was becoming clear that Ana could not take much more—she was exhausted. However, the monitors attached to Ana's belly were telling us that the baby was not stressed at all, in fact it was sleeping comfortably.

Bravely, Ana wanted to persevere, but naturally.

Nobody wanted a Caesarean.

During the pregnancy Ana had developed thrombocytopenia, not in itself dangerous but it did mean that the number of platelets in Ana's and therefore the baby's blood were so low that it would not clot, so the hospital didn't want to operate. Ana did not want a Caesarean either, as she wanted ten babies—or at least she did before today.

But now the alarm had sounded as the baby awoke and became distressed. A full surgical team was quickly assembled with plenty of spare blood on hand, as both mother and child were in danger.

The clock to my left silently ticked up to ten to midnight. Will its birthday be 23 or 24 February 1989, I mused. A few more silent minutes passed before the peace was shattered as the swing doors burst open. In marched a nurse; she gently placed a baby wrapped in a white towel into the clear Perspex cot. She didn't notice me sitting among the medical equipment and quickly returned to the theatre without saying a word. Their concern was for Ana now. Throughout the day we had met many couples, who had arrived and then left with their babies; we were the first and last. This was finally our baby. I froze as I realised that I was now a father.

The baby's head slowly turned around to look directly at me. I was struck by the beautiful round face; it was a boy's face. He had lots of black hair and wide-open big brown eyes. I felt that he was examining me as closely as I was him.

I began to feel uncomfortable. I felt unable to move, pinned back against the chair by the intensity of his stare. What should I do? I wanted to move but felt I shouldn't break this contact. Was I experiencing parental bonding? Nobody had warned me of this.

Newborn babies that I had previously seen on TV cried when they were slapped and then they went to sleep. I had heard no cry and he was very much awake and focusing on me.

Laurence was the name we had chosen for a boy and it was Laurence who broke the impasse by slowly turning his head to face the other way. Relieved, I stood up and walked over to him, but he wasn't interested in me anymore, I was dismissed.

He had a full head of thick black hair on top of a long conical head; he looked like an Egyptian pharaoh. It was five to midnight, so I wished him a happy birthday and apologised for it being so short. He was absolutely gorgeous.

4

The nurse returned and assured me that Ana was going to be OK. The bleeding had stopped and she was going to be transferred to a ward soon to sleep it off. The nurse checked Laurence over and took a bit of blood from his heel. She assured me that his head would quickly return to the normal shape and told me to come back in the morning as they were both doing fine and there was nothing more that I could do here tonight.

It was all over as suddenly as it had begun. I floated out of the hospital into the cold night air. It was snowing. That seemed apt; after all, a star was born this night.

The next morning, mother and baby were fine. Laurence's blood had already normalised and Ana's did the same over the next few weeks. Ana's smile was from ear to ear despite still being in a lot of pain and exhausted. She had what she wanted more than anything else in the world: a healthy baby boy—and she wanted to tell her family in Colombia.

I wheeled her around the hospital to the public payphones and with a handful of pound coins she rang her mother. Ana burst into tears and cried until the money ran out. She had said nothing and I asked her what her mother had said.

'Nothing,' she replied, 'she just cried as well.' I went away to get some more pound coins and we tried again but with exactly the same result. Ana tried several times to interrupt her mother's flow but her mum's crying just made Ana cry as well. It was hopeless so we decided to try again tomorrow once everybody had calmed down, as emotions were clearly running too high.

I put it down to the excitable Latin temperament, but that night I received a telephone call from Ana's sister, Nancy. She was staying in our flat in London while we tried to sell it. She was crying too, as she had heard from Colombia and it was bad news. On the night Laurence was born their sister Luz Maria was murdered.

Luz Maria had stayed with us over Christmas and left us just five weeks previously. She was a pretty woman in the prime of her life, a wonderful bubbly personality with a good business brain as well.

I first met her a few years back in Colombia when we visited to get Ana's parents' blessing. She had a young daughter; she worked hard and had a good job with a very nice car. Unfortunately somebody else wanted her car and she was shot dead whilst sitting at traffic lights on her way home from work.

It was not road rage; it was simple theft and the robber didn't bother to ask. It was all so senseless.

The family were utterly devastated when they received Ana's call. Nobody could talk.

Some horrible no-win decisions had to be taken. We decided that I would tell Ana but not until she was well enough to come home. We would keep the news away from her while she was in the hospital. Somebody in Colombia would have to answer her mum's phone, put on a happy voice and congratulate Ana. During this call I stood behind Ana, expecting the secret to come out, but it didn't. At least she would be able to mourn in the privacy of our own home. All too soon the hospital said that Ana and Laurence could leave, then they checked my baby seat and allowed me to drive home with my most precious cargo. I'm an experienced driver but I still felt very nervous.

Home at this time was a top-floor one-bedroom flat in a large Georgian house on the edge of a park in central Gloucester. The previous year I managed to arrange a transfer to Gloucester at work and we were renting this place until we could sell our flat in London. We had hoped to have sold our flat and bought a house in Gloucester before Laurence was born.

We were renting our flat in London to Nancy to give it a lived-in feel through the winter months, on the understanding that she would have one month's notice once a buyer was found, but it didn't happen.

This flat was not ideal, one flight of stairs to the front door and then a further two flights indoors to our flat. On the plus side it was literally a stone's throw to the health centre and a short walk to the town centre, and our front garden was a huge, beautiful park.

Years later we were to find out that the owners of the garden at the end of our rear garden were the infamous murderers, Rose and Fred West. We were neighbours. I recognised the front of the house as soon as it came on television as I had walked past it most days. We never became friendly and I never saw anything suspicious, but I remembered him as being a very keen DIY man. He was often crashing about both indoors and in the rear garden until late into the evening, but I suspected nothing.

I waited until Ana had settled in and the baby was asleep that evening before breaking the news to her. Her pain was awful to behold. She wanted answers. Answers to questions that I could not answer and the questions that I could answer made the pain no less bearable. She was angry, angry at the crime, angry with me, and angry with her family for concealing the news.

Over the next couple of days she was inconsolable, but despite all this she never neglected Laurence's needs, carrying him and her grief. A heavy burden for a person still recovering from an operation.

Laurence had a good appetite, he put on weight fast and over the next couple of weeks transformed from an Egyptian pharaoh into a Roman Catholic monk as his skull returned to a normal shape and he wore out the thick hair on the back of his head.

He was the star of the show as friends and family paid homage. My mother came over from Essex and stayed for a week, Nancy stayed for a while and my colleagues at work helped me take my annual leave between their stays. There was no such thing as paternity leave in those days.

Ana was soon left alone to look after our month-old baby during the daytime. I was working six days a week managing a busy betting shop. My transfer from London was a promotion, but there was no extra money as I lost the London weighting allowance. However, I had gained a great improvement in the quality of life. I had swapped commuting daily on the 56 bus between Walthamstow and Hackney for a ten-minute walk across the park.

I couldn't have been happier as I walked back to work. The park was illuminated by swathes of bright yellow daffodils, the birds were singing and now I too had an extra mouth to feed. I relished the new challenges ahead.

Ana was not so happy. She still mourned for her sister and she was finding out that Laurence was a very demanding baby. She was struggling to cope with Laurence's need for constant attention. Over the next few months I failed to understand Ana's problems, as did the health visitors and the nurses in the medical centre who checked Laurence's development regularly. They all said that he was progressing quite normally.

Ana noted in his baby book that he smiled for the first time at 2 months and he slept through the night at just 2½ months. Laurence first reached for a toy at 3½ months and began crawling in July at 5 months. All of this was quite nicely within normal parameters.

From as early as six weeks Laurence was supporting his big head easily and he was getting a good view all around him, and in the following weeks he quickly learnt to lift his head even more with the aid of his hands underneath his chest supporting his body. With such an adequate view of his surroundings, he seemed to have no desire to sit up.

Whenever we sat him down on the floor he would prefer to lie down and rest on his back or lie on his stomach and lift his head up to have a look around. From this position, it only took a few kicks and he was crawling of sorts.

We were learning that Laurence did things his own way.

With food, he knew what he wanted and he expected it immediately. If you didn't make enough you had to make some more because he would not give in. Once fed, Laurence was a very happy and alert baby and he interacted well with any visitors and with us. He didn't really play much, he preferred to meditate, but he loved us to play with him and he always wanted more, whether it was shaking one of his rattles or tickles or rough play—he never seemed to tire of attention.

With this never-ending regime of feeding, playing and cleaning, by the time my day off came around Ana was exhausted. All she wanted was a break from him, telling me to take Laurence out for the day so she could have a proper rest.

So began a family tradition. We had a state-of-the-art Maclaren Turbo pushchair with suspension and all the trimmings. It was Laurence's throne; he loved the wind in his face, the traffic, the people, and the people loved him. It wasn't just the shopkeepers who saw him often who made a big fuss of him; it was also complete strangers who would stop to comment.

If Laurence caught someone looking at him in his buggy he would enchant them with his big brown eyes and innocent face. It was as if he was flirting for the attention he craved. Strangers certainly felt a strong urge to respond to him. I called this behaviour 'beaming'— Laurence would beam out to people and they would be hooked, just as I was when we first met.

With all these people commenting on how wonderful Laurence was, it made us very proud parents. He was a 'wow!' child and I was certain he was going to be a star, maybe a bit eccentric but definitely a star.

Ana, on the other hand, had a different perspective. She was running around after Laurence six days a week, she knew him better than anybody and she was not happy. He seemed to be trying to dominate her.

Ana cried as she told me that she felt her beloved son was reading her mind, that he knew what she was doing when they were in separate rooms. As soon as she sat down with a cup of coffee in the lounge, he would cry out from the bedroom. He did this repeatedly. Trying to make light of this, she said that we should have called him Damien.

However, as the summer wore on Ana found it harder and harder to make light of these matters. She complained that nobody listened to her. She claimed that Laurence always put on a good show for the health visitors and for me when I came home from work, but he was different with her. She said that only she could know what a little devil he really was.

I tried but I could not understand her claims — he was just a baby. We all put it down to her grief, as there was obviously nothing wrong with our very popular, beautiful and healthy child.

Everybody said so.

I have to admit that I knew very little about babies, having spent most of my life trying to avoid them. However, Ana grew up in the middle of a family of seven sisters and seven brothers, first helping her mother with the younger siblings and then helping her older brothers and sisters with their children. She was a natural with babies, she loved babies, and she always wanted lots of babies of her own. However, her own ambitions had lowered from ten to three since having Laurence.

At weekends I would try to persuade Ana to come out with Laurence and me. She rarely did so as she preferred to take a break from Laurence, but she did like to visit Prinknash Abbey just outside Gloucester. It is run by a group of Benedictine monks who conduct their services in Latin, just as they do in Colombia. Ana liked to spend time inside the abbey listening to the services and talking to the monks while I entertained Laurence in the surrounding gardens and bird park.

Sadly Ana was to find no answers to her grief here.

In August I noticed they were holding the British Open Horse Trials at Gatcombe Park, which wasn't far away. Ana was interested in the royal family, so she came along with us. It was a very good day out; besides the cross-country course, there was a large arena surrounded by stalls selling arts and crafts, food, and of course equestrian items. Inside the arena bands regularly marched up and down between displays of motorcycles, police dogs and parachutes, among other things.

As I struggled to push and pull Laurence around the cross-country course in his throne, I had to marvel at the athleticism of the horses competing.

While we were watching a horse traversing a tricky triple fence I noticed out of the corner of my eye Ana recoiling away from us as if she had been stung. I turned around to see a TV camera on a cherry picker zooming down, pointing at us. Laurence was beaming again and Ana need not have worried about her windswept hair. The cameraman was only interested in Laurence.

At six months old, Laurence was a big baby. He started out in life under the average weight of three kilos and now he was nearly ten kilos; only 1 in 20 babies would be bigger. Laurence had been crawling now for a couple of weeks and was getting around quite well.

He started teething early—he seemed to take the pain quite well and his first two teeth popped up one after the other at the end of August. Ana had been forced to give up breast-feeding at three months because of his firm gums and his preference for chewing rather than sucking.

Laurence was cooing, giggling and making all sorts of funny noises, so we felt it was only a matter of time before we would get a 'mama' or 'dada' and we gave him lots of encouragement.

Laurence's playing still seemed a bit unusual, as he preferred to lie on his back, seemingly meditating with his fingers rather than playing with any toys. However, he was still more than happy for us to interrupt and play with him.

I do remember whilst playing peek-a-boo with Laurence getting an uneasy feeling that he did not really understand the game, he just enjoyed the attention.

I could not let such a silly little feeling upset my first wonderful summer of parenthood.

The cold winds of autumn blew in some harsh realities about our situation. Ana was feeling isolated in Gloucester. She had made a few new friends but with Laurence getting heavier by the day, the stairs to our flat were becoming a mountainous obstacle to her going out and socialising.

Nothing had happened with our flat in London and it was becoming clear that we were not going to be able to sell our flat while Nancy was living in it. The rent she was paying had now reduced to a trickle and we were falling behind with the mortgage.

With Ana protecting her sister from me asking for more rent, it was becoming clear that we would have to take the flat off the market and move back in.

Our London flat was a two-bedroom first-floor maisonette in Walthamstow. It was in a quiet tree-lined residential road with a register office at one end and the Samaritans at the other. Our flat was nearer the Samaritans' end.

It was a short walk to the shops, medical centre and schools, and with an extra bedroom and only one flight of stairs it would be a big improvement for Ana. Also, if we were living in London, both Nancy and my mother would be able to give her more support.

An old friend in London had offered me work. I didn't fancy the job as it meant going back to my old career in contract cleaning management. That meant working long anti-social hours but it was more money, which would be useful when it came to repaying the mortgage arrears.

Ana agreed that we should move back to London where she had more friends, but what she really wanted to know was when we would be going to Colombia. She needed to see her mother and family soon; she wanted to show them their new grandson and they had a lot to talk about. Hopefully at the same time she would get a few tips from wise old Grandma on how to handle a child like Laurence.

It was clear from the nature of my new job that I would not be able to take a long holiday once I started, so if we were to go in the near future we would have to go before I began.

By November I had sorted out the passports, organised the inoculations and I had arranged a bank loan to pay for the holiday. I handed my notice in and agreed to work until Christmas. I would start my new job at the beginning of February.

All I had to do now was do a deal with the building society over the mortgage arrears, with the promise of more money in February. The building society was not giving me any extra time but nothing could stop us now. We were going to Colombia and I would have to sort the fininicial mess out when we got back.

I finished work three days before Christmas. Although I had been there for only a year, I had made some good friends. We made a good team, in and out of work time. It was a sad last walk home across the leaf-strewn park that had so gloriously welcomed Laurence in the spring. It had given us many happy afternoons and evenings throughout that summer. I liked Gloucester.

We decided that Laurence should spent his first Christmas in surroundings that he knew. We were flying to Colombia on 28th allowing us to spend Christmas Day and Boxing Day in Gloucester, travel to London with the last of our belongings on the 27th ready to fly out from Heathrow the next day.

Christmas comes alive when children are around and so it did that year. Obviously, Laurence didn't understand what was going on around him but he thoroughly enjoyed all the extra attention he was getting.

On the 27th, we headed off to London leaving our flat empty but still resplendent with Christmas decorations.

Our flat in London was a mess. I had dropped off carloads of rarely used but essential possessions on previous weekends without stopping to sort them out before returning to Gloucester. Our luggage was already packed with summer clothes and ready to go, so it was just a matter of sorting out all Laurence's paraphernalia and trying to get some sleep. This mess could be left until next year as well.

I first went to Colombia five years ago to meet Ana's family and get their approval for our marriage. That done, some of the younger members of Ana's family and I went trekking in the wilder more remote parts of Colombia.

It was a real adventure travelling across the Andes and beyond the final army outpost into Marxist guerrilla-controlled territory. We passed through several spaghetti-western-like towns and then, travelling mainly by boat as there were no roads, we went 500 years back in time staying in some thatched wooden huts in a jungle clearing next to an Indian settlement. We lived off the land with no electricity or toilets, the only running water being the nearby river.

I was told that the only gringo the local people had seen before was a missionary and so with my beard I was considered a missionary. The locals gave me a wide berth. I think it was a case of once bitten, twice shy.

It was tough and fulfilling. I lost a stone in weight but it was the experience of a lifetime. It was a different way of life; it was real life. I would not be going native on this trip as I had responsibilities now.

Considering the length of the journey and the fact that the cot supplied by the airline to hook on the wall in front of us was much too small for Laurence's bulk, the journey went well with no real problems. Laurence behaved himself throughout. He loved to stand on my lap looking over my shoulder, gurgling and beaming at the rows of heads behind us.

Colombia is a roughly square-shaped country, sitting between the equator and the tropic of Cancer. The climate varies greatly around the country depending on the altitude. It has coastlines on the Caribbean and the Pacific Ocean where it is very hot. Ana's home city, Medellin, is cooler as it is situated in a large valley halfway up the Northern Andes. Some people call Medellin 'The City of Flowers' in 'The Land of Eternal Spring', while others call it 'The Cocaine Capital of the World'.

Ana's family had moved since our last visit, downsizing the family home, as the children were now setting up homes of their own. Her parents now lived on the top floor of an eight-storey tower block in a semi-residential part of the city. It seemed a far cry from the sprawling house in the quiet suburbs of five years ago but I soon saw the benefits.

There were just two large flats on each floor and Ana's family had the entire top floor. Her parents had one flat and her eldest sister Mercedes had the other. There was a lift to the ground floor where a 24-hour security guard sat in the reception and there was a supermarket nearby that did home deliveries. It was an excellent arrangement for Ana's ageing parents in this dangerous city.

Over the next couple of days I was quite happy to sit out on one of the balconies, relaxing with a beer watching the hustle and bustle of the city below, while Ana and her family caught up with five years of gossip.

From our safe vantage point on a roof in the centre of the valley, this was a vibrant, glistening, money-soaked city to live in. However, down on the ground and up in the shantytowns clinging on to the mountainsides there was a different view. Away from the lights a vicious war was being fought where a life was worth as little as $100. Twenty murders in one night was not big news in this beautiful but deadly city.

Ana's father was a big bear of a man with a huge hug, filled with warmth. Escaping from the women, he would come out onto the balcony to join me. He would just sit and talk. He knew that I could not follow his rapid talking but that didn't seem to matter to him. I wished I had put more effort into my 'learn at home in 24 hours' Spanish course. This man had a lifetime of experiences to tell me.

Ana was born in the countryside and they were very poor. He had

13

brought his young dependants into this city and worked hard all his life providing for his ever-expanding family. He could now look back with pride as all of his children, without exception, had grown up in this violent city without succumbing to the ever-present lure of crime or drugs. He was an excellent role model for his children and most certainly a wise old man.

Ana's mother on the other hand was a small wiry woman. It was difficult to imagine how she could have had the strength to bring up all those children but she was still full of energy, always fussing around doing something and nowadays being told off by her daughters for not resting more. If anybody could give Ana advice on Laurence then it would be her.

I didn't see much of Laurence whilst we were in Colombia as there was always an auntie or niece wanting to make a fuss of him. He was beaming and he lapped up all the extra attention.

Ana's brothers and sisters took turns to show me different attractions in Medellin and the stunning Andean countryside.

We spent a week in Cartagena on Colombia's Caribbean coast. As a boy I had read books and seen films about the good old English pirates stealing the nasty Spaniard's gold from around the Spanish Main. It was too hot for Laurence to go but Ana's mum and a couple of her sisters quickly volunteered to look after him.

It was Ana's first real break from Laurence and an excellent opportunity for her to relax. We knew that Laurence had been all right during our stay in Cartagena as Ana had insisted on queuing for the pay phone each evening, just to check, but it was still great to see him safe and sound on our return. Laurence on the other hand appeared quite unfazed by our return; he was happy before we returned and he was happy after we returned. For the first time I felt that the hugs were only one way. Why did I worry like this when everybody, including Ana's mother, agreed that we were very lucky to have such a big, healthy and happy baby boy.

Laurence was now eleven months old and we had hoped that he might take his first steps or say his first word for his grandmother but he wasn't interested in trying to walk or talk.

It was a very sad farewell at Medellin airport. I sincerely hoped that one day I would be able to return to this magical but dangerous city.

2

New Beginnings

Our flat felt cold and had a damp, unlived-in feel. Nancy had cleared out. There was a pile of bills on the doormat and no food in the fridge. It was raining. I discovered that I had lost my prized Panama hat that Ana's father had given me, I had a raging toothache and I had to start my new job the very next day.

We were both wondering why we had bothered coming back at all.

I could not phone in sick on my first day in the new job. I didn't want Mick thinking that I was abusing his friendship as he had already waited for over two months for me to start.

Mick owned his own small office-cleaning business. He had recently started to rent some offices and wanted the business to expand. It would be my job to take over the day-to-day running of the cleaning contracts and Mick had also employed a salesman to get the new business he needed for the expansion.

I had to be in the centre of London before 6.00 a.m. dealing with the morning cleaners, checking that everything was done properly before seeing the clients when they turned up for work after 9.00 a.m. I would then pop into the office in Tottenham for paperwork and stores before heading home for a few hours off in the afternoon. I would return to work later to supervise the evening cleaners until about 9.00 p.m. I didn't like the split shifts, but the money was good and I had a company van. I was a white van man.

Having the use of a van meant that I could sell my car, my trusty old Saab which had never let me down despite its enormous mileage. I didn't get much for it, but what I did get I gave to my building society, whose needs were clearly greater than mine. There had been no threats of bailiffs before Christmas but in the new year the menacing demands had thudded onto our doormat and I had not been there to hear them.

I could not expect any sympathy or patience if I told the truth to explain my silence for the month of January, whereas now I was on the phone nearly every day pleading for more time. It was my plan to protract proceedings long enough to show that regular repayments were being made, but it was tough as I also had to make regular repayments to the bank for the holiday loan.

I had hoped that after the holiday with her family, Ana would settle into a more normal relationship with Laurence but she still complained that he was an exceptionally difficult child. She was desperately worried that there was something seriously wrong, but our GP, the health visitor and I could see nothing wrong with him.

Laurence was approaching his first birthday when out of the blue he decided that it would be quicker to go across the lounge rather than walking around it, holding on to the walls. He ran from one side of the lounge to the other, landing on the settee. After getting Ana in I called Laurence over to me in the armchair and he ran back across the lounge, landing in a heap in my lap. Laurence was a natural runner. Within a week he was running all over the flat, but he still wasn't walking.

Yet again he had reached a developmental milestone at the right time but in his own way.

He was bouncing off the walls, the furniture and us without seemingly doing any damage to himself or causing him to try to slow down. 'Walk' became the most commonly used word in our family. In the time you could say, 'Laurence walk please' he would already be where he wanted to be and so it became a loud, 'Walk!'

Laurence's high-speed life needed high-speed communication but it made no difference to his behaviour. We said, 'Walk', 'Walk', 'Walk' all day and Laurence ran everywhere all day.

If you stood him on the ground and let go he was like a toy car with wheels that you spin round faster and faster before releasing. They would both shoot off in the direction that you pointed them in.

He was a funny child.

We did not consider him to be hyperactive, as when he finally did run out of petrol he would just lie down and meditate peacefully for hours until he succumbed to sleep. He was simply a very happy, contented, stubborn child who liked to get where he was going fast.

He was a thrill seeker; he loved the feel of the wind on his face not just outside but indoors as well. He would scream and laugh at the same time as I spun him round or threw him in the air. He always wanted more than was good for him.

Ana gathered some friends and family for Laurence's first birthday party. I didn't take time off work, as we needed the money. I felt that first birthday parties are really for the mums to have a good gossip and compare notes, so I left them to it.

Later that night we discussed our main concern about Laurence, his lack of speech. They had been talking about it earlier and Ana was now really concerned about how quiet Laurence was. He had a few onomatopoeic words like 'broom broom' but that was it. Ana spoke to our GP, who said that it was much too early to start worrying about that sort of thing.

We bought flash cards with pictures and words and whenever we could get Laurence's attention we would work on him, but we couldn't get him interested very often or for any length of time. Similarly, Laurence did not seem interested in books, of which he had many.

He was, however, interested in simple jigsaw puzzles and was quite good at them. He liked to play with bricks, stacking them up and then knocking them down; he was quite good at that too. However, he was quite hopeless stacking the beakers, the ones that can be fitted inside each other; he just didn't seem to have any concept of bigger and smaller.

I remember testing this idea with broken rusks, offering him a piece from each hand. The size didn't seem to matter to Laurence as he always took the rusk from the nearest hand. However, all I could really conclude from this test was that Laurence was not greedy.

Now that we had moved back to London my mum was able to visit more often, and whenever she did she always had a pile of things for Laurence. He was my mum's first grandchild and she wasn't going to let him want for anything.

As a substitute for the lack of grandchildren she kept Dalmatians, usually two or three. The dogs were always excited on their visits and charged around the flat. This behaviour reminded me of Laurence's frantic antics.

Laurence enjoyed stroking them and sitting on their backs. Initially he seemed relaxed in their company and dangerously oblivious to their fast wagging tails.

It was a different matter when we were out. If I shooed away some pigeons with Laurence in the pushchair he would hold up his hands and wince as they flapped away. It would only take a pigeon to walk towards him and he would run back to me for protection.

My son was a wimp.

I had managed to drag out the discussions over the mortgage arrears into March, but the building society's patience was exhausted. They wanted our flat; my small but regular repayments did not impress them and they would listen to no more sob stories. Only immediate full repayment of the arrears would stop them repossessing the flat. We had no choice—we had to re-mortgage.

It meant that we could repay the bank loan and the building society, keeping a roof over our heads. However, it also meant that we lost all the equity in our property, which was effectively the deposit for our family home. We were already feeling cramped in our two-bedroom flat. Laurence was so full of energy he needed space to run around, he needed a garden. After remortgaging we would probably be stuck here for at least three years, depending on property prices.

I had hated being in debt with all the associated humiliating grovelling that I had had to put myself through. It was going to be a tough few years, nothing like the future that we had originally planned for ourselves in Gloucester, but we did now have a fresh start.

Through the spring and summer a familiar family routine developed. I was working usually six days a week, splitting my spare time between DIY and playing with Laurence. Ana was at home full-time and still struggling to cope with Laurence. He was exhausting her. If he wasn't demanding attention then he was requiring attention. Within seconds he could be anywhere in the flat and he seemed to be fearless. Or was he?

Laurence had his own way of getting down stairs, head first on his stomach. This form of body surfing made him appear totally fearless. However, during the hours I spent trying to train him to safely crawl down backwards I realised that he was totally terrified of not being able to see where he was going. To him, the safest way down was his way, eyes first.

I was beginning to recognise that he had an odd way of thinking.

When I came home from work in the afternoons I would take

Laurence out for a walk. That would please both Ana and Laurence. He thoroughly enjoyed being pushed to the park or the shops. He would be beaming as he sat in his mobile throne, but Londoners seemed to be immune.

I was not going to be his chauffeur all the time so I made him walk until he was too tired. I wanted to wear him out before returning him to Ana. Laurence enjoyed running along the pavement. I always kept myself and the pushchair between him and the road. It was not a problem to keep up with him because at every open garden gate he would stop and close it.

He wouldn't go past an open garden gate and he was soon able to run all the way from our flat to the park on the next block, closing all the gates along the way without the help of the pushchair. Yet he never bothered to close a door indoors.

It was weird. I remember some of the gates were difficult for him to close and all of them were bigger than he was, but he persevered. Nobody complained about their gate being closed and I couldn't see any harm in it so I let him carry on.

I was beginning to think of Laurence as my puppy. Indoors the training was starting to have an effect. The command 'Walk' was beginning to work. He would shoot off and we'd say, 'Walk' and he would slow down to a walk before running off again to his destination. At least we were slowing him down at the most dangerous part of his journey, when he was changing rooms.

We now knew that he could understand some of what we were saying.

Like all puppies, Laurence loved to play and with two of us at home he would run between us for attention. If I sat down in the armchair he would come over and climb on my lap but he wouldn't sit there. He would silently keep on climbing up onto my shoulders and he even tried to balance on my head. He loved to get a good view. It was impossible to ignore him; he liked having rides on my shoulders, horsey rides, being rolled over, being chased, having scary tickles and any other form of rough play that we might have stumbled upon.

When I sat down tired he would just start silently climbing up on top of me again. Sitting on my shoulders, he would rock back and forwards as an unmistakable sign for me to get up and give him another ride; he was remorseless. He didn't seem to see me as a parent; I was his interactive plaything. It was only when he was too tired to play with us that he would settle down with his jigsaws and bricks, but still he showed no interest in books.

He would give a book a brief glance, chew on it and contemptuously throw it over his shoulder. He was still teething but he rarely complained. He would prefer to gnaw on his wooden bricks or chew a toy than munch on some soggy cardboard book.

While I was beginning to feel like his plaything his mum had felt for a long time that she was just his dresser, cleaner and cook and like all puppies he had a big appetite and a marvellous ability to make a mess out of anything.

He loved his food and seemed to take particular delight in slowly disintegrating it in his fingers. He would crumble it onto his plate before holding it to his nose and finally putting it in his mouth. He was a very messy eater. When we tried to give him a spoon he expected us to feed him. If I held the spoon in his hand he would politely allow me to feed him but as soon as it was left to him he would drop the spoon and carry on eating with his hands.

Everything went into Laurence's mouth. If he considered it was edible, it went down; if not, he spat it out. We quickly learned that Laurence was a good judge of what he could and could not swallow. Despite all our concerns he rarely made himself sick.

Above all else our puppy liked his walkies but he was becoming much too agile to be allowed to run freely so we kept his wrist tied to a lead until he was safely in a park. Other people's puppies urinated up against the gatepost along the way, whereas my clever puppy closed their gates.

At first Laurence didn't mind where I took him just so long as it was out of the flat. We all enjoyed going shopping; we were becoming very proud parents indeed, silently tut-tutting as other parents struggled to cope with their unruly terrible two's in the supermarket. We thought that our son could never be like that as he was much too quiet.

I started taking Laurence further and further afield, travelling on the buses and the Underground. Laurence enjoyed travelling on the top deck of buses, standing on the seat watching the scene below; but most of all he liked the Underground.

I could feel the excitement in the air as we heard the distant rumble of a train down the tunnel. As the train approached it felt like Laurence would explode. His small body would start jumping up and down on the spot whilst squeezing my hand trying to relieve the pressure. Once the train burst onto the platform the pressure was released, and Laurence would calm down and sit attentively on the train, studying the stations as they passed. Between stations Laurence would sit quietly beaming at the other passengers. There was no escape; they could not avoid his gaze and the compliments flowed in.

So Londoners were not immune to Laurence's beaming. They avoided looking at other people in the street, but sitting on a tube train, they were trapped.

We would travel to different parks near stations and once there he enjoyed the swings and being bounced up and down on the seesaw. Laurence did not appear to like slides or the baby climbing frames, but what he did like most was the wide-open spaces to run in. On windy days he would run into the wind, gulping the air. The wind had to be tested in his mouth just like everything else.

He seemed to be having so much fun that he didn't appear to notice the other children playing in the parks and occasionally he literally bumped into them.

It was on one of these trips to the park that Laurence spoke his first word, 'Gudju.' Laurence was approaching eighteen months old and we were getting desperate for a word. But what was gudju? I looked in the same direction as him. Where was gudju? We were looking across the park—there was a fence then a road with parked cars with houses behind and a few trees, but I could not see anything like gudju. I pointed in the general direction saying gudju, gudju, but Laurence had lost interest.

This excited me and when we got home I asked Ana if she could think of any Spanish connections. I suggested that maybe Laurence had picked up on Ana swearing in Spanish after discovering yet another mess that he had created.

She didn't swear and there were no Spanish connections, she assured me.

Laurence continued to occasionally use gudju and each time it felt like it was directed at us, unlike all the other sounds that he made, which felt like they were floating on the wind. We were desperate for any verbal contact. So what was gudju? Laurence was giving us no further clues. We needed another word or some sign from him to make any further progress, as we were baffled.

It was another sunny summer's afternoon in the park when Laurence gave me that sign. Laurence was sitting on his throne as we were about to leave when he started chanting, 'Gudju . . . gudju . . . gudju,' in a deep rhythmic way. I looked towards Laurence; he was pouting his lips as he pushed the words out. 'Gudju . . . gudju,' he continued. He had his head back and was looking straight up in the air. I followed his gaze; it was a clear blue sky and there wasn't a cloud in view.

'Gudju,' Laurence seemed to emphasise and I looked again. There was a minute plane without a white trail travelling across the clear blue sky. It was flying very high, definitely not landing in this country, or maybe it was a military jet. Was this small black dot gudju or was it the clear blue sky or even the breeze? I pointed up at the jet and said, 'Gudju.'

'Gudju,' Laurence replied and, raising his arm up, he pointed just like me.

'Gudju,' we said as the penny finally dropped. Laurence wasn't just eccentric—he did have a problem. Ana instinctively knew when Laurence was a few months old and now I had to agree with her because that was the first time that Laurence had ever pointed at anything.

I couldn't understand why I hadn't noticed this before and the past year flashed before me. We were always pointing out things to him quite naturally without giving it any thought and yet Laurence had never pointed at his food or toys or people or even the dreaded pigeons.

Although Laurence didn't speak or point in order to communicate, we still knew what he wanted. It felt like we had been trained to look after his needs and it seemed that we were doing quite a good job because he rarely complained even though he was a non-stop exhausting child. We could read him like a book, an open book, and we were impatiently waiting for another word to fall out, as surely gudju would open the floodgates.

(We eventually established that gudju did mean aeroplane, using photos from a book.)

With all the attention on Laurence's speech, we had no reason to give any thought to his MMR vaccination. At eighteen months it was, after all, just another inoculation and he'd had so many. He had screamed with his earlier jabs and this was no exception.

'You would think we were trying to kill him,' Ana reported. 'He fought the nurse and he screamed the place down.' He was becoming a very strong little boy.

As the autumn nights closed in we conceived our second child and the morning after the night before, Ana was sick. A second day of sickness confirmed our fears that Ana was due for nine months of illness. We didn't need a pregnancy test—Laurence had set the pattern with nine months of sickness, but this time round she would have to cope with him as well.

It was going to be a miserable winter for Ana and now we both knew that Laurence had something missing and it might be serious. But what exactly was he missing? There was no doubting Laurence's eyesight was good after the gudju incident, but what about his hearing? He only seemed to hear what he wanted to hear and he shut out everything else.

Ana spoke to our GP, who again reassured her that there was nothing to worry about and that Laurence was probably a bit delayed due to him trying to learn two languages around the home. We immediately dropped the Spanish at home; we would give him every bit of help that we could to get him through this barrier.

As we tried to get Laurence into the habit of pointing we found that he grasped the concept of pointing quite quickly but he insisted on using our hands to point with.

For example, if I was sitting in the lounge, Laurence might silently pull on my arm and lead me by the arm to the kitchen where he would place my hand on the fridge door handle. Letting me open the door he would take my hand again and point my finger at what he wanted inside the fridge, maybe a yoghurt. He would then stand back and wait to be handed the yoghurt, repeating the actions if he considered I was too slow in following his instructions.

Were we too stupid to know when he wanted yoghurt so that he had to get up and show us what we should be doing?

It certainly felt like we were being trained.

With the worsening weather, and feeling weaker as the pregnancy wore on, Ana was struggling to take Laurence out. Cooped up indoors while I was at work, Laurence and Ana were becoming stressed.

At home, Laurence was no longer building tall towers with his bricks. Instead he would stack no more than two or three bricks before smashing them across the room with a great sweep from his arm. His jigsaw-puzzle pieces were breaking as he persistently tapped the pieces in place with his knuckles. Laurence used to enjoy his Thomas the Tank Engine video. Remarkably he had effortlessly learnt how to use the video recorder, but now he was only interested in one scene, the crash scene.

He would repeatedly play the same scene, rocking back and forth while tapping. In fact, whenever he was stationary he was now tapping something against something else or just tapping with his knuckles. His eccentricities were definitely worsening.

Probably the most dramatic change came in Laurence's eating habits. He became fanatical about spillages; if he knocked his drink over he would start panicking and screaming. It would take lots of coaxing and reassurance before we could calm him down and return to the table.

He went from scoffing everything and anything that he alone considered edible, to eating only white foodstuffs. He went from being the first to finish, to last to finish, to not finishing at all as he would sit eating a bowl of rice one grain at a time, stopping every few grains to tap on the plate. After a couple of weeks of living on rice, fish and milk, even peeled apples weren't white enough. We were getting worried and Ana took him to the GP again.

The doctor laughed at Ana's concerns when he saw Laurence. He told Ana that he was clearly a very healthy energetic little boy, a little overweight, but definitely thriving on his food. He said he could see no reason why we should try to change his diet. 'If he's happy, let him carry on,' he said.

Regardless of the weather, once I'd returned home from work for the afternoon I would take Laurence out of the flat for some exercise. He seemed to revel in the weather, running in the wind, licking the rain, splashing in the puddles and eating the snow, he loved it all.

It was not all plain sailing, however, as Laurence grew tired of his quest to close everybody's garden gate. He had found himself a more important job—checking manhole covers. Laurence would bend down and tap each manhole cover with his knuckles, even the tiny BT ones. I never noticed before how many of those damn things there are along a residential pavement. As I was always holding his hand, the constant stopping, stooping and starting was very annoying.

Why couldn't they be like garden gates, with just one utility cover per house? If allowed, Laurence would give each cover a thorough examination, but I would slowly continue walking, gently pulling him behind me, hurrying him along until we eventually reached a compromise where he would only give each cover a quick single tap.

When I returned home from work after the evening shift Laurence would hopefully, for Ana's sake, be in bed. Too tired to resist being put to bed, he would lie there resisting falling asleep. Other people might say he was waiting for his daddy to come home, but we knew otherwise. He had always done this and we felt he needed these quiet hours to reflect on the day's adventures. I would go in to say night night and try not to get him excited and then leave him alone to meditate in peace. Laurence was still asleep when I left for work at 5.30 each morning.

It was to be the same story for Christmas and then Laurence's second birthday. Ana was feeling awful. We tried to put on a good show for Laurence, but whatever we did he didn't notice it. He blanked the decorations and didn't understand the concept of presents at all. Laurence didn't understand possessions full stop.

If I took something he was playing with he would silently move on to something else without complaint and if there was food on my plate that he wanted he would just help himself in complete innocence.

So when it came to giving Laurence a present, it was a matter of whether it was an interesting item to tap or not. When we tried to show him how to open a present he got upset when we started tearing off the wrapping paper and when we did manage to carefully open a present he was more interested in the wrapping paper than the toy. He made no sense.

I took Laurence to see the Christmas lights in the West End on the Underground. No matter how many times we travelled on the Underground he still got ridiculously over-excited whenever a train approached. Holding on to him tightly by the hand, I could tell that he was jumping up and down for maximum height rather than trying to jump rhythmically. He would also flap his spare arm up and down much faster than he was jumping.

Once seated on the train, I soon found that my elbow could overlap onto Laurence's seat and discreetly pin his shoulder to prevent him rocking with excitement. He did not object and proceeded to beam at our fellow passengers. Compliments about Laurence's face, smile or eyes were common, but the most popular comment of all was, 'Is this his first trip?'

I could tell that even more people than said it were convinced by Laurence's look of excited innocence that he was seeing the Underground for the first time, when in fact he was a regular traveller.

Laurence's beaming gave many travellers a memorable journey.

As soon as our train started slowing down as it approached Walthamstow, he would stand up ready to get off, and one day as we disembarked a suited gent with a leather briefcase approached us and, apologising for the intrusion, asked in a posh voice, 'Is his name Henry?'

Sensing no danger, I told him that it was Laurence.

He stepped back, looked down at Laurence and said with a smile of approval, 'Yes, first class,' and disappeared into the throng of commuters at the bottom of the escalator. Laurence had been beaming again, but God knows what ideas he had managed to put into that chap's head.

One day we were travelling on an Underground line that we hadn't been on before. As the train approached our connecting station Laurence stood up to get off while we were still in the tunnel. I wondered how he knew that it was time to get off. He must have been following the line map on the train, which meant that he was reading the station's names.

Over the next few weekends I tested Laurence by travelling all over the network. I would say to him, 'Going home now,' and he always knew the way home. I couldn't lose him even if I wanted to. I followed his line of sight; he focused on the station names on the platforms as we passed by, his eyes flicking faster and faster as we left each station.

He wasn't talking but he was reading at two years of age. Laurence was getting more and more confusing as each discovery about him was made.

We shouldn't have wasted our money buying Laurence toys when a simple free Underground map gave him hours of pleasure tapping the map or tapping something else with the map. I learned to keep a reserve supply of maps because he wore them out very quickly and he carelessly often lost these treasured possessions.

Following on from Laurence's birthday comes spring, with its better weather and more opportunities for walking around above ground rather than travelling underground.

Whilst out on these walks I found that Laurence had a good

memory for our routes. When we were walking along the road he would lean in to me to indicate for us to cross the road or turn left, and he would pull me to turn right.

But the clever part was the intensity of his pushes. At either end of our road he would only gently push in his preferred direction, as there were different places in each direction that he would like to visit. However, towards the end of a long walk where the options were either left to the park or right into unknown territory, Laurence would push my thigh with all his might to go left.

Over the following months I was able to build up a pretty good idea of Laurence's likes and dislikes. By changing the routes I was able to calculate his preferences. I started to push back. We were communicating, sometimes going where he wanted and sometimes where I wanted.

Throughout this Laurence quietly continued tapping the utility covers wherever we went and he also developed an obsession with crossing the roads in exactly the same spot each time. I quickly realised that this would not be good in the long term and I set about upsetting the habit.

Knowing where his favoured crossing points were, I would cross over early, taking him by surprise if a safe opportunity arose. Laurence would quite politely start pushing gently as we approached a favoured crossing point but once past it he would rapidly increase pressure and become more anxious. I made a point of walking at least one or two metres past his favoured crossing point, careful not to raise his anxiety levels too high. Over the years Laurence learnt to live with irregular crossing points. At two years old he couldn't do any harm, but in a few years' time I didn't want him pushing Mummy or Nanny into the road because I had crossed there the previous week.

Ana had many visits to the GP during the pregnancy. They had to monitor her condition closely. It was on one of these routine visits that Laurence started to get bored and began removing all the books from the doctor's bookshelves. The doctor, seeing that Laurence was doing no harm, allowed him to continue until there were no more books left on the shelves. With all the books heaped up in a pyramid on the floor, Laurence then began to put them back onto the shelves.

The doctor was amazed, it looked like Laurence had replaced every single book in exactly the same position as they had been before, but he couldn't be one hundred per cent sure as he couldn't remember the exact layout himself. But Laurence wasn't happy; he was anxious, desperately looking around the floor until he found what he was looking for, a book that had slid down the pyramid and been hidden in the shadows under the GP's desk. Laurence placed it in its correct position on the shelf and sat down contentedly rocking and tapping his knuckles.

He had made his point.

The GP had ignored Ana's concerns for the past eighteen months but now he listened to Laurence's silent demonstration. Whilst assuring Ana that it was still much too early to be worrying about such things, he agreed to refer Laurence to a specialist. We weren't worried — we were relieved that somebody else would now be looking at Laurence, and maybe now we would start to get some answers.

The speech therapist whom Laurence was referred to quickly realised that his problem was more than a simple language delay. I think his violent aversion to going anywhere near her office might have tipped her off. She referred Laurence to a centre nearby where he would be assessed by a wide range of professionals, without actually examining him herself.

We would get our answers there, she assured us; however, we would have to wait another three months for an appointment. In the meantime she gave us a few tips on how to develop Laurence's attention skills and suggested we put Laurence in a playgroup.

Ana had been trying to get Laurence in a play scheme for a long time to no avail. The good ones didn't want Laurence and the not-so-good ones were content to leave him sitting in the corner tapping and rocking, just waiting for Mummy to come back. Ana preferred no relief rather than allow Laurence to suffer the abuse of neglect. She asked the speech therapist if she could exert some pressure in the right places.

At home things were going from bad to worse for Ana, as the thrombocytopenia had returned. This poor woman who had so much wanted to have lots of babies seemed to be living in a body that was allergic to having them. The hospital decided to try to maintain Ana's platelet count with regular transfusions. However, as Ana grew bigger her platelet count inevitably shrank, no matter how many times she went to the hospital.

Laurence enjoyed his trips to the hospital with Mum as there is a forest nearby, but Mum didn't enjoy taking Laurence with her. He appeared oblivious to Ana's condition, her bump being no more than a climbing aid. We tried to explain to him what was about to happen but he showed no interest or understanding. He expected Ana to carry on as usual and he was relentless. Ana vowed she would never go through this living hell again; this baby would be her last.

The operating theatre was booked; nothing was being left to chance. Ana spent the last week in hospital hooked up to a drip, but still her platelet count hovered just above zero. The doctors had lost the battle. It would be dangerous for Ana.

The date that the doctors had decided to put Ana out of her misery was 12 June 1991. Laurence waited impatiently with me. He wanted to go to the forest that he knew was just outside the hospital. He didn't have a clue as to what we were waiting for.

It wasn't long before a nurse brought our baby girl out of the theatre. She had lots of dark hair and looked just like Laurence had but she was a special baby, she was a normal baby. She had cried and then half opened one eye before screwing up her pretty face with a yawn and quickly falling back to sleep. I knew that this little girl would not turn into a Damienella, which had been Ana's biggest fear.

Bianca was the name Ana had chosen for a girl, and over the previous nine months she had earned the right to call the baby whatever she wanted. I showed Laurence his new sister but he wasn't impressed, although I am sure he would have given her a tap with his knuckles if I'd given him a chance. He pulled me in the direction of the exit and I tried to explain that we had to wait to see Mummy, who was still in the operating theatre. Laurence ran up and down the corridor as I paced up and down the waiting area.

It was over an hour later before Ana came out of the theatre. Still hooked up to the drips and wired up to a monitor that clattered along beside her trolley, Ana lay motionless. She had lost a lot of blood and her skin was white; she had been through a lot but she had made it. Ana was right—she couldn't go through this again. I didn't know if she could hear me, but I walked beside the trolley telling her that Bianca was fine and that I was sure she was going to be a normal baby. That would be music to her ears as they wheeled her away into the lift.

I picked up Laurence and said goodbye to Bianca, who was still sleeping. We walked to the forest and I gave him a celebratory run about followed by a big ice cream.

That way we could both be in a happy frame of mind.

3

Labelled

A few days before Bianca's birth I was sitting at home reading the newspaper with Laurence tapping on an Underground map beside me. Ana was in hospital. I noticed a women's interest story about a mother and her son. I would not normally have given it a second glance, but something caught my eye and I read on.

She described a child with wild behaviours and strange routines. There were some similarities to Laurence. She said her son was autistic. I had never heard of autism and I wondered if this could be what we were looking for. I rang the helpline number at the end of the article and the National Autistic Society (NAS) sent me an information pack with more details about autism.

Amongst all the papers in the pack was a leaflet of illustrations that depicted the principal ways in which autism is displayed.

AUTISTIC		LAURENCE
Handles or spins objects	YES	Tapping with objects in his hand
Bizarre behaviour	YES	Jumping up and down, arm flapping
Talks incessantly on one topic	NO	Silence
One-sided interaction	YES	We always felt it was one way
Doesn't play with other children	YES	Ignored other children in the park
Displays indifference	YES	Often in his own world
Shows need by using adult's hand	YES	Wow
Copies words like parrot	NO	Silence
Inappropriate laughing	YES	I hadn't worried about this before.
No eye contact	YES	It seemed to hurt him!
Variety is not the spice of life	YES	Crossing the road, garden gate routine
Lack of creative play	YES	No painting, no making things

The leaflet made it clear that you cannot diagnose autism by counting items on the checklist, but I did.

I felt that ten out of twelve was pretty conclusive. Laurence was autistic and on top of that the two no's indicated that he was behind with his speech. We could look forward to Laurence mimicking us and or endlessly repeating himself on one subject. We considered either would be preferable to the deafening silence that we currently had to endure.

The no eye contact was a shock. With our attention drawn to Laurence's bizarre behaviours we never thought about the lack of eye contact, just like his lack of pointing earlier. The only time I could positively recall having solid eye contact with Laurence was in the hospital the day he was born, and it was me who felt uncomfortable then.

I tested Laurence there and then. He resisted and when forced into eye contact he reacted as if it was painful. It was a quick test, but why was I the first person to test Laurence for this at the ripe old age of two years and four months? Why hadn't the GP, a health visitor or a nurse noticed this and mentioned for us to monitor and encourage his eye contact?

Was this why we felt so disconnected from Laurence and why we couldn't get through to him?

So much time had been wasted unnecessarily, but now we had something to work on. Laurence's bizarre flapping, tapping and so on was no longer a list of eccentricities; it was a list of symptoms. He was not unique; there were other children just like him. We now had a label that we could use to explain Laurence's behaviour to friends and family.

The more we read about autism the more convinced we were that he was autistic. We watched the film *Rain Man*, joined the NAS and sought out more information on this mysterious condition. We read *Nobody, Nowhere* by Donna Williams. I found it a painful book to read. Her childhood was so different from Laurence's that I could gain no insights into his autistic world.

Autism was rare but on the increase, with approximately one in a thousand children affected at this time. There were many theories about the possible causes of autism but little seemed to be known about it and even less was known about what to do about it. The literature made it clear that this was an awful incurable condition and Ana was devastated. She blamed herself, saying it was a punishment for a past wrong.

I couldn't see it and she accused me of being in denial, a common reaction. To me it didn't seem that bad—after all, there was nothing life-threatening. Yes, of course I wanted a real son to play football with, but if that was not to be then I was happy and currently having a lot of fun bringing up my puppy. The word 'incurable' frightened Ana, but it felt like a challenge to me.

The date for Laurence's assessment finally arrived. They had written to us informing us of what to expect. The assessment would take a full day. Laurence was to be studied by a paediatrician, a speech therapist, a physiotherapist, an occupational therapist, an audiologist, an orthoptist, an educational psychologist, a social worker and a health visitor, with a nursery nurse on hand to keep Laurence amused through the day.

With such a wide range of professionals looking at him this had to be our D-Day. Although we already thought we knew what was wrong with Laurence we hoped that we would find out more about the full extent of the problem and what we could do about it.

It was nice to be with Laurence but have somebody else there to deal with him. We were out of the front line, for a day at least. That relief highlighted how we were already habituated to constantly monitoring him.

At the end of the day there was a discussion between the team and us to plan any help that Laurence might need. We patiently listened and awaited the results of their assessment, but they were talking like our GP.

They couldn't say exactly what was wrong with Laurence. Yes, there was a mild delay in his speech but he was still only two and a half years old and it was not unheard of for children to suddenly start talking at four years old.

'Einstein didn't speak until he was three,' one said. With regard to our concerns over his behaviour, they said he might just grow out of these odd phases. However, they did want to keep monitoring his progress.

They proposed that the health visitor and the speech therapist would visit Laurence regularly. I asked about Laurence's hearing and they explained that the audiologist and the orthoptist were unable to attend that day and Laurence would be tested by both at a later date. They added that nobody else had expressed any concerns about his hearing.

Ana asked about a play scheme for Laurence to give her some respite during the day. They said they would look into it, but I think she knew that with a child like Laurence it would be many months (six in fact) before a place could be found. The social worker offered us marriage counselling.

I felt they were trying to apply a sticky plaster when in fact a triple bypass was required. At no time did anybody mention autism. My patience snapped. I am not a violent man but I do like to slap a desk to get people's full attention. Taking the NAS list out of my pocket I slammed it down hard on the desk.

'Never heard of autism?' I snarled sarcastically. I was angry that they had tried to withhold such an obvious match of symptoms for Laurence's behaviour.

Asking for calm, they explained that Laurence was still much too young to be labelled autistic and that we should carry on monitoring him to see how he developed. Exasperated, I showed them the list again and explained that we were just a parrot impersonation short of an autistic full house. That told me that Laurence had already developed, and he had developed autistically.

They assured me that I didn't want Laurence labelled so early as the label couldn't be removed later. They were the experts, they knew what was in Laurence's best interests and they told me to leave it to them. Unable to convince them of my ability to remove an inappropriate label, and being new kids on this block, we agreed to differ but I was very angry.

I suspect that they attributed my anger to a typically male response to Laurence's condition, but my anger was aimed directly at their complacency and incompetence. This day had cost the NHS thousands of pounds.

All I wanted was a place to start and all they wanted to do was sit back, have another cup of tea, monitor the situation and do it all again in six months' time. The cosiness of this situation inflamed me; they were ripping off both the NHS and the parents, giving no value for money to either.

There was only one question that needed to be answered that day: Did Laurence need help?

There was only one decision that needed to be taken that day: Where was the best place for him to start getting that help?

The pathetic waffle these experts were feeding me about irremovable labels and so on to justify doing nothing was tantamount to child abuse. They were actively seeking ways to deny a child the help he so obviously needed.

I didn't know what help he needed; I expected them to know that. I did know that giving him some extra teaching, training or other therapy now couldn't do any harm if it later transpired that he hadn't needed it after all. All their arguments were totally false.

We took Laurence home none the wiser, leaving the experts to carry on assessing without labelling. Nobody wanted to use the 'A' word and I got the impression that they were used to parents finding things out for themselves, the hard way.

At home we were making some slow progress. Although the command 'Walk' still meant run at both ends of the journey, Laurence was beginning to respond to other commands, like, 'Gently.' We were worried by the increasing violence in his rocking. He would throw his head back as hard as he could into the padding of the armchair. I couldn't help thinking of the padding in a boxer's glove impacting with his head.

Initially using physical intervention whilst saying, 'Gently,' we helped Laurence learn to slow the rocking down. Gradually he learnt to ease up when I said, 'Gently,' without the need for my physical intervention.

Laurence also began to howl like a cross between a wolf and a boiling steam kettle, getting louder and louder all the time. By graphically saying, 'Quietly,' I got Laurence to learn to turn the volume down.

None of these behaviour modifications lasted for any length of time and he would soon start speeding up or getting louder again until the command was repeated or he was distracted on to some other occupation, like climbing all over me. He was a full-time child.

We were also becoming aware that Laurence understood more than he let on. During conversations he would become attentive on hearing certain words like 'out'. If anybody was going out he wanted to know about it. Mention of certain food items also caught his attention. But although our words were going in, still nothing came out. Gudju had not opened the floodgates.

We were having a complete communication breakdown when it came to potty training. It took several months just to get Laurence to sit on it; he was very nervous. It would have been easier to train a real puppy to sit in the potty than Laurence on it. When we did finally manage to get him seated he would sit there tapping or rocking with a look that said, 'You can't expect me to do anything without my nappy on.'

Through these opening months of potty training Laurence developed good bladder and bowel control. He knew that sooner or later we would give up and put a nappy on him. With the nappy on he could relax and relieve himself because to Laurence that's what a nappy is for, isn't it? Laurence liked to be clean, so he always waited for a nappy before going. If we did push him too far, not only would we have a big mess to clear up but we would also have a very distraught child to deal with.

Ana saw it another way; she felt Laurence was doing it in a fresh nappy to deliberately annoy her. Laurence might indeed have done it deliberately to get the extra attention, with the sideshow of Ana getting angry as an added bonus.

He didn't seem to understand our emotions at all.

Ana was having a particularly hard time of it when I was at work. Laurence was fearlessly bouncing all around the flat climbing everything, regardless of whether it could take his weight, including us. He was howling at the top of his voice while he tested everything to its breaking point, including us.

Surrounded by all this chaos, Ana had to protect our precious little baby. It got to the point that Ana felt she had to take Laurence into the toilet with her for his own protection and for the peace of mind coming from knowing that Bianca was safe.

We knew there was nothing malicious in Laurence's actions but also there was no common sense. He could decide to climb on Bianca, tap her in the eye or lift her up by the hair. They couldn't be left alone together for a second. Laurence was running rings around Ana and she was at her wits' end.

Out of this maelstrom of madness one thing did become clear. It was Laurence's strange howling, which had evolved from a boiling wolf into a fully grown underground train. It was no ordinary underground train: Laurence's impression became so accurate that it was clearly a Victoria line train. At this time, passengers were complaining of the intolerable noise on this line and there was talk of 'uneven wheel wear' and Laurence captured it all. You could even hear the doors opening when the train was in a station.

I said 'a fully grown underground train' because he didn't scale anything down, so we had the full intolerable volume. As the train gathered speed in the tunnel Laurence would crank up the volume. Reaching full speed, we became concerned for his voice with all those mechanical sounds pouring out of his throat with such force.

The echolalia train had arrived. I wouldn't have been surprised if somebody told me that Laurence was travelling in real time, but I never checked his timings. We had foolishly looked forward to this, thinking that anything would be better than the silence, but we were already trying to stifle his early vocal expressions.

But the really bizarre part of this little tale was Laurence's reaction to our attempts to stifle him. He took to kneeling behind the settee. Then, rocking towards the floor, he would screech out his journey at full volume into the carpet. Did Laurence innately understand that this was the best way to muffle his sounds, giving him the best chance to complete his journey without interruption from us?

Unsurprisingly, Ana was depressed and spending more and more time on the phone to her family in Colombia. I explained that if we gave our money to BA rather than BT we could go to Colombia for a holiday every year, but to no avail. I needed to earn some bonuses, but the plum-in-the-mouth salesman that Mick had hired to get the extra work was useless. The big one was always just around the corner and all we were getting was little jobs tucked away in the middle of nowhere that nobody else wanted.

The end was all too inevitable; the small business could not support all of us, and when the salesman went there was no realistic hope of sizable expansion, so Mick didn't need me either. I didn't mind losing the job with its long hours, but it was a shame that it happened in such a way that I lost a good friend who was clearly feeling very guilty about laying me off with Christmas approaching and a young family to support.

I decided not to rush out and get a Christmas job. There would be plenty of jobs in the new year and I was confident that I would get one then. I looked forward to spending two or three months at home on the dole with the children. It would give me more time to take the pressure off Ana and to learn more about autism.

There are plenty of books on teaching children to read, write and count but I could find no instructions on how to teach a child to talk. With Laurence seemingly deaf to our endeavours it seemed an impossible task. Laurence was showing signs of reading on the Underground but we were having no success with the flash cards. He didn't like us matching the sound, written word and picture together. He would try to drown us out with howls of his own and if we tried to impose some eye contact he would run away.

We discovered that Laurence liked photographs. He would sit excitedly tapping the photograph with his knuckles and he allowed us to sit beside him and talk about the picture. We could do with ordinary photographs what we had been trying and failing to do with flash cards and simple books; I think they were too abstract for him.

We had found a chink in his armour and for the first time he was allowing us to sit with him and communicate to him. We could tell that he loved his photos, so it was even more of a shock when he started to tear them. As he sat contentedly tapping the photos, a tap could turn into a rip in the blink of an eye. Even when we were sitting next to him, he was too fast for us to prevent it happening. Why was he destroying the one thing that he had shown us he cared for?

Nothing in this autistic world seemed to make any sense.

We needed to keep on using the photographs, as they were our only gateway into Laurence. I spent many evenings taping the photographs back together again and again. Even though I started buying an extra set of prints, Laurence nearly managed to destroy the entire photographic record for this crazy period in our lives.

It was quite by chance that I spotted a small ad in the evening paper for a job that I could do, so I decided to give myself some interview practice ready for the new year job search. It had been nearly ten years since my last one.

I attended the interview in Knightsbridge suited up but without bothering to shave off my beard. I would do that in the new year when the job search got serious. I have experienced a lot of beardism in my life and I do feel very fortunate that, unlike victims of racism, I can shave off my beard for an interview. Working with the general public, I have always been interested in how different people make initial judgements of others by their appearance.

My interviewer explained that he represented a northern-based company that wanted to expand into London. They currently had just one small shop in London but would be acquiring another twenty in the new year, with hopefully more to follow after that. Although he was only looking for one manager to run their one shop at that time, I quickly realised that this job had good prospects.

I set about explaining how I was the right man to have around during this rapid expansion. With my range of experiences I would be very useful. He bought into the idea and we had a long chat about the way forward. I knew before I left the office that I'd got the job; the letter following me home was just a formality to let me know that I could start on 1 December.

I was really chuffed with myself; it had been the first time that I had been unemployed since I had been married. Ana was not so happy; she needed my help at home, as there was still no play scheme and she had expected me to be around until January at least.

I could see some good opportunities coming out of this job, though. I would have every Sunday off and, working ten 'til six, I would see the children in the evenings. I would be a commuter and Ana would have to keep her job of dealing with all the different agencies that we were finding you have to deal with when you have a son like Laurence.

I volunteered to swap jobs with her any time if she could match my salary. As I got into the routine of commuting between Walthamstow and South Kensington six days a week, the idea of becoming a househusband became ever more appealing.

Sadly, Ana didn't take me up on the offer.

Starting work in December meant that I received a wage packet just before Christmas, so shopping was a last-minute rush. Top of the list was the London Transport Museum shop in Covent Garden. Laurence and I had discovered it earlier during our travels. This year I was determined that Laurence would get some Christmas presents that he really liked. I bought a full-size map of the Underground, some Underground books for children and a plastic Underground train.

It was a crazy Christmas, with Bianca at six months too young to understand what was going on. The map didn't impress Laurence initially, but he did start taking an interest in it when I stuck it up on his bedroom wall (just like it appears in the railway stations).

He gave the books just a cursory glance and the plastic train made an interesting noise as it disintegrated while he tapped it on the floor. However, with a tricycle and other ignored toys he had plenty of wrapping paper to play with. This year he loved the wrapping paper. He liked to roll in it, cover himself with it and tear it. He especially liked to tear it and wrapping paper was one thing we didn't mind him tearing, so we were finding little pieces of Christmas wrapping paper for weeks to come.

Babysitters were out of the question for Laurence, so Ana went out with some Colombian friends to see in the new year while I stayed in. I wished myself a happier 1992, as I couldn't see how things could get any stranger than they had been over the past year.

By now we had virtually no social lives. Friends and family didn't really like to visit us and we didn't wish to visit them for fear of what damage we might do. I rarely socialised with my colleagues after work, as I was needed at home.

When I arrived home from work our dinners would be on the table, with Ana retiring to the back bedroom saying, 'I have had enough, I have looked after them all day, it's your turn now.' It had become a regular routine, just like on my days off when I was still taking Laurence out to give Ana and Bianca some quality time together.

I tried to entice Ana to join us on our travels but she was always too tired. It was becoming clear that not only did we no longer have a social life but also there was no family life either. Laurence had turned us from parents into shift workers, exhausting us each in turn.

I returned to the London Transport Museum shop for Laurence's birthday presents. I had picked up a few cheap items for him to ignore or destroy, when I found a beautiful coffee-table book packed with large photographs of Underground trains. It was expensive; it would be criminal to allow this book to undergo the Laurence treatment. It would be like giving a puppy a beautiful handmade tapestry for a doggy blanket.

I bought it—we had to get him interested in books somehow, and he loved it. He studied each photograph in minute detail, excitedly tapping them even while he was turning the pages causing them to crease and rip. The book died a slow lingering death, but it was all in a good cause as we got a lot of communication out of it before other similar books replaced it.

Nothing could beat the real thing, however, and when we were out Laurence was always steering me towards the underground station.

At three years old Laurence, had stretched out and was a tall, skinny, very agile little boy. The compliments were becoming less frequent but they still came. One lady actually did say, 'Oh, he's so cute. I want to pick him up and take him home to show to my family.'

I knew that he would happily have gone along with her without a thought for me. She would have returned him quick enough. However, I also knew that I would have missed him.

*

Laurence's good looks couldn't last. He tapped a local cat just a little too hard, and the cat retaliated by slashing its claws across his right cheek. He yelled for a little while but it was mainly shock rather than pain. My little puppy had learnt that cats can move faster than he could and he gave them a wide berth from then on.

More serious was his flying head butt on the corner of a cabinet in the lounge. Laurence had decided to leave the room, but just as he was picking up speed I shouted, 'Walk' as usual and he seemed to trip on his own shadow. Blood spurted out from a cut above his eye and he screamed.

We pinned him down to apply pressure with cotton wool on his wound and we phoned for an ambulance, as we didn't know how he might react. The ambulance men arrived quickly and we explained the situation.

They fascinated Laurence. He stopped crying immediately and calmly allowed them to look at his cut; it was deep, down to the bone behind his eyebrow. They felt he should be checked over and have stitches at the hospital. Laurence loved the ambulance ride and proved us liars with his very best behaviour; it was as if there was nothing wrong with him at all.

Inside the hospital, however, Laurence managed to shame us with his very worst behaviour. He didn't want to sit down, he was excited, he could see a long corridor and he wanted to run down it. I tried to hold him in my lap but he was squirming and wriggling so much that the cut started bleeding again and when he started screaming I had to let him go.

He was so happy he was laughing as he ran down the corridor with blood pouring down his face. I felt so helpless; I could feel the scorn being heaped upon me from all around.

Laurence was not running up and down the middle of the corridor but alongside the walls, grazing the radiators and fire extinguishers. Of course the inevitable happened—a nurse walked out of one of the cubicles and he was unable to avoid her. Laurence went flying but he was having too much fun. He just picked himself up and ran off down the corridor laughing again, with blood still running down his face.

The nurse was not amused; her pristine uniform was now splattered with Laurence's blood. I tried to apologise and explain at the same time. She looked sternly at Laurence and decided to deal with him personally there and then. At least she understood.

*

With the improving weather I started taking Bianca out in the pushchair with Laurence to give Mum a complete rest. I soon noticed that Bianca wasn't getting the attention from strangers that Laurence had received. The children looked so similar when they were young that their baby photos are almost indistinguishable. People who knew us made a big fuss of her, but she definitely wasn't pulling strangers off the street. She was not beaming.

Laurence seemed to have Bianca classified as an object of no usefulness and blanked her most of the time, whereas she was becoming fond of her big brother. Even if she crawled up and took something that he was tapping with, he would quietly move on to something else. It was very sad to see her advances not just being ignored—he seemed to look straight through her as if she wasn't there.

Despite this I think he liked having Bianca along on our travels as it gave him a bit more freedom. In the park he had more time to brush past the bushes and fencing around the perimeter while I played with Bianca on the proper play equipment. I enjoyed her enjoyment and started to learn about what I was missing from Laurence's enjoyment of the park.

On the Underground I did have a few problems coping with them both. Once the train had stopped at the platform and the doors opened I had to let Laurence loose to carry Bianca and buggy onto the train. This wasn't a problem on half-empty trains because he always ran to a seat, but it could be a problem on the busy trains.

Laurence was always eager to get on, but I held him back to allow the impatient commuters to bustle on board first, before releasing him and lifting Bianca and buggy onto the train. But he was an experienced commuter in his own right and he could hustle with the best of them.

One day he weaved around and through a sea of legs, squeezing past them all before sliding underneath an old man's slowly descending posterior onto the last seat that had been left empty for him. Putting Bianca down I looked up to see the old man frozen halfway down with Laurence sitting nonchalantly on the seat. Laurence of course was immune to the daggers that were flying towards him from all directions. I called him over to me, immediately making myself the target for those daggers.

He looked up at me with his innocent face as if to say, 'What did I do wrong? I got there first.' I couldn't tell him off so I gave him a quiet little lecture on how little boys should give up their seats for older people. It didn't matter that he didn't understand what I was saying as it was not for his ears.

Similarly, Laurence was too fast for me on another occasion. We were standing on a crowded train when it started to slow down as it approached a station. Laurence spotted a little old lady starting to get up. He had to move fast as there were a couple of women standing near to the old lady. He managed to weave around them and slip into the old lady's seat before she had even fully got up. She walked towards me on her way off the train saying some not very ladylike things. I waited before calling Laurence over, as I didn't want him pushing past her on his way back to me. He was a bit miffed when I did call him over as one of the women that he had so neatly sidestepped took his seat.

How could I expect him to understand our funny little ways?

Ana's persistence in her search for help finally paid off. At the end of March Laurence was given a place in the local under-fives' play scheme with his own keyworker. At least it gave Ana a couple of hours' respite a day.

We still had two years before he was five but we asked to see a potential special needs school to see if this was really what we should be aiming for. Secretly I also wanted the chance to see some other children with the autism label.

Laurence's social worker arranged for us to visit a local special needs school called Whitefield. The buildings were all modern and purpose-built for teaching children with special needs. Each of the large classrooms had its own washing and toilet facilities and access to its own little outdoor play area. They also had built-in observation rooms, which doubled as distraction-free one-to-one areas. They seemed to have thought of everything.

The children certainly lived up to their label of having severe learning and behaviour difficulties and yet I soon noticed that Laurence did that and that and that. I realised that Laurence would fit in here. There was a gym, a swimming pool, a soft-play room and an outdoor adventure playground. We wanted to leave Laurence there, there and then.

While we were looking at them they were looking at Laurence. The school wanted to know everything about him so they could be fully prepared. It was so good to talk to people who understood our problems. We told them of our worries, about his funny ways, his strange noises, his lack of speech and his white diet. We were worried about his knuckles—calluses were forming and we were now concerned about long-term damage. We had serious concerns about his feet, as ever since he had learned to slow down and walk, he had walked on tiptoe. It was like he was always ready to spring away at a moment's notice.

We were embarrassed that he was still not toilet trained. Laurence seemed to be quite literally petrified of letting go without a nappy on. They explained that for Laurence wee and poo were parts of him and as such felt warm and good, for a short while. We were asking him to sit on the toilet and irretrievably throw his innards into the cold water below. He was frightened of what he might lose.

The teachers reassured us on all our worries; it was all part of a day's work for them. I was beginning to understand how differently Laurence thought compared with us and appreciated how well the teachers understood children like him. It was wonderful to hear them saying, 'Don't worry, leave it to us.' They shared our problems now and we were feeling better already.

Children from all over London and the nearby counties travelled to this school daily so we felt fortunate to have this place so close to home. The school wrote to us a couple of weeks later saying that Laurence could start in September. He would be going into their nursery observation centre for children with severe learning and behaviour difficulties until he was five, when they would assign him to an appropriate class.

This was brilliant news. We had only gone along to have a look and we never expected him to be admitted so quickly. I was beginning to think that this system wasn't so bad after all.

We were as impatient as any other parents for the school holidays to finish. We hoped that we could start living a more normal family life, for part of the day at least.

We seemed to be having some success on the dietary front. Initially we had tried to bribe Laurence with brightly coloured sweets, but with no effect. He was a boy with principles. He did, however, like white chocolate buttons and they became his sweet of choice. So we started with the off-whites, greys and creams. Eating the white stalk of a lettuce leaf slowly led to the whole leaf if it wasn't too green. Peeled apples, pears and cucumbers followed.

Bananas were another early success and Laurence didn't need any help peeling them as he had his own superior method. You almost needed a slow-motion replay to see how he did it. He took the banana in both hands and, applying just the right pressure, he twisted, giving the banana a Chinese burn. This caused the skin to split the length of the banana in several places simultaneously, allowing the whole banana to pop out and disappear into his bulging mouth. He would dispose of the banana skin by throwing it over his shoulder with his spare hand. It was no wonder that he looked at me so strangely when I peeled a banana. How could we expect him to understand our funny ways?

I read in the local paper that for the school holidays there was a children's funfair in a park on the other side of Walthamstow. We had visited the park the previous summer and Laurence demonstrated that he remembered the long route by leading me the last part of the way. Neither of us was prepared for what we saw when we turned the corner into the park.

Right in front of us was a Thomas the Tank Engine ride going round and round its circular track. I was holding Laurence's hand and I could feel him trembling; he was standing on tiptoe, his left arm flapping excitedly. This was no video—it was the real thing. As we were now safely in the park, I released him.

He didn't run off; instead he put his arm between my legs around the thigh and squeezed. He couldn't have produced more tears if he had squeezed elsewhere! At 3½ years old Laurence had acknowledged me—he had said thank you in his own silent way. It was the first time that Laurence made me feel like a parent, as opposed to a machine employed to meet his needs. Laurence was a playful, cantankerous puppy, he was a weird alien doing bizarre things in strange ways and he was a tireless robot continuously repeating tasks, but now I knew that underneath all those layers there really was a little boy inside.

I bent down to give him a hug and to say thank you for his thank you but he pushed me away. This was no time for sentimentality—he had a Thomas the Tank Engine train to explore.

That day I vowed that one day I would get him out of there. We must have made a strange sight, a grown man crying and a little boy trying to fly.

We walked around the ride a few times and Laurence tapped the train when it stopped but he didn't want to get on. Being viewed very suspiciously by the ride operator, we moved on. The next time we visited the park Laurence was happy to ride on the train, over and over again. I think the first time we visited he was just too excited to sit down on it.

After all that effort to get Laurence started at the play scheme, it was almost a shame that he had to leave so soon to join Whitefield. But in the five months that Laurence was there Juliet McCusker, his key-worker, had done more for Laurence than all those highly paid experts who had been hovering around monitoring and assessing him for the past year.

We knew that she had some rough times with Laurence in the early days, but despite this she developed a genuine affection for him and chose to write about the good things. I have printed her short report as Appendix 1.

It was all that we had been asking for—somebody to stand in the front line for long enough to establish a good relationship with Laurence—and Juliet did just that. She was the first person to try to help.

I think it was probably Laurence's own observations of the other children in the play scheme that caused him to give up on the white diet rather than our efforts at home. I wonder if those squeaks that she reported were Laurence's first attempts to say hello.

Laurence was to travel to and from his new school escorted and strapped into a special school bus. I knew Laurence would be no trouble on the bus as he loved travelling and I was confident the school could handle anything Laurence could throw at them. A home/school book travelled with him, and his teacher Carol made a point of writing an eagerly read note in it each day. It soon became clear that the school was having a big influence on him in all areas.

Laurence single-handedly demolished any lingering arguments concerning the merits of doing nothing.

At the start of term Ana was sending Laurence to school with white packed lunches and she was still concerned that he wasn't eating enough. Within a week Carol wrote that Laurence was eating a school dinner as well as the packed lunch so could we send in dinner money next week. The white diet and finicky eating quickly crumbled at home as well.

Within two weeks we noticed Laurence making an effort to try to dress and undress himself with often hilarious results. He had shown no previous inclination to do this—Mummy had to do it.

After three weeks Carol reported Laurence's first tinkle in a potty; he didn't like it, but it was a start.

During the summer Laurence had been making all sorts of weird and not very wonderful sounds while tapping and rocking. Now some of the sounds were starting to evolve into distorted words.

It was a strain to pick them out at first but once we'd recognised a word we would hammer home the proper pronunciation over and over, getting him to repeat it as often as possible. Gradually each word in turn became clearer. It was a few favoured food items at first, followed by 'Mama' and 'Dada' which we had pushed for with renewed vigour. With these mastered, Laurence started on 'Bye', 'Out', 'Shoe' and 'Coat'. It was clear that talking did not come easily to Laurence and he was choosing to concentrate on the words that really mattered to him. We would have been happy with progress in just one area, but to see the developments in all these areas was very encouraging indeed.

By contrast, things were not going well at work. The expansion into London had not worked out and the company was bankrupt. Fortunately the receivers put together a rescue package. The terms were tough; one was no holidays for the next three months. We had to turn the company around into a profit-making organisation. My colleagues and I joined up, as we were confident we could make it work.

Again Ana was very unhappy, as we had been hoping to go to Colombia that winter. We had even toyed with the idea of moving to Colombia and starting a business over there but I felt that we had to live in England while we learnt more about autism.

Ana's father was ill, however, and she wanted to introduce him to Bianca sooner rather than too late. What could I say? She would have to go without me, as the best I could hope for was two weeks next spring. We decided that Ana should go as soon as possible, stay for a month and get Laurence back into the school routine as quickly as possible.

We also decided that Laurence should be baptised whilst amongst the majority of his family in Colombia. There was a lot to organise— the children needed passports and they had to be fingerprinted at the Colombian consulate on Park Lane. I too had to take a day off work queuing in there to sign some papers. I couldn't complain, however, as it was all to do with some new Colombian law to prevent child kidnapping so it was in a good cause.

Everything was arranged. They were to leave on 25 October, returning a month later. I borrowed a friend's car and drove them to Heathrow. I helped with all of the luggage up to the check-in desk and waved them off through the passport control.

Laurence never looked back—he was having too much fun in this enormous building with lifts, escalators and vast open expanses of shiny floors for him to run across and explore. He had no time or need for me, but Bianca looked back from her pushchair and waved.

4

Another New Start . . .

I rang Ana approximately once a week. Everything was fine, Laurence was baptised, it was a lovely ceremony and then when it was time to return, she wanted to stay in Colombia for Christmas. Her father was still very ill and it was only another month.

More than anything else I was unhappy about Laurence missing more school time. After three years of stalemate we had a tantalising taste of progress in the two months he had been at school and I wanted more. I relented, on the understanding that Laurence would be in school for the first day of the new term.

A couple of days after Christmas Ana rang me. That was the first surprise. Apparently, there was a problem with the children's passports. She told me that they would not be allowed out of the country without additional papers. Before I could erupt she went on to tell me that I could easily sort this out by going to the Colombian consulate and signing them there. She had already spoken to them, they were expecting me and they would fax the signed documents straight back to her.

I did not relish the prospect of queuing at that place again and I asked why she hadn't done these papers when we did all the others. Ana blamed it on the woman at the Consulate, saying that she had not given her all the papers.

I tried but couldn't get the next day off. That evening Ana rang again and this time she was very agitated. She was annoyed because she hadn't received the papers and yelled down the phone, 'Don't you want your children back?'

That hurt. I was surprised by the panic in her voice and suspected that they may have overstayed their welcome. I calmed her down and reassured her that I had swapped my day off with a colleague and would be launching an early-morning assault on the consulate tomorrow.

48

The queue was enormous and moved very slowly. I could see that the concept of customer service had not stretched to this outpost of the Colombian empire. Eventually, when I actually got inside, I could see that there was only one woman dealing with the public. When I finally sank into the seat in front of her I was not in a good mood.

'Does the Colombian government make a habit of kidnapping English children?' I enquired.

'*Que?*' She looked puzzled and I proceeded to tell her my name and why I was there.

'Señor!' She interrupted and smiled. 'You should not have queued, you should have come straight up to me.' Now that didn't improve my mood and I snapped back that I wouldn't have had to come here at all if she had done her job properly in the first place.

'No, no, señor,' she retorted. 'I remember you, I remember you very well. It's very unusual to see a man sign away his children like you did.'

'What?!'

She explained that she had even queried the lack of any papers allowing the children to return to the United Kingdom with my wife at that time and was told to mind her own business in no uncertain terms. I recalled that there had been a short altercation between them and when I had asked Ana about it later she told me that the girl had been rude to her. But now that altercation gave her story a ring of truth.

I thought back further. It was only after Ana knew that I couldn't get time off work that she insisted that she had to go.

I was stunned.

'Look, señor,' she reached over behind her and, picking up some papers, proceeded to show me how the in and out papers came together. She went on to demonstrate how she had to throw away the 'in papers' because today we would only need the 'out papers'. It was the opposite of last October, when she had to throw away the 'out papers'.

I was convinced that she couldn't have forgotten, as Ana had claimed, and I meekly signed the papers. She stamped them and wished me good luck.

As I slumped out of the consulate into a grey Park Lane, there was still some of the afternoon left but I buried myself in the Underground, going straight home. I was happy that the children would be home in a couple of days but I felt devastated and betrayed.

Ana had planned all along not just to stay in Colombia for Christmas but to stay for good. She didn't even have the decency to just disappear; she had allowed me to help her with her plot. How could she?

I could think of nothing else. But no matter how bitter I felt about this betrayal, I had to consider the future and in the near future they were coming home.

I eagerly awaited their arrival at Heathrow; it seemed to take an eternity from their arrival time to when they appeared in the arrivals hall. Ana was pulling a trolley full of luggage and pushing Bianca's buggy. Bianca was toddling along holding on to the side of the buggy while King Laurence was sitting in the buggy. *Typical*, I thought; it was hard to believe that a child with so much energy could be so lazy.

We were only a couple of yards apart when Laurence spotted me approaching through the crowd and, climbing out of the buggy, he ran towards me. He staggered forward and then wobbled one way and then the other before collapsing into my arms. *What's wrong*, I wondered, *is he drunk?*

No, I realised he'd been drugged to keep him quiet during the long flight. I bit my tongue and hugged him, for this was not the time for recriminations. As I held him I could feel that my puppy desperately wanted to run across this vast hall, brushing past all the people.

Inside he was so excited but he could barely walk; it was so cruel.

Forcing a smile, I turned my attention to Bianca who had seized the opportunity to reclaim her seat in her buggy and was sitting there looking up at me with a puzzled expression. We had been apart for a long time in her short life. Still holding Laurence, I knelt down and made a big fuss of her too.

That night, when the children were asleep, I confronted Ana. She vehemently denied everything and wanted me to go to the consulate with her so that she could prove her innocence, but I had to go to work. I knew whose story I believed.

Laurence slept off the effects of the tranquilliser and was back to his bouncing best form the next morning ready for the start of the new school term. Carol reported that Laurence settled back into the school routine very well.

Ana and Bianca had to get into the routine of getting as much done as possible before Laurence returned from school, as nothing could be done once the whirlwind arrived home. I was still taking the children out on my days off and relieving Ana when I came home in the evenings. Despite Laurence now going to school, we still seemed to have no time for family activities.

I decided that we should take a family holiday as soon as possible to try to pull us all together again. I had my two weeks' winter leave booked around the half term, to help Ana while Laurence was at home. I searched through Teletext and found a bargain, rang them up and it sounded ideal.

Playa Blanca in Lanzarote was a quiet resort suitable for families. We would be staying in a brand-new time-share complex. They were looking for a dozen families to give the place a lived-in feel while they showed prospective buyers around. We would be free to come and go as we pleased and there would be no pressure to buy. It sounded ideal, for the fewer people around, the less likely Laurence could cause trouble. I signed up. If he did manage to put off any potential buyers that would be their problem.

The week before we went I had some free time so I arranged to attend Laurence's class for a morning. The school encouraged this and the staff were very helpful. Ana had already been in a few times. I travelled into school with Laurence but skipped the morning assembly so that I could hide in the observation room before the children arrived in the classroom.

Although there were only six children in the class it seemed more like sixty when they arrived. Laurence and his classmates were bouncing off the large classroom walls. Carol and her three assistants seemed happy to allow the children to burn off some excess energy while they formed a circle of chairs for the first activity of the day.

With all the children rounded up and sitting in a circle they sang their daily greeting song. Passing a hat around they all sang a good morning greeting to each child in turn. Laurence wasn't singing but you could see that he was following what was going on and he got very excited when his turn to hold the hat approached. It was great to see him fitting in with the other children.

After the song there was a one-sided conversation on the day, date and weather before Carol went through the day's timetable with the compic symbols for each subject.

By this time a couple of the children were requiring help from the assistants to remain seated. Laurence was rocking on his stool and I

51

could tell that he was about to burst. Carol expertly pushed them to the limit before calling for the next activity. Laurence sprang out of his seat, as did a couple of the other children, and they ran across the room instead of going to their desks to do some work.

Again the teachers didn't try to inhibit this behaviour, preferring to settle the other children before calling Laurence to his desk. Laurence complied immediately. I was amazed to see him being so obedient as he sat down and proceeded to do the work in his workbasket. I realised that if they had taken Laurence from the greeting circle to his desk he would have been very agitated, just as I had expected him to be. By being allowed his little outbursts, he was able to settle down much better.

With everybody working Carol took the opportunity to pop into the observation room to explain to me what they were doing. They were using a new teaching programme, which had been producing good results through the 80s in the USA. It was called TEACCH, which stands for Treatment and Education of Autistic and Communication Handicapped Children. They were one of the first schools in this country to use it.

Carol explained that TEACCH is a very structured programme so that the pupils know exactly what is expected of them, with each task broken down into such simple steps that even a child like Laurence could understand. He didn't object to these short series of tasks because he knew that on completion of his work he would get a reward like a little run around in the playground attached to the classroom.

With the work all done, the next lesson was a session in the soft-play room. Trying to keep out of the way, I followed the class across the adventure playground to this room. On the way I met a pupil a few years older than Laurence hanging on one of the climbing frames.

'Hello,' he said cheerily.

'Hello,' I replied.

'What's your name?' he enquired in a perfectly normal voice.

'Stuart,' I answered.

'Where do you live?'

'Walthamstow,' I told him and with no more questions forthcoming, I said goodbye and hurried to catch up with the class. I was very impressed with the clarity of his talking and asked Carol if he had Asperger's syndrome.

'No,' she smiled, 'they're all autistic here.' She explained that I had just heard his entire vocabulary. The last flickering embers of hope that Laurence might have Asperger's syndrome died as I realised that he wouldn't have been here if he did.

In the soft room the air was thick with the yells, squeals and howls of excited children flying around the room. Out of the chaos Carol organised a turn-taking game. Each child in turn would roll onto a blanket on the floor, which the assistants picked up at either end and swung from side to side for one verse of a song.

The hard part for the children was that they had to queue for the ride. Jumping up and down and flapping in the queue was allowed but if they left the queue they had to rejoin it at the back. I was surprised at the number of times a child would approach the front only for the excitement to get too much for them to bear. They bounced around the soft room again to rejoin the queue at the more relaxed tail end.

Such excitement is usually only seen once a year at Christmas with other children, but with these children it was every day and it was wonderful to watch. I understood that this wasn't playtime—they were learning patience.

On the way back to the classroom my little friend was still on the same climbing frame.

'Hello, what's your name?' he asked again as we repeated our conversation exactly. I was still impressed. If Laurence could talk like that I felt sure that we could build on it.

Carol invited me to stay for lunch, but I declined as I felt they had enough on their plates without looking after me as well. I left the school feeling happy and confident that Laurence was in the best place for him. At the same time I felt disappointed that, by the end of the twentieth century, the best we could offer these children was the horribly simple TEACCH. I could see that it worked but it also felt like an admission of failure. Maybe I still had my head in the clouds looking for the magic bullet that everybody was telling me didn't exist.

Laurence was very excited when we got our luggage down from the loft. It slowed him down as he insisted on carrying it around the flat all day. He had us in stitches as he struggled to run with it. He even fell asleep that night curled up inside the suitcase—he was going wherever the luggage went and was determined not to miss out.

Ana tried to pack the luggage but whenever she turned her back

Laurence would nip in, pick up a nicely folded item and then stuff it back in the case all screwed up. It was impossible to be cross with him as this was one of those rare occasions when he appeared to be trying to join in. No matter how often Ana showed Laurence how to place the clothes nicely, he insisted on stuffing them in and then firmly tapping them down just to make sure they stayed put. We decided that it would be easier to take a travel iron with us.

Laurence thoroughly enjoyed and consequently was very well behaved during the taxi ride, Underground trip and train journey to Gatwick Airport. I packed him a small rucksack with items to amuse him during the 3½-hour flight to Lanzarote.

The airline gave both children some crayons and a picture to colour in. Bianca produced a rough picture with appropriate use of colour, whereas the marks on Laurence's paper were more to do with his attempts to destroy the crayons than any artistic endeavours.

However, the steady destruction of the crayons kept him amused for a long time and by being allowed the occasional run-up and down the aisle, he was able to sit still for most of the flight. I allowed him to run his heart out in the airport concourse after the flight.

We expected everything at the time-share complex to be new, but were surprised to find that each apartment was a detached chalet with its own little black lava garden and potted plants. Paths wound around the gardens leading to the central complex with its tennis courts, swimming pools, underground gym, bar, shop and restaurant. With only a dozen families scattered around the sprawling site, we had no neighbours to annoy. It was perfect.

The next morning we decided to go and explore the beach. It was a gently sloping, artificial beach with a sea wall on either side. This ensured the waves were no more than ripples when they hit the beach. It seemed perfect for young children, with the only danger coming from the topless German grannies swinging around.

Ana was disgusted and was also unimpressed by the rugged volcanic scenery. Bianca refused to get out of her buggy, as she didn't like the feel of the sand on the soles of her feet. Laurence started flapping as soon as he saw the sea and once on the beach he had no such inhibitions, leaving a trail of clothes behind him as he raced down to the water naked.

I left the girls to their moans and followed Laurence to the water, picking up his discarded clothes along the way. He was very happy running through the shallow water, kicking up as much spray as possible.

He wouldn't let me get near him, running away whenever he considered that I got too close. I thought that he was worried that I might take him away from this giant bath so I kept an eye on him from a mutually acceptable distance.

As he splashed around he seemed to be deliberately catching some splashes in his mouth and I began to wonder just how much of the seawater was going down his throat. I came to realise that there was a clear distinction between his general splashing about and his scooping the water into the air to catch on his tongue. The significance of this often repeated behaviour eluded me for several years.

By the second day Bianca cracked. She had watched her big brother laughing and having fun for long enough and she wanted to be carried to the waterfront. From there we were able to gradually desensitise the soles of her feet so that she was soon running all over the beach chasing her big brother. We found that the only way we could lure him peacefully out of the sea and off the beach was with food.

After the beach each day, we ate at different restaurants along the waterfront. Laurence was eating adult portions as he had a lot of energy to replenish. He behaved himself very well in the restaurants just so long as we didn't try to stay for too long. Despite him eating these giant meals I sometimes had to take him for a walk, allowing Ana and Bianca time to finish their meals in peace. It was a far cry from his pre-school finicky eating.

Behind our chalet a distinctively shaped extinct volcano dominated the horizon and I had seen people walking up it. It didn't look too difficult, so on one overcast morning I suggested we take a walk.

Ana told me to take Laurence and give them some real peace. I felt that this went against my plan to spend the holiday doing things together, but I could see no point in having an argument over this. I packed a few items in a travel bag and we set off.

There were no road signs pointing to the volcano so we followed a dusty road that seemed to be going in the right direction. There was no traffic so I allowed Laurence to run loose, scampering off in different directions but always returning to me before going too far. The road petered into a rough dirt track and then into a single-track footpath as the gradient increased.

I set Laurence off in front of me and followed closely behind, ready to prevent any deviation from the narrow path. He walked and walked without deviating or complaint until about halfway up, when he stopped in his tracks. He didn't try to turn or move—he just silently stood still. It was unheard of for Laurence to stand still, so I patiently stood behind him, giving him quiet reassurance while he rested.

We don't have hills like this in London. I suspected that he was puzzled by the strange feelings in his legs but he made no complaint. After a short rest he was happy to carry on up the path. We were nearly at the top when he stopped again. Again he didn't try to turn, move or speak, so I stood behind him and reassured him again that we were nearly there now and after another short rest he marched on. We soon reached the top and Laurence was free to run around, but as he turned he froze.

'Ooh, ooh, ooh!' were the first sounds he had made since leaving the chalet.

Try to imagine going to bed and waking up to find yourself standing on the top of a mountain; that is how Laurence reacted. He had gone for a walk just like many times before, only this time he ended up on top of a mountain. The poor boy was petrified by the view that spread out below him and he cowered under my arm.

I eased him over to a smooth rock and sat him down on it with the full panorama in front of him. He seemed to feel better sitting down and his worries magically disappeared completely when I produced a carton of Ribena and a packet of white chocolate buttons from my bag.

We had discovered that if you make the hole too big in a bag of buttons they can disappear in one mouthful but if the hole was small enough he would hook each button out individually with his little finger even after the hole had grown bigger through repeated use.

I heavily praised him for being a good boy as I watched him studying his rewards. I noticed that he was also giving the view some short furtive glances between buttons. It had been a horrible shock for him, having no preconception of what to expect. The view from a double-decker bus was no preparation for this new perspective on his world. But now that we were here he was starting to take it in, in small chunks at a time. He needed time to take it all in and I needed the rest.

Before leaving, I pointed out the distant beach and beyond that the large ferry boat, which we had seen close up previously and was now toy size, leaving the harbour for the island of Fuerteventura. I pointed down to the tiny blue circles that were our swimming pools and asked him if he could see Mummy down there. I couldn't, but I could see that he was having a good look.

When we stood up he started to feel nervous again. He held on to me as we walked around the crater rim despite it being wide enough to drive a car around. Youngsters had climbed down inside the crater and written their names with small white stones set against the grassy crater walls and floor. That exercise would have been pointless with Laurence, so after one lap around the crater rim we headed back down.

I led the way so that he couldn't try to go down too fast and he followed just behind, holding on to my belt. He was a very relieved puppy, skipping around with delight, when we eventually got back down to the dusty road.

I spent the rest of the afternoon relaxing poolside, keeping an eye on the children playing in the pool while Ana slept off her headache in the chalet. There was no sign of the other families who were staying here so we had the pool area to ourselves.

Occasionally I noticed a suited salesman and a couple of pretty young girls escorting a potential buyer around the site. We were promised that the salesmen would not approach us and they kept their promise. They even gave us a password to use when we were off site. I was sceptical at first, but without exception the time-share touts apologised for troubling us and disappeared. I was impressed.

I had to keep calling out, 'Walk' all afternoon. I was worried about Laurence slipping over around the wet poolside. He would not let me get close to him; yet again I suspected that he was worried that I might take him away from the water.

However, whenever I did catch his attention I would point up to the volcano, saying things like, 'Did Laurence go up there?' 'Did Laurence see the little swimming pool down there?' And I pointed to the pool he was standing in. I didn't know how much he understood but I felt that it was important to keep reinforcing the memories.

It was only a one-week holiday so all too soon it was time to go home. Ana felt that we could have better spent the money getting a desperately needed bigger house. Unfortunately, property prices hadn't increased since we re-mortgaged, and we were lucky that we weren't in negative equity. I explained that we would be stuck for at least another year probably two, regardless of whether we had had the holiday or not.

I felt that the holiday experience had been very beneficial for both the children, but it had failed to reunite the family.

The return journey home was troublefree, with Laurence being unusually subdued.

The following day Laurence was straight back into the school routine as if he hadn't been away. Carol wrote in the home school book on his first day back, '. . . he has used the potty a couple of times here— so far only a little but he is indicating when he needs to go to the toilet.' It was always good to hear of Laurence using the potty but it was fantastic to hear he was indicating his needs. It meant that he really wanted to use the potty, although so far he was cautiously trying a wee bit at a time.

The next day Carol wrote that they had a cake and class party for Laurence's fourth birthday. He had a cake and a few presents at home as well. We made a big fuss of him, which he didn't appreciate, but there was no party. He had no friends of his own age.

The developments kept coming. Carol wrote, 'Laurence is showing some good doll play now. Also using more words appropriately though sometimes when he "talks" to us, we don't understand what he is saying!'

Laurence uttered his words in a whisper as if frightened by the sound. We had to get close and then listen carefully but not too close or else he would run away. When we caught the semblance of a word and guessed right we repeatedly encouraged him to pronounce it correctly. Very slowly, word-by-word, his vocabulary was growing and the teachers were now also aware that he wasn't just saying the words, he was talking to us but we were unable to understand or answer him.

The tables had been turned—he could understand us but we couldn't understand him. I was baffled.

At the end of March we were due to attend Laurence's Special Education Advice Conference. The report from this conference would form the basis of his Statement of Educational Needs, which was apparently crucial to getting the appropriate educational provision. We had put the cart before the horse but the school staff had taken one look at Laurence and were confident that he would be placed with them.

A couple of weeks prior to the conference we received the draft report. It was Laurence's first school report and it was twelve pages long.

It made fascinating reading. They had studied all aspects of Laurence; it made us laugh and it made us cry as we read about his progress. I felt strangely proud of my little puppy, he was being trained and he was learning. Prior to us attending the meeting, Ana and I sat down and highlighted the points that we wanted to query. Ana highlighted in yellow and I in red. It soon became clear that we disagreed on our disagreements as the draft report was covered in separate red and yellow stripes.

But there were areas where we could agree; the Gross Motor Ability section was a wonderful description of Laurence's behaviour at home. Sitting in a chair with my legs outstretched was an invitation to Laurence to walk up the sloping beam onto the horizontal bench called my lap.

Recently he had brought 'Ready ... Steady ... Jump' home from school and was happily experimenting with this off all items of furniture. When Laurence said, 'Ready,' we jumped to see what he would be jumping from this time.

Laurence was doing his first homework and the steady destruction of beds, armchairs and settee was, in the wacky world of autism, a good sign. It meant that he was bringing home things that he had learnt at school.

There were also many puzzles in this report.

How was it that he needed physical prompting to imitate even simple things like clapping and stamping and yet he was anticipating the consequences of another child's misbehaviour?

How was it that he 'does not readily learn from experience or demonstration by an adult' and yet he was teaching himself to read on the Underground and now in the classroom?

How come he was reading more than he was talking?

By the time we arrived at the conference we had a lot of questions. It was held in the school after lessons so that everybody who worked on Laurence could be there. A classroom assistant amused him in the playground while we talked. The finalised report of the conference is reproduced as Appendix 2.

First up on the agenda was his hearing. Yes, I was still going on about it. The assessment centre had agreed to test Laurence's hearing, which they did and the report had come back saying 'normal' but I didn't believe that they had tested him properly. They couldn't have, not without somebody who knew Laurence well, like me, to manipulate him through the tests.

The school agreed to have Laurence re-tested at the next opportunity. We received the full handwritten audiology report later that summer. It showed Laurence's responses in decibels but they noted that his responses were inconsistent and they were unable to do an impedance test.

Now that sounded like my boy. Despite these problems, their conclusion was emphatic: 'Definitely has no significant hearing loss.' It also stated that they would review his hearing again in six months. I could see that they had tried and they were going to try again so I couldn't complain.

As the meeting went on it became clear that in school Laurence was presenting differently just as he behaved differently with Ana and me at home. He appeared to be happy to trade periods of work for periods of play in school. The report is littered with the phrase 'on his own terms' and indeed everything was on Laurence's terms. They could not dictate to him, but they could negotiate and the teachers were experienced negotiators. He was enjoying their challenges. We would have to learn their techniques and strategies to use on him at home.

They were satisfied that Whitefield was the right placement for Laurence but they would not comment on the nature of his condition. Despite the fact that they obviously knew him very well indeed, they were not qualified to make a diagnosis. He would have to join the six-month waiting list at Guy's Hospital in south London for a formal diagnosis.

We could have spent £600 and had a private diagnosis at the same place within weeks but we did not see the point of spending all that money to hear something that we already knew.

I mentioned that the NAS was organising a conference in the summer for families with a newly diagnosed autistic child and asked if they thought it would be good for us to go. They advised us not to miss it but they still wouldn't comment on the nature of Laurence's condition.

Still nobody wanted to mention the 'A' word. I booked our places on the course the next day.

When we started discussing Laurence's future at the school we found that they were very unhappy with us as they thought that we had conned them over Laurence's age. We protested our innocence. Apparently when we visited the school the previous year the school was in the midst of individually interviewing and showing four-year-old prospective pupils and their families around the site. Deceived by his height they gave us that wonderfully understanding interview and a place for Laurence in September '92 aged 3½. It wasn't until Laurence had his fourth birthday the previous month that the school realised their mistake. They had thought it was his fifth.

They accepted our truthful plea of 'ignorance of how the system worked' and they also accepted that it would be churlish to turn Laurence away now only to re-admit him in September as, with his condition, they inevitably would have to.

What a result! Laurence had fooled the State into giving him an extra year of education.

What nonsense!

With just one exception (i.e. the State), it is universally accepted that children with problems like Laurence benefit from early intervention. In fact, the earlier the intervention the better. Laurence demonstrated this wonderfully for us.

From eighteen months onwards Laurence started getting frustrated, and we were failing him. With my work commitments, I couldn't give him more time. He already had all of my spare time but he still needed more attention. As he grew our friends and family melted away, they didn't want the responsibility even for a short time. He frightened them; isolated in his own world, he was very physical, fast, and oh so fragile. Nobody could blame them.

He needed two mums and two dads. With us, the parents, becoming more and more isolated and exhausted, the State should have stepped in then.

Look at what happened when it eventually did step in a year later.

Juliet at the Under-5s' Centre (Appendix 1) suffered for her early efforts while Laurence tested her out, but then she started making real progress with him. Despite only having him for a couple of hours a day, in a few months she helped to beat the white diet and got him to use a spoon, play with toy cars and even take notice, however fleetingly, of other children.

But how could this part-time amateur succeed when we, full-time dedicated loving parents, had ground to a halt with his development? Where did we go wrong?

When the professionals from Whitefield moved in, steady progress was made in even more areas. Progress in self-help, potty training, turn-taking games, the reading of flash cards, doll play and generally allowing himself to be manipulated was amazing considering the school only had him for 52 school days before they prepared that report.

What could have been in that report if they'd had him for a year and a half plus those 52 days?

From the age of two years old, any child falling outside the parameters of normal healthy development should be given the assistance they require to make sure they start out on the school ladder at the age of five on an equal footing.

We have equal education for all but only if the child can reach the start line under their own steam. With up to three years to introduce autistic spectrum disorder (ASD) children to the concepts of school and what exactly is required of them, many more children would be able to join in mainstream education and reach higher levels of the academic ladder with lower levels of support. The subsequent savings made in educational and welfare expenditure would multiply for each child helped for every year of their life and would soon far outweigh the initial costs.

Unfortunately we have had successive governments becoming increasingly paralysed by the proliferation of experts with an ever-widening range of titles, intent on minutely analysing our children before doing anything. But for what purpose?

Is it a) in the hope of discovering a new syndrome?

Is it b) in the hope of not making a mistake before gaining a rapid promotion and moving on?

Both of the above seem to occur all too often, they take up too much irreplaceable time and they give the family no real assistance. All we hear is, 'It's far too early to worry,' 'I'll see him again in six months' or 'I'll make an appointment for him to see another specialist.'

Or is it c) to save money?

Now we all know it cannot be c) because of all the money currently being spent on graduate therapists, consultants, and managers with their salaries, transport and offices.

So let us start saving money.

It took a superhuman demonstration from Laurence to get our GP to take any notice of our 'silly worries'. Cutting out all the middlemen, the GP should then have been able initially to prescribe three months in the local primary school special needs nursery unit. Placing Laurence straight into the hands of educationalists charged with preparing all their children to be ready for mainstream or modified mainstream education, they would soon determine whether he was a genius or autistic, whilst working to solve the problems he would encounter either way.

Therapists should be based in these pre-schools, spending as much time as possible carrying out their therapies on as many children as possible. They could write up reports after school hours rather than spending half their day stuck in traffic trying to return to their offices to complete the paperwork from their last couple of home visits.

Educational, behavioural and paediatric psychologists and so on could observe several children in one visit to the school rather than summoning each child individually to their own suite of offices for tests. This would not only boost productivity enormously, but these psychologists could impart the benefit of their experiences and observations from other units in their area directly to the teachers in the front line.

Everybody benefits with this zero-tolerance approach. Even the normal children attending the primary school would learn consideration and understanding of the smaller children with learning difficulties around them. They might even gain a greater appreciation of how lucky they are.

Successive government policies of procrastination and placing ever-increasing numbers of experts between our children and the education they need cannot be considered a do-nothing policy—it is far far worse, it is torture.

Torture for the family as this cuckoo in the nest steadily destroys everything that is destructible right down to the bonds between friends and family. The cost to the state? Enormous.

Torture for the child as, frightened and alone, they are sucked into the black hole of autistic behaviour. Such behaviours seen in a zoo would create a public outcry to help the animal, but seen in a human, they must be studied. We must learn all that we can. We must make sure that we label them correctly.

But what is the cost of a mistaken label?

Answer: Possibly three months of unnecessary education for the child.

What is the cost of doing nothing for the child?

Years of howling, rocking and headbanging before the teachers are allowed to begin to deal with the child's problems. Nobody should expect a young child to go through this terrifying rite of passage, possibly lasting years, without sustaining severe long-term damage.

This State-sponsored torture of these young children has to stop.

4A

. . . and the Quest Begins

Dr Leo Kanner first coined the term autism in the 1940s. Shortly after that, Bruno Bettelheim claimed that the cause of autism was 'refrigerator mothers'. This theory was accepted for the next twenty years without any evidence to support it. This idea also contributed to the under-recording of autism during those years. It was much easier to tell a mother that her child was mentally retarded than tell her that she was the mother of an autistic child.

Were we an example of those emotionally sterile parents who had failed to bond with their children like he described? The evidence was stacking up against us.

It seemed that anybody could deal with Laurence better than we had been doing. First Juliet and then Carol and her assistants all made progress in many areas of development, while we consistently hit a brick wall when we tried.

We couldn't even teach him to put his socks on, and yet it took Carol and her team just two weeks to get him interested in dressing and undressing. (However, it still took Laurence many years to learn and remember, 'heel at the back'.)

I realise now that with no verbal clues, our attempts to dress him and our attempts to teach him to dress himself were indistinguishable to him. It simply required the introduction of a third party to get him started.

Like most people, we dismissed Bettelheim's outdated ideas. After all, Ana was a natural first choice for babysitting other people's babies, she loved being with them and had desperately sought loving interaction with her own child, but her love flowed over Laurence like water off a duck's back.

Bettelheim had to be wrong, but not necessarily by much.

Using my words to explain his behaviours and express his percep-

65

tions, let us try to consider this from Laurence's perspective. He started life in a very strange world indeed:

I study them, as much as I can, they are indeed alien objects. I have tried to communicate with them but they do not answer. I have beamed to similar aliens that we encounter on our travels but they are all unwilling or unable to communicate.

I have noticed that when these aliens approach each other they have increased levels of sound emissions but I can find no pattern in their volume or frequency. Maybe they are using these emissions for manoeuvring and to avoid collisions. I have found that if I create loud emissions one alien is drawn towards me and when I stop, it drifts away from me. I have been experimenting with this alien for many days and have found that no matter how many times I do this it keeps coming back to me, sometimes taking longer, and sometimes it creates loud emissions of its own. However, its sound emission generator is clearly inferior to mine. I must study this behaviour pattern still further to see if I can improve my manipulation of this alien's movements.

I have begun to detect several different short behaviour patterns amidst the chaos of their general movements. They are so unpredictable.

I have also found that each alien has a different smell. As these aliens appear to be able to alter this smell at will I have been unable to find any reliable pattern to these emissions either.

There is still a lot to learn about these strange alien objects moving around me.

By the time Lawrence was six months old, Ana's maternal instincts were screaming. We were not connecting, it seemed like Laurence had no idea what we were.

Andy Meltzoff at the University of Washington and co-author of the book *The Scientist in the Crib*, showed that newborn babies as young as one hour old could imitate facial expressions like poking the tongue out. These babies were too young to have seen themselves in the mirror. How could a newborn baby's brain map out what it saw from another human's face onto its own?

Normal babies must be born with some sort of basic template as to what they are. They must know that they have a face like ours when they imitate our facial expressions.

Or is it simply an assumption that Laurence never made?

Laurence certainly behaved as if he had no built-in preconceptions.

Newborns quickly learn to recognise and prefer familiar faces, voices and smells, but Laurence seemed to have no preferences and he was equally open to all.

He seemed to study us as we would study frogs. Starting from scratch, he learned quickly, but to us frogs it was very slow progress indeed and it often seemed irrational in our illogical world.

While Ana floundered trying to connect with her emotionless son, Laurence continued his studies:

I'm sure that this alien's primary purpose is to feed, clothe, clean and play with me, indeed I can find no other purpose.

This alien is not robotic; nothing could be programmed so badly. After all this time it still tries to clean me when I want feeding and sometimes gets so mixed up that it even tries to give me the wrong food. I throw it back but this only seems to confuse this simple creature even more.

Am I alone in this world?

Another of these alien creatures visits me twice daily. It alternates its smell between visits and I have been unable to ascertain any purpose for its presence. However, this alien does play with me on these visits and it picks me up a lot. I like this and I must find ways of encouraging this behaviour.

If only they could communicate.

Over the next year Laurence pigeonholed me as his chauffeur and playstation in the armchair. He did not allow Ana's status to alter. As he and his needs grew, his isolation and fears grew too and then came the cruellest blow:

I have detected amongst all the random sound emissions a few small groups of sounds being repeated. I believe that this is a rudimentary form of communication; maybe they are teaching each other. I want to be involved with this process and have worked very hard to mimic these small groups of sounds.

My copies of these sounds are good, yet they ignore my efforts. Why?

Remember that we often couldn't understand what he was saying to us. This scenario fits with our observations of Laurence's behaviour and attitude towards us, but our stories do not match. We say we communicated a lot and Laurence says that we made no effort to communicate. Laurence agrees wholeheartedly with Bettelheim—we were cold, unintelligible, alien surrogate parents.

I recall my old English teacher saying to me, 'Stuart, it's not what you say that counts, it's what other people think you say that matters.' This was very true for Laurence in his reality. Laurence thought that we had said nothing, so that is all that mattered.

Laurence was trying to read with very little or no verbal input while we were stumbling along with our verbal communications, but to him we were still at the basic labelling stage. We had achieved about 30 labels, all of which were words that interested him: coat, shoe, out, bus, train, car, rice, milk, etc. He learnt to read the word during the time it took him to perfect a recognisable pronunciation. We had labels all over the flat but he refused to look, it was too much like school. He insisted that we stuck to our functions, resisting all our efforts to diversify into schoolwork.

I suppose he had to have some order in his autistic world.

Shortly after returning to London, I had joined a book club called Books for Children. They sent a magazine once a month and I had to buy a minimum of four books a year to receive various discounts. That was not a problem as I bought something most months. Books didn't last long in our house. These days we made sure that Bianca had the benefit of them before allowing Laurence to chew and rip them.

The day came when I needed to order different books for Bianca as she was ready to move past him, but then, something strange happened—Bianca stopped progressing.

We had never had any worries about her development. She was at the labelling stage and she could name many more objects than Laurence. She was ready for the next stage by talking in two- or three-word sentences, but she stopped. It was as if she was waiting for her big brother. She was spending more and more time working with him, bless her, but could she? Where we had all failed, could she succeed? I was out of bright ideas so I didn't intervene, I watched.

Bianca could get closer to Laurence than we could. He had her classed as harmless and insignificant and continued to ignore her even when she sat right beside him. Getting close to him was one thing, but getting his attention was another. If she persisted too much he would jump up, bend down, kiss her on the head and run off to another room giggling. Bianca toddled along in his wake, waving her ABC book and calling after him.

It was a funny sight for such a sad situation.

Sitting down reading with Bianca, I made no progress; I found her to be as stubborn as her big brother. She was determined not to leave him behind. I could tell that she was about to burst; she was too bright to hold back much longer, so I allowed her to carry on.

The alert health visitor noticed Bianca was falling behind and recommended her for the next available place in a play scheme. But the dam burst and Bianca was catching up fast, so that by the time she arrived at the play scheme she was in line with her playmates.

The play scheme seemed a good reward for her heroic efforts.

It was sad to see how easy it was for a child who might develop a problem to get in a play scheme, and yet Laurence, who at the same age clearly had lots of problems, was rejected, repeatedly.

While Bianca was fighting her battle with Laurence's autism, we found that the school was engaged in a no-holds-barred war with the local council and prejudice. Whitefield School had already taken a budget cut, resulting in three unfilled staff vacancies, and now they were hoping that next year's budget would restore that cut at least. Parents were lobbying members of the Education Committee outside the Town Hall. I took Laurence along to show support. It was a pleasant early summer evening and a good long walk for him.

I found out later that inside the Town Hall tempers got very heated indeed. The Education Resources Committee rejected a report recommending a partial restoration of the budget cut and asked for another report outlining even bigger cuts. They wanted blood and very nearly got it when the chairman of the committee, Councillor Radcliffe, inflamed the meeting with some outrageous remarks. The councillor was quoted as saying that special schools were 'sucking the money away from mainstream schools' and that 'there are children in mainstream schools with equal problems to those in special schools'.

Parent and teacher outrage was chilled by the prospect of another 14 teaching posts being lost. Fortunately Councillor Radcliffe was only a chairman and not a dictator. It would be the committee that voted and the parents set about lobbying them individually to visit the school. One by one they agreed and one by one they saw the true facts for themselves.

The new wave of swingeing cuts was defeated but the old budget cut was not restored and the school had to limp along until the time when it was allowed to control its own finances.

I don't understand why these Councillors, clearly ignorant of the facts, should have any say in the quality of our children's education. The State already employs lots of experts called educational psychologists who make clever calculations such as, 'This child requires 0.2 of a teacher' and 'That child needs 0.3 of a teacher'. A simple calculation would give these councillors the total number of special needs teachers required, end of discussion.

Good councillors should have been trying to reduce their special needs education budget by making an effort to reduce the numbers of children requiring special needs education. Give them access to the early support they need to survive and thrive in mainstream education and the long-term special needs budget would steadily fall.

It seemed ironic that while the school was fending off the wolves snapping away at its finances they were also preparing for a visit from the Queen to officially open a new library and resource centre. It was good to see that she appreciated the school's work.

Laurence accepted this invasion into his school routine calmly, despite the presence of the parents, with all the flag-waving and cheering. I watched him from afar as he sat down and monitored his teacher's attempts to maintain a flag-waving line up for the Queen's walk-by. Some children, Laurence included, were not entrusted with a flag to wave. He seemed bemused by all the fuss and had no idea what it was all about. Fortunately he didn't decide to get up and see if the old lady had any sweets in her handbag.

The school wanted to get to know Laurence better and they invited him on a school trip to Herne Bay in Kent. It would be his first time away from us and at £48 for four days and three nights of peace, it was a bargain. Apparently it was a quiet place close to a farm and the beach. They planned to visit Canterbury and a zoo, as well as assessing Laurence's self-help skills in the evenings and mornings.

We tried to explain to Laurence what would be happening but he blanked us as usual until we got the luggage out. Jumping up and down with arms flapping, he became very excited. He dashed about the flat collecting clothes, towels and even blankets to pack. We watched, bemused by his frantic efforts to stuff everything into one small suitcase. Through the evening he struggled while we quietly laughed. We offered our help but he would have none of it, this was his task and it was much too difficult for the likes of us, so we left him to it.

The flat was a mess, it looked like a storm had blown all of the clothes out of the wardrobes and drawers, but he slept well that night while Ana packed the items he would need.

The next morning with luggage firmly in hand he was more than happy to get on the school bus as usual. He was not bothered at all that we weren't going with him as he had the luggage, which was all that mattered to him. If we had planned to take his luggage separately to the school we would never have got him on the school bus without it.

We had no worries about Laurence being away from home. The teachers had known Laurence for a year now and we were confident that they would fulfil our functions, to Laurence's satisfaction.

A knock on the door four days later signalled the end of Ana's holiday. Carol was at the door but before she could say anything Laurence burst past her. Clutching his precious luggage, he silently pushed past them both and ran into the flat and up the stairs. It was clear that he was happy to be home. Regaining their composure after Laurence's fly-by, Carol told Ana that there had been no problems, he enjoyed the holiday and had behaved well.

We knew this to mean that he was no more trouble than the other kids and there had been no 'incidents' to report, which nevertheless was good to hear. Carol did, however, have one worry. Laurence was happy and healthy but hadn't done a poo for the entire holiday. This was unusual for Laurence, who was normally as regular as clockwork. I imagine they tried every trick in the book, but this was one function he would not allow the teachers to fulfil.

As Ana stepped back into the flat she could smell her 'welcome-home present' from Laurence. Despite it being wrapped in the nappy Carol had put on him that morning, she did not accept it graciously.

When I returned home from work he displayed the same indifference to me as he had to his mum, showing more interest in the food on my plate than in me. He followed each mouthful with his big brown eyes as it travelled from my plate to my mouth. He behaved as if he hadn't seen food for the last four days. Over the years I have developed immunity from his silent pleas.

Having spent the last four days missing him, his behaviour on return had been too much for Ana to bear silently. Later that evening, with the children asleep, she vented her feelings and frustration.

'Is this all he thinks I am worth?' she moaned. 'Cleaning up his shit and sticking food in front of his nose. Is that my life?' she sobbed.

It was a conversation that we had had many times before and I had no comforting answers for her as I was just as bewildered as she was. The cold, hard answer to her questions seemed to be—yes. We had our duties that he expected us to perform properly, and that was that. He sought and wanted nothing else from us. Ana wanted love but she would have been happy with just a glint of appreciation from him.

We hoped for answers at the upcoming conference organised by the NAS. It was a three-day workshop in Hertfordshire for families with a young child with autism. It was held in a big old country house with large grounds. A Christian group ran the facility so there was no alcohol on the premises and the place was somewhat spartan. That was good as it meant we didn't have to worry about Laurence breaking expensive fixtures and fittings. It seemed to me that the NAS had got the venue just right and their line-up of speakers was first class. I had read papers and articles written by these people—they were leaders in their fields.

The first day didn't begin until mid-afternoon, giving us plenty of time to get there and settle into our bedroom. We were to meet for tea at 3.00 in the main hall.

The hall was about the size of a school gymnasium. Immediately in front of us was the crèche facility with an enormous ball-pool with inflated sides. There were a couple of small children playing inside it. Down at the other end of the hall were the refreshments and chairs, but most people were standing around the crèche. The far wall was mainly glass with large French windows; it was a beautiful July afternoon and they were wide open, sending a pleasant breeze through the hall.

Laurence was nervous and held back, not wanting to go through the doorway. I left him and followed Ana and Bianca into the hall and encouraged Laurence to follow us. We had barely said hello to a young couple standing by the ball-pool when Laurence made his grand entrance.

Accelerating to full speed in a couple of strides, he leapt onto the inflated wall of the ball-pool. I suspected that Laurence had planned on a couple of strides along the wall before leaping off and quickly racing through the French windows into the safety of the empty garden. But Laurence didn't plan on the bounce and after a couple of strides he found that he couldn't leap off. He was on the wrong foot and the bounce was tilting him inwards.

It was for this reason that Laurence treated us to a truly virtuoso balancing act by continuing around the ball-pool to complete another circuit. A hush swept across the hall as by now all eyes were following his bouncing progress. I felt strangely detached from the situation and watched people's reactions to his seemingly slow-motion bounce around the perimeter.

Most people were transfixed, gawping at his antics, but a look of horror spread across the faces of the crèche workers. An unknown larger child had appeared out of nowhere and was compromising the safety of the children in their care inside the ball-pool.

Wisely they chose not to interfere, as any distraction to Laurence's concentration could have had painful consequences for those children. For the same reason I didn't bark out his name and fortunately for us all, Laurence got his calculations correct and after one and a half laps was able to execute his original plan and leap off the ball-pool wall and run out into the garden. A collective relieved sigh signalled the resumption of conversations around the hall.

'That's my boy!' I said proudly to the young couple and, explaining that I had to follow him to check on the safety of the garden, I made a swift exit.

Laurence had found another wall, this time it was made of stone and enclosed a lily-covered pond surrounding an ornate fountain.

'No,' I barked instinctively, 'no go in the water,' and to my surprise, he didn't. He just stood there panting and leaning over the low wall, peering down into the water. When I got closer, I could see that he was intently studying some goldfish swimming between the lilies. With hindsight I suspect it was the presence of the goldfish that stopped him climbing into this new bath rather than my command.

With the hall no longer new to Laurence I was able to coax him back indoors, allowing me to introduce him and Bianca properly to the crèche workers prior to sitting down for the introductory session. I was surprised to find there were only a dozen families attending such a star-studded line up. There were three families from London and the rest came from as far afield as Aberdeen and Devon. The autistic children were from 2½ to 5 years old, with siblings from 1 to 13 years old.

After the introductions there was an excellent presentation from

Dr Barbara Kugler entitled 'What is Autism?' Now that was a question that I had asked many times over the last couple of years and it would be a few more years before I realised that nobody was really answering this question.

Dr Kugler's talk was clear and thorough and was presented at just the right level for parental consumption. She included a history of the definitions of autism, a description of the range of ASD, the statistics of autism and a full description of the symptoms and manifestations of autism, but she didn't say what autism is.

Ask any expert, 'What is autism?' and you are given a list of three essential impairments and a list of half a dozen variable features, which are not essential for diagnosis. To define autism as a list of symptoms graphically demonstrates our complete lack of understanding of this condition.

Medieval people described a plague by its symptoms because they had no understanding of viral infections attacking the immune system. Consequently they concocted many wild and weird cures for the plague. I do hope future generations will judge our fumbling attempts to treat and understand autism just as sympathetically.

The following morning was for me the highlight of the event—a lecture by Rita Jordan entitled 'Enabling Communication'. This was a subject that Ana and I both felt was so important. We felt that communication was crucial to our understanding of Laurence.

Rita opened with a chilling message for us. Our children's communication clock was ticking. From the age of six a language learning function in the brain known as the language-acquisition device (LAD) stops working and progress after that is limited and determined by what has been achieved in the first six years. (The LAD was first proposed by the great psycholinguist Noam Chomsky.)

If we wanted better than phrase speech then we would have to achieve phrase speech before the LAD stopped working or we would be left with just an ever-increasing list of labels. We only had eighteen months left; it seemed an impossible task to achieve phrase speech in such a short time, especially considering our current rate of progress.

None of the experts had bothered to tell me about this ticking time bomb, but I wondered what I might have done if I had had this important information earlier. I suspected that it would only have resulted in me worrying for even longer.

Rita Jordan's lecture went on to describe the different language and communication difficulties experienced by autistic children and their different treatment approaches—she was very thorough. She gave us many practical suggestions, several of which I recognised from Laurence's schoolwork. Her principles for enabling communication were clear and simple.

'Start where the child is.'

So straightforward, so obviously correct and yet so difficult to do. We had studied Laurence intently and still didn't have a clue where our child was. He was reading words which he couldn't say and probably couldn't comprehend. He had started counting at school and yet still showed no understanding of quantity, more than or less than.

So where do we start?

'Play.' We certainly had done that. I had been happy to play with Laurence at his level, the puppy-level, which basically consisted of lots of walkies and rough play indoors.

'Use the child's play interests and expand,' was music to my ears. This was a subject that Ana and I had been unable to agree on. She felt that it was wrong for me to feed Laurence's obsessions and felt that I should have been trying to diversify his interests.

I felt that these obsessions were my only route into his world and I was happy to follow this path, hoping to bring some of my world into his.

Watching his favourite scene in the Thomas The Tank Engine video for the millionth time and noting his mounting excitement at the inevitability of the rapidly approaching crash, I would try to introduce other perspectives with an emotional emphasis on the words. Things like, 'Ouch! The train is hurt, poor train' seemed to have a calming effect but, 'The fat controller is upset, the fat controller says "naughty train"' only seemed to heighten his excitement. I didn't know how much went in but I did seem to have some small effect, which was much better than being constantly blanked on other subjects.

Later that day I had the opportunity to have a chat with Rita, who is now a professor. I had read her papers amongst many others and I suppose I was fishing for a new direction. She smiled and advised that I should throw away the books and look elsewhere.

'We've given you all that we have found out up to now,' she said and then emphasised, 'You're the expert now.' She explained that, armed with their knowledge and dealing with autism on a daily basis, we were the researchers now.

Mischievously, she added, 'The next time we meet I will be asking you for the answers.'

The tables had turned again; I didn't feel like an expert but if this was all they knew then yes, she was right, I was an expert now.

As an expert I knew that I didn't understand much about autism. There seemed such a wide range of problems and contradictory conundrums. I suppose that is how the idea of an autistic continuum or spectrum developed, but I could make no sense of it all. I had read the research papers, analysed the results and failed to find a hint of commonality for a clue. I had to narrow down my field of study, so I decided there and then to concentrate on just Laurence. I had failed to understand autism; I would not fail to understand my son.

I would study him and to understand him would be my quest.

As an expert I knew about the subject of the next lecture. There was a special guest speaker from the USA who was an expert on TEACCH and was travelling around the United Kingdom spreading the word. After her talk I invited her to visit Laurence's school. Although they were already using TEACCH, they were very keen to learn more.

Carol had asked me to send in everything we picked up at the workshop. They were as desperate for new information on this perplexing condition as we were. Their thirst for knowledge was very refreshing.

The lectures kept coming but the parents started turning to each other as sources of more ideas. We made some good friends and started to discover just how fortunate we had been with Laurence's early school placement. They were envious that he was already in a special school and told us horrendous stories of long battles with their local authorities trying to get their children an appropriate education.

During our stay, I noticed several children try to emulate Laurence's feat but none got close to completing one lap of the ball-pool. Ana spent a lot of time chatting with the other mums, while I spent most of my spare time patrolling the grounds keeping an eye on Laurence.

It was on one of these patrols that I met the man from Aberdeen taking his daughter Rebekah for a walk in the garden. She had Rett's syndrome which is a regressive form of autism that only affects girls. With a moist eye, he explained how she had been a normal bubbly little girl who was slowly being taken away from him. She could no longer talk and she could no longer walk. She lay slumped in the pushchair peacefully like a baby.

We had never 'had' Laurence to lose him, but I could understand that it must be an awful situation for any parent to face.

He was a desperate man; he had sold his business and he had sold his house. He was now flying to the USA for one last desperate roll of the dice. I wanted to hug this brave man but I shook his hand instead and wished him good luck.

I hoped that if it ever came to the crunch with Laurence then I too could show the same 'true grit'.

PART 2

5

Auditory Integration Training

That workshop in Hertfordshire was our summer holiday that year. A new boiler and plumbing work combined with essential repairs to the roof had ensured that money remained tight.

Our local authority was still collecting specialist reports on Laurence, to add to his school's comprehensive report, for their Statement of Educational Needs for him. It would take them another year to complete their investigations and I wondered why they didn't trust the school's report.

Fortunately as Laurence was already in a Severe Learning Difficulties (SLD) school, we were not waiting on this Statement for an appropriate educational placement, unlike many other parents. For that reason we allowed them to plod along following their dogma of 'children require comprehensive specialist assessment' while we followed our belief that 'autism requires comprehensive specialist assistance'.

Laurence appeared to enjoy being tested by all these experts, with one major exception. We were advised that Laurence would require an EEG test because many autistics suffer with epilepsy as well. We both knew that this would be tough on Laurence as we were well aware that he hated us touching his head. We decided that I should take him and I arranged my day off to coincide with the appointment.

It was at Oldchurch Hospital in Romford, so we travelled by train. Laurence was a happy, excited little puppy throughout the journey and I allowed him to run freely up and down the near-empty carriages. He was doing one of his quaint erratic skips as he happily entered the hospital grounds.

Oldchurch Hospital is an old dark-brick building made even darker by the mature trees filling the small grounds. It felt like the sun never shone here and I had good reason to feel that way. Twenty years previously the doctors here had fought a long, desperate and eventually futile battle against a tumour lodged in the heart of my sister's brain. She was buried in the cemetery across the road to the hospital, at the age of seventeen after a brave three-year fight.

We followed the signs to the EEG Department until we arrived outside a small group of dilapidated Portakabins. Laurence was starting to become nervous and was reluctant to go through the door. I coaxed him inside but when he saw the big black chair and the man in a white coat, he panicked and tried to escape. I caught hold of him and held him close to me, saying, 'No dentist, no dentist,' and after a while he calmed down.

He trusted me and sat in the chair, nervously whimpering. I answered the doctor's questions and then explained to him that he would have to be extra gentle as Laurence had a sensitive head. He smiled and showed us one of the electrodes. Laurence tapped it while he assured me that Laurence would feel no pain at all.

Ha! That's what he thought.

He gently placed the first electrode on Laurence's head and Laurence yelped. The second and third followed before he yelled out and pulled them off. 'That's naughty,' I said. 'Be a good boy now.' And I held both his hands while the doctor started again. Laurence was not getting used to the electrodes — he was getting more and more upset, crying and yelling in pain or fear, I didn't know which. He was shaking his head so violently that they were coming off as fast as the doctor could place them. I did know that I would never get him in this place again, so this job had to be done here and now.

'Right, let's do this as quickly as possible,' I told the doctor. Taking hold of Laurence's head with both my hands, I smothered his arms with my body and elbows whilst my head pinned his chest to the chair. He was unable to move except to stomp his feet and he screamed and screamed. He was screaming right into my ear and it was the worst sound I have ever had to endure.

I was saying repeatedly, 'It's OK, nearly finished now, it's OK,' but I couldn't say as to whether I was saying it to him or to console myself. With my head on Laurence's chest I couldn't see the doctor's progress, so I had to endure the entire torturous process blind, just like Laurence. When the doctor said a relieved 'Done', I climbed off Laurence and felt drained but he sprang out of the chair and raced to the door. He didn't know that it was all over and he was taking his chance to escape. Snapping out of my torpor, I chased after him, catching up with him just outside the door.

I didn't make him return inside and spoke to the doctor from the doorway. I didn't understand how Laurence's extreme distress hadn't distorted the EEG test but he said it didn't and Laurence was given the all clear. We would never have to return to this awful place again.

As we made our way out through the shadowy grounds I couldn't help feeling, as Laurence did, that we were escaping from a terrible torture camp. We had both been through a horrible ordeal. We dodged the security guards and men in white coats and nipped through the gates to the freedom of the open road.

I took Laurence's hand, and told him that as he was a good boy he could have a McDonald's. He knew what McDonald's meant and his face lit up. 'Dodos,' he repeated.

I knew that I shouldn't have said that as he hadn't been 'a good boy', but I was feeling so guilty that I had to try to make it up to him in some way.

Laurence likes burgers, but in 'Dodos' there was only one item on the menu for him—chicken nuggets with the obligatory chips and tomato ketchup. He always wanted Coke and I always said no and gave him a milkshake instead, but today I was treating him so he got his Coke.

He appeared to have forgotten the traumas of the morning as he happily tucked into his routine by eating the nuggets first. He would hold each one in front of his nose while peeling it whole and then, whilst eating the peel, he would break the nugget in half and examine it closely before popping it into his mouth and starting on another. Only with all the nuggets gone would he start on the chips and ketchup. He was adept at scooping large dollops of ketchup with half a dozen chips at a time and he was soon eyeing up my chips as well. I was in no fit state to resist his silent pleading eyes and he had most of my chips as well.

I have always found McDonald's to be a wonderfully autistic-friendly operation. All the outlets look the same so that Laurence was never worried before entering an unfamiliar site. He could order using my finger rather than utilising his small vocabulary, the menu was always the same and the food always tasted the same. A remarkable feat, considering the high turnover of low-paid staff in their large number of outlets.

The use of cutlery was not required and we were never thrown out for making too much mess or noise. Although Laurence was an efficient eating machine he was still messy. Tomato ketchup could be accidentally flicked remarkable distances and his hands seemed to move faster than he could think, resulting in regular spillages of drinks.

There were no mini-dramas on this visit and Laurence was content to play with the ice cubes from his long-gone Coke while I sucked up the last of my milkshake. He loved to repeatedly run the ice cubes in and out of his mouth. It couldn't be the taste, so it must have been the sensation that he was enjoying.

As we left the restaurant I discovered that he still had a couple of rapidly melting ice cubes clutched in his hand as well as the one he still had in his mouth. I took his other hand and led him towards Romford station still clutching his precious ice cubes. He was so happy and excited on the platform that I deliberately missed our first train home to give him more time to take it all in.

Ana wouldn't have appreciated our early return so I treated him to a run around in the park and an ice cream before eventually arriving home to give Ana the good news. It felt like the first bit of good news that we had been given and from now on we would be able to say, 'It could be worse, he could have been epileptic as well.'

Other than that, it had been a bad year for bad news about Laurence.

His speech clock had ticked down to 15 months with little progress. Parents who had been in this game longer than us gave dire warnings of what we would have to face in the future as he grew bigger. They said things like, 'You'll wish he was physically handicapped rather than autistic.' I couldn't believe that any ailment could be so bad as to make a parent wish that on their child.

However, we did believe that Laurence's young body couldn't take much more punishment and we were becoming increasingly concerned about his overall health. He always seemed to have bruises, cuts or grazes somewhere on his body and we were becoming paranoid that we might be suspected of abuse. He could spot a pin in the carpet, yet regularily crashed into doors and tripped over shadows. He appeared to make no attempt to cushion his falls with his hands and he would just run off laughing.

Back in March he caught something and went very quiet. We knew he was unwell and then rashes of red spots appeared all over his body, under his arms and on his face. Our GP couldn't say exactly what it was but thought it might be a form of chickenpox.

We used gallons of calamine lotion in the battle to stop him scratching and picking his spots and scabs, but only constant monitoring and physical intervention throughout his waking hours brought success.

Left alone for a couple of minutes, he would pick off a scab and poke around inside the wound curiously exploring the inside of his own body seemingly without pain. In April, with the battle nearly won, some new strange-looking spots appeared around his ankles. The school nurse thought they looked like bites and asked if we had any pets, which we didn't.

Our GP thought it was a form of eczema but wasn't exactly sure what type and gave us a different cream to put on them each month until we found one that helped.

Laurence developed a cough and wheeziness that intermittently kept returning throughout the summer. The GP decided that he was asthmatic and gave him an inhaler, which didn't seem to have much effect either.

It seemed like Laurence was an alien to our GP as well.

His constant running on tiptoe was making him knock-kneed and his left arm appeared lifeless while he was running, causing him to throw in the odd hop between strides, which probably caused a few of his crashes.

Now he had started coughing and vomiting, hardly surprising considering what went in his mouth, but we couldn't work out what was causing it and he always seemed fine immediately afterwards. After careful observation we decided that he had probably discovered how he could make himself vomit after coughing hard. It was just childish curiosity. We set about discouraging him from this habit by distracting him when he started coughing.

We were having some success with his tapping; he still tapped things with his knuckles but not with the same ferocity. He still had thick calluses over his knuckles but they were not getting any worse.

I suppose we were lucky that none of this self-inflicted harm was life-threatening, but it was becoming increasingly worrying. Laurence had a lung test, thyroid test, blood tests as well as the EEG and the regular psychological tests that year, and now it was time for Guy's Hospital to do their assessment for Laurence's official diagnosis.

Prior to the appointment we received a letter advising us of the different people we would be meeting during the assessment. There would be a professor of child psychiatry, a paediatric doctor, a speech

therapist, an occupational therapist, a psychologist and a senior regis-
trar. These people were all very good at their jobs, but what could
they tell us about Laurence? I scribbled down three questions on the
back of that letter to keep me focused while they bombarded us with
their professional opinions:

1) What is Laurence's IQ and what is his potential?
2) What is the cause of Laurence's difficulties?
3) Was Laurence's hyperactivity a separate problem requiring
   a separate solution?

I have typed out these questions because they show how I was
thinking at that time. I was still naïvely expecting too much from
these eminent experts. The third question demonstrates how important the issue of his hyperactivity had recently become. Originally we
were not concerned by this element of his problems, but as he had
grown bigger his high-speed lifestyle was creating ever-greater damage to his young body and we were terrified that he would soon be
breaking bones.

As we told one expert our problems and worries, another expert
was testing Laurence in a different room and so we spent the day
playing a game of musical chairs from room to room, occasionally
bumping into Laurence as our paths crossed. He was clearly enjoying
playing their games and we all met up at the end of the day to hear
their conclusions.

They explained that their full, considered opinions would be sent
on to us in due course. In the meantime, yes, he was autistic and yes,
he had many severe difficulties, but during their tests they were
surprised by how well trained Laurence was. We explained that he
had been attending Whitefield School for the last fifteen months.

'That explains it, they are always well trained from there,' one of
them said, and I passed the compliment back to the school. In their
final report, the speech therapist stated: 'We were impressed by how
well taught Laurence has been in the early learning skills, for example,
sitting down at a table and paying attention during an adult-directed
task. This shows that Laurence is capable of learning providing the
teaching style matches his learning style.'

This must apply to all autistic individuals—find the teaching style
that matches the learning style and expand. Our children should be
rising up the educational ladder rather than being labelled disruptive

and falling down it just because they don't fit into the one-size-fits-all dogma imposed by politically correct ideologies.

Fortunately Laurence's teachers had found the right teaching style, without the help of the experts, and had been pursuing it using the latest technique—TEACCH.

The report was thorough and full of suggestions for interventions and advice specific to Laurence and his problems. It made interesting reading, but it was only a snapshot of Laurence on that day and we had heard most of it before from his teachers. After all, these experts could only report to us best practice methods that had been learned from teachers in the first place.

Most certainly, these experts learnt more from Laurence than he did from them and they could not give me direct answers to any of my three preset questions.

I felt strangely cheated by their one-word diagnosis. Autism seemed too simple to describe a child like Laurence. I felt that he should have some tendencies or an extra syndrome or something.

I found it hard to accept that he was pure and simple—autistic. Even though it seemed an open-and-shut case and we had been convinced for some time that he was autistic, it still didn't feel right. I could see he had all the symptoms and I could see that to the experts he was a classic case of autism with SLD, but there was more to him than that. Inside he wasn't simple. He had a complex character that I had only caught glimpses of so far.

I was convinced that he was more than autistic, but maybe it was my image of autism that was wrong.

It was with a sense of déjà vu that I started reading a story in the newspaper about a mother and her autistic son. She was one of a group of ten parents whose autistic children had undergone a radical new therapy from the USA. Some of them were reporting unbelievable improvements in their children. Some claimed that their children had been 'awoken'. I remember thinking at the time that that couldn't apply to Laurence, as he was obviously very much awake already. I had seen autistic children who looked like they needed awakening, but this was not what caught my attention.

It was their method that had me hooked; they were playing distorted music through headphones. They were working on the ears. I had never believed the reports of 'normal' regarding Laurence's hearing and decided that we had to try this. At the end of the article it said that the therapist, Aditi Silverstein, was returning to England in January for further therapy sessions and there was a phone number if you wanted more details. I was on the phone straight away and arranged for the order form and information pack to be sent to us.

There were reams of paperwork—the Americans like their waivers and consent forms, and they wanted them for every eventuality. We also had to agree to participate in their research programme and fill in stacks of questionnaires for nine months after the therapy. They wanted to know all about us, and a $250 non-refundable deposit would secure us a time slot, with the rest of the $1,200 fee to be paid weeks in advance of the therapy.

The company was called Innovative Therapies Inc, which hardly inspired confidence, but I didn't care. They were dealing with the ears; any other part of the body and I might have hesitated and suspected a con, with hundreds of us paying up and then turning up at the clinic with no therapist in sight.

I signed all the forms, completed all the questionnaires and transferred the deposit into their bank account. It was a matter of first come, first served, and I was desperate to get into the next group of ten families to be treated on Aditi's return.

We soon received a reply saying that we were in the programme. There was another pile of paperwork to be completed and there were also details of an initial blind placebo evaluation of auditory training on seventeen autistic individuals. It was carried out by the Autism Research Institute in San Diego, which was now carrying out a much larger study of 500 children, but I wasn't going to wait for the results of that.

In this first small study, five of the eight children who actually received the auditory training showed significant improvements, which translated to better than six out of ten for our group. I liked these odds; they were so much better than the 'no-hope' message we had been receiving from everybody else.

I rang the NAS to see what they could advise. I was very disappointed with their response; at best you could say they sat on the fence, but in reality they were very negative. They said things like, 'We've heard of it—there's been no large-scale controlled trials— we've heard claims like this before with other alternative therapies— don't get your hopes up.'

They couldn't put me off, but I would have preferred to hear something like, 'If you are sure it's not harmful, go for it.'

There could be no harm in playing music to him.

I had learnt enough about Laurence to realise that he would need to be trained to sit in the chair properly and keep the headphones on for half an hour. His favourite sitting positions at this time were sitting upside down in the armchair or kneeling on top of the back of the settee. I suspected he felt safe with a good view up there, but I couldn't understand his desire to sit upside down.

Every evening, when he was running out of petrol, we had a short session, taking great care not to introduce an element of trauma into wearing headphones. He was very nervous at first but surprisingly he soon started showing an interest in the music. I used to sit on the floor at his feet to stop him springing from the chair pulling the hi-fi with him and to stop him from chewing the headphone lead while I counted the minutes. I chose easy-listening pop music, as that was what they were playing in the therapy and by Christmas, we were already up to half an hour.

It was a Christmas filled with hope and joy. It was a joy to see the wonder in Bianca's face as we spent our first real Christmas together and we were full of hope that at last we could do something for Laurence. But for him it was a normal day with an extra big dinner, chocolate buttons and lots of new things to tap. Unfortunately, that year his favourite present was Bianca's doll's pushchair. He wasn't interested in pushing a doll around—he expected us to push him around in it.

He still had no practical concept of bigger and smaller, which Bianca had learnt to use to her advantage, but now it worked against her as he insisted on precariously perching himself on it and expecting to be pushed around in it. The lightweight axles soon gave in under his bulk and the dolls never got a look in.

Like most children, Laurence liked to play with cardboard boxes. He seemed to like being enclosed. I remember watching him with a shoebox. He placed it on the floor and stepped in it, first with one foot and then the other. He started whimpering and tried again, first one foot and then the other. To my amazement he then tried to squat down into the shoebox. He was trying to get into the shoebox and was working himself into a tizzy because he couldn't.

It would have been just another inexplicable tantrum if I hadn't been there and stepped in to distract him.

*

In the new year Laurence started in a new class at the school. He was approaching his fifth birthday and, having seen other children arrive and leave, it was now his turn to leave the nursery observation centre to join the department for children with specific behaviour and communication difficulties.

He had had several lessons in the new class during the previous term. It soon became clear that Carol had done her job well in preparing him for the move. Nikki, his new teacher, reported that Laurence was 'settling in very quickly'. He knew all his classmates from their time in the nursery and there was no discernible interruption to his progress. He was happy in his new class.

His vocabulary was growing; we now had 'peeze' and 'tank-u' which he would say after prompting, and a steadily increasing list of labels, such as cat, dawg, burp (bird), cow, car, crips, appul, cake, etc. Some of the children in the class benefited from using sign language but Laurence usually seemed to resist it. However, he was quick to recognise the advantages in learning the signs for 'drink' and 'more'. His communication clock was ticking down towards one year and there was no sign of phrases or even a glimmer of the concept of conversation coming from him.

Carol used to write a short note most days but Nikki regularly wrote half a page or more; she was very thorough and we felt obliged to keep her thoroughly informed of what Laurence was doing at home in the evenings and at weekends. We worked closely to try to synchronise our approaches and responses to problems encountered at home and school.

It was therefore with a guilty sense of betrayal that I informed her that we would be depriving Laurence of school for a week for what could be considered a quack therapy. I left it until the week before the therapy started when I wrote in the home schoolbook:

'It is clear to us that Laurence has settled in well and is enjoying his new class. He seems to show steady progress in many ways and music seems to be having a big effect on him. However, we feel that no matter how much progress is made the underlying problems remain the same. We have therefore decided to give Laurence a course of auditory integration therapy (AIT). We DON'T expect a miracle but maybe it could help a little with one or two of the underlying problems. I do hope that this will not cause too much disruption to Laurence's school work for what is after all a long shot.'

I gave them lots of other information about it and invitations to a lecture by Aditi for professionals dealing with autism. After receiving the negative comments from the NAS I was surprised by their enthusiasm; both Nikki and Laurence's speech therapist wanted to attend the lecture. They had read Annabel Stehli's book, called *The Sound of a Miracle*, which had started it all back in 1990; they wanted to know more and they were happy to help with the questionnaires.

The Hale Clinic in London's West End was just a stone's throw from Regent's Park and Harley Street. Ana told me that it was famous because Princess Diana went there for her colonic irrigation.

On the first day the ten families met up for an introductory seminar. We were told that although some parents reported odd things happening shortly after starting the therapy, we should not expect to see results for several months. They might well train his ears to listen during this course but it would take months for the brain to make sense of all this new input it was receiving. That made sense to me.

There was plenty of time to meet the other families while they conducted each child's initial audiogram. We were a motley group but we were all on the same quest—to do the best for our children. It soon became clear that most of the parents were paying a lot more than us for this therapy; they came from all over the country, and ten days in a reasonable hotel in central London isn't cheap. Added to that all the problems created by living in a hotel with a young autistic child for ten days and I could tell that this was a major undertaking for most of them.

Laurence's audiogram did not go well; we could find no way to make him understand that we wanted him to do something only when he heard a tone. Aditi tried many tricks but the more we tried the more anxious he became.

We didn't try to force him, as we didn't want to make him wary of coming to the clinic. There was to be another audiogram halfway through the course and then one at the end, yet they were both equally futile. This confirmed my suspicions that the English audiologists could not have tested Laurence properly. They guessed 'normal' because he could hear a sweet wrapper in the next room.

It seemed to be too complex a concept for Laurence to understand. Aditi assured us that this was quite common with the autistic children and not to worry. Some of the preliminary results from the large-scale study of auditory training showed that the children did not necessarily benefit from tailoring the music to the results of the audiogram.

We didn't see much of the other families after that day until the end of the course. The therapy was two half-hour sessions each day for ten consecutive days. We each had time slots; ours were 12.30 and 5.00 p.m. each day, so it was only if the therapist ran late that we had time to chat in the waiting area.

It was an obscene waiting area. On one side there was us, the families spending their holiday money in a desperate bid to help our incurable children; on the other side were the women hidden beneath layers of make-up wearing expensive clothes that were one size too small.

As I sat wondering what therapy they thought they needed I sensed their discomfort at the proximity of our 'badly brought up' children. That amused me, but sadly Laurence ignored them. I was beginning to realise that he was a good judge of character. I was pleased that we did not bump into Princess Diana there.

I had organised my winter leave to coincide with the therapy. I liked the late starts—not that there was any chance of peace in our house once Laurence woke up. It meant that we had plenty of time to get him clean, dressed and in a relaxed frame of mind for the therapy.

Travelling home in the rush hour was not a problem either, as Laurence was a competent commuter who always considered there was plenty of room for one more. Between sessions we spent our afternoons travelling around central London killing time, eating and running between rubbish bins in the parks. In these beautiful central London parks he was only interested in the rubbish bins and their contents. He had also recently started running around howling while patting his mouth.

I realised that to a passer-by he would have looked like a normal five-year-old playing cowboys and Indians, where he was a Red Indian looking for the cowboys hiding in the rubbish bins. It was a scene so divorced from the reality of the situation that I wondered what really was reality.

What on earth was Laurence's reality?

What I did know was that the combination of tapping the bins and patting his mouth was not a healthy one and our time in the park was limited to short visits as I taught him that going in the rubbish bin meant going out of the park. It worked—in time.

The training sessions at home paid off and the therapy sessions went well; however, the last five minutes of each session were always difficult. Aditi had several items to distract Laurence from trying to leave the chair and together we were reasonably successful in keeping him calm for the full half hour. After each session I was relieved to have completed it and Laurence was just as relieved to get out of there. He was, however, thoroughly enjoying this holiday with all its tube and bus travel and was generally on his best behaviour.

Even so, we were amazed by his behaviour on the evening of the fourth day. We were walking home from Walthamstow station, having done some shopping after the therapy. I was carrying the shopping, Ana was pushing Bianca's buggy and Bianca was sleeping.

Laurence was skipping around us as usual, closing gates and tapping utility covers, when suddenly he silently brushed Ana aside and proceeded to push the buggy along the pavement. He struggled with the steering but persevered for approximately 100 metres without ejecting Bianca and with only a few minor scrapes with lampposts and garden walls.

It was so out of character that we were shocked. We didn't want to interrupt his endeavours and curiously followed him closely to prevent any excursions into the road.

We had on countless occasions tried to encourage him to carry a small bag or push the buggy when we were out with absolutely no success. As soon as we removed our hands he would drop the bag or allow his hands to slip off the buggy handle and then run away. He was an unchained free spirit who, for a couple of minutes, had become part of the family.

That night we discussed Laurence's behaviour and decided that he could have decided to push the buggy any time, it was just a coincidence that it happened during the therapy. However, over the next few days we couldn't escape the feeling that something was different. We couldn't explain it—just as we couldn't explain what was missing during his early months, so now we couldn't explain what we had gained.

I wrote, 'We think Laurence is taking more notice of what is being said to him and around him,' and I reported, 'increased vocal repetition'. We felt that he was more aware of what was going on around him and yes, I had to say it, he seemed to have 'awoken'.

After the twenty sessions there was a post-therapy seminar for all the families and an individual consultation with Aditi. There were three families who had noticed no change but the rest of us had the same strange feeling that something had started happening and Aditi reminded us that we would see the real results in three to six months' time.

She also warned us that there could be some negative reactions in the next few months. Our children perceived their reality differently now and they might not like some of this new input.

Whilst organising the distribution of the questionnaire packets containing the one-, two-, three-, six- and nine-month evaluations that we had agreed to complete, she wanted to talk about auditory training and its effects. We were not interested. We wanted to take this opportunity to find out what else she knew.

With no Internet we were desperate for new information and wanted to know what else was happening in the USA. She understood our thirst for gossip and told us what she knew about various supplements, diets and ABAs (applied behaviour analysis schemes) that were being tried with varying degrees of success over there.

In the private consultation with Aditi I wanted to know more about what she thought Laurence's hearing problem was. I had always assumed that a hearing problem was just a matter of degrees of deafness but she explained that this was far from the case. Of the possible scenarios for Laurence's hearing that she suggested one seemed to fit with my observations of him.

She said that his ears might be processing sounds at different speeds to each other, resulting in him initially hearing a blur while his brain struggled to synchronise the differing audio streams.

A fraction of a second difference was all that was required to make the world seem a strange place, and speech was made totally incomprehensible.

We didn't need more tests. It was enough to know that it fitted in with our observation of Laurence's attention kicking-in mid-sentence. We had learnt to always say his name first, usually several times, before telling him something. The school had noticed he was enjoying music, which would have been easier for him to synchronise and understand than the sound of voices. That is why when he sang nursery songs at school the words were not there.

We thanked Aditi, promised to complete all the questionnaires and wished everybody the best of luck with their quest before leaving the clinic to continue our own. I couldn't help feeling that we had reached the frontier. AIT was new and at the forefront of the technological battle against autism.

The next day it was back to school for Laurence. We hoped that he would settle back into the school routine quickly and wondered if the teachers would notice any changes in him. That day Nikki wrote, 'Laurence was so pleased to be back today. He was giggling and went all shy when he walked in this morning. He's been cheerful all day and pointing and naming children in the class.'

Compared with his usual entrance, bursting through the door and bouncing off all the walls before settling into his chair, this was a remarkable change of behaviour. Apparently when he walked through the door he covered his face with his school bag, quickly sat down and, with the school bag still covering his face, he started giggling. Why was he suddenly so shy with his classmates? It had to be his heightened awareness of his surroundings, his 'awakening'.

But what was this 'awakening' that so many other parents had also reported?

I believe that the answer lies in Laurence's reality. Prior to the therapy he showed no change in his behaviour towards us. He was still analysing these 'strange aliens', trying to understand us while he puzzled over where he fitted into this crazy world. He was still trying to establish communications with us using our 'sound emissions', but progress was hampered by our inability to understand his distorted vocal repetitions of what he was hearing from us.

Once the therapy started to train his ears to listen, he started hearing our conversations for the first time. He quickly realised we were communicating, and the realisation that he was one of us finally followed.

His sudden shyness with his classmates demonstrated that he was seeing them for the first time as people like himself and not as aliens to study and occasionally interact with. His sudden desire to assist with the pushchair demonstrated that for the first time he saw himself as one of the family.

In the weeks and months following the therapy Laurence's vocabulary continued to grow steadily but phrase speech still seemed a long way off. We couldn't help noticing that Laurence was finding it easier to copy our sounds. Prior to the therapy it would take twenty, fifty, countless attempts before he could reproduce a recognisable copy of the word we were trying to teach him.

Within a couple of months of the therapy the number of attempts required fell to a steady six. I boasted that Laurence could reproduce any short word in six attempts. I know that doesn't sound too impressive but it was a massive improvement on what we had before. Long multi-syllable words were still a problem for him and things like Pica-pica Circus (Piccadilly Circus) produced hours of entertainment for Bianca as she tried to help him with his pronunciation of the longer words.

Some might say that all this and our feelings regarding his apparent greater awareness do not prove that the auditory training worked. All that progress could have been coincidental normal development, but the proof came four months after the auditory training.

We had been working on Laurence's newfound ability to copy our words by labelling everything—floor, ceiling, carpet, wall, etc.—but Laurence was also listening to our conversations. To our amazement and very quietly at first all the little words like 'a', 'the', 'to', 'is' and 'in' started tumbling out of his mouth in all the right places. He was using all these little words appropriately and soon after that, plurals and tenses started to appear as well. It seemed like a miracle— Laurence appeared to achieve phrase speech almost overnight, when in reality it had taken him four months of hearing our conversations to start duplicating them appropriately.

To achieve phrase speech before the age of six had seemed like an impossible dream but now we had reached it with eight months to spare. It felt wonderful. We could now hope for better than phrase speech, maybe even normal speech, in later years.

I felt that we had taken our first step in rescuing that little boy who squeezed my thigh when we met Thomas in the park all that time ago. He was certainly no longer an alien in our midst but he was still autistic, he was still my robotically inclined puppy.

It is so sad that Laurence had the auditory training just before his fifth birthday. That meant that he only had about a year of hearing with the benefit of the LAD in his brain. I couldn't help wondering, if he had the therapy when we first complained about his hearing, what his speech would be like now.

It wasn't just his speech that was developing. Now that he knew he was one of us he became fascinated by other people's emotions and we soon found him trying to provoke emotional displays.

I remember him being fascinated by a toddler bawling his eyes out in the supermarket checkout queue because he had been refused sweets. Laurence bent down and planted his head inches in front of the toddler's face intently studying the tears streaming down the cheeks, completely oblivious to the child's feelings and loud screaming.

We also noticed Laurence in mid-tantrum suddenly stop, jump up and run off to the dressing table in the bedroom and continue his screaming tantrum in front of the mirror. We laughed at this mid-tantrum silent dash and marvelled at his attempts to control this newfound emotional aspect of our lives.

He was also trying to control his laughter by lying on his back in front of me, pleading, 'Tickle, tickle.' When I obliged I could see him grimacing, trying not to react to my tickles. Unfortunately for Laurence he is a very ticklish boy and his efforts were doomed to failure. Despite his best efforts I always managed to reduce him to a helpless giggling mass.

Laurence's annual school conference was held in June that year so these speech and behavioural developments were only just starting to appear while his report was being compiled. Consequently, it was reported that Laurence had made good steady progress throughout the year in all areas, especially in English, but it was of little relevance as it was already out of date.

I believe the behaviour report was the last to be written for the conference. I have included it as Appendix 3 as it shows the embryos of his developing behaviours and introduces our principal weapon in the war against them, 'The Stern Look'.

That summer Laurence, Bianca and I visited places of interest, museums and parks all over London. Many of these places were well known to Laurence but this time he was seeing them from his new 'awakened' perspective. I was well aware that more often than not it was the travelling rather than the destination that interested him the most.

He enjoyed parks, preferring to run around aimlessly while Bianca explored the different sets of equipment in each park. We often encountered funfairs on our travels. At first Laurence was nervous of the flashing lights and loud noises but he grew to like the excitement of a funfair. It was lovely to see them sitting side by side enjoying the same rides.

We visited London Zoo. It started off very well in the aquarium; the fish fascinated Laurence. He stood and stared as they swam from side to side, but Bianca was soon bored. To a three-year-old a fish is a fish, and having seen the sharks and piranhas, she wanted to see some different animals. It was dark in there and it was impossible to keep Bianca interested and at the same time follow Laurence flitting between his favourite tanks. For the first time ever he was out of my sight while out in public. It was scary but each time I soon found him pressed against a different tank; he was going nowhere.

He wasn't interested in the small fish or the large ones. He liked to watch the ones that were about the size of a hearty meal. It seemed that my puppy had feline tendencies too.

I enticed him out to look at the rest of the zoo with the lure of an ice cream. He wasn't interested in any of the other animals, with the exception of the white pony that he had a ride on. He sat quietly for the duration of the ride, beaming brightly. At the end he climbed off and dashed across the green, skipping and flapping. He really enjoyed that. It wasn't his first horse ride, as he had been horse riding with the school.

The school took the children out a lot, recognising their need for hands-on learning experiences. They even took the children to Thorpe Park in Surrey, staying overnight at an independence training facility. It was an excellent way for the teachers to assess and help with the children's domestic skills. Nikki reported back that he went on and loved all the roller coasters and water rides.

'He was far more daring than us adults!' she exclaimed.

That night he was well behaved and slept well, but Nikki was sorry that they hadn't been able to get him to use the toilet, either with or without a nappy. Holding it in for one night was no problem for Laurence. His poos were still a matter between him and his mummy.

He also had good bladder control, and when we were out he would say, 'Toilet' clear and loud. I noticed that when I didn't find a toilet quick enough he would tap his shoulder as if to say, 'Don't you understand English? Look at my sign—TOILET.' It wasn't as if I could explain to him why I couldn't present him with a toilet straight away.

The school also ran a summer-holiday play scheme on the premises. What a wonderfully sensible way to utilise the school facilities during the summer months. However, due to the budget cuts they had to scale it down and Laurence didn't get a place.

The school advised us to try the local authority, but we held out little hope of success—they were, after all, still labouring over his Statement. Fortunately, nearby there was the North East London Autistic Society (NELAS) and Ana was able to get Laurence a place in their play scheme. To her disappointment it was only for one week, which, added to my two weeks of summer leave, still left her looking after Laurence for three weeks during the long school holiday.

Relations between the pair of them had been steadily getting worse. Laurence's newfound awareness of his environment was making him even more assertive and their clashes grew stronger and more frequent.

Almost every evening, when I returned home from work, there was a dispute to resolve whilst I ate my dinner. On one side was Laurence with the trials of the day forgotten. He was solely interested in my food going from plate to mouth. On the other side was Ana, recounting all the details of his trail of destruction and misbehaviour for that day. Demanding that I punish him, she would retire to the bedroom for some peace—she was exhausted. To her annoyance I rarely did, as I couldn't punish him without being absolutely sure that he understood what the punishment was for.

Compare that misbehaviour to the daily reports we received from Kim and Leigh at the play scheme. Their purpose was clear: to give these poor disabled kids a good time. Laurence was now able to 'determine their purpose' and he was able to fully exploit them.

I suspect they received some severe beaming from him, and they were enchanted.

Day 1:
Laurence had an excellent day at the farm. He enjoyed stroking and feeding the animals, the bouncy castle and his lunch! Laurence is such a good boy. No problems at all!

Day 2:
Laurence has had yet another good day. He is communicating beautifully with mostly words or directions. Once he arrived here he was very happy. A great day!

Day 3:
Laurence had an excellent day!

Day 4:
Laurence has had an excellent day. With encouragement went through child assault course on own. Enjoyed absolutely everything!!!

Day 6:
Yesterday's park trip was great!
Laurence has been extremely verbal and has definitely come out of his shell. Water and sand play and foot print painting was thoroughly enjoyed today.

Day 7:
Laurence had an excellent experience in the Sea-life Centre at Southend. He was extremely verbal and excited. Laurence is a dream of a boy and has proved to be so happy with us. I will miss him. An excellent day all round.

Day 8:
Laurence had yet another excellent day. He was very verbal and loved feeding the animals.
Laurence has been a pleasure to work with.

Kim 'n' Leigh

These girls had been playing with my puppy. I could have written similar comments returning from our own day trips. He was my special puppy, to those girls he was 'a dream of a boy' and yet he was Ana's nightmare child. Ana was full of love for him, so how could that possibly be?

Laurence knew that those girls' purpose was to entertain him and he made damn sure that they did, not that they needed any encouragement. Their enthusiasm was rewarded; if they had been slackers they might have encountered a different Laurence.

Laurence also knew what his mum's purpose was and he made damn sure that she did just that. She was his cleaner, dresser and cook and any attempts to diversify were seen as not doing her job properly and were vigorously resisted. Ana wanted more interaction, she wanted to share her love, but to Laurence that wasn't in the job description.

She felt powerless to affect his behaviour, so it was a shock when in the last week of the school holiday Laurence stopped asking for a nappy.

On the first evening he did it on the bathroom floor, but on the second evening he did a little plop into the toilet and on the third evening he let it all go.

Hurrah, we lavished praise on him; he was such a good boy. After five and a half years Ana was finally free of dirty nappies. On the next couple of evenings he produced nothing and by the time I reported this situation to Nikki on his return to school we were on the fourth day without a poo and getting worried.

Nikki wrote back that they had no success in enticing him to go even when they offered him a nappy.

After another poo-less evening Ana wrote back insisting that they didn't offer him a nappy. She was determined that we had come too far to return to the old ways.

The following evening I wrote in the book, 'After five days of deliberation Laurence took mum to the toilet, very nervously sat on the toilet and held mum's hand. He said, "Here it comes." '

We were all very relieved.

Laurence had finally overcome another of life's hurdles.

6

A Statement

It was the end of the road for our management team at work. The company had a new owner and he didn't seem interested in the running of the company. We suspected he was an asset stripper; the writing was on the wall. So when I was offered a job with less responsibility, the same money and half the commuting time, I jumped the sinking ship.

Yet again Ana was unhappy when I came home and proudly announced that I had a new job. She had had enough. She needed me at home. She wanted us to give up and fall into the arms of the State. She told me social services couldn't help us while I was working and we owned our own home. She claimed that we could be better off if I was not working.

I wasn't ready to roll over just yet. I had seen what the AIT had done for Laurence and I wanted to be ready for the next opportunity to help him. I couldn't do that on the dole. I felt that I had to keep working. We had terrible rows over this but I was pushing forty and worried that work could be getting harder to find.

The pundits were talking up property prices, which hadn't moved over the past four years. Maybe in the spring demand would push up prices giving us the equity we needed to move into a family home with a garden of our own. That is what Ana really wanted, but the best I could offer her was 'maybe next summer'.

Ana's patience was wearing thin and Laurence kept pushing. It was becoming a war-zone and my conciliatory manoeuvres in the evenings went unheeded by both sides. It seemed like Laurence couldn't and Ana wouldn't understand what I was saying. She accepted that some of his bad behaviours could be seen as deliberately provocative towards her but she couldn't accept that he was deliberately trying to manipulate her. She couldn't see past the mental handicap label.

Now I understood why she had called him Damien when he was a baby. Her strange claim that he was psychic, that he knew what she was doing even when they were in different rooms, was explained simply by what we had learnt at the AIT course.

Laurence's hearing was in fact very good, but it was also distorted. Whereas the sound of our voices with a rapid echo made our speech unintelligible to him, the almost silent sound of Ana sitting down on the armchair for a five-minute tea break was unmistakable to Laurence, even with an echo.

As a baby, he experimented and found that if he yelled out when he heard that sound, Mummy responded quickly and noisily, but if he yelled out when he heard the almost silent sound of her pulling down her knickers in the bathroom he found that she took much longer to respond. He was manipulating her even then.

Then and now, Ana wasn't getting a minute's peace, but Laurence was only trying to establish some form of communication and understanding of these '*strange aliens and their erratic behaviours*'. He was looking for patterns in her behaviour.

As he grew up he began to recognise our short commands, like, 'Wawalklk' to mean slow down, but he was getting no clues to our communicative intent from our encrypted conversations. He was keen to learn short names, but only of things that interested him. Progress was painfully slow and made worse by our inability to understand him.

At times it was difficult to tell who was teaching whom.

The lack of progress must have been even more frustrating for Laurence than it was for us; after all, he was alone while we had each other. How cruel could life get?

I didn't know how the auditory training adjusted his hearing, but it was becoming clear that he could now understand our words. The communication was still one way, as he didn't seem to share our desire to converse. He only spoke to satisfy his needs as he continued to study us.

Since his 'awakening', his awareness of emotions was developing. We had already seen him trying to control happy and sad, but now he was studying other emotions.

We began to see greed and jealousy creep into his personality. He was no longer interested in sharing biscuits with Bianca—he wanted the whole packet. I noticed during tickling sessions that Laurence kept glancing towards Bianca. He was looking to see if she was showing any signs of jealousy with all the attention that he was getting, but Bianca was not so easy to manipulate.

He had found that Mummy was a good source of the angry emotion. He found this emotion exciting. He would empty a rubbish bin on our bed or tip milk down the stairs while she was distracted. He stood back, chuckling in anticipation of her emotional reaction upon discovery of his handiwork. We learnt to recognise that chuckle. It could only be described as a naughty chuckle and in our reality it was very naughty behaviour, but I struggled to see it this way. It was premeditated, it felt too artificial, which made me feel that he was simply exploring and experimenting in his reality.

In this sea of strange realities I felt that this introduction of human emotions was a positive development. It made him more human, a bit more normal, but Ana could only see a never-ending spiral of decline.

Amid all this mayhem, our local council finally produced their draft of Laurence's Statement of Educational Needs. All thirty-three pages of it. It was over two years since Laurence started at Whitefield School and over three years since he first became known to the local council via the assessment centre.

Now they had the cheek to give us just two weeks to respond if we had any disagreements. The Statement was hopelessly out of date. They were describing a child that we struggled to remember with all our current problems.

I spoke with the head of Laurence's department at school who had also received a copy of the draft for her comments. They were going to say nothing and asked me to do the same. The only part of the Statement that really mattered was where they stated specifically that Whitefield School was the appropriate school for Laurence. We needed that to allow him to stay in the school.

It had taken the experts over three years to come to the same conclusion as the Whitefield staff did in that original interview. The other thirty-two-and-a-half pages didn't matter as they could be updated on his next Statement review, which the council rather optimistically claimed would be annually.

What an appalling waste of time and money—it's no wonder that people complain about the size of the special needs budgets. I agreed to ignore this out-of-date white elephant, but it was an interesting document for other reasons.

Despite it being nearly a year since Laurence was diagnosed at

Guy's Hospital, the council inexplicably decided not to include this expert advice, and summed up his problems like this:

'Laurence has severe difficulties with all aspects of communication and has associated learning difficulties. He has difficulties also with attention and hand-eye coordination as well as a mild delay in basic skills.

'He is generally physically healthy with normal vision and hearing. His general difficulties are of an autistic nature affecting communication. He is fairly independent with self care and does not show exaggerated difficulties in behaviour.'

When I read that last line I couldn't help thinking, 'Yes—but if we'd done nothing for long enough we would have seen those "exaggerated difficulties".' We learnt so much from his teachers when he was three to four years old. They had some understanding of him, whereas he was an alien to us and we were aliens to him. Oh yes, 'exaggerated difficulties' would have been inevitable if we had blundered on alone until the arrival of his Statement to receive a place in a specialist school.

As this was all that the council wrote about his condition, I studied it carefully.

The last three sentences came from his GP's report, who wasn't sure if Laurence was autistic because of the lack of these 'exaggerated difficulties'. These were reasonable comments for a GP and it was why a clinical diagnosis was required from Guy's Hospital.

The first two sentences were harder to pin down until I realised that the council had simply paraphrased the 'Summary of Special Educational Needs' in Laurence's first school report which was now over eighteen months old (see Appendix 2).

After three years, our hopelessly inefficient local council listened to Laurence's GP and his teachers. Bizarrely, they light up the true path. Parents go to their GP; the GP sees that the child has some form of learning or behaviour difficulty and sends the child to a special needs pre-school. Not a bad place to send a child with learning difficulties.

Within weeks, these teachers working full-time with the children would get to know them, begin to understand them and develop a full- or part-time educational programme to prepare the child for entry into mainstream education.

There would be plenty of time for a clinical diagnosis to give the child a label and back up the teacher's judgement. If the child still required a supported or modified curriculum, then a Statement of Needs could be prepared much more efficiently and quickly. That would be the simplest, cheapest and shortest route for our children to follow. However, we are being forced to follow along our local council's path.

In accordance with the Children's Act, the Education Act and countless other rules and regulations, all designed with the children's best interests at heart, the local councils steadfastly collect reports from as many 'experts' as they can find—hence the thirty-three pages. They collected reports from us, the teachers via the original school report, two reports from his GP and one each from a speech therapist, a school nurse, a social worker, a health visitor and an educational psychologist.

As I said, I couldn't agree with the council's decision to ignore the diagnostic report from Guy's Hospital, but I wholeheartedly agreed with their decision to ignore all the reports on Laurence compiled by the experts at the local assessment centre.

Therapists, paediatricians and psychologists with many different titles all saw him. Some were based at the centre and others were based at sites scattered around the borough, so between regular trips to the assessment centre, Ana and Laurence were sent all around the borough for monthly or quarterly examinations with further experts.

In fact, the assessment centre seemed intent on sending Laurence anywhere other than where a child with learning difficulties needs to go—SCHOOL.

Shut these other places down and retrain the staff to work in the schools. Speech and other therapists should be based in the schools, applying their so-called therapies to the children, six hours per day, five days a week, filling out their reports after the children have gone home.

It should be illegal for a speech and language therapist to say, 'I'll see him again in a month's time.' To any child under six years old that's another month off from that child's language-learning countdown.

The council's path ensures that contact between these therapists and the children is kept to a minimum before the child reaches six.

Psychologists should also be based in the schools. A school psychologist working in conjunction with the teachers would soon get to know the schoolchildren much better than they could do working from an office block. The educational psychologist who prepared the report for Laurence's Statement readily admits to having met Laurence only once.

No matter how good this psychologist was, I'd never met him; he could only comment on how Laurence was on that day and rely on the teacher's comments for the rest of the year. It's a nice report, I'm sure it's a good professional report, his comments are valid, but he mistakes Laurence's desire for physical interaction as displays of affection and he tells us nothing new about our son.

If he were based in the school, during the year he would have noticed at some time Laurence smashing plates whilst having a tantrum in the canteen. He would have noticed Laurence trying to trip children in the playground (an efficient way to produce tears) and maybe he could then have written a report that gave some meaningful input to our son's education.

Unfortunately, our council employs psychologists as educational auditors rather than to help our children. I have reproduced the report in Appendix 4 to demonstrate that he says nothing new about Laurence.

The entire system is a SHAMbles. A plethora of government laws and regulations are rigorously enforced by an army of experts employed by the local council at considerable cost, only to run out of money when it comes to actually supplying the special education that our children need.

Instead, after extensive observations, our children are thrown into the much cheaper option of mainstream education with the help of a part-time assistant. The authorities cling to the moral high ground, claiming the politically correct policy of 'Inclusion for all'. This is precisely what autistic children don't want or need at this age. They only have to ask the autistic children, but instead they keep shouting, 'Inclusion, inclusion,' as they have no arguments or figures to show that this cheap form of inclusion is an effective method of educating autistic children.

In the run-up towards the Statement completion we had been looking at the different types of schooling available to children like Laurence.

Head and shoulders above the competition was Daily Life Therapy. At this time it was only available at the Boston Higashi School in the USA, so we needed to win the Lottery before we could consider taking Laurence there.

Likewise, schemes like Lovvas were coming out of the States at this time, but the American quasi-religious sales pitch put me off. I remember seeing an awful film about an immaculate apple-pie mom who refused to listen to the authorities and have her young autistic son locked up. Instead, without damaging her hairstyle, she loved her son back to normality and started the Son Rise programme and lived very comfortably ever after. These schemes did have some good points though; I noted the useful ones from the literature but rejected the rest of the mumbo jumbo.

These schemes are generally known as ABAs, which stands for applied behaviour analysis. Because of their success, there has been a proliferation of these schemes in the United Kingdom, but they all have the following in common. They all start early, they are very intensive and then pursue purely positive approaches. They are also very time-consuming so they are very expensive.

The best education on offer in this country at that time was provided by the specialist autistic schools and units. According to research carried out in 1993, the SLD schools were lagging some way further behind. However with the flood of autistic children entering the SLD schools, they were catching up fast in their understanding of autism, as I witnessed in Laurence's school.

But they could never completely catch up, as the hierarchy is clearly defined by the teaching ratios.

Laurence's class had a teacher-pupil ratio of 1:5, which is usual for an SLD school. In a specialist school the teacher ratio is normally 1:3 and therefore the head-to-head teaching time is that much greater. Laurence was happy in his class and being unable to afford an American-based treatment, we were happy to leave him at Whitefield, especially as there were nearly 8,000 autistic children chasing just 1,000 places in those specialist schools.

If their autistic child was not in one of those places the parents saw it as a failure and they would appeal against the decision. There is a very fair, long-winded appeals process all the way up to the Home Secretary, but by then the child's childhood has slipped away, and the LAD is long dead.

Meanwhile Lovvas, Higashi and other ABAs utilise a teacher pupil ratio of almost 1:1. With the programme continued after school hours by the parents in the home, the results can be staggering. In the 80s, Lovvas claimed that with early intervention nearly half of their children achieved normal intellectual and educational functioning by the end of their first year at primary school, with decreasing levels of support required thereafter. These children are still autistic but they learn to function in the educational and home environments.

These types of treatment are now available in this country, but at a cost. Parents don't mind putting in the time, but if you haven't got the money the well-oiled local authority defence team of psychologists, doctors and therapists ensures that the due process of assessment, diagnosis and statementing allows time for only the minimum of early intervention.

The local authorities are terrified of the cost of these ABAs. Each child would require two years of pre-school full-time 1:1 training with initially only the successful ones integrating into mainstream primary schools with continuing but reducing support. The cost of teachers for two years and the early years mainstream support could be an additional £100,000 for each child, with no guarantee of an individual's success.

With the numbers of autistic children growing rapidly, the local authorities needed a cunning plan. I doubt if anybody would admit to dreaming up the 'inclusion' policy, which has been so enthusiastically embraced by the local authorities. Well, it is cheap: just an assistant to help the child through the school day whose hours are determined by a psychologist employed by the local authority.

Again it's a fair system: if you disagree with the number of hours help your child is receiving, you can appeal and appeal, again and again. By adopting a policy of inclusion, all the children who failed to get a place in a special needs school are magically transformed into successes. Success, that is, for the policy of inclusion, but there is no evidence to suggest that dramatically cutting access to specially trained teachers is beneficial to these children.

The local authorities trumpet that these children are autistic and autism is incurable, and yet with their policy of inclusion for all, these poor children are able to sit in a mainstream classroom and have access to the National Curriculum, just like normal kids. These people are cynically sucking the special education out of our children's lives, leaving future generations with an ever-growing bill of care.

Councillor Radcliffe would be so proud of his successors, but what is the price of all this success? The cost of life-long institutionalisation or care with special facilities soon runs to over a million pounds, and with a full life expectancy the bill for each autistic person could easily be over two million pounds. The one-hundred-thousand-pound bill for each child's intensive early intervention immediately looks like a bargain.

Figures for the autistic population of this country are shrouded in mystery. Nobody is counting. Even when the Commons Health Committee recommended in 1997 that Britain should start a register of autism the government refused to do so and continues to bury its head in the sand to this day. Instead, volumes have been written about 'the difficulties of counting' because of the differences in definitions of various autistic conditions.

We have to rely on extrapolating the prevalence rates in small population studies conducted over the last thirty years, like the Camberwell study by Wing & Gould in 1979 and the Gothenburg study in Sweden in 1986.

From these and other small studies, the NAS estimates a total prevalence rate of ASD in the UK as 91 per 10,000. A mid-2002 population estimate gives this country an under-sixteen population of 11,750,000 children. With a prevalence of 91 in every 10,000, we reach a frightening figure of 107,000 children aged under sixteen with ASD.

We have an epidemic and nobody is even bothering to count the casualties.

Most of these children have average or above-average abilities with an IQ of 70 or above, and with the right help and understanding they can grow up to lead partially or fully independent productive lives. These children have Asperger's syndrome and other similar conditions.

The NAS estimates that approximately 20 of the 91 per 10,000 are like Laurence, with an alleged IQ under 70. This gives us about 25,000 under-sixteens who will require a high level of support throughout their lives. The figure of 8,000 quoted in 1988 has already trebled and yet many would argue that this 25,000 figure is still too low, as prevalence rates are still increasing. I would agree that this figure of 25,000 couldn't be any lower, and it could easily be double that.

Nobody knows.

So 25,000 children times £2 million each equals £50,000,000,000. In other words a £50 billion bill of care for the lifetime of the children in the education system right now. Every year increasing numbers of autistic children step onto the educational ladder without the appropriate preparations and they innocently add another couple of billion pounds to the bill.

Nobody is counting.

We are crippling this generation's healthy children with a future astronomical debt of care for their old classmates. Politicians are not interested in spending money to save fortunes for people in 20, 30, 40 or even 50 years' time. They cling to the hope that the pharmaceutical companies might come up with a cure next year.

Elected officials are interested in policies that will help to give them a second or even third bite of power. For example, cutting half a million pounds from the education budget by depriving half a dozen autistic kids of intensive pre-school training might cost twenty votes. Being seen spending half a million pounds on much-needed new facilities in local schools without raising local taxes wins hundreds of appreciative parental votes.

Maybe we shouldn't be so concerned about the pension time bomb looming in front of us and be more concerned about the much bigger autism bomb rolling up behind us. I say 'bigger' simply because the autistic population has a much longer life expectancy than pensioners. Numbers of pensioners can easily be culled in the future by raising the retirement age from 65 to 70 to 75, but how will they reduce the numbers of autistics? There are no shortcuts.

The drug companies lick their lips at the prospect of a lifetime of profits when they offer to zonk these children so that they are no trouble during their waking hours. Most parents find the idea of Stepford children abhorrent, but presented with no early interventions and no help or understanding from the State, they are often forced to choose between drugs and giving up on their child altogether.

I have a nightmare vision of the twenty-second-century nanny state converting the old royal palaces and castles, which nobody has time to visit anymore, into huge 'monasteries' to house 'God's children' for the rest of their special lives.

Children who failed to learn how to talk during their inclusion in mainstream education could join a silent 'order', while others could be trained to chant and pray their simple spaced-out lives away.

Busy citizens of that future could even sponsor a special child to pray on their behalf, with all proceeds going towards maintaining this sanitized efficient solution to the legacy from the previous century.

But we have been there before, in the nineteenth century. We called them asylums.

*

If the intensive early intervention programmes like Lovvas and Higashi can help these children as they claim, then combined with the full backing of the State, it wouldn't be unreasonable to expect half of all these children to fully integrate into mainstream education and have a productive life.

Having invested the money preparing the children for the school experience and having a thorough working knowledge of each child's special needs, the policy of inclusion could blossom from primary to secondary and beyond when required.

Inclusion is not a cheap option. When done properly it is expensive, but if it is done badly it is an astronomically expensive option.

The system is currently set up to create handicapped individuals. It is designed to assess, label and make a statement about the needs of an individual without the slightest pretence of giving assistance along the way.

We must stop saying autism is incurable; there is so much that we can do to better their lives.

With that attitude, Laurence would never have been 'awoken'.

Whichever way we look at this, the solution is always the same. We must put the children in school first, then have the diagnosis and the Statement comes a long way third, if required.

Put simply, in school by 2 to 3 years of age, formal diagnosis between 4 and 5 years and a Statement by 6 if the child is still struggling to integrate into mainstream education.

7

Diets, Supplements and Poison

The AIT had undoubtedly delivered. When we saw the changes to Laurence we were impatient to try and give him another boost and even though we still had the six- and nine-month post-training reports to complete, we started on the range of supplements that Aditi had told us about.

I was adamant that we would use no drugs.

We started with Dimethylglycine, or DMG for short, which sounds like a drug but it isn't. It is a naturally occurring substance called pangamic acid, otherwise known as Vitamin B15.

During the cold war some Russian scientists started giving pangamic acid to children with learning difficulties. They noted that some of the children showed considerable improvement in their speech. When the Americans got hold of this information they tried it out on some American kids, some of whom were autistic, and just like the Russians, some of their kids' speech improved too.

Since then there have been extensive tests to ensure its safety even with massive doses. The literature suggested that if DMG was going to work, then the effects would usually be seen in the first week and occasionally, quite dramatically, some children spoke for the first time within the first couple of days.

We persevered for a month, but DMG could not work a miracle on Laurence. We saw no effects. Each dietary and supplementary intervention was said to affect a different percentage of the autistic population. It was potluck.

Vitamin B6 with magnesium was next up on the menu for Laurence. It was easy to get hold of in the local health shop, which was handy, as we had to keep this one going for three months.

Aditi had given us the results of a survey conducted by the Autism Research Institute in California on parental evaluations, comparing the effects on their children's behaviour by different drugs, diets and other interventions. Parents were asked to say if their child's behaviour had got worse, stayed the same or got better for the interventions that their child received.

Supporting what I said in the previous chapter, head and shoulders above the rest was 'behaviour modification', or ABAs, with 83% of parents saying their child's behaviour improved with this type of therapy; 14% said no change and 3% said their child got worse. You have to feel sorry for those 3% who spent all their money and invested all their time only to see their child's condition get worse.

Autism does not respect our money. This fact was highlighted by the 48% of parents who saw an improvement to their child's behaviour with cheap and simple 'vigorous exercise'. This fact is often overlooked and with hindsight I think our travels were crucial to Laurence's development. With a child's behaviour deteriorating, there are fewer opportunities for the child to go out and get the rigorous exercise they need. Buying an exercise bike is not the answer, as the real benefits of vigorous exercise come from the autistic child getting lots of opportunities to study and understand their environment.

The Higashi behaviour modification plan is centred on the need for plenty of exercise to tire the children before they settle down to learn.

The sugar-free, milk-free and wheat-free diets all scored well and should be tried individually in order to ascertain exactly what the child is intolerant to. The white diet was not on this list but I read about it elsewhere. It is well known that some children have an intolerance of artificial colourings, but some children have an intolerance of natural colourings as well.

Laurence put himself on a white diet. I wondered if he instinctively knew something and initially I felt terribly guilty about trying to tempt him off it. This was potentially a very serious mistake by us and it highlights the importance of respecting the child's instincts, if it's not harmful. The white diet couldn't be harmful; it was simply not normal, so we tried to correct it. At the same time, however, it is important to remember that a child will often crave something that they are intolerant to, so parental instincts must also be respected. When I thought back, we saw no benefits during his spell on the white diet and in fact his behaviour was deteriorating at that time.

*

The survey conducted by the Autism Research Institute contained a long list of drugs given to autistic children in the United States and Canada. They were placed in order of decreasing behavioural improvement and I was surprised to see Ritalin one off the bottom of the list, with only 21% better behaviour and a whopping 46% worse. The only drug listed below Ritalin was amphetamine, with 20% better and 51% worse. I could not believe that anybody would prescribe amphetamines to an autistic child. But of the 315 prescriptions for amphetamine, 20% of the parents saw an improvement in behaviour, so who am I to argue?

It demonstrates just how diverse the autistic spectrum is.

Moving up the table of drugs, among others were Phenobarbital, Thorazine, Valium, Benadryl, Dilantin and, with 724 prescriptions, the most popular drug of them all was Mellaril. Even though this drug was high up on the list, only 34% said it produced better behaviour, while 23% said worse and 43% said it had no effect at all.

This whole set of poor figures for drug interventions reinforced my decision to avoid drugs. It seemed like the doctors were guessing which drug should go to each child. Many of these drugs were more likely to produce a worsening of behaviour than they were to produce an improvement, so no doctor could say with any degree of certainty what effect any of these drugs prescribed would have.

We talk about the dangers of children experimenting with drugs, but here we have a clear case of doctors experimenting with dangerous drugs on children.

I accept that the data was collected in the late 80s and that in the last 20 years drug interventions must have improved, but they were not honest with their guessing games then, so why should we believe them now?

I also accept that, as parents, we are predominantly unqualified to make expert assessments of these drugs; however, we are experts on our children and we know when they are not right, better than any doctor can.

On top of the list of drugs was the vitamin B6 and magnesium supplement, with 43% of parents reporting an improvement in behaviour while 52% saw no change, with a still worrying 5% saying their child got worse. They were not messing around with the small dosages that we had been using on Laurence. These parents had been giving their children alarmingly high dosages, not just of the B6 but of many

115

other vitamins as well. For this reason it was known as the megavitamin diet. For many years parents had to grind away making their own concoctions, but now there was a product on the market for this megavitamin diet.

I looked at the list of contents; this supplement contained large doses of vitamins A, Bs 1, 2, 6 and 12, C, D and E. It also had several other ingredients and large quantities of calcium and magnesium. Apparently they were needed to help the body cope with all the vitamins being introduced and a lack of these minerals was responsible for the 5% of children getting worse.

There was also a long list of items that it didn't contain, for children already on special diets.

There was nobody to turn to for advice.

We had seen no improvement to Laurence with the small dosages of B6, so at the risk of him exploding with surplus energy we decided to follow the megavitamin approach by filling him with vitamins. The daily dosage was six large capsules and Laurence quickly adopted a chew-and-spit policy.

He enjoyed this game.

Six capsules produced a heaped teaspoon of dark powder when opened. That might not sound much, but it was an awful lot to get past Laurence's eyes and nose every day. Ana had to become very inventive, as Laurence soon realised what was happening and he conducted regular search-and-reject missions around his plate. He learnt so quickly and we learnt so slowly.

I came to realise that if Ana had started out by openly putting the powder on the side of his and our plates and eaten it, he would have eaten it too. It didn't taste too bad and he would have eaten it just as he would eat a bag of plain flour, given the chance. This meant that Laurence was rejecting the powder because it was hidden.

Was this an instinctive mistrust of something in the wrong place or was he using logic and understanding beyond his years?

We slowly realised that Laurence was deficient of nothing. He certainly had excesses of many things but he didn't need any supplements. I suspected that Laurence ate what his body needed just like wild animals, which have been observed seeking out the minerals and salts that their bodies needed. Everything, dirt, fluff, hairy sticky old sweets, pins and anything he could get his hands on from the kitchen, went into his mouth. It was then either swallowed or spat out. He rarely got sick.

If he wasn't swallowing or spitting he was chewing—his clothes, a toy, the furniture—it didn't seem to matter. His mouth was always busy. He had no time for talking except to demand more food. Despite all this oral activity he didn't put on weight. He was reasonably fit and healthy, so after a couple of months with no apparent changes we stopped the megavitamin diet and allowed him to enjoy his food without having to worry about where Mummy had hidden the powder.

I wanted to take Bianca to a firework display but there was no way Laurence would let me take her out without him coming too. I wasn't going to deprive Bianca because of my concerns as to whether he could handle the fireworks and large crowd.

We walked to the display. Along the way we tried to explain to him what was about to happen but, we only received a disinterested 'yeah' in response to our bangs and whooshes. As usual he had no interest in the destination, he was just happy to be out.

We ended up near the middle of the crowd. I avoided the front where they were packed in tight. Laurence had enough space to jump around us while the disco music and laser beams pulsed across the dark field. As we waited while the field filled up, I wished I still had a lead for him so that he couldn't get lost. I had hoped that the fluorescent bendy tubes we bought at the entrance might interest him, but he was only interested in chewing them.

He needed my constant attention. I was resorting to chocolate-button bribery to keep him at heel, when I was relieved to hear the disco music fade away, heralding the start of the show.

The opening explosion of fireworks sent Laurence reeling round to shelter behind me. As the first salvo of rockets exploded high in the sky above, flowers of multicoloured flares floated down towards us. Laurence must have realised that his trusted old shield was useless against this aerial bombardment and sank to the ground behind me in terror. Almost immediately he rose up again, this time inside my coat. He wormed his way right up and peeked out from under my arm. He held my coat in front of his face, taking in just a small part of the display. He was frightened and fascinated.

I looked down to Bianca; she had followed Laurence's antics with some amusement. She was enjoying the display but found the bangs were too loud and had her hands firmly clasped over her ears.

What a family, I thought; she can't listen and he can't look. I was suffering too. The frightened whimpering and whining coming from my petrified puppy inside my coat had attracted the attention of our neighbours. The people in front of us looked around, exchanged whispers and then looked again. Then later they looked again to see if I had done the decent thing and withdrawn with my poor mites.

I hadn't—I couldn't, because for once I was ahead of the game.

I figured that he was already very stressed and introducing any more uncertainties by moving could cause Laurence to produce a firework display of his own. The situation was not satisfactory but it was stable. He had found a way to handle the situation and I was going to support him through it. I didn't move, not even to shuffle my cold feet. I was his rock.

The fireworks lit up the sky; it felt like broad daylight and even after they had finished it felt like there was still a spotlight on us as we slowly made our way towards the exit.

Bianca said that she enjoyed the display but it was too loud and her arms ached from covering her ears throughout. Laurence was skipping around like a newborn lamb. His relief at surviving that bombardment was obvious for all to see. My mind was spinning. Had I been stupid, cruel, thoughtless or just irresponsible? I didn't know. During the walk home I asked him if he liked the fireworks.

'Yeah,' was his consistent emotionless reply.

It was a year later before I found out how he really felt.

He was determined not to be left behind; he definitely wanted to go to see the fireworks again. Now, however, he was ready for them, as he wormed his way inside my coat before the display started.

He was able to take in more and more of the display each year as Bonfire Night became as important to him as his birthday in the annual calendar of events.

I had been right to take him there after all. Now he could grow up to enjoy fireworks just like other kids. The path seemed clear; Laurence was to be left out of nothing. We would expose him and his emotions to as many different sensory experiences as possible.

A week before Christmas we attended a two-day AIT booster course. Research had shown that children who benefited from the original course sometimes benefited from a booster. I was happy to give it a go, it couldn't do any harm. Laurence was relaxed about returning to the Hale Clinic and was happy to comply with sitting in the chair and listening to the music in return for the train and bus trips around central London.

We still couldn't get him to react to hearing the beeps on the audiogram. I felt that at this time it was important to be aiming at his weaknesses, but Aditi assured me it wasn't important and the two days passed without serious incident.

This course was also a good opportunity to catch up with any transatlantic developments. Aditi was selling CDs of music called Spectral Activated Music of Optimal Natural Structure, or SAMONAS for short. She explained that the modified music was based on similar processes to the AIT.

Laurence liked listening to music and I had continued using the headphones on him. It was lovely to see him sitting still, tapping the pages of a book while listening to the music, even if it was for just half an hour or so. He looked so peaceful locked in his musical world.

He almost looked normal.

I bought two CDs, one with the natural sounds of a forest and one with orchestral music. Although Laurence liked to go for runs in the forest he didn't like the nature CD. He started to pull off the headphones, saying, 'No burps.' He didn't like the sound of birds flapping in the forest canopy. I hadn't thought of that, but he did like the other CD. I can't say I saw any improvements, but there were a lot of things happening around us at this time. The important thing was that they couldn't do any harm and they just might have done a little bit of good.

Between the therapy sessions I took Laurence around central London looking at the Christmas displays. One afternoon we walked around Hamley's toy store on Regent Street. It's huge, five or six floors as I recall, and we walked around every one. Nothing interested Laurence—I tried, but nothing got more than a cursory tap before moving on. I remember thinking that I had the only child in the world that would swap the contents of a toyshop for a routine bus ride.

His Christmas presents came from the London Transport Museum, again.

Laurence knew Christmas was coming; he liked the decorations and he was getting excited. We wondered what he was anticipating. It wasn't the presents. He had learnt that we expected him to tear the wrapping paper off from his Christmas presents, which he dutifully did—silently and emotionlessly—one after the other, only pausing to look if he suspected there were sweets inside.

119

That was what he was anticipating, extra food and especially Christmas dinner—he loved roast dinners, and Ana hated cooking them.

The long, aromatic build-up to the roast dinner was too exciting for Laurence. Flapping, jumping and flitting from room to room, he nearly wet himself by the time the food was served. Undercooked, burnt or lumpy, it didn't matter to Laurence; he scoffed the lot and blatantly eyed our plates for potential leftovers without a trace of gratitude. I didn't expect any, but it was heartbreaking for Ana.

He was talking in phrases and he even put phrases one after the other, but they never quite blended into a sentence. Despite this progress Laurence and Ana's communication was getting worse. She didn't understand him. She found it impossible to tell the difference between his questions and his statements, and yet he expected an appropriate response from either. He was struggling to cope with his newfound emotions—they seemed too strong for him and he could easily slip into 'emotional overload' after an inappropriate response. Simple things, mundane situations to us, could create an emotional overload or, in other words, a tantrum.

Laurence appeared to have no sense of time; his life was a sequence of events set out in front of him, just like in school where his day was sequenced. It was interesting to consider whether the TEACCH programme fitted into his way of thinking or whether TEACCH gave him a way to think and organise his life. Which came first?

I might say to Laurence, 'Come on, we're going to the park.' To Laurence this would mean shoes on and then coat on and then go out of the house and then turn right and walk down the road and then cross over and then turn left and then . . . etc., etc., all the way to the park. He understood that park was shorthand for that sequence of events.

Ana might say to Laurence, 'Come on, we're going to the park', and his excitement levels would rise as he understood exactly what that meant. But Ana might have said that to get him on her side before telling him that they had to go to the post office first. Laurence knew that this was not possible—they were in opposite directions, nowhere in the park sequence was the post office—and an emotional overload would build up. If Ana persisted with the post office idea a tantrum was inevitable. Observing Laurence rolling on the floor, kicking and screaming, 'No post office, no post office,'

Ana's conclusion was that he had a strong aversion to the post office.

On the other hand, I had evolved an evasive strategy with Laurence. I would say to him, 'Come on, we're going out.' That was enough to get him excited. The sequence had started: shoes on, coat on and go out of the house, but that wasn't enough information for Laurence.

'Going,' he would demand, holding out his leg for me to tie his shoelace giving no clue as to whether he was making a statement, 'We are going out,' or asking the question, 'Where are we going?'

'We are going out,' I would reply evasively, knowing that he really wanted more information. He must have thought I was a dopey creature who didn't know where I was going most of the time. But it worked; it helped to avoid long sequences.

In time, though, he learnt to counter this.

'Going to,' he would say, staring at my lips for the slightest clue to our destination.

With his shoes on at least, I would suddenly remember where we were going.

'We're going to the post office,' I'd say, without upsetting him, as he had a sequence for that and if I did get some 'that's not very exciting' whines from him, I countered with, 'Do you want to go out?' and, 'Must be a good boy then.'

I would hold back the 'park' option for as long as possible. I would ask him, 'Where shall we go after the post office?' He was always bereft of ideas and replied with, 'Going,' which was now Laurence-speak for, 'Where are we going after the post office?' If I could keep him guessing until reaching the inevitable queue in the post office, then I could be reasonably confident of him being a good boy there. He would wait, tapping with the free brochures on a writing shelf, happily contemplating the sequence of post office-to-park for the duration of the queue.

It was easy if you did things his way and correctly filled in the missing words around his bland words and phrases. It was not easy for Ana, whose English was far from fluent. It was not easy for Laurence, whose effervescent emotions erupted all too easily.

While I was happy to chip away at the edges avoiding confrontations, Ana clashed repeatedly head on with Laurence's autism. She was losing and she blamed me for that. She accused me of taking his side all the time and she did not appreciate my understanding and translations. The school had warned us not to react to his deliberate misbehaviours as it was what he wanted and he would only do it more. Ana, though, couldn't help reacting.

The teachers and I found that a stern look frightened him into changing tack. It was strange, if not surreal, how any other reaction to his pranks would give him satisfaction and encouragement to do it again, but a stern look would see him scampering away every time.

Ana didn't seem to possess a stern look, just an angry one. I thought that autistics couldn't read faces, but Laurence was learning very fast, and we were all getting very confused.

We had made no special plans to welcome in 1995; well, I had made no plans. I came home from work carrying a couple of bags of shopping and the flat was empty. As I wandered around the flat it was so quiet, so empty and I felt empty too.

Ana had taken too much stuff to have left the country; she hadn't even left a note. I felt I should do something but could think of nothing that I could do. I could only wait for her phone call.

A couple of days later the phone finally rang. It was Ana and she was on the offensive, she was spitting fire.

It was my fault that the family had split up. I was just like my father, who had separated from my mother when I was young. She failed to mention that he was still happily married to his second wife after 25 years.

It was my family's fault that Laurence was autistic, she claimed, as there was nothing like that in her family. I chose not to argue; we had been over this ground before when we first discovered that there might be a genetic element to autism. We are not a big family and I had studied my family closely for traces of autism.

My father started out as a TV repairman just as people were switching from black and white to colour. He moved up through the ranks to become an export sales manager for EMI. He was a very good salesman, selling broadcasting equipment to developing countries. I always suspected that his regular business trips abroad were the cause of his first marriage breakdown.

He only had one brother who was a bilingual teacher and a gifted musician. He was married and had two musical girls who in turn had normal children. My father's father was a cobbler and a polio victim and not much else is known about him. My father's mother's side definitely had another musical gene but I could see nothing unusual on my father's side of the family.

My mother's side of the family was larger, with one sister and two brothers. All the women seemed normal housewives bringing up normal kids who in turn have had normal kids themselves, except for Laurence, of course.

There was, however, my mother's elder brother; he was a quiet, solitary man. I only met him a few times at family get-togethers that he couldn't avoid. He was a long-distance lorry driver and he appeared to be married to his truck. You could say he was a bit eccentric or reclusive and that was enough for Ana. It was all the proof she needed to justify her accusation that it was my family's fault.

She carried on, claiming they were much better off without me, the children were happier now. She went on and on before finally saying that I could take the children out on Sunday if I was still interested in them.

'Of course I'm still interested,' I jumped in, interrupting her flow. She gave me the address and times to pick up and return the children. I took down my instructions and didn't argue; there was no point, as she wouldn't listen in her current mood.

They had moved to a quiet part of Leytonstone, but it was an awkward bus journey away. They lived in a tree-lined side road some way from the shops but with a good primary school nearby for Bianca. It was a terraced house with a small front garden, three bedrooms and a large rear garden. I understood why Ana felt they were better off without me. I couldn't compete.

After a couple of Sundays exploring the local parks I decided that I needed a car if we were to get the most out of our days together. My battered old Saab had been so reliable when I was travelling between London and Gloucester every week that I decided to get another old Saab. The 3-door version had the advantage of no doors and windows for Laurence to tamper with in the back while I was driving.

A Saab locks into reverse gear when the ignition key is removed, so I could leave Laurence in the car fiddling with the handbrake amongst other things without worrying about the car rolling away. The seat-belt alarm was also useful, as Laurence did like to undo our seat belts whilst travelling to get a reaction. Having said that, he was generally well behaved in the car, just as he was on public transport.

He enjoyed travelling and I felt it was so important to his development. He could not learn from books or from our conversations as to how the world works. He didn't have the imagination to build up the mental images needed to comprehend our crazy complex world. He had to see it for himself. The more he could see and take in, the more he could begin to understand.

Laurence's sixth birthday came and went. I delivered some presents, he efficiently ripped the wrapping paper and I left. One of the presents was a large map of the Underground for his new bedroom wall. Bianca told me that he liked that but I doubt the rest of the presents got a second glance.

Through the rest of the winter and spring we visited many parks, funfairs, museums and other tourist attractions, as the weather dictated. Sometimes we travelled by car and sometimes we parked the car near a station and used the trains. I always tried to make the journey interesting for Laurence and the destination interesting for Bianca.

Although my Sundays were full, the rest of the week felt empty. I filled my days with my work and in the evenings I studied autism. I could no longer play and experiment with my puppy in the evenings but I could get up to date with all the paperwork that we had collected over the last couple of years.

I had read, met and listened to the best of the experts. Professor Rita Jordan's 'You're the expert now' was a challenge to me. If I was to fulfil that challenge I felt that now was the time to do it while I didn't have Laurence trying to climb onto my head.

Something positive had to come from this mess.

We had now had three failures (DMG, Vitamin B6 and the SAMONAS) since the initial success with the AIT one year ago. Ana was now trying the gluten and casein diets on Laurence. We needed another success, but it became increasingly clear that supplements and diets were not the answer for him. Nowadays there are many good books on special diets for autistic children packed with much better advice than I can give. So my advice on tackling these diets is buy a good book and do it right.

The more I read, the bigger the autism problem seemed to get. I knew it wouldn't be easy, but this seemed a classic case of the more you know, the more you understand how little you know.

It was while I was getting stuck into this quagmire of quandaries that I heard about a group of parents who claimed that their children had been made autistic by the MMR vaccination.

My first thought was Laurence. A quick search of the school papers showed I was too late; he had received his second MMR last November. Anyway, Laurence was autistic before his first MMR; it may have helped to increase his stress levels at that time, but there were too many odd behaviours prior to this and other injections to give us any real cause for concern.

My second thought was Bianca; she had not yet had her second MMR, so I looked into these parents' claims.

The measles, mumps and rubella combined triple vaccine had been given to children since 1988. It was launched as a revolution in child immunisation, but having been used on over a million children, it was withdrawn in 1992 over concerns about the mumps part of this vaccine.

I realised that Laurence would have had that one!

At the time there were acrimonious exchanges about exactly when and how much the government knew about the risks of this vaccine triggering viral meningitis. Government experts produced figures to show that the meningitis risks were not as high as some concerned parties claimed and said that they acted just as soon as they identified the cause and effect. They wasted no time in launching a new improved safe MMR. Now, after three years of this new safe MMR being used, a growing band of parents were claiming that the measles part of the vaccination made their children autistic.

I read the parental reports. They were sad stories of apparently normal toddlers lost to autism within days or weeks of receiving the MMR. They spoke of charming, happy children beginning to talk, with minds enquiring into everything. They were normal kids who passed all their developmental milestones before having the MMR and regressing into an autistic world.

They went on to describe Laurence—the obsessive routines, the flapping and tapping, the chewing everything, the destructiveness, the hyperactive behaviour, and they mourned the loss of their child's personality.

But there was more. These parents spoke of their children appearing to be ill after receiving their MMR. Consulted GPs would tell neurotic parents that it was probably just a cold and sent them away to watch in horror as the 'cold' developed into autism, epilepsy and all manner of bowel problems. These children were sick, some with very serious medical problems on top of their autism. The question was, were these sick children poisoned, and could I learn anything about Laurence from these possibly poisoned autistic children?

I could see little in common between these parents' stories and our own experiences. They had 'lost' their child after the MMR, whereas we had 'found' our child after the AIT.

It seemed that Bianca had nothing to fear from the MMR other than the needle, but there was still a niggling worry. With an autistic brother and the possibility of a genetic link to autism, was Bianca more susceptible to the perils of the MMR than other children?

There was nobody who could reliably answer this question. I decided that it wasn't worth the risk and spoke to Ana. For the first time in a long time she agreed with me and we decided that Bianca should skip the second MMR. It was unthinkable that there was even a remote chance that we might lose her to Laurence's world.

Sometime later, Ana admitted that under enormous pressure from her GP, she gave in and Bianca had the second MMR. I was annoyed that Bianca had been vaccinated against our wishes and relieved that she had come through it unscathed. It was such an unnecessary risk to take with our precious normal daughter.

Our GP was the first to admit that he knew little about autism; it was still considered a rare condition, although numbers were increasing. Any increased risk of autism to siblings would not have shown up in the drug company's tests carried out on general populations. Our GP could not have known what was in the best interest of his patient, so he followed his own best interest and boosted his MMR bonus payment.

I had always been a supporter of vaccinations and we had happily authorised the school to give them all to both children. They had a lot more experience than we had in those situations and with the way Laurence resisted injections as a baby we were happy to let them get on with it.

Vaccination programmes are carried out with the consent of the population and the population gives its consent on the understanding that the inevitable casualties are kept to a minimum. From this experience and my initial investigations into MMR, I was beginning to wonder exactly whose best interests these programmes were serving. I had no axe to grind with the MMR; it had not harmed my children, but my curiosity was aroused and I resolved to follow the fortunes of the 'poisoned' autistics. They could just be a vociferous blip in the statistics or they could hold a hidden clue.

For now, I felt there was no connection to Laurence. He was too healthy to be one of those children.

He was always happy to see me on Sundays. However, it was difficult to ascertain his behaviour during the rest of the week. Ana continued to assure me that everything was fine, but I couldn't believe that the introduction of a garden could have resolved all their disputes.

I would not ask Bianca. I grew up in a broken home and I vividly remember being pumped for information when I travelled between my parents. My mother was up front and honest about it, but my father was more devious, trying to use his well-oiled sales techniques to gain information from me. I hated it but felt obliged to give them both some titbits to demonstrate my loyalty. I would not put Bianca in that position.

Confirmation that everything really was going well with them came when Ana announced that they were moving to Colombia and not coming back, and she informed me that her solicitor had said that there was nothing I could do about it.

I had already hired a solicitor because Ana had decided to start divorce proceedings, so I hastily convened a meeting. Abi was a tall young African woman, probably fresh out of law school, and she was full of enthusiasm. She showed none of the prejudices that I have come to expect in matrimonial battles and she took down my story without assuming that the mother was probably in the right.

'She's wrong,' she said, 'there's a lot that we can do about it.'

There was no time to waste. Within days, Abi had us in the Principal Registry of the Family Division at Somerset House. It was the top family court in the country. It was less formal than a normal court, with discussions and decisions taken around antique tables in wood-panelled offices.

We were in room 53. We sat opposite Ana's team around the perfectly polished table while the judge and his team sat down the end.

Ana's team were immovable—she was going to Colombia with the children and they weren't interested in talking. We spent most of the afternoon in the corridor while the legal arguments raged inside. Occasionally our solicitors were sent from the room while the judge conferred with his team, which allowed us to get updates on the battle.

It was not going well; they were intransigent. Despite Colombia's concerns over child kidnapping, it had not signed the Hague Convention. If she went, there was no way I could get the children back. At the end of the afternoon, with no deal in sight, the judge decided to put the matter to the High Court.

I couldn't believe our little case was going to the High Court and I don't believe Ana's team expected it either.

I had never realised how many courtrooms there are in the High Court, and when we found ours I felt dwarfed by its size and by the judge sitting high up in his pulpit. He started with Ana's team, and they seemed to have completely lost their bottle.

'Of course she's coming back, your honour,' they grovelled. I was stunned.

'Of course you can trust her, your honour, after all, she came back last time.' I was outraged, how could they say that? She never intended to come back last time. I was desperate to speak out, but I had to keep quiet and let my body language do the talking.

Ana's barrister went on, but this particular High Court judge was no fool. He quickly realised they were bullshitting as we wouldn't have been there if they had said this previously. He was furious, and with cold, calculated precision he launched volley after volley of sustained scathing chastisement for wasting his and the court's time. He did not believe one word of their assurances that Ana planned to return. He would not allow the children to leave the country until he had received a letter from Ana's parents giving their assurances that the children would be returned.

Ana's team couldn't object as they had already said she was coming back anyway. I was happy to agree with that and it was all over. It was so quick—it was a rout. Ana's legal team crawled out of the courtroom with their tails between their legs; they had taken a terrible mauling from the judge and it wasn't even lunchtime. Ana, however, didn't care about the judge's silly letter, as she still wasn't coming back.

I skipped down those famous High Court steps. I had met Ana's parents twice and I trusted them. They were decent, honest people. They were honourable people who would now know that I really cared about the children no matter what Ana said to them about me. It was an unbelievable victory pulled from an impossible situation.

*

It was still sad to say goodbye to the children when they flew off from Heathrow, but I was confident that they would be coming back despite what Ana was still saying. I rang once a week; I didn't speak to Ana— I'd chat with Bianca and then get her to give the phone to Laurence. He would get very excited listening on the phone but was too nervous to talk. Instead he would listen and then skip away and then return to the phone to listen some more. I never knew whether he was listening or skipping, but I did know that I could still make him happy all those miles away.

8

Ears, Eyes, Nose and Neck

Six weeks later, in early August, they returned.

Hell hath no fury like a woman thwarted, and Ana was incandescent with rage.

'How dare you interfere with our lives,' she ranted. She had obviously underestimated the judge's letter and her own parents' strength of character. She was furious that she was back in this country and was determined to get her revenge.

We had both read horror stories of the Child Support Agency (CSA), a new government agency that was zealously hounding separated fathers with exorbitant demands for maintenance, regardless of their means to pay.

'I hope they screw you,' she snarled, but more importantly, she didn't prevent me from seeing the children on Sundays. I think she would have liked to, but she needed the break from Laurence.

I guessed that Laurence was pleased to see me. He didn't show it, but he was his usual self, which was good enough for me.

Bianca was sporting a new, very short hairstyle that I'm sure was fashionable and expensive, but it looked absolutely awful on a four-year-old girl. I bit my tongue. I could tell that she was not impressed by it either. As we travelled around different parks and other places on my days off during that summer, she kept an eye out for another little girl with a boy's haircut. I knew that because I was desperately looking for one as well, but to no avail.

The highlights of that summer were trips to Chessington and Thorpe Park. Laurence appeared fearless, wanting to go on all rides that his height allowed; however, I suspected that he usually didn't realise what he was queuing up for and was often taken by surprise by the ride. Despite the look of sheer terror on his face during the ride, he always wanted more. He liked the adrenaline rush, and familiarity with a ride didn't diminish it.

Queuing was a bit of a problem, but he was still young enough to jump up and down flapping his arms if the tension got too much. I noticed normal communicative kids exhibiting the same behaviour when they got near the front of a theme-park queue. The only difference between Laurence and them was he would be jumping and flapping at the end of the queue as well.

Queuing is a part of modern life which he would have to learn to cope with, and the only way I could think of to help him was to keep practising.

I was aware that some of these amusement parks allowed autistics to jump the queue with the physically disabled kids. That would have made our visits to these places a lot less stressful for Laurence and for me.

Long amusement-park queues are expected and they are where you can develop distraction tactics and coercive strategies to handle the unavoidable queues elsewhere. In other words, you learn what works and what does not. Pushing Laurence to the limits of his endurance would inevitably create failure and that unavoidable walk of shame. Other parents are forgiving of toddler misbehaviour, but in a six-year-old it could only be the parent's fault.

The bad-parenting daggers rain down as you march, drag and carry the screaming child away from the queue. My advice is keep marching, don't hesitate to consider which way, don't pause, just walk. The regular pace of the march forces the child into a gentle trotting rhythm. The child has to concentrate on this and as their anger subsides, their breathing settles down into a normal pattern. It is very difficult to remain angry when jogging.

Just as importantly, this march gives the parent time to cool down so that when they are back in full control they can calmly explain the consequences of the incident.

Only then will the becalmed child listen to what you have to say and, having listened, you can slow down, clean up his devastated tear-streaked face and cheer him up with some upbeat messages.

I found that dishing up a sub-standard evening meal because 'the dinner was still in the supermarket' was a useful graphic re-enforcer of the day's lesson. Those tut-tutting parents left in our wake are of course correct—their Johnny would never behave like Laurence had, and weren't they lucky. It was their mutually shared unspoken inferences that were so wrong, insulting and ignorant.

There is never time to explain in these situations and I do

wholeheartedly support the principles behind the 'Autism Is . . .' business cards that you can buy from the NAS to leave behind as you lovingly frogmarch the child away. Not only can they help the parents feel better in these stressful situations, but they also spread the autism message to the poorly informed public. Having said that, however, I never got round to purchasing any of these cards and have become, like Laurence, immune to all of this telepathic bullying.

If I had to do it all again I would use the cards.

I would lie awake at night analysing the run-up to each failed queue incident, searching for clues as to the cause of the eruption. We were so close together, I should have seen everything, but so often I saw nothing. However, I knew that he did everything for a reason. Were those children in front of us annoying him as much as they annoyed me? He hadn't seemed to notice them. Did he mishear something I was saying to Bianca? I tried so hard to remember. Bottled up in a queue, it would take the slightest uncertainty to tip him over the edge.

Poor Bianca, she never got a say once an eruption started. She was left to follow on behind us, probably trying not to look related, another trip ruined by her big brother. But no matter how many times he ruined her day out, she still loved him. She couldn't begin to understand his naughty behaviour and why he didn't learn from his mistakes or from her demonstrations. She was well ahead of him in all areas and was developing a caring, understanding personality.

To Bianca, Ana and the general public a tantrum in the supermarket, deliberately destroying a marketing display, was construed as naughty. So too was an unprovoked assault on another child, pulling their hair, with his other arm around their neck to prevent escape. Again I couldn't agree that these behaviours were naughty.

These 'physical outbursts', as his teacher euphemistically called them, were beyond his control, set off by sensory overload or local environmental triggers. He needed help, not punishment. If I was to help him handle these situations, I had to get ahead of the game and understand my son much better than I did already.

It was clear that autism was not an illness. Laurence was not sick; his body had struggled to cope with his high-speed, bizarre lifestyle during the early years, but apart from the odd bout of asthma and regular grazes he seemed physically healthy now.

However, he did have problems with his senses.

132

We already knew more about his hearing than the audiologists. I suspected that he was still experiencing some distortion with his hearing as it still took him more goes than Bianca to correctly pronounce a new word. There was still some room for improvement here.

Laurence's senses of smell and taste were certainly different. His need for oral stimulation was clear from his tapping the lips, his constant chewing, and his liking for Ana's hot dishes. I didn't see how this could cause any developmental problems.

I could only see his enhanced sense of smell as a bonus. I remember one day in a McDonald's he refused to eat one of his chicken nuggets. This was unheard of and I investigated. When I opened the nugget I found that some of the chicken inside had turned brown. He didn't need to open it, he had smelled it.

I did think that we could help with his constant craving for chewing with chewing gum. It is not a habit that I ever enjoyed but clearly lots of people do. Perhaps Laurence was one of these people, but with an increased need to chew. Unfortunately when he examined the chewing gum he classified it as a sweet and ate it accordingly. Our attempts to show him how to chew the gum were in vain and he continued to bite pieces off the stick of gum, taste them and swallow. The solution to this impasse may well have been tasteless chewing gum, so that it would not be classified as a sweet, but my search for truly tasteless chewing gum failed.

Laurence's eyesight was an enigma. I felt that there had to be a something wrong, but as much as I looked I couldn't see any problems. He could spot a 'gudju' as a tiny speck in the sky, he was unfazed by the flashing lights of a funfair, and he could see a word like 'Paddington' in a magazine if there was a picture of a train nearby to grab his attention.

It was from Donna Williams, author of the book *Nobody Nowhere*, that I first heard of fractured vision. She described it as like looking through a shattered pane of glass.

This could explain how he could see small areas in detail but could not make sense of the bigger picture. Donna and other individuals had found that wearing tinted lenses helped many types of visual dysfunctions. Since the 1980s the Irlen Centre had been using these filters to help people with dyslexia and other reading problems. It was only recently that they had found that these filters might help the autistic population as well. So I phoned them for more information. They were being swamped by calls from parents of autistic children wanting to try their coloured lenses.

I explained that I had no specific reason to suspect my son would benefit from the filters, but I wanted to eliminate this line of investigation from my enquiries. They sent me an information pack with some self-testing ideas to carry out before making an appointment.

Great—we were on another mission in the pursuit of my quest.

I bought a red, blue, green and yellow light bulb and blacked out a room. Using each colour in turn, I monitored Laurence while we carried out various activities such as puzzles, drawing, catching and throwing balls and general playing. I had to take notes on his behaviour, any squinting, his abilities to perform the tasks and any other differences that I could observe between the different-coloured lighting sessions.

I allowed him a good runabout to let off steam while I changed the hot light bulbs and at the end of the last session, I thought I could see a pattern. It certainly wasn't clear-cut, it could be a blip, and it could be wishful thinking. A repetition of the tests the following weekend would be needed to confirm the pattern.

Bianca was very interested in this important research into Laurence's eyesight and was keen to help by retrieving wayward balls and so on. She was very helpful, as her presence allowed me to sit back occasionally to monitor where he was focusing. The second set of tests showed an even more pronounced pattern but for a different colour. I was desperate for a positive result, but I couldn't ignore the first set of results. Hopefully a third weekend would confirm the second set of results.

By the time we had finished the third session the novelty factor had disappeared for all the parties. I combined all three sets of results and the conclusion was clear: the results were random, there was no positive preference for any colour.

I decided not to make an appointment at the Irlen Centre, but I would give Laurence a range of coloured sunglasses next summer in case a preference developed.

We also knew about Laurence's skin sensitivity, his sense of touch. We had already conceded defeat with clothing labels. Ana had found it was better to cut out labels neatly first, rather than have him rip a hole in the garment trying to remove the label. He was incredibly ticklish, despite his best efforts to control it, and he hated having his head touched. I also suspected that his love affair with water was purely a sensory thing.

For an insight into tactile and other sensory problems, I found the writings of Temple Grandin invaluable. This autistic professor with many sensory issues built her own squeezing machine at the age of eighteen. She went on to get her PhD in animal science and created a 'stairway to heaven' responsible for the humane slaughter of most of the western world's cattle. She did this by looking at the cow's perspective.

An Inside View of Autism by Temple Grandin is essential reading for anybody trying to understand sensory issues.

I didn't feel that Laurence's tactile problems were urgent enough to require a squeezing machine, although I appreciated that they could make his life more difficult than it needed to be.

My puppy didn't like being stroked. I had tried stroking him very gently but he soon ran away. To my surprise he was less bothered by short periods of firm stroking. I suspected that the gentle stroking was too tingly for him. Having found what he could tolerate, the de-sensitising could begin and I stroked him as often as he would allow.

Some areas were more sensitive than others. He was already de-sensitising his mouth by chewing hard objects like Lego bricks. However, the rest of his head was still very sensitive and he didn't like having his hair stroked at all. We had to pick our moments carefully.

The most sensitive area of all was the back of his neck; there was no chance of giving him a neck massage. I only had to touch his neck and he would collapse to the ground and then roll away from my reach. The way he dropped reminded me of one of Mr Spock's handy tricks in Star Trek. Although I applied no pressure, I felt it was still a bit cruel and used it only to bring him under control in emergencies.

It was certainly no party trick.

In the same vein, Laurence could often be seen apparently giving himself a Vulcan mind-meld, and I tried it.

With the little finger of the left hand in the corner of the eye, middle fingers bent under the palm and the first finger blocking the ear the thumb naturally rested on the jaw.

He was picking up the vibrations. He seemed relaxed when he sat doing this. His howling was barely audible; in fact, it was relaxing for the whole family. I tried it with him. As we hummed quietly together in a mind-meld, I desperately wanted to take a bite out of his autism and to give him a mouthful of my understanding in return.

There was another sense that he really struggled with—his sense of fear. It had started with pigeons and had progressed to dogs. 'Dawg ... Dawg' was the alarm call from Laurence to alert the family whenever one of these unpredictable creatures headed our way. I suspected that he was frightened of dogs and pigeons because they moved faster than he could run away. In other words, he felt vulnerable.

He still had a faint scar across his cheek from his close encounter with a cat all that time ago but he didn't appear to be frightened by them. They were lazy cats around our way and rarely moved fast enough to bother him. He left them alone and they left him alone. They had a truce, but toy dog breeds, that were even smaller than a cat, still frightened him. I wondered how he differentiated between tiny dogs and big cats.

It didn't make sense, and each time Nanny's dogs came to visit it was like he had never met them before. 'No dawg, no dawg!' he would scream while standing on the table or on the back of the settee as the tail-wagging monsters milled around below trying to lick his ankles.

However, there was a lot of nervous laughter between his screams whenever a dog put its feet up on a chair to get closer to him. He was enjoying all this excitement, he loved the adrenaline rush, and it was like the amusement park had come to his turf. By the end of each visit Laurence would nervously stroke the dogs, but on their next visit he was back to screaming, 'No dawg!' He liked it like that.

On his own turf, he had a measure of control, but if caught by surprise in a park he had no qualms about using his little sister as a human shield if I wasn't immediately available to use.

It was good to see his sense of survival was programmed too strong as well.

Ana's revenge arrived on my doormat a couple of weeks after she returned to England. The large brown envelope from the CSA was more terrifying than any firework display. During the breaks in the battle to keep the children in this country, my solicitor Abi had told me of some of the cases she had been working on involving the CSA. One poor father had custody of his daughter and still had a bill from the CSA for £10,000. They were intransigent and if they wouldn't listen to her, what chance would I have?

I questioned, argued and stalled at every opportunity, but they were relentless. They were not interested in my bills, they were only interested in what money I had coming in and where I kept it.

A colleague of mine was screwed by the CSA with a demand for £93 per week maintenance for his nine-year-old daughter plus a five-figure bill for the arrears. An unemployed adult didn't receive that much on the dole, so how could they justify this figure for a child? He was taking home around £200 per week and, faced with regular additional deductions from his wages to repay the arrears, he was forced to abandon his career, go on the dole and get his CSA assessment reduced.

It was madness.

I was determined that the State would not crush me in the same way. Like my colleague, there wasn't much money for the CSA to find, but there was some. I had been working overtime saving some money for a holiday and to cover our moving expenses when the time to move came. That move was obviously not going to happen now, but I wasn't going to meekly hand over my hard-earned cash. I would prefer to spend the money on a holiday or some therapy for Laurence. But what?

The latest craze in the world of autism was Facilitated Communication, so I investigated.

They were sitting young children with autism in front of a computer with a facilitator standing behind them supporting the child's hands over the keyboard. Some of the work produced on the computer this way was quite extraordinary and produced many arguments among parents and experts. The believers in Facilitated Communication claimed it was all the child's work, while the disbelievers suggested that the facilitators subconsciously assisted the children without realising it.

The truth in these arguments seemed clear. Whereas some of the facilitators might have been a touch too eager to produce a success story, there were undoubtedly a few children who did benefit from having this kind of physical support to communicate. This wasn't surprising, as we had already seen Laurence needing physical support to do even the simplest things, such as holding cutlery and pens.

Even with the entire class stamping their feet in PE, Laurence had no clue as to what he was supposed to be doing when the teacher said, 'Stamp your feet.' A teaching assistant had to get down on her knees and physically manipulate his legs to get him started. Likewise with catching a ball and clapping, Laurence needed an assistant or facilitator to move his arms appropriately. He was physically capable of doing these things but needed this support until he had the confidence to do it on his own. So I could easily understand how some autistic children needed physical support to type on a computer.

At the same time I realised that Facilitated Communication was not for Laurence. He couldn't see any correlation between his tapping on the keyboard and what came up on the screen, despite all our efforts. It was similar to our problems getting Laurence to complete the audiogram; he could not associate tapping on the table when he heard a sound.

I had tried to help him overcome this mental block by buying him remote-controlled toys. No matter how hard I tried I couldn't get him to understand that it was his tapping on the remote control that caused the car to move. I had to accept that this was too complex a concept for him to understand, for now.

Like everybody else in the country at this time, I had been following the horrifying case of Nurse Beverley Allitt. She had murdered four infants and seriously harmed nine others, a truly evil woman who preyed on the weakest of them all, sick children in hospital.

The experts disagree; they said she is not evil, she is sick, and declared that she was suffering from Munchausen by Proxy Syndrome. No doubt the taxpayers are paying for her to be studied by highly qualified experts with a view to curing her while she serves her thirteen life sentences. Why is anybody who commits an abominable act declared sick and not evil?

Among her victims were baby twins, the same age as Bianca; one died and the surviving twin was growing up with permanent brain damage and was partially paralysed. The experts agreed that she had no chance of any significant improvement.

Of course her parents were not going to give up on their precious little survivor and they turned to the United States, where there is always hope.

The newspapers followed her story as she underwent dolphin therapy in Florida. It was a real tearjerker of a story. The Make-A-Wish Foundation sends terminally ill children there. Crash victims paralysed from the neck down are taken there in the hope of getting the first flicker of movement. When the experts said no hope, the staff at Dolphin Human Therapy (DHT) started working on these children and they regularly performed miracles.

In this instance I define a miracle as the movement of an arm or the first words uttered after a lifetime of being told no chance. If it was incurable they tried to help and autism is incurable. They saw a lot of children with autism.

I sent off for an information pack.

It was immediately obvious that they were oversubscribed. They were already fully booked for the following year but they did have a two-week slot in April due to a recent cancellation. If I wanted that slot I would have to act fast. I needed to, as I had the CSA breathing down my neck.

The basic idea behind DHT was simple. It was a motivation-based behaviour modification programme. They utilise the child's natural desire to interact with the dolphins by offering rewards for improvements in behaviours related to each child's specific disabilities. So each programme was different, but they all used the same reward of interactions with the dolphins.

Was this the right therapy for Laurence?

I tried to think logically, putting aside all the emotional considerations as I weighed up the pros and cons. Laurence was frightened of all fast-moving animals from pigeons to dogs, so I doubted that he would be motivated to interact with the dolphins. However, I had previously asked at his school for poolside speech therapy as it was clear that Laurence was highly motivated by the prospect of going in the water. It was clear that this was prime learning time. Of course I was laughed at, but the principle was the same here.

On balance I was confident that he would get used to the dolphins after a couple of days, just as he got used to Nanny's dogs during each visit. He would soon get to like the thrill of being pulled through the water by the dolphins.

Then there was the cost of the therapy; at $5,000 for two weeks, it was more than I had expected and on top of that, there were the flights, accommodation, car hire and living expenses. There were no package deals. The final payment would be due in March, six weeks before the therapy. I could take out a bank loan to cover the shortfall. It was financially feasible but it would leave me with nothing except for a large debt.

The CSA would be welcome to that.

My other concern was the practitioners. Where they experts in the field or were they jumping on the bandwagon in a lucrative field? I decided to invest some money on the telephone and try to find out more about the man who ran the show, David Nathanson, PhD, or Dr Dave, as he preferred to be called.

I found the Americans refreshingly open and I was surprised at how often I got straight through to people without having to negotiate obstructive secretaries.

As I built up a picture it became clear that for many years Dr Dave had been a pioneer in this field. I don't know how, but I ended up having a long chat with a lady who was working with dolphins, studying inter-species communication. When I said that I was from London she told me that she was travelling to Europe to work with a disabled boy and dolphins but she couldn't tell me exactly where she was going because her research was funded by the military.

The American military were spending millions on inter-species communications research, to be better prepared for when ET arrives. The theory was that if we couldn't communicate with a species living next door like dolphins, what hope would we have communicating with a species from billions of miles away?

Being unable to discuss specifics didn't prevent us having a fascinating chat about her work in general. It seemed that they were interested in the communicative intent of certain behaviours shared by dolphins and autistic subjects. At this time I was out of my depth with the idea of some strange 'seventh sense' shared by different species, but we did share common ground.

I was trying to communicate with my puppy and she was trying to communicate with the dolphins. They are both intelligent mammals and can be trained to make appropriate responses to an ever-widening range of commands, but they displayed no desire to communicate, as far as we could see.

Laurence's phrases were just that, pre-learnt phrases which he uttered when he thought we expected it. There was nothing coming from inside him, there was no apparent communicative intent, just never-ending demands and pre-learnt tricks. Dolphins made demands and performed pre-learnt tricks. In fact, there were many behavioural similarities.

They suspected that we were missing out on something.

When I mentioned that I was going to see David Nathanson she replied, 'Oh, you'll get a bang for your bucks with Dr Dave all right.' She knew him well. I hadn't heard that expression before but as soon as she said it I knew that that was what I had wanted to hear.

A bang for my bucks was what I was looking for, miracles happen to other people.

I rang DHT straight back and spoke to Dr Dave, who happened to answer the phone. We discussed Laurence's love of water and fear of animals. He didn't try to sell the therapy; he explained that a fear of either of these could put limitations on what could be achieved with this type of therapy. He stressed that there is no magic bullet.

He explained that only I could decide whether his fear was more that of sheer terror or just exaggerated natural apprehension. I felt that Laurence fell into the latter category. I had caught him laughing between screams with the excitement of a dog's presence. The decision was made. I told Dr Dave to book us in. I would be wiring the deposit to them the next day. For the second time in my life, I was sending a chunk of money to the USA with my fingers firmly crossed.

Dolphin Human Therapy is based at Key Largo in Florida. Key Largo is the first and largest of a chain of small islands stretching out over a hundred miles into the Gulf of Mexico from the southern tip of Florida. The DHT team were accustomed to receiving visitors from all around the world and their next information pack was comprehensive.

Of course there were all the waivers, disclaimers and other legal stuff in triplicate to plough through, but they also wanted lots of information from me. They wanted the latest school, medical and psychological reports plus any other recent reports from relevant areas of treatment like speech and occupational therapy in order to prepare Laurence's programme.

There were some add-ons that you could purchase and I felt that their 'Reefling' programme for the siblings was an essential extra. With all the attention focused on Laurence, this would make Bianca feel special too. They taught the children to recognise the local marine life and at the end of the course they had an hour's snorkelling lesson before going on a four-hour boat trip to snorkel over a coral reef. She was the minimum age so she would be mixing with the big girls. She would like that.

There was also Dr Dave's guide to all the local amenities and the list of hotels graded as expensive, medium and cheap, which was a great help to finding accommodation. I was surprised to see that many of the big name hotels were there. Key Largo has its own Sheraton and Marriott and I was relieved to see a Holiday Inn down in the cheap section. I rang around a few other places in the lower priced section getting quotes and checking availability and I was confident the Holiday Inn would be cheaper than them.

It wasn't. 'You're not one of those nice cheap Holiday Inns like I've stayed in before?' I commented while I recovered from the shock of the price.

'Nothing is cheap in Key Largo, sir,' was the cheerful reply. I was beginning to get the picture. I decided to compromise and booked the first five nights of our stay only. I hoped that once we had settled in we might find somewhere better and cheaper for the second week.

There was so much to organise, with just enough money to pay all the booking deposits until the bank loan arrived. It was an exciting time.

My biggest problem was getting hold of the children's passports, as a still-bitter Ana had handed them to her solicitors. Ana's solicitors were also bitter and they were determined to get revenge for their High Court humiliation. They advised Ana that it was in her best interest for them to retain the passports, so I rang them.

'You mustn't talk to us, you must speak to your solicitor.'

So I did. We had a little chat and she knew me well enough to know that I could understand a legal document. She couldn't see why she should get involved if I was prepared to sign anything they demanded. If I wasn't happy with anything, she would be happy then to get involved.

I wrote to Ana's solicitors explaining that we weren't going on holiday. I told them we were going to the United States for potentially life-altering therapy that wasn't available in this country for my autistic son and I was happy to agree to whatever conditions they saw fit to impose. They did not reply, so I telephoned again. The woman I spoke to sounded quite hysterical because I had rung her again and frantically repeated that I had to get legal advice, while I shouted over her voice, 'Screw me if you want, I don't care, I'll sign anything you want!'

We were getting nowhere. I could see their game. They wanted to make a string of queries and clarifications, extracting as many letters as they could from my solicitor before the flight date. They would make a nice profit from Ana's increasing legal aid bill and their revenge would be my additional stress and large legal bill. I didn't have the money to play this game.

To me those solicitors were evil. It was extortion. Masquerading as 'family solicitors', they were threatening to prevent my son from having potentially life-changing therapy unless I handed over a sizable chunk of money.

Despite all this hassle, things started to look up. First, the CSA bill arrived; they wanted £47 per week, which wasn't as bad as I had expected. My colleague had been screwed for double that for just one child and yet he was on the same wage as me. It didn't make sense. They also wanted arrears dating back to the day Ana walked out. They even had the cheek to expect me to pay for the six weeks she spent in Colombia. I started making the weekly payments to show good faith while I argued about the arrears. At the end of the argument there would be no money left for them to take, anyway.

A few weeks after I had started making the payments there was a knock at the door. It was a dark, wet and windy evening. I opened the door to be confronted by a completely soaked Ana with the children on either side and her sister Nancy standing a few paces behind in the rain with some luggage.

Ana burst into tears; she spluttered out that she was sorry and wanted to come back. I was happy to have the kids back, so I ushered the children inside and left the door open for Ana to follow us in.

Oh, how I wanted to slam the door in her face but I knew it wouldn't solve anything. I was very angry with her; she had put us all through a lot of pain following some airhead social worker's vision of a better life living on the State. Now was not a time for arguing, though— it was a time for listening.

I had said little to Nancy since she abused our hospitality so badly. She was uncomfortable in my presence, but while Ana was sorting out the children's beds she came over and said, 'She is much better now, you will see.'

'I will see,' I nodded with a raised eyebrow. With that she said her goodbyes and left—she had a long drive home. Despite my misgivings I could tell that she was a good sister to Ana. She had driven all the way across London after work to help her with this theatrical production.

I listened to Ana once the children had gone to bed. Her repeated claims that everything was fine had been a façade. She had had problems with the council and the neighbours, and Laurence's behaviour was getting worse. She couldn't cope with him any more.

We agreed to try to live together peacefully and see if time could ever heal the wounds that were preventing us from loving each other.

My biggest headache immediately disappeared as there was now no need for the solicitors to hold the children's passports, and they meekly handed them over without gaining any concessions from me.

The evil legal-aid blackmailers ended up with nothing.

It was great having the kids back. The flat had felt so cold and empty in the evenings when I came home from work. I had missed trying to read to Bianca with Laurence clambering onto my head or demanding, 'Horsey, horsey' sitting on my crossed legs.

He was getting too heavy for these toddlers' games but he couldn't understand that and he always wanted more. He had become used to getting his own way and several negative behaviours had crept into his life. He was pulling hair, spitting and kicking.

It would take a long time to heal the damage to this family and it wasn't long before the fragile family bonds were put to the test. Ana wanted to go to Florida; she had friends in Miami and cited my attempt to rebuild the family with the Lanzarote holiday as a good reason for her to come on this holiday.

I couldn't use any of the emotional reasons why I didn't feel she deserved a holiday. Therefore, I was relieved that the simple truth of the matter was that I couldn't afford an extra passenger. The financial facts and figures were clear—I was skint, and she had to begrudgingly accept that she wouldn't be going.

As our departure date drew near we were all excited. I was because the next leg of my quest would take us to a place where miracles sometimes happen. Bianca was because she was going to see some dolphins. And Laurence was because he was going to Heathrow Airport. I don't think anything else we said was understood, but he had picked up on the word Heathrow and that was enough for him.

When we got the luggage out of the loft Laurence was ecstatic. He needed to jump up and down, flapping to burn off the excitement, but he also wanted to curl up inside the luggage and he wanted to start packing, all at the same time. He could be such a clown sometimes and this was one of those occasions. We stood back bemused as he frantically flitted around the flat.

It was apparent that as his thoughts switched from flapping to packing so his body switched too as if he had no control. There was no buffer between thinking and doing. He was in overload mode and it was best to let him burn it off.

It was Saturday night and Ana would have to pack the luggage while we slept as we had an early start for what would be the longest day of my life.

9

Dolphin Human Therapy . . .

The taxi arrived at six in the morning. Laurence was bouncing off the walls, Bianca was sleepy and Ana was tearful. She had been up all night packing and crying. She was still upset that she wasn't coming with us, but she had to bottle it in for the children's sake.

It was a short taxi journey to Walthamstow station and then a lengthy Underground ride to Heathrow. Laurence knew the way. There was plenty of space on the train so I allowed him to bounce around the compartment to burn up his excitement. He wouldn't stray too far as he always kept the luggage within his sight.

We arrived at Heathrow half an hour earlier than I had planned, giving him more time to run around the terminal, brushing past people and their trolleys. Thankfully there were no collisions and there were no tears when we said bye-bye to the luggage at the check-in desk. Laurence was on his best behaviour; he had been a delight to be with.

We wandered around the shops wasting time, with Laurence skipping around us burning up more energy. It was only nine o'clock in the morning and he was full of it.

He coped well throughout the boarding procedures. He quietly sat down in his seat, but as the plane started to move his excitement levels rose. His rocking became violent and his knees kept crashing into each other. I put my hand over his knee to cushion the impacts and slid my elbow across his shoulder and chest restricting his rocking.

He didn't object to me doing this, he never tried to push my elbow away. It was as if he needed the rocking convulsions but didn't need the movement that came with it. As the plane took off and rose up into the sky he gave my hand a big squeeze and the tension ebbed out of his body.

I started feeding them boiled sweets to keep Laurence in his seat

146

until the seat-belt light went off and to help their ears adjust to the altitude. Bianca had the window seat with Laurence in the middle and me on the end to prevent him escaping with a head start.

When I allowed him to take his seat belt off he jumped up and then immediately got down on the floor.

'Laurence, what are you doing?' I asked.

'Sleep.'

'Do you want to go to sleep now?'

'Yeah.'

'Is Laurence tired?' I couldn't believe that he wanted to go to sleep; he had been so full of energy just a few minutes ago.

'Yeah,' he lied.

'OK, Daddy help Laurence.' I couldn't believe my luck; this was an unexpected bonus, no matter how short his nap was.

Bianca explained to me that he had slept on the floor during their return flight from Colombia. It made sense now and of course he had no trouble sleeping then, with the aid of Mother's little helper. Today was different; he was full of beans, so for the next eight hours between meals we played 'It's time to go to bed now'.

Aarrgh! Hour after hour we repeated the same conversations followed by night-night and a short period of squirming and wriggling on the floor as he attempted to go to sleep. Each time he was soon back up on his feet to have a quick look around before initiating the whole process again. It did keep him occupied and out of trouble, but my patience wore thin and with an hour to go I introduced the idea of 'finish soon'.

'No there, no there,' he screamed.

I had started the descent too soon and he exploded. That last hour seemed longer than the whole of the rest of the flight. As soon as I could get a hand free I produced the rather sticky chocolate buttons that I kept in my pocket for just such situations.

They gave him something else to think about. I realise with hindsight that to Laurence the flight couldn't end, as he hadn't been to sleep yet, despite his hours of trying. It was a disaster for him and I had failed to see it coming.

It was such a relief to let go of his hand as we disembarked. I knew he wouldn't go far as he scampered up the gangway into Miami International Airport, free to roam at last.

Bianca and I were still nursing sore heads from his attack. He had grabbed a handful of her hair and as I forced him to let go he made a grab for mine. Despite the shambles at the end, I felt that overall the flight had been a success.

There were long queues at immigration, but with Laurence able to skip up and down along the queue there was no problem. The man at the desk was very nice and he even allowed the children to stamp their own passports. Bianca did hers followed by Laurence, but he stamped his with gusto. The stamp crashed down onto the desk causing everything else to bounce up. Laurence had clearly done 'stamping things' at school and was keen to show what he could do. The man was taken aback by the force of the blow and took another look at our passports before returning them. I smiled and thanked him as I quickly ushered Laurence away.

I allowed Laurence some time to run around the terminal to burn off some of his pent-up energy and then caught a courtesy bus to the Alamo car rentals.

The name 'Alamo' conjures up feelings of foreboding and this was heightened now by copious newspaper reports in England about tourists being singled out by robbers after leaving the car-hire centres. We were seen as easy pickings.

The car-hire centre was huge, one enormous car park with several large cabins at the centre of a sea of cars. A large fence surrounded it and beyond that it looked rough. I had visions of the baddies circling the compound waiting to pick us off one by one as we made our dash for freedom.

The atmosphere inside the cabins was feverish. The air conditioning didn't seem to be working, it was hot and stuffy and the queues seemed all tangled up. Laurence would have to be loose and I told Bianca to keep an eye on him while I found the right queue. She would let me know if he started doing something outrageous. I didn't need to worry, as he found two empty seats in a corner and he curled up on them. He got some funny looks but he was no trouble. I wondered if the excitement of the day had started to catch up with him or was he still trying to take that nap?

Behind the counter it was all hands on deck and the queues moved quickly. At the counter the girl was polite and efficient and zipped through the details.

These were dangerous times; Laurence could get up at any time in a bad mood, especially if he was tired. I wanted to get out quickly and get Laurence safely strapped inside the car without pushing my luck any further. She wouldn't give me the keys until I had heard all the dos and don'ts for my own safety. The car-hire companies were going to great lengths to ensure we all knew of the dangers out there. They had even removed their advertising from the number plates to make us less obvious; we had to blend in with the Miami traffic as quickly as possible.

'Where you heading?' she enquired.

When I told her that we were heading for Key Largo she muttered that she would have to write out some instructions for me. It seemed that few people headed south from here. The instructions were long and complicated. I was getting very concerned and she handed them over with a pile of guides, maps and the car keys, while pointing in the general direction of our car. Having put the fear of God in me, she had the gall to say, 'Have a nice day now,' before swiftly moving on to the next customer.

As I walked back towards Laurence he sprang up—he hadn't been sleeping. He had been keeping an eye on proceedings safely curled up in his corner of the heaving room. It was great to get out of that oppressive atmosphere and breathe in the car fumes outside. It took a while to find our car, but once the luggage was in the boot and the kids were strapped in the back, I felt I could breathe a sigh of relief even though we still had the badlands in front of us. To hammer home their safety points, there was a list of the dos and don'ts attached to the steering wheel.

I was tired and I don't mind admitting that I was scared. This was my first visit to America. As I twiddled with the knobs and adjusted the mirrors I tried to memorise the route, but it wouldn't sink in. I realised that I would have to hope for a road sign south after a few turnings.

I didn't see a sign and I got lost while we were still in the badlands. The Alamo car rental site was at the heart of a sprawling grey industrial estate, which on a Sunday afternoon was deserted. I expected to see tumbleweed drifting down the lifeless roads, but I did spot a police patrol car parked at the end of the road and I pulled up beside him. He gave me some simple instructions which I was able to follow, and we were soon turning on to the elevated freeway and back into civilisation.

I noticed in my rearview mirror that the patrol car discreetly followed me, turning back only when they saw that we were safely on our way. What a good example of preventative policing, I thought.

As we travelled further south the number of lanes in the road reduced. It was a pleasant journey with little traffic; in fact there was a lot more traffic coming the other way. The children were tired. Bianca was asleep—she was always falling asleep in the car—and Laurence was sitting staring blankly out of the window in silence. As we approached the southern tip of Florida the road reduced to one lane each way and it was a solid jam coming the other way.

As we sailed past boat after boat, it became clear that these people lived in Miami and had spent their weekend fishing and playing with their boats on the Keys. Now they were hauling their toys home. For every small dinghy and jet ski there was a pocket battleship-sized powerboat being towed by a super-size family truck. They wouldn't get far on our roads, I thought, but now I realised why everything was so expensive on the Keys. We were entering the Miami residents' playground.

A causeway took us onto Key Largo, where the road opened out again into a three-lane dual carriageway with a wide grassy central reservation. All business premises on the Keys give their address with a mile marker figure. Mile marker 1 or MM 1 was at the end of the island chain in Key West and then every mile along the road was another MM post all the way up and onto the mainland.

This made it easy for outsiders who don't know the names and order of the islands. Spotting an advert for Mary Beth's Diner, Pigeon Key, MM 48.4 you knew exactly where it was without having to wonder in which direction Pigeon Key actually was.

The Holiday Inn was at MM 100 and just after MM 101 I spotted the logo in the distance, on the other side of the carriageway. I would have to execute an American U-turn, as I had seen many do already.

It was a tricky manoeuvre: speed up moving into the outside lane, then break hard into the crossover lane on the central reservation, spin the car round and choose your moment to shoot across three lanes of traffic into the hotel car park; safe. We had reached base camp.

I wished I could slump into the sumptuous armchairs in the reception area as the children did, but I had to stand at the counter and allow the receptionist to fill me in. Eventually she handed over a handful of paperwork with the keys and a map of the resort.

It wasn't a hotel, it was a Holiday Inn Resort. I wondered what the difference was and realised the receptionist had probably just explained that to me so I didn't ask. We walked through the reception following the map and found ourselves in a large open-air quadrangle with two floors of rooms in front and to our right. To our left were tropical gardens surrounding a large rectangular swimming pool. Our room was over the back, in the cheap seats. As we walked around the serene blue pool we could hear loud gushing water.

Behind the pool on the other side of the thatched poolside bar was a large children's pool with a wide waterfall cascading into it. The children were transformed; all signs of tiredness vanished immediately. Laurence was jumping up and down, flapping his arms and struggling to take his clothes off all at the same time while Bianca was bombarding me with pleases.

'OK, OK,' I quickly surrendered, telling them they could have a little swim after we had found our room and unpacked their costumes.

The room was an icebox with the air-conditioning full on so I switched it off, as I didn't want the children catching a chill. There was no time for organising; Laurence was on an urgent mission so it was a quick change, pick up the water wings and towels and head back to the pool.

Despite all the excitement and urgency in Laurence's actions, Bianca was frolicking in the water long before he was. He flapped around the edge of the pool on tiptoe. He kept going to jump in but kept pulling back at the last moment for some more flapping. He was ripe for a push but I didn't and I led him to the concrete steps leading into the shallow 3-foot section. He stood flapping on the first step with his ankles in the water for a while before stepping down and cautiously exploring the extent of the three-foot area. Only when he was confident about the extent of the shallow area did he relax and start jumping up and down laughing.

I remember thinking that he looked like a fish when he leapt up and crashed down into the water; however, he didn't have the agility of a dolphin. His was more like a whale belly-flop than a dolphin dive.

It was six o'clock in the evening here and miles past their bedtime in British time and yet there wasn't a trace of tiredness to be seen in either of them. Watching them laughing and splashing made all the trials of the day disappear. Although the air was still hot the shadows stretched across the pool and I could see that the children were getting cold, but they didn't care. It was the promise of some dinner that finally got them out.

Our room was like a sauna so I turned the air conditioning back on. Dried and dressed, they had children's portions of fish and chips beside the pool. They could only eat half, their eyes were getting heavy and they were in danger of falling asleep into their food. I whisked them back to our room and they were asleep before their heads hit the pillow.

I wanted to do the same but there was so much to sort out. The therapy started at 10.00 a.m. and the room was already a tip. It was a large bed-sit comprising a lounge/dining area by the door with two double beds in the adjoining sleeping area, a bathroom and a small kitchenette. I was smugly pleased with my choice of accommodation.

Laurence was awake at 6.00 a.m., bouncing around the apartment, but Bianca was so tired that she managed to sleep through the commotion until 7.30. We had plenty of time to look around the locality.

On the block adjacent to our resort there was a parade of shops including a diner, a couple of small gift shops, a supermarket and a water sports shop that was the largest and busiest shop on the block. There were also a McDonald's in a petrol station and a Burger King on either side of the carriageway. We appeared to have landed in a good spot.

We needed provisions, so we explored the supermarket. It was more like a large Londis than a super Sainsbury's, but they had fresh fruit daily and the children were soon demanding water melon, bananas that hadn't crossed the Atlantic and freshly squeezed Florida orange juice for breakfast. Laurence's eyed popped out of his head when he saw the size of American crisp packets. He wasn't bothered whether they were called chips or crisps, as he knew exactly what was inside. We had to buy some but I made out that it was on the understanding that he had to be a good boy with the dolphins. However, I realised that he would say anything for a bag of crisps that size.

After breakfast I drove the short distance to the Dolphin Human Therapy centre. In England I would have insisted on walking, but nobody walks in America. It was a lovely sunny morning with the temperature in the 80s, a beautiful mid-summer's day to us but just a normal spring day to the locals.

The DHT centre was in a residential area and surrounded by a high wooden fence for privacy. I was surprised at how small it was on the inside. There were a couple of offices above the changing rooms, a couple of thatched huts for shade and two large seawater pools, which were separated from a sea channel by fencing. There was a floating pontoon at either end of each pool, allowing a maximum of four children to have therapy at any one time.

I took a firm hold of Laurence's hand as the pools were deep and we could see dolphins swimming around beneath the surface. Bianca squealed with delight when she spotted a baby dolphin, but Laurence was very unhappy, saying, 'No dolphins,' with growing conviction as we contradicted him.

I started preparing him for the therapy with plenty of sunblock and his fully inflated water wings. In his school swimming pool he was swimming with the wings virtually airless, he just needed more confidence and I wanted him to have plenty of confidence today.

Bianca's tutor on the Reeflings programme was Elizabeth, a young and very pretty blonde multilingual teacher who was experienced at working with children from many different countries. However, this week Bianca was the only sibling on this time slot so they would be working one to one. She led Bianca by the hand to a thatched wooden hut that was the classroom and I didn't have to worry about her anymore.

Donny was Laurence's therapist. He was a tall, handsome young man dressed in a brightly coloured wet suit, with long blonde hair and a golden suntan. He was a genuinely nice guy who you couldn't help liking.

He explained that today was an introductory session so he wouldn't be pushing Laurence, just helping to make him feel comfortable. He had read the reports on Laurence that I had forwarded and he asked me what I wanted.

'What do you want?' is a simple question, an obvious question and yet I realised that I had given it no real thought. I couldn't say, 'I want a bang for my bucks.'

'What do I want?' I asked myself aloud, feeling stupid, as the answer didn't roll off my tongue.

'I want ... I want him to talk, not just repeat phrases. I want him to talk to us, not at us. I want him to answer me and I want him to ask me questions. I want him to communicate,' I blurted out.

His appropriate copying of labels in short phrases only gave an illusion of communication.

For example, Laurence was always first through the door when we arrived home after a walk. Quite often when I caught up with him he could be found kneeling on the settee.

Seeing me coming he would say, 'No shoes on the seats,' cover his ears and cower down.

To an outsider Laurence was being naughty. By his own mouth he had shown that he knew shoes shouldn't be on the seats, and yet they were still on the seat and he was apparently expecting to be punished for it. But Laurence was just repeating the label that he heard whenever I caught him in this situation. He would cower down, covering his ears in anticipation of my loud angry bark, 'For the hundredth time, no shoes on the seats.' Only then would he run off into another room as if frightened. It was all labels. It was as if nothing was coming from his heart, he made no effort to remove the shoes, it was all coming from memory banks.

I wanted him to communicate with us.

Donny smiled, took Laurence's hand and led him around to the pontoon on the other side of the pool giving him warm words of encouragement along the way. Laurence was whining but not resisting. As they approached the pontoon his 'No dolphins' got louder and he was crying and stamping his feet, but still he didn't resist.

Donny told Laurence to kneel down beside the water on the pontoon and Donny sat down beside him, wrapping his legs around Laurence, enclosing but not constraining him. Sitting beside Laurence and facing Donny was his assistant, Marcie, who kept him supplied with teaching aids. Standing behind her was the dolphin trainer, Lynn, and sitting up on the dock looking down between Donny and Laurence was Janna, recording every comment and response Laurence made. This was the team that would be working on Laurence for the next two weeks.

Laurence was crying when Donny started work.

Elizabeth had found a life jacket to fit Bianca and she was on another pontoon having her first dolphin encounter. The dolphin slowly glided across the surface, allowing Bianca to stroke its entire body length. It fetched a ball and stood up in the water, offering a flipper to shake hands before leaping over a pole that she was holding, soaking them all. She was enjoying her special time.

Laurence was not enjoying his and he was making sure everybody was well aware of that. His screams rang out whenever the dolphin approached, shattering the serenity of this sunny morning. Donny steadily worked through the crate of teaching aids. Despite his distress, Laurence recognised that Donny wanted to do schoolwork and was happy to oblige, but he objected strongly to Donny's choice of location so he kept up his crying and screaming whilst answering the questions. Donny tried to calm Laurence with a little effect, but he didn't waste time on it. He worked through Laurence's screams.

Occasionally Donny would throw the ball into the water and the dolphin would retrieve it. He would then ask Laurence to take the ball from the dolphin. With a look of terror in his face, his arm tentatively reached half way while his screams reached a new crescendo; but he did try.

Dr Dave came over to have a chat with me. He was a tall, pleasant, grey-haired man with a fish stuck on the top of his baseball cap. He told me more about the programme. He assured me that Laurence's behaviour was normal for an autistic child in these circumstances. He told me not to worry, as there were already glimpses of a good relationship developing between Donny and Laurence.

Another couple came by and Dr Dave introduced us, as they were from England too, before continuing on his supervisory patrol. They were a friendly couple from Macclesfield with a son a bit older than Laurence who had a rare condition called Global Deficiency Syndrome, which I had never heard of but it sounded awful. The experts had said there was no hope of improvement and that he would never say a word. The people of Macclesfield had a whip round and raised enough to send him here for three weeks of therapy.

This was the start of their third week so I couldn't help asking what they thought of this place and the therapy. With her emotions rising and whilst Dad prepared their son for the therapy, Mum explained that they were very, very happy. At the end of the previous week their son had said his first word and given them their first real hope. It was a very emotional time for them. They already had a 'bang for their bucks' and they desperately wanted another word before they returned to England. I was so happy for them.

I was beginning to realise that this was a very emotional place.

Laurence's emotions were wailing out across the pool and they were cutting right through me. Donny and Laurence were holding a pole over the water.

He will begin to enjoy it more when the dolphin leaps over the pole and splashes him, I thought. I couldn't have been more wrong. Any pleasure he felt from being splashed was drowned out by the realisation that this giant fish could jump out of the water any time it wanted. His screams intensified and Donny returned to more conventional teaching methods to calm him down.

At the end of the session when Donny told Laurence they were finished, he jumped up to escape. Donny caught hold of his hand and pulled him back, making him wait to say goodbye properly. The dolphin glided past on its back, flapping its flipper, and Laurence was more than happy to flap his arm in return. It was natural to him.

Donny called me over; he thought that if Laurence saw me with the dolphin he might feel better about it. I went onto the pontoon and knelt down where Laurence had sat facing the water. This was my first meeting with these creatures and I felt a tingle of excitement in their presence.

The dolphin's name was Genie; she was the mother of the baby dolphin called Alfonz that Bianca had spotted earlier. She was the dolphin that would be working with Laurence for the whole fortnight.

Genie rose up in front of me; supported by her tail, she was as tall as me kneeling. We looked eyeball to eyeball and she held out her flippers for me to shake.

With a big grin I turned and said, 'Laurence look, nice dolphin, Daddy shake the hand with the nice dolphin.' But he screamed even louder. I turned back to see that Genie had opened her mouth wide and she was now talking to me. Nobody has been able to translate their clicky language but I felt those clicks were said with an intent to communicate that was absent from Laurence's talking.

I was mesmerised by the size of her mouth—my head would fit in there, and her jaws were lined with teeth. OK, so they were not jagged sharp teeth like a shark's, but they were still teeth and there was plenty of them. There was a flash of, 'What am I doing entrusting my son to this creature?' which had to be swiftly suppressed to maintain a positive image for Laurence. I could show no doubts or fears.

Although Genie was an alien-looking creature we had things in common. We were both mammals and we were both parents.

I trusted the sincerity of her clicking.

Back on terra firma Donny was pumping Laurence full of praise and he spoke positively about the chances of making real progress over future sessions. I gave Laurence some white chocolate buttons and Ribena for being such a brave boy during his frightening battle with fear.

We were there for over three hours on that first day, there was so much to take on board. All of the DHT team were very thorough, filling me in not just about the therapy but also on surviving our stay in the Keys with topics as diverse as how to handle the intense media interest in the place to what to do if you hear the hurricane warning siren.

I asked what happened to the dolphins when a hurricane hit. We just let them go was the simple answer. We don't know where they go, they probably take shelter in deep water, but they always return for their wages when it's all blown over. The fact that they are only penned in during the day to ensure they were present and on time for their appointments helped calm those niggling worries at the back of my conscience about these beautiful creatures being confined.

Laurence wanted to get out of this place and I ran out of bribes, so we said our goodbyes and Laurence said, 'Yeah' to Donny's, 'See you tomorrow, buddy.'

I thought that was a real result considering the traumas of the morning.

We returned to the hotel and the children only had eyes for the pool. They didn't even want to eat. We had a sandwich anyway and spent the rest of the afternoon in the pool.

The children's pool was shaped like a club in a pack of cards. The waterfall was at the stem of the club and was about five feet wide. The leaf on the left of the waterfall was the shallow end at three feet deep. In the centre it went from four to five feet and the right leaf went down to six feet.

Bianca jumped straight in while Laurence teetered on the edge flapping around on tiptoe. He was too excited to jump and kept pulling himself back from the brink. He would spend all day jumping into the pool but that first leap caused such excitement that he was reduced to performing this crazy poolside dance. Bianca was the first to snap. She went over and pushed him in. He laughed, quickly climbed out and jumped straight back in under his own steam as if to demonstrate that he really could do it without her help.

Laurence jumped and splashed around, staying in the shallow end—he wouldn't go an inch beyond the four-foot line. This kept the waterfall tantalisingly just out of reach for him. He would hop up and down on the four-foot boundary, stretching his arm out to catch the edge of the waterfall. He desperately wanted to play in it but he needed to be a lot braver.

Bianca had pinched Laurence's water wings and was swimming. She was doing really well and having a whale of a time. Yet again it was hunger that drove them out of the pool. Back in our room, while I was getting Bianca dried and dressed Laurence collided with the corner of the metal casing on the air-conditioning unit, cutting his head. Fortunately I had a first aid kit, the bleeding soon stopped and I eased the pain with some crisps and chilled orange juice. With the pain/crisps all gone we went back to the shops. Laurence had already broken his flip-flops and he also needed a sun hat, although a crash helmet would probably have been more practical.

With the shopping done we decided to have our dinner in our local Burger King. We were the only people eating in—everybody else was driving in and driving off—but it was a nice little restaurant with tropical fish tanks around you. It was a nice relaxing reward to end our first day of therapy.

The next morning I looked through the tinted apartment windows to see that it was another cloudless day. Bianca had discovered the Cartoon Network on TV and was no trouble, allowing me to keep Laurence out of trouble. We had what was to be our regular breakfast of fresh fruit salad and digestive biscuits washed down with Floridian freshly squeezed orange juice, which Bianca craved, just like Sunny D.

We arrived at the DHT centre early to give me time to prepare Laurence. As soon as we arrived, Bianca skipped off to her class hut to meet Elizabeth. I thoroughly covered Laurence with suntan lotion, as there was no shade sitting out on the pontoon. Going through the routine of swimming trunks on, suntan lotion on and water wings on should have alerted him to the possibility of going in the water but I don't think it did. He was crying and whimpering, 'No dolphins' but he was not resisting me like he does when I try to get him to do something that he doesn't want to do.

It was as if he knew that this had to be done.

Donny greeted Laurence warmly. 'Hiya buddy, how you doing? Have you come to do some work?'

'Yeah,' Laurence whispered.

'All right, gimme five,' and Laurence slapped Donny's hand. If he had learnt anything yesterday it was how to 'gimme five'.

Donny took Laurence's hand and they walked around the pool to their workstation. Laurence's complaints rose in volume as they sat down in exactly the same position as yesterday. Genie came by to say hello and Laurence screamed. It was not getting any easier but Laurence was working well and he was earning rewards that he didn't want.

Donny asked if he wanted a kiss from Genie. 'NO!' he shrieked in horror.

Donny asked if he wanted to hold the pole, but Laurence wanted nothing to do with the stick that summoned the dolphin out of the water.

Donny asked if he wanted to throw the ball and he said yes. Donny made Laurence work hard before throwing the ball, which he did, but he still shirked at retrieving the ball from Genie.

Near the end of the session Donny asked Laurence if he wanted to go in the water. Laurence let Donny know that he definitely didn't want to go in the water, but Donny put on his flippers and stepped into the water anyway.

He started enticing Laurence to come and join him. Laurence began to get excited. He was rocking and noisily smacking the wet pontoon with the palms of his hands. It was as I had figured back in London — he was scared of the dolphins but he couldn't resist the lure of water. Donny recognised this and realised that although Laurence was screaming out, 'No, no, no,' he really did want to go in. He encouraged him even more.

'Come on buddy, you can do it, yeah. Go for it buddy, you can do it,' Donny urged.

Laurence inched towards the edge of the pontoon, rocking further over the water and then suddenly he jumped. He leapt straight into Donny's arms and looped an arm around his neck.

'Hey, you did it buddy, well done, gimme five buddy,' Donny gushed.

As soon as he hit the water Laurence realised what a terrible mistake he had made. He desperately clung to Donny's neck pointing towards the pontoon.

'Ergh, ergh, ergh,' was all he could say as his head swivelled around searching for that dreadful dolphin.

Donny ignored Laurence's frantic urging to return to the pontoon and stuck his arm out as if he was hailing a bus. From a deep unseen approach Genie flashed by, Donny gripped her dorsal fin and they were away. Surging across the surface of the water Laurence shrieked with a look of sheer terror on his face and I laughed. I was so happy that he was doing it and I had seen that look of terror before, on a roller-coaster ride. It had never stopped him from wanting to go again. Laurence couldn't control his emotions like us; he exhibited all his feelings, holding nothing in.

Genie deposited them both safely back near the pontoon.

'Ergh, ergh, ergh,' Laurence urged again, frantically pointing towards the pontoon. Donny helped him up, showering him with praise. Laurence scrambled out of the water and lay down on his stomach as if he was trying to hug the ground. He was lying down looking straight at Donny who was still in the water. Laurence was beaming and he was giving Donny some really good eye contact. He started rocking on his belly like a rocking horse, which was always a good sign that he was feeling pleased with himself.

Donny climbed on board and they went back to work and the crying returned. Laurence's anxiety levels rose and then the screaming returned. The joy of the ride made the pain from hearing his cries of, 'Daddy, Daddy' even harder to bear.

I was as relieved as Laurence when the session ended. He happily flapped bye-bye to Genie and skipped around the pool holding Donny's hand as if they were best of friends.

'That was good work buddy,' Donny praised him. 'Are you coming back to see me tomorrow?'

'Yeah,' Laurence replied.

'All right! Gimme five.' Donny turned to me and said that despite all the screaming he thought Laurence enjoyed the ride and I agreed. He felt that we were making good progress.

Back to the hotel, and it was straight into the pool for an hour's play before lunch.

I had seen signs to Harry Harris Park, so that afternoon I decided that we would investigate what else this island had to offer.

I drove into the large car park to find what was basically a recreation park with a few swings, a large barbecue area and a small sandy beach with a sea wall surrounding it, making the sea inside the wall nothing more than a shallow salty lake.

It was a big disappointment; the kids would have preferred to stay in the hotel pool. The place was deserted, but I could imagine that it would be buzzing at weekends. There were slipways into the sea on either side of the beach for the motor boats and jet skis and I realised that the sea around the beach area was walled in to keep the paddling children safe from the water-sports fanatics speeding around outside.

I couldn't keep the children out of the sea and they happily splashed around—it didn't take much to amuse them. While they were sitting beside each other in the water I noticed that Laurence appeared to be biting Bianca's shoulder. She didn't seem to mind and when she moved I could see that he was actually chewing the shoulder strap of her costume. It slowly dawned on me that he was sucking the salt out of her costume, but what I couldn't understand was how he made that discovery in the first place. We didn't stay long; we had a little picnic and drove back to our hotel.

On the way back we saw the famous yellow school buses. I was impressed when they stopped, the red lights started flashing and all the traffic stopped. Each time we saw them not one car, in either direction, tried to sneak past. The Americans value their children's safety and put us to shame. Why can't our little country do this, I wondered? We shrug our shoulders as over 100 child pedestrians are killed and over 3,000 child pedestrians are seriously injured on our roads each year. The carnage is even worse if you add on the child cyclists killed and maimed on our roads as well.

Every day thousands of special needs children are transported to school in special buses. Why can't this system be expanded on? Are our normal children considered not worth it?

No, even now local councils furtively attempt to scrap the special school buses and force these children onto public transport as well. All in the name of inclusion.

I'm not saying that public transport is unsafe but the stops are often one, two, three or four hundred yards away from the school entrance and half of the time they are on the wrong side of the road.

Local councils are steadily reducing the population of lollipop people helping the children cross the road outside of schools. Essentially they are right, as these well-intentioned people are inefficient. Children don't die under their wing; they die a hundred yards down the road when they jump off the bus and dash across the road to catch up with a friend already on the other side.

The Americans recognise this, and provide a dedicated bus service, taking children from the school gates to the end of each child's road.

*

Safely back at the hotel, we watched a couple of small fishing boats unloading at the dock beside our resort. We decided to have a freshly caught fish supper. The portions were enormous. Laurence really didn't like leaving some chips on his plate, it was unheard of, but he had to accept that he didn't have room for any more.

We made our way back to the poolside bar and had a drink to allow that big meal to go down. It was dark but the air still felt hot. There was a local band playing to the accompaniment of the children's waterfall behind us.

Lights under the surface lit up the swimming pools and gas flames on torches, which were safely out of harm's reach, illuminated the gardens with their flickering light. I liked this place, the children loved this place and I thought it would be nice to stay here for the rest of the therapy. It meant we would have to carry on with the self-catering to keep within budget but the children were enjoying our fruity breakfasts and picnic lunches, so the next morning I booked us in for the rest of the fortnight.

It was another beautiful day. Bianca skipped into school and Laurence grumbled and whined but was fully compliant as I rubbed the sunblock all over. He trotted down to the pontoon holding Donny's hand, still complaining noisily. The complaints turned to screams again as Donny got to work. Laurence was adamant that he wanted nothing to do with the dolphin but he did nervously make a lightning grab to retrieve the ball from Genie.

Part-way through the session Laurence was distracted from Donny's enveloping presence by another child enjoying a dorsal ride at the other end of the pool. Donny didn't try to grab back his attention and allowed him to watch the child's pleasure. After a bit more work Donny invited Laurence into the water.

'No, no, no,' Laurence shouted, but his body language gave away his true desire. Donny asked Laurence to pass him a flipper and Laurence threw it, hitting him in the face. Donny calmly said no, replaced the flipper and requested it again. On the third time of asking Laurence realised that he wouldn't get in the water playing this game and he handed over the flippers nicely.

After an excited rocking routine he made the leap towards Donny in the water. Clinging to him, he nervously looked around for the dolphin. Genie flashed out of the water and Donny grabbed her dorsal fin. This time Laurence was silent, with a look of concerned awe on his face. At the end of the ride Laurence shouted, 'Finish now' and pointed to the pontoon. He had had his ride and he wanted to get out of the water as quickly as possible.

At the end of the session everybody felt that we had made good progress that day and the volume of his screams was not an accurate reflection of his feelings.

Back at the hotel pool I noticed how brown Laurence was. He was a chameleon—in three days his skin colour had blended in with the locals. Bianca was like a fish confidently snorkelling around the deep end with her water wings on, I was turning pink and getting sore and we all had burnt ears thanks to our baseball caps.

Our hotel organised many boat trips for fishing, scuba diving and gambling out in international waters. I booked us onto a glass-bottomed boat trip over a coral reef. Bianca was probably the most knowledgeable passenger on board as she had been learning about these fish in the Reefling programme and she squealed with delight when she spotted a queen angelfish. Laurence enjoyed this trip as well. With all the passengers lined up and looking down into the middle of the boat he had an unimpeded run the length of the boat and he made the most of it.

That night both the children fell into bed exhausted. I felt that it had been an excellent day.

Ana phoned at 05.30 a.m. and the children wouldn't go back to sleep. Bianca watched the Cartoon Network, Laurence had an early break-fast and I must have dozed off while watching the cartoons. I became aware of Laurence chuckling, it was his naughty chuckle. His teachers reported that he was the school grass. If a child was being naughty, Laurence's chuckling would give the game away.

Who was being naughty, I wondered, and leapt off the bed, sliding across the wet tiled floor. I couldn't prevent myself from falling. On the way down I crashed into the bathroom doorframe, which spun me round so that I ended up in a heap on the wet bathroom floor with my back pressed against the side of the bath. I had stubbed my toe, banged my chest, hit my head on the toilet and my shoulder hurt from taking the brunt of my fall. I was in a lot of pain and very uncomfortable lying on the cold wet floor; and yet, I had to chuckle.

Laurence's distinctive naughty chuckle of anticipation had turned into a raucous laugh. My leap up to confront his naughtiness and my ungainly hasty disappearance into the bathroom was a better result than he could have anticipated.

I could imagine myself as one of Bianca's cartoon characters and although Laurence had never taken any interest in cartoons he could appreciate good slapstick in real life. His favourite TV programmes showed home movie clips and he got especially excited prior to people falling into water. 'Splash!' he would shout, rocking on his belly. He wasn't rocking on his belly this time—maybe he was concerned for me—but he couldn't control his laughter.

I fully accept what the psychologists tell us about autistic children not understanding that we have separate minds, but Laurence had spent his entire life observing us ignoring everything that was on his mind.

Nowadays he was anticipating that we would ignore what was on his mind.

He had thought about using all of those lined-up toilet rolls in one go, so therefore I knew about it and I had not expressed disapproval. With them all stuffed into the toilet, he had repeatedly tried to flush them away. I had been warned but I only heard the naughty chuckle that followed his warning thoughts.

It felt so good to share a joke with my son, a joke that everybody could understand. A joke that Bianca could share with us. Laurence and I had shared jokes before but they were body language or silent jokes. They were rare precious moments when our minds met which I couldn't explain when I was asked, 'What are you two laughing about?' They were precious because I got a feeling of togetherness when we laughed together. They were rare because I needed him to be sitting quietly and I needed to know exactly what was on his mind.

A thought like, 'There's still some ice cream left in the fridge' would bug Laurence, so it would be easy to read his mind from his prior body language and I could play with that. On the rare occasions when I could silently demonstrate to him that I knew what was on his mind it amused him.

His eyes would flicker into life, a look of acknowledgement would spread across his face and he would giggle an 'I've been found out' laugh. I laughed too because I knew that he knew I knew what he was thinking. These were our silent jokes, nothing was said, as nothing needed to be said, it wasn't mind reading, it was just a shared understanding.

We also shared some humorous moments and learned a lot about each other in the process, whilst playing simple non-verbal games.

Sitting opposite each other with a bunch of grapes between us, he obviously wanted to eat them. I can see nothing wrong with occasional 'grape therapy', though not too often because it can be habit forming. If an autistic child wants to eat a grape they will do good work between grapes.

Carrot, broccoli and even lettuce therapies would also have worked on Laurence. He would happily munch his way through a whole cucumber given the chance.

So with the grapes on the table I had his full attention. 'Wait,' I told him. 'Wait' was such a good command to teach him when he was young. If I had said 'No' he might well have done a snatch and dash, but to Laurence the command 'Wait' meant 'Yes, soon' and I had his full attention ready for the command, 'Go.'

I remember playing with our collie dog as a child. If during play I froze she would freeze as well, attentively watching me for a clue to what I planned to do next. A twitch of my shoulder would be covered by a twitch from the dog, but her patience snapped with a bark much quicker than Laurence. I was able to maintain the time warp for longer periods with him.

So I slowed things down and presented my face to him one frame at a time. He studied my face intently as it slowly changed from a look of disapproval through a neutral look to an expression of approval when I silently signalled him to eat one grape. Although he appeared to be focused on my lip area, he was aware of tiny movements in other areas such as eyes and hands. I was amazed at how well he understood the tiniest muscle movements.

Laurence was happy to play along with the time warp. His hand moved slowly towards the grapes as my face gradually turned to approval, and away from the grapes as it turned to disapproval. I had an accurate measure of his understanding of each of my facial expressions. With his remarkably accurate interpretations of my face muscle movements I realised that during the first five years of his life, when he couldn't understand what he was hearing from us, he had probably taught himself a form of lip or face reading to give himself some insights into our intentions.

It must have been such a frightening and uncertain world for him.

His teachers had also noticed him intently studying their faces for clues to the answers of questions. They found that asking him questions that they knew he knew the answers to, he was much more likely to give a response if their lips made the shape of the first syllable of the answer. Even though he could now understand our speech he still sought out those little physical clues.

Recent research has identified micro expressions. These are intense facial expressions that last for only a fifteenth of a second. They tend to occur when people conceal or suppress their emotions. Most people do not notice these fleeting micro expressions, but people who are good lie detectors are very good at spotting these involuntary give-away micro expressions.

Further to his research into micro expressions, Paul Ekman, emeritus professor of psychology at the University of California, found superior lie-detecting abilities in people with damage to the left side of the brain that had impaired their ability to understand sentences.

It would seem that our normal heavy reliance on verbal communication hinders our ability to spot lies. Just like Laurence, these people were forced to rely on non-verbal cues like facial expressions, and they scored better than us.

The autism experts tell us that autistics cannot tell the difference between happy and sad faces. With an autistic mind Laurence had failed their tests when shown drawings and photos of happy faces and even acted happy faces, but in the time warp he could spot the slightest changes in my expressions and he could interpret them accurately.

It occurred to me that in normal time he was probably still trying to do the same. Reacting to hundreds of conflicting signals, including micro expressions that we were blissfully unaware of, his frantic flitting around began to make sense.

Reacting to a frown on my face as I read the newspaper he flees to the kitchen where he finds Mum with a look of frustration because she can't find something and he scampers off to the bedroom where he finds Bianca scolding one of her dolls. Add to this all the micro body signals that we were inadvertently emitting and it was no surprise that he behaved as if stuck in 'fast forward' mode.

Laurence didn't have time to properly digest all the inconsistent data streaming in, causing him to overload and crash frequently. We seem to have filters to prevent such information overloads so that we just take in the information that we need to proceed with our lives at our own pace.

The concept of time flowing seems to be governed by our processing of information.

Asleep, we take in no data and have no idea of time. With just a little information to process, we get bored as time drags by, but with a heavy workload the increased data processing makes the time fly by.

With so much data coming in, time was always flying by for Laurence; he never had time to process all the information coming in so it could be no surprise that he had no time to learn the things that other children learned naturally, in their own time.

He was a child out of time.

9A

. . . The Agony and the Ecstasy

This was no time to lie around laughing on the cold wet bathroom floor, as water was still pouring over the toilet rim. I pulled my aching body up onto my knees and called out to Bianca to start picking things up off the floor as the water had spread right across the apartment. As I started scooping clumps of sodden toilet paper out of the toilet bowl I mused that a clever cartoon character's head would have ended up in the bowl and not clumsily head butting the side.

There was a little mop in the kitchen for spillages; it certainly wasn't designed for clearing up floods. I had no time for breakfast as I was at full stretch to get the place presentable for the maid. She knew our timetable so she did our room in the morning while we were out at the therapy.

It was the hottest day so far; when we arrived at the DHT centre it was already 86 degrees, rising well into the 90s by lunchtime.

Today was also Bianca's big day; after her normal lesson she was going to have an hour's snorkelling lesson followed by a boat trip out to the coral reef. I was to pick her up at the end of the afternoon at a quay near our resort.

It was the fourth day of therapy and Laurence was much calmer. He was still nervous, with intermittent crying, but he wasn't screaming. After correctly answering a couple of questions Donny decided to reward Laurence quickly and invited him into the water. 'No, no, no,' he said rapidly, but we all knew he meant yes. He meekly handed Donny his flippers and without much fuss he jumped in.

Because of all his good work and reduced crying they had three dorsal rides spaced across the session. After the second session, while still in the water, Laurence actually stroked Genie. He was still very nervous and keen to get out quickly.

'Let's get up now,' he said and I thought, 'That's good talking.' He scrambled onto the pontoon and knelt down, waiting for Donny to pull himself out of the water.

'Who were we in the water with?' Donny asked.

'Fishie,' Laurence replied and I had to laugh. He knew the correct answer was Genie but in order to express his feelings he had chosen a more contemptuous answer.

My laugh turned into a gasp as Laurence then urinated on the pontoon. I immediately remembered that in my rush I had not checked if he had wanted to go before starting the session. I felt it was my fault—he was usually so good and I couldn't remember when we had the last accident.

Donny pulled himself up onto the pontoon and in doing so he washed off that corner of the pontoon and he carried on working without allowing Laurence to deflect him. Laurence continued to work well, earning more rewards through to the end of the session.

I apologised to Donny when he returned Laurence to me, but he brushed it aside, preferring to talk about all the great improvements we had seen that day. He was full of praise for Laurence; it had certainly been very different to the first three days.

Laurence and I returned to the hotel. We had time to kill before picking Bianca up so I put his water wings back on and we played in the pool. With the aid of the water wings he had the confidence to go out of his depth and he happily splashed around under the waterfall. At lunchtime he complained of a headache so we returned to our room. I put him to bed and he was soon asleep. I put it down to too much sun, as he refused to keep his hat on for more than a couple of minutes. He hated wearing hats. I was happy to have a peaceful lie down in the air-conditioned bedroom as well.

It was too hot for me too.

At four o'clock he was still asleep and I had to meet Bianca. I couldn't possibly leave him alone so I had to wake him. He was a bit groggy at first but after a drink of chilled orange juice his hyperactive motors kicked in and he skipped along to the quay. The waterway was lined with beautiful white houses and it was so clean and peaceful. Between hurricanes, this was definitely a beautiful place to live.

Bianca was the only child on the excursion and had been spoilt rotten. She had found the seawater cold so she did her snorkelling in ten-minute stints between sunbathing spells on the deck to warm up. On the way back the captain had allowed her to steer the boat.

She was gushing; she had seen so many fish and had even seen a couple of giant turtles. Elizabeth quickly explained that they were 'dancing'. We returned to the hotel and Bianca desperately wanted to show off her new snorkelling skills. Laurence seemed to have fully recovered and was eager to jump in the pool as well.

While we were at the pool Janna and a couple of her friends came by for a dip. She was the student who was recording all Laurence's responses and comments during the therapy. She explained to me that having spent the day sitting out in the sun taking notes, this was the best swimming pool in Key Largo to cool off. The large waterfall ensured that the water was always really cool, whereas the adults' pool was empty in the afternoons because it was like swimming in a hot bath. I was pleased that Janna had a chance to see Laurence in a relaxed mode.

We had another big freshly caught fish dinner. It was lovely to see Laurence wolfing down all the fish before starting on his chips. I wondered if there was an element of revenge in his mind.

The next morning Laurence started protesting, 'No dolphins today.' It was the first time he had complained like this before leaving the hotel. He was crying and he had wet the bed so I had little patience for him. While I was driving to the DHT centre Bianca called out, 'Daddy, Laurence is doing wee-wee on me,' and I snapped. I slammed on the brakes, jumped out of the car, pulled him out and smacked his leg. I was furious.

'How could you do that to your sister?' I demanded, futilely. He was giggling and I smacked his leg again asking him if he found that funny. He hastily replied, 'No' and we finished the short journey in silence.

I made sure he did wee-wee again, this time in the toilet, before handing him over to Donny. Laurence worked well despite his apprehension. He was still whining and crying, but excited smiles were also appearing during the session. While he was having his first dorsal ride he even laughed out aloud and choked with a mouthful of seawater. He was on an emotional roller coaster; his shrieks of delight on a ride turned to shrieks of fear when stationary in the water as a dolphin brushed past him. He was saying, 'Stay in the water,' and yet his body language was saying, 'Get me out of here.' Back on the pontoon he urinated again. I couldn't believe it; he had been three times already that morning.

I glared across the pool, my face set on maximum stern look. If there was any telepathy between us he would have looked up and seen my displeasure, but he didn't. There again, maybe he knew not to look up at me.

I was furious, first with him and then with myself. What had I done?

I realised that I had put my precious puppy under too much pressure. The stress caused by his conflicting desires to play in the water and to avoid the dolphins had torn him apart, reducing him to scent marking. I felt that I had pushed him over the edge.

Dr Dave came by and I told him my concerns. Laurence's screaming on the first three days had cut me up badly and now his scent marking everywhere had me questioning myself: Had I gone too far?

I no longer knew that I was right. Like Laurence, I was all mashed up inside. I could not put him under even more pressure.

'I don't think we can take any more,' I blubbed.

Dr Dave was reassuring; he had seen this behaviour pattern before. He told me not to think of his mind being torn apart, but rather to think of it as being tossed into the air.

'We don't know why, but when all the pieces settle back down they connect together a little more normally,' he rather unscientifically explained. He was confident that we would see good progress next week now that Laurence was calming down.

At the end of the session Donny was, as usual, very upbeat. 'Did you hear him laughing today?'

He too felt the hard work had been done and was looking forward to next week. He would deal with the urinating just like he did with the screaming, using the minimum of fuss.

Donny and Dr Dave picked me up off the emotional floor and within minutes I was on the ceiling, as it was time for Bianca to be presented with a certificate for completing her course.

At five, she was too young to be able to read it properly. It said that she had demonstrated an exceptional understanding and appreciation of the marine ecosystem. Elizabeth presented her with the certificate while we all stood around applauding her. It was a lovely moment.

On the way back to the resort we stopped at a gift shop, and as Bianca and I looked in the window discussing what present she wanted to buy for Mummy I felt warm water running down the back of my leg. It was Laurence scent marking again. Argh! I whisked him back to the hotel and allowed Bianca to go swimming while making Laurence sit on the sunlounger beside me. He really didn't like watching Bianca enjoying herself but I had to try to make him understand that his behaviour was totally unacceptable. That afternoon we visited a bird sanctuary, with Laurence on a promise that if he was a good boy he could go in the swimming pool when we got back.

In London we are plagued by fat greedy pigeons. In the Florida Keys they are plagued by fat greedy pelicans. Not the pretty white ones seen in the zoo but ungainly dirty-looking brown ones. Their greed resulted in frequent collisions with boats, fishing lines and cars. The casualties ended up in the bird sanctuary.

They were a sorry-looking bunch with missing wings and legs, but Bianca was enchanted by this 'birdie hospital'. We bought a bird identification chart and went around again so that she could identify all the different types of birds, as Daddy didn't know his herons from his stilts.

Laurence wasn't interested in the birds but happily skipped around the cages and enclosures. I repeatedly reminded him of my promise of 'swimming pool later' but that didn't stop him trying to scent mark around the place. By now my eyes were glued on him so I was able to catch him each time he lowered his shorts. If he was not within arm's reach I found smacking my hands together loudly was enough to snap him out of it and he would hurriedly pull up his shorts. It was clear that he had no control over this urge, just as the pelicans couldn't control their natural greedy urges.

There was no way Laurence would risk 'no more swimming pool' if he could help it.

At the time I considered myself to be rather clever to have worked out that the stresses of the DHT had caused Laurence to revert back to this primitive natural instinct and that it was not misbehaviour. But with hindsight I wonder if I was in fact nowhere near clever enough.

I had often observed Laurence in the sea and swimming pool scooping water into the air and catching a few drops in his mouth. This behaviour was distinctive from his general splashing around, with a dozen wild splashes between the accurately aimed scoops. This constant behaviour gave me cause for concerns regarding the quality and quantity of the water entering his mouth. It was impossible to prevent him from doing it, and as he wasn't making himself sick I felt that very little was actually going down.

At the DHT Laurence had screamed for the first three days and then after a couple of swimming sessions with Genie the screaming stopped and the urinating started. Each time he urinated just after he left Genie's territory and returned to his own territory on the pontoon. (He might have urinated in the water as well. He certainly seemed to have an inexhaustible supply at this time, but only Genie could have told us if he did.)

I am sure that if Genie had been chemically communicating then Laurence, with his enhanced senses of taste and smell, would have received those messages through the splashes on his tongue during his water sampling.

For the American military the million-dollar question was, did he understand those messages?

When he climbed onto the pontoon was he sending Genie a reply or was he warning Genie off by saying, 'This pontoon is my turf'? Laurence instinctively developed the water-sampling technique years before he met the dolphins, but did Genie show him what it was for?

While we blindly fought to encourage him to communicate with us, was the air and water full of communications that we were blissfully unaware of?

Having discovered that he could communicate this way, Laurence wanted to communicate with Bianca, Donny, the car and me. He wanted to leave his messages everywhere for all to taste or smell and yet again, it seemed to him that we were trying to prevent him from communicating.

The evidence for chemical communication between Laurence and Genie is only circumstantial but it explains the autistic theory of mind and why autistic people keep repeating themselves.

Consider two dolphins swimming along. There is no need to click away with social chitchat. The answers to such questions as, 'How are you?' 'Where have you been?' and 'What have you been doing?' are wafted around by their tails in the water around them. There can be no deception; the information is freely available for any dolphins in the area.

A dolphin would expect a human entering the water to know what it knows just as Laurence expected me to know the answers to the questions above. These intangible dolphin messages would need to be constantly updated, just as Laurence did when he kept on repeating what was on his mind.

Are we the dumb animals here?

Laurence and other mammals could see no use for the high-functioning chitchat that we so highly value. Dogs and dolphins are happy to learn tricks to demonstrate that they understand the dumb humans, just as Laurence was happy to learn our spoken labels to demonstrate his understanding of us but we humans could see no desire from them to communicate with us.

Nowadays humans no longer smell their partner to see if she really does have a headache. We seem to live in fear of others detecting how we really are and we mask our natural communications with artificial odorants. Ana's love of perfumes and deodorants could only have made her behaviour harder for Laurence to understand.

The dolphin's clicks are indecipherable because they are just a small part of their communications, just as speech used to be only a small part of our communication.

In recent years we have only begun to re-explore body language, and who knows what further communicative insights, like micro expressions, are still to be uncovered?

Some people describe an autistic individual's inability to understand that we have separate minds as 'mindblindness'. Seen in the context of the animal kingdom, it would appear that it is us who have mindblindness, bedazzled by our over-reliance on speech.

I was beginning to understand what the military were investigating.

With no DHT over the weekend, we were free to travel further. I wanted to drive down the island chain and visit Key West, but we didn't make it that far. The scenery was stunning. The modern long white bridges bisected the tranquil turquoise sea, each one pointing to the next mangrove-green splash of land in the distance. One bridge was seven miles long. It was all so peaceful. I felt like I was driving along the straight lines in a Kandinsky painting, but the children were soon bored with yet another bridge. They were not interested in admiring the scenery—they wanted to be part of it, so we stopped off at a picnic/barbecue site beside the sea and didn't get any further.

Over the weekend the hotel was full and the pool was alive with children. I was concerned with how Laurence would behave with all these interlopers, but he coped well.

There was a group of young boys his age playing in the pool. They liked to walk around the shallow end to the edge of the waterfall and jump into it. This was such a popular pastime that there was often a queue and Laurence joined it. It was lovely to see him mixing with the normal kids.

A couple of the boys tried to talk to him but he just blanked them. They were puzzled by his silence and funny behaviour but they didn't trouble him. Laurence copied them right up to the edge of the waterfall before flapping and leaping back into the shallow end rather than leaping into the deeper water under the waterfall like the other boys. He could have jumped into the shallow end anytime, he certainly didn't need to join a queue, but he repeatedly waited patiently in the queue before going right up to the brink and then leaping back into the shallow end at the last moment. It was very funny and a bit sad to watch. I was by now getting used to having my emotions twisted.

Bianca, on the other hand, was having no trouble making friends with the little girls in the pool. Over the last week I had steadily deflated the water wings and she was now swimming without them. She was so proud of herself and now all she wanted to do was swim.

I was watching Laurence like a hawk and several times I caught him lowering his swimming trunks around the pool. Each time I caught him I would march him off to the toilet but he always seemed to be able to produce more.

He kept trying to communicate and when I was asleep, I could not stop him communicating with me. Since the first accident the maid had put plastic sheets over the mattresses and we needed them, as on one night he wet the bed three times. I was at my wits' end, I even considered making him sleep in the bath, but I couldn't be that cruel.

I trawled the shops looking for jumbo-sized nappies to no avail. I did find some small incontinence sheets, which were somewhat ineffective due to the way he tossed and turned through the night, but they were better than nothing.

Laurence didn't seem worried by the prospect of dolphins the following week. In fact, when we were in our apartment he liked to sit down and tap some postcards with pictures of dolphins on them.

The second week followed a similar pattern to the first. Fresh fruit salad breakfasts and DHT in the mornings, followed by picnic lunches and trips to local beaches and parks in the afternoons, interspersed with frequent sessions in the hotel pool. We ended each day by eating out at a different restaurant. Inevitably, wherever we went we visited the toilets as Laurence persisted with his attempts to communicate with us and any other people we encountered on our travels.

I was full of hope for the second week of therapy. Laurence was whining, 'No dolphins' but when we arrived at the DHT he was happy to skip off with Donny. They had become best mates. Laurence worked well, his talking was really improving. When asked what he wanted to do with the ball he said, 'I want to throw the ball.' It was so clear it was lovely to hear.

Although he was not motivated by contact with the dolphins he really did want to have a ride and he got one for that bit of good talking. He was still very nervous in the water with the dolphins swimming around him, but when he was on the ride there was now no doubt that he was really enjoying it. Back on the pontoon he left a message for the dolphin and Donny washed it away without fuss before continuing.

Genie had gone out over the weekend and didn't turn up for work on the Monday morning so Laurence had to interact with another dolphin called Dinghy. Although I had been told that this was very unusual behaviour for Genie, nobody seemed too concerned about where she was and her absence didn't seem to affect the session.

While they were working a big cheer went up at the other pool, with high fives all round. I had seen them wheeling an American boy round there and struggling to get him down onto the pontoon every morning. There was a media crew following him as his story had touched the hearts of America.

His entire family had been wiped out in a terrible car accident. He alone survived and was paralysed from the neck down. The experts had said that there was no hope of him ever regaining any movement.

He had just independently moved his arm to stroke the dolphin.

The atmosphere was electric, his therapist excitedly explained that his arm hadn't just flopped down onto the dolphin, he had lifted his arm up to touch it.

Dr Dave told me that they didn't have a clue how it worked, but somehow these kids' brains find a way to rewire and get a message through to the limbs. All we do is give them the stimulus to make a connection, he explained. He had seen it all before, but to me it was miraculous.

*

Genie returned back to work the next day. With no means to communicate we couldn't know where she went or why she took a long weekend off but I wonder if Laurence knew. They worked so well together—it was a wonderful session, the best so far, and I was seeing the therapy working properly for the first time. Donny was asking questions like, 'What do you want to do?' and Laurence replied, 'Go in for a ride.'

They spent a lot more time in the water compared with the previous days. In the notes for this session it was recorded that Laurence only gave one incorrect response during the whole session. He was no longer working well because he had been trained to do so at school, he was working well because he wanted to interact with Genie.

It was wonderful to watch, but I realised that it was probably too late to make a big difference; we needed this kind of interaction last Tuesday. I was devastated. I wanted more; we needed another week.

The pain and anguish I felt now matched the pain of the previous week when I felt that I could take no more. I knew that I couldn't afford an extra day let alone another week. I was heartbroken again.

We had lunch with Dr Dave that day and he soon put me out of my misery. It didn't matter how much I offered, they couldn't possibly fit us in next week or the week after, they were booked to capacity. I should have booked three weeks originally but I hadn't, and now there was absolutely nothing that could be done about it. He saved me from robbing a bank or bankrupting myself. (I would strongly advise anybody considering DHT to plan for three weeks.)

We talked about autism at length. I asked him what type of autism he thought Laurence had. Laurence's diagnosis had stated 'autistic' and not elaborated further. From what I had read I had to agree that he fulfilled all the criteria for classic childhood autism, but somehow I hoped for him to appear as having atypical autism, otherwise known as PDD-NOS (Pervasive Developmental Disorder, Not Otherwise Specified), especially considering the improvements after the AIT. This rather stupidly named and renamed condition is still autism, but with one or two of the symptoms missing, and from my biased parental perspective I had sought reasons to place him in this category. However, even though Dr Dave had only seen Laurence under stress, his response was swift and confident.

'Oh, he's a classic all right,' and he went on to explain why they didn't see many like him these days.

I listened intently as he described a few ABAs like Lovvas, some dietary interventions and AIT. He told me nothing new about the different therapies on offer, but he was well informed on autism and had been a pioneer of motivation-based therapies since the seventies, developing a good understanding of the autistic mind.

He had found that by using dolphins to motivate children with all kinds of learning and attention difficulties, they learnt between two and ten times faster than in the normal classroom setting. Obviously it is impractical to have a pool with dolphins beside each classroom, so this therapy had to be seen as a springboard for more conventional teaching methods. The objective of the therapy was to motivate and increase the confidence of the child so they could get the maximum benefit from help by other professionals dealing with the child in the future. A useful analogy would be to think of the DHT as a tantalising opening paragraph of a story.

Although Laurence had lost a week overcoming his fears, Dr Dave was very pleased with Laurence's progress and was confident that when he settled back in school he would be better able to learn from his teachers.

Dr Dave had led a full life. He was born in Scotland and moved to New York to teach gifted kids in a private school before deciding that that was no big deal. He felt that a big deal would be to actually teach a child to speak and he changed his career. He got a doctoral degree in psychology specialising in behavioural medicine and had spent the last thirty years working with handicapped children. He was a font of knowledge and consequently was invited to consult on many unusual cases.

He told me of a recent case involving a local mother and her non-verbal autistic son who was about Laurence's age. One day they went for a picnic in the Everglades. They found a nice spot beside the water and were enjoying a pleasant picnic. The mother said that she turned away for just a moment to get something and when she looked back her son had disappeared. She searched desperately and her frantic calls alerted others who called the police and a full search was conducted, but no trace of the boy could be found.

They concluded that he could only have gone into the water so they gave up hope of finding him alive as the Everglades are infested with alligators. To emphasise the dangers of the Everglades, three soldiers had recently died when they got lost during military exercises in the area.

You might wonder about the wisdom of having a picnic beside alligator-infested waters, but I did find the Floridians quite blasé about living with these creatures. On a couple of beaches that we visited with children happily splashing around in the water I noticed signs saying, 'Please don't feed the alligators.'

It was a tragic tale—except that seven days later the boy was found miles away, still in the Everglades and apparently unharmed by his adventure. The police tried to piece together the story of the missing week and they called in Dr Dave for advice.

Dr Dave struggled to get any information out of the non-verbal boy. Forensic tests found bear hairs on his body, suggesting that he may have been in close contact with bears. They concluded that to have covered such a distance he had to have travelled extensively in the water and quite possibly hitched a ride with the alligators!

Dr Dave explained that an autistic child wouldn't give off the same fear signals that we and other potential prey send out to alligators and bears. I found this hard to understand, having watched my son screaming in fear of the dolphins, but I could understand that Laurence would behave in the same way whether it was a dolphin, an alligator or a duck in the water. So therefore if this autistic child had no fear of ducks and dolphins then they probably would have no natural fear of alligators and bears as well.

This crazy theory of the boy hitching a ride with the alligators during the days and snuggling up to the bears for warmth in the cold nights was the only way they could explain the distance covered and his survival for a whole week in such an inhospitable wilderness.

Dr Dave gave me a lot to digest that lunchtime.

The children played in the pool for the rest of the afternoon. Bianca was swimming around the deep end without the water wings, showing off her swimming and snorkelling skills, while Laurence had the courage to jump up and down under the waterfall with the water wings on. It was heavenly to watch them having such fun, marred only by Laurence's attempts to leave messages whenever he left the pool. Poor Bianca had to get out of the pool each time until I returned from marching Laurence off to the toilet. He didn't seem to get my message.

Throughout this holiday the children had been collapsing into bed around nine o'clock exhausted, but that night Laurence couldn't sleep. He was behaving strangely as if he had something weighing heavily on his mind. I suspected that with all the extra time in the water, Genie had made a big impression on him that day. Maybe she had fetched him a special message from her long weekend.

The following morning Laurence seemed his usual bouncy self. He worked well with Donny and Genie, giving all the correct responses, and they spent more time in the water again.

Bianca was still attending her classes and she showed me a bracelet that she had made. I suspected that she wasn't enjoying this second week as much as the first because she had to share Elizabeth with two German girls. You find many autistic German children at the dolphin therapy because they get the DHT on their health insurance.

The DHT team employed a professional photographer to take pictures and make a video to give us as a record of our stay. Today was the day for us to receive our photos. Bianca had her own little album with her name printed on it and there was a similar one for Laurence. There were some beautiful pictures; the photographer had done brilliantly to capture the few smiles that there had been in the first week. It was difficult to choose one photograph to be blown up and sent on to us with the video.

During the week I had noticed an English girl in her late teens having rides with the dolphins. She was having a wonderful time and was very verbal and emotional, often bursting into tears. It was clear that she couldn't believe this was happening to her.

She was collecting her photos at the same time. Before handing over her photos the photographer pleaded for no more tears and the young girl eagerly agreed. She opened the album, shrieked, 'That's me!' and burst into tears of joy. The photographer quickly followed suit and I found it impossible to focus on our photos. We all had an emotional overload. She was such a lovely girl, I could see nothing wrong with her, but I couldn't ask, as she was on the Make-A-Wish programme.

It was our last day in the Keys as tomorrow we had to check out of the hotel before going to the therapy. We bought some souvenirs and presents and I stocked up with the incontinence sheets as we would have two nights in Miami before flying home and I didn't think that other hotels would be as understanding as the Holiday Inn had been.

The children spent their last afternoon in the hotel pool, of course, and Laurence spent the entire evening excitedly tapping his photos, which allowed me time to pack.

It was a sad morning as we squeezed everything into the car, checked out and drove to the therapy. I couldn't talk as I rubbed the suntan lotion over Laurence for the last time. I was happy with the progress made but saddened by the thought of what might have been with an extra week. Donny was demanding so much more from Laurence. He asked for, 'I want to go in the water with the dolphins,' before allowing him to have a ride and Laurence said it. He would say anything for another ride.

At the end of the session Bianca and I were invited down onto the pontoon to say our goodbyes to Genie. Laurence didn't like this again and when Genie rose up out of the water clicking away at me, he screamed. It was a timely reminder of how he had been last week.

It was as if he didn't want me to hear what she had to say. He needn't have worried, as I was just a dumb human who didn't have a clue what she was saying, so I simply beamed back my thanks for all her efforts.

In return, I got the strongest feeling that this was unfinished business.

We said a sad farewell to all of the team. Bianca gave Elizabeth a thank-you mug but Laurence showed no emotion, skipping up and down while impatiently waiting to go. Donny and Laurence had built a strong bond of trust over the past fortnight and he had worked hard to get inside Laurence's mind. Now he looked genuinely sad to be saying goodbye to his emotionless buddy.

Only now did I understand something Dr Dave had said to me during the first week. He told me that Donny was one of the best he had ever met but he couldn't hold on to him and he would be leaving soon. I couldn't understand how anybody could be unhappy working in such a beautiful environment alongside dolphins that produced the odd miracle. Now I could see that intensely working on each child for two, three or four weeks and then saying goodbye for good took a heavy emotional toll.

I do hope that Donny found the level of job satisfaction that he so richly deserved.

I shook his hand and thanked him for all his efforts and Laurence gave him several high fives before we headed north on Highway 1 towards the mainland and Miami on the first leg of our journey home.

We stopped for lunch at what looked like a 'super size' McDonald's. When we walked inside I was surprised to find the restaurant area was quite small as there was a huge indoor kiddies' play area with a ball-pool, slides, climbing nets and elevated padded walkways. The children's hunger disappeared but I foolishly insisted they eat their lunch before having a play. Laurence ate his nuggets and refused his chips; unbelievably he claimed that he wasn't hungry and Bianca was the same, so I gave in and allowed them to go and play. After all, our work was finished and we were on holiday now. When they eventually returned to the table Laurence scoffed his cold fries and we continued on our way after another precautionary trip to the toilet.

The number of lanes started to increase as we approached Miami. I decided to turn off right towards the sea just before hitting the city centre to start looking for a hotel and we ended up crossing a bridge onto an island called Key Biscayne. The first thing we saw was the Miami Seaquarium and we decided that we would visit it the following morning.

I was unimpressed with this island; it felt like a penal colony for the rich. Locked away in their expensive high-rise heavily defended apartments, the inhabitants were safely segregated from the general population of Miami. The manicured streets were deserted.

I remembered seeing a hotel on the approach to Miami with a large neon sign advertising a pool, so I decided to drive back there as, at the end of the day, the presence of a pool was all the children were interested in. By Miami standards, it was a drab hotel and I checked that the pool was working before booking us in.

However, it was in a pleasant area called Coral Gables, the room was basic but it had air conditioning and TV and the children were happy playing in the large rectangular pool during the evening.

The shallow end was a bit deeper here but Bianca leapt straight in full of confidence while Laurence carefully explored the area around the steps with his water wings on. Having explored the depth and extent of the shallow area, he was soon happily jumping in, holding Bianca's hand to create an even bigger splash. I decided that this hotel would make a good base for our last couple of days in Florida.

The children slept well in their new surroundings and for the first time in over a week, I awoke dry. The beds were dry and the screwed-up incontinence sheets were dry. Laurence hadn't left me any messages.

I was engulfed by a tremendous sense of relief. I felt like I had been bent over, ploughing through a hurricane for the last ten days, and now I could stand up. It felt great.

There were no more messages.

We were back to normal, but of course Laurence wasn't normal, he was still autistic, but he was definitely different. I couldn't figure what the difference was but just like immediately after the AIT I knew something had changed in his head. It was as Dr Dave had predicted, everything had settled back down and it had settled down differently.

We set off early to the Miami Seaquarium in order to arrive at opening time. The morning rush hour was in full swing and, being an experienced London driver, I enjoyed the hustle of four lanes of cars undertaking and overtaking. I felt good cruising through the traffic in the sunshine with my elbow resting out of the open window.

We arrived safely at the Seaquarium to see a notice saying 'No killer whale show today', as it wasn't well. but there were many other shows. There was a sea lion pantomime, some alligators and sharks, and I was pleased to see my first manatee or sea cow. These huge creatures spend their lives slowly chewing seaweed just below the surface of the waterways around the Florida Keys. They are nearly extinct and there are now draconian punishments for speeding motorboats in manatee areas, but the manatees don't know where the safe boundaries are.

When you consider how much we get from land cows, I wonder what discoveries we will deprive future generations of, if we fail to save these harmless sea creatures.

There were two very different dolphin displays. The first was held in a large very deep circular aquarium. The show was full of American razzmatazz and was a brilliant display of synchronised dolphin acrobatics. The kids in the front rows were getting soaked. I had chosen to sit further back where there was more space for Laurence to move about.

I didn't want him to worry that we might make him swim with these dolphins as well and I didn't bring any waterproofs either. Half way through the show a dolphin made a huge leap right in front of us. It was as high as we were up in the stand and it appeared to look across as if to say, 'This one's for you.' There was no time to run. I stuffed my camera under my T-shirt and ducked as the splash cascaded over us. The children were delighted.

The other dolphin display was held beside the sea and was more of a getting-to-know-dolphins show. I immediately recognised the scene, as it was on the set of the TV show, *Flipper*. What the TV cameras don't show you are the three large concrete stands facing the warden's beachside cabin.

The show was informative and it ended with what I could only describe as a chaotic game of flipper ball. About ten dolphins were leaping in and out of the water flicking large beach balls into the stands and sometimes even over the roof of the stands. The chaos in the water was matched by the melee in the stands as at least a dozen children chased after each ball as they bounced erratically around the half-empty stands.

We left the Seaquarium late in the afternoon, went for a walk along the beach, found a place to eat and got back to the hotel at eight. Laurence then expected to go for a swim in the pool. I couldn't deny him, as he had been such a good boy all day. Not once had I caught him trying to leave a message—it was over, and that night I didn't bother using the incontinence sheets. I left them for the maid when we checked out the next morning.

Our flight home wasn't until the evening. I noticed on the map that the Miami Metrozoo was close by and it was a simple journey from there to the airport. I had heard how American zoos put ours to shame and was immediately struck by the scale of the place; London Zoo would fit comfortably into the car park of this zoo.

The Miami police were holding a children's safety week and Bianca was keen to take part. She had to visit booths scattered around the zoo collecting stamps while receiving various safety messages.

As we walked through the entrance there was a large lake with a beautiful island of pink flamingos in front of us. Following the path around the lake we saw the white bengal tiger enclosure. There appeared to be nothing between them and us except for a small neatly trimmed hedge. I noticed one of the tigers behaving like a domestic cat preparing to pounce. I followed its line of sight to see that a pelican had landed at the edge of the enclosure. There was no cover to hide its approach so the tiger had to rely on speed. It bounded out of the shadows, rapidly accelerating, and leapt, with its outstretched paws missing the pelican by inches. The pelican rather cheekily flapped away to safety in the nick of time.

The tiger skidded to a halt at the edge of a large moat that prevented it from picking up an easy lunch from the other side and trotted back to the shade. These large moats were used extensively around the zoo to separate humans and animals and the hedges cleverly hid them from view.

In the baking hot sunshine it was not difficult to imagine you were in Africa as you looked out on giraffes, zebras and gazelles grazing in the same huge field. It was as close as you could get to a safari in a city. There were no bars.

Of course Laurence wasn't impressed by any of this, he was even unmoved by the bareback elephant ride in the children's petting zoo which left Daddy walking like John Wayne for a week.

The only wildlife that interested him were the hot dog sellers, the drinking fountains and the largest creature in the zoo, the air-conditioned monorail train that travelled around the zoo above us. Laurence stood in awe looking up as the train ran over our heads and he insisted on doing several laps of the four-station circuit. It was like a huge toy train set just for him and we left the zoo with him in tears because he wanted to go round yet again.

Bianca had collected her safety stamps. I had censored a couple of the booths: I felt the 'Dial 911' booth might confuse her, and the 'What to do when you find your parents' handgun' booth was totally unnecessary in our family. She was given a small pencil set and the policeman stuck a Miami Police badge on them both.

To my complete surprise Laurence's mood was transformed by this act. I would have expected the badge to be lost in the car park long before we found the car.

However, he was happily skipping around again, tapping the badge on his chest saying, 'Miami police Daddy.' His tears had disappeared and with a beaming smile, he said it again, 'Miami police Daddy.'

'It's not real, it's just a sticker,' scoffed Bianca, but for me his words were real.

He was talking TO me. For the first time he displayed a desire to inform me. His words were coming from his heart and they pierced mine.

It was the first evidence of Laurence's second awakening.

185

PART 3

10

Speech Therapy

The journey home was relatively uneventful. It was a night flight, so after his long run around in the zoo Laurence was able to complete his mission and sleep on the plane.

They say no rest for the wicked and I was straight back to work the next day. Colleagues and customers could not understand me. I was physically and emotionally shattered. I needed a holiday now more than I had ever needed one, and yet they all said how wonderful it must have been and then they asked if it had worked. I had to be honest, and said that I didn't know if it had worked, I just knew that he was different somehow.

Laurence returned to school. Nikki reported that he was shy when he walked into the classroom and then he gave everybody a big hug. Her reports over the coming weeks were positive and encouraging. She regularly reported that Laurence had concentrated really well today, was well focused today and was very cheerful or interacted well with the other children. It seemed like he understood better what school was about and he was enjoying it.

Nikki also noticed the change from labelling to communication in Laurence's speech. Here are a couple of extracts from the home schoolbook at this time:

'Laurence is now beginning to tell an adult if something has happened to him in the playground, which is good. Today he said that a child had pinched him.'

'He ate well and asked for more dinner, "Fish fingers please Nikki" without me even asking him.'

'Laurence is getting much more aware of children's emotions and commenting on them. Today he said that someone was "upset" and that another child was "sick", which was nice.'

Dr Dave appeared to have been correct, the DHT had acted like a springboard and his teachers were getting more out of him now, and this newfound desire to communicate rather than label seemed to be an added bonus. However, I felt that the DHT had a more profound effect on him but it was hard to explain exactly what it was. It was as if Laurence went to Florida as a seven-year-old terrible two and came back as a seven-year-old aged three.

The DHT claims to give some children a six-month to a year's boost in their educational development. Laurence got a boost to his educational development, but he also appeared to have gained a boost to his behavioural development.

I have mentioned before Laurence's distinctive chuckle which communicated to people around him that somebody was being naughty. Because of our need to rely on verbal communication, we had managed to instil in him the idea that he could communicate with us via words. But I have to wonder if his saying, 'Andrew is being naughty' was any more communicative than him emitting his distinctive chuckle of anticipation.

Post-Florida Laurence had now taken this one step further. While walking along the road on a class trip to the local shop, he told another child, 'Cross the road now.' Laurence picked on a normally good well-behaved little boy and he said it just as a teacher would. The boy did as he was told and went to cross the road.

Nikki said that obviously there was no chance that the boy would have made it into the road, as they had it well covered, but it gave them a shock and Laurence was hysterical. He had made the child naughty.

Everybody had behaved just as he had anticipated—at last he had found a means of communication that we responded to and which allowed him to manipulate us. He was no longer simply reacting to events happening around him, he was now experimenting with creating events.

He had jumped from a terrible two to a manipulative three.

I wanted to capitalise on the springboard effect.

I was very impressed by Donny's in-your-face speech therapy. I felt that during those two weeks Laurence had taken in more speech therapy than he had done previously in his life.

The school was struggling to provide adequate speech therapy. The parents and teachers of children in the Behaviour and Communications Difficulties Department held meetings to try to find ways to improve the availability of speech therapy.

The parents viewed the current provision as totally unacceptable as it amounted to one half-hour session per week every other term for each child. The school employed one speech therapist, whose contract was due for renewal. The school didn't want to renew her contract; instead they wanted to spend the money saved to replenish the teaching complement. Speech therapists are expensive.

As parents, we had a different perspective and we weren't interested in the budget battles going on around us. To us it was simple. Our children were in this department because they had severe problems in two areas, behaviour and communication. The children needed a high level of staffing to control the behaviours and they needed a much higher level of speech therapy to help with their communication problems.

The school explained that this was simply not possible; it was struggling to cope with the current teaching levels, and speech therapy was a luxury that it could no longer afford.

The problem was how the parents could have the teaching levels that their children needed and also have a meaningful level of speech therapy. The solution was not difficult to find, and I put it to the next meeting.

The speech therapist already spent a lot of her limited time with each child assessing the child's progress for the annual reviews. I said that she should continue doing these assessments, but the rest of her time should be spent training the parents to give their child the relevant therapies that their child needed. I wasn't asking for us to be trained as speech therapists—we all had our own careers—all I wanted was to learn the exercises and therapies that she would have used on Laurence in her office if she had the time.

Each parent would receive the exercises relevant to their own child and we would report back to her if we had problems with an exercise or when we successfully completed one and wanted more. I felt that half an hour of speech therapy every night delivered by an amateur had to be a significant improvement over the once-in-a-blue-moon professionally delivered speech therapy that our children were currently receiving.

Absolutely not! The speech therapist was adamant—it was a ridiculous idea that was a non-starter, and there was to be no discussion on this matter. The parents were keen, the teachers remained knowingly quiet and the speech therapist moved the meeting along. I suspected that I was being a bit naïve.

All I wanted to do was help our children to talk, so why did the speech therapist refuse to give us some tools to do this?

191

In my experience of dealing with skilled professionals, they fall into two groups. One group rely on a few clever tricks or tools and don't like you to see what they are doing because you will copy them and deprive them of future business. The other group are happy for you to watch their skills because they know that if you try it you'll make a pig's ear of it and give them extra work.

The speech therapists seemed to behave like the first group; they performed their therapies in their offices away from the eyes of the classroom and wouldn't divulge what they did. But what little tricks could they possibly be hiding in their offices? It didn't make sense.

I wasn't going to be put off. If the school's speech therapist would not help us to help our children then I would find one that would. I got the number of a place that was an institute of speech therapists or something similar, I cannot remember its exact name.

I explained that I was looking for information regarding the therapies that speech therapists used on autistic children. The woman seemed more interested in who I was than in dealing with my enquiry. When she found out that I was just a parent, she politely told me that she couldn't help me. I asked her to put me through to somebody who could help and she swiftly informed me that there was nobody in the building who could help.

I was finding these so-called experts in communication to be very uncommunicative, so I changed tack. I explained that I was making these enquiries because I was considering hiring a speech therapist who specialised in dealing with autism and could she give me the number of somebody who could advise me on this. Her response reminded me of Ana's solicitor's response to me having the audacity to try to talk to her direct. Her polite composure wilted; she couldn't help me at all and she ended our conversation abruptly.

I knew that I couldn't have been the first person to try to hire a speech therapist, so there had to be another way. I made an appointment to see the school speech therapist again.

I explained that I was just trying to maximise the benefits to be gained from the dolphin's springboard effect. All I wanted was a skilled professional to work once a week on Laurence and his speech. If the therapist was working on pronouns, then for the rest of the week we would use and emphasise the usage of pronouns. It seemed logical to me, but to the school speech therapist it was out of the question.

I asked if she knew of any speech therapists who were not as busy as she was, maybe newly qualified and looking for some experience with autism. No matter what I asked the answer was always no, and she couldn't or wouldn't point me in any direction to help me continue my search.

I had hit a brick wall and I was convinced that it had been built to hide something.

Donny had been so open, helpful and genuinely interested in Laurence's development, in complete contrast to the English speech therapists.

I haven't bothered to reprint any of Laurence's speech-therapy reports as they all say the same and tell us nothing new. Their comments on Laurence's communication and comprehension skills only echoed his teacher's observations in his annual school reports. Their conclusions were annoyingly predictable and uncommunicative: 'Laurence continues to require a classroom communication pro-gramme designed by teacher and therapist. In addition, he requires access to individual and/or group speech therapy, according to need.'

But if a speech therapist could not conclude what type of speech therapy their patient requires and how frequently they require it, then how beneficial can it be?

About a month after we returned from Florida we received the final report from the DHT. They concluded that Laurence would benefit from DHT three times a week. Although that was blindingly obvious, it was out of the question. At least they did quantify it, though!

Much more helpful was a personalised exercise video for Laurence. On the tape Donny explained ten exercises whilst giving lots of encouragement to Laurence, and between each exercise there was a video clip of Laurence interacting with Genie.

The idea was simple: while Laurence was doing an exercise the video was put on pause, and when it was completed he was rewarded by restarting the video, allowing him to see himself interact with Genie.

Well, that was the theory. In practice Laurence became much too hyper in anticipation of viewing the tape, shrieking and rocking on his belly just as he did in Florida. We were able to use the tape as a reward for good behaviour, but not in conjunction with the com-pletion of the exercises. However, I was able to incorporate the exercises into daily life.

The exercises covered all areas of his development. One exercise was called 'Near and far'. I hadn't realised that Laurence had a problem switching his focus between distant and close-up objects, but it was easy to practise this when we were out.

There were also exercises to help his maths, his hand–eye coordination and his speech. The speech exercises were called 'Pick a pronoun' and 'What do you want?' and were designed specifically to follow on from the work that Donny had been doing with Laurence.

It was exactly what I had been asking of the school speech therapist—some simple exercises to support her infrequent work with Laurence. Donny hadn't given away any secret therapies, but he had given me some relevant exercises to work on.

With the speech therapists refusing to help me help Laurence, I turned to his teachers for some additional help. Their schedules were already full but one of them put me in touch with an agency called Top Tutors.

They had tutors for primary to degree-level students and they took on children with special needs as well. (Unsurprisingly, they had no speech therapists on their books, but I had to ask.)

The first tutor they sent didn't last long, but then they sent Lynette. She was a primary teacher with no special needs training but she had tremendous natural ability and had quite a few special needs children on her books.

Unlike the speech therapists and the psychologists, Lynette wasn't interested in his diagnosis. She read his latest school report, identified his area of least development and set to work.

Laurence had made great progress with his speech, rising from the least verbal to one of the most verbal children in his class. However, his writing skills had not kept up and after four years of schoolwork all they had achieved was that he could now 'scribble within preset boundaries' (i.e. the edge of the page).

Lynette had the patience of a saint and she needed it as she set to work on Laurence's writing skills. Laurence was a good student during her weekly visits, he liked Lynette, but progress was painfully slow over the two years that she worked on him.

With hindsight, the money would probably have been better spent working on Laurence's strengths rather than on his weakest subject. I had foolishly ignored Rita Jordan's advice to find a subject that interested him and to expand on that. Writing certainly didn't interest him; he was compliant and did his best doing the exercises for the teacher, but he had no motivation to develop his writing skills.

It was as if Laurence could see no point in writing other than to please the teacher. It was the same with his reading books—he didn't seem to improve, but when it came to reading menus and maps he was very interested and learnt to read them quickly. Laurence's talking followed the same pattern—he was happy to talk about what's for dinner or where we were going, the things that interested him, but it was impossible to get him to say what he had done at school that day.

Although none of the diets and supplements that can benefit autistics had any apparent effect on Laurence I decided to give him children's vitamins, the sort of vitamin supplements that normal parents give to their normal children. I felt that if they did have any beneficial effects for normal children then they would help Laurence in the same way. They certainly wouldn't do him any harm and I felt the same way about giving him cod liver oil. Unbelievably, he liked the taste—he lapped it up.

These days I give him a product called 'Eye Q', which is supposed to help with eye and brain function with a mixture of fish oils and evening primrose oil. Laurence likes the micro capsules. He chews them like 'hundreds and thousands' cake decorations, but like the other supplements, they seem to have had no appreciable effect. However, some parents swear by them, so they should be tried, as it cannot do any harm.

We are forced to become amateur scientists as we study the claims of these products, as there is very little impartial help around. This is an area where I feel the NAS has let parents down. They send out a comprehensive information pack to all new parents, but there is no list of things to do while you're waiting for the experts to watch, assess, diagnose and Statement your child. If there were such a list, it should be in order of effectiveness, but the NAS has only just begun to look into the relative effectiveness of different interventions.

I was determined to give Laurence every ounce of help that I could post-DHT. I felt that there was still some distortion in Laurence's hearing, as he still took longer than Bianca to correctly pronounce a new word. New words to Laurence were like foreign words to us. He said them correctly, but only after several attempts.

I booked us in for another course of auditory training but we had to wait for the October half-term holiday. That was a blessing in disguise as I really couldn't afford it right away, but I was due a bonus in September.

I had hoped to get the AIT on the NHS this time around, but despite years of promising results the health authorities were running scared of the costs. Some claimed that as nobody knew if the therapy would help any particular child then it was a speculative therapy. The NHS doesn't do that, even when over half the children were benefiting from this potluck therapy.

This policy was so short-sighted that even the most myopic could see through it. When you're talking about spending money, any excuse not to will do.

The school held regular relaxation lessons. At first Laurence was a hopeless pupil, but over the years they had taught him the concept of relaxing, which he desperately needed. Even when he was sleeping he seemed so rigid and tense.

When he was feeling stressed his tapping could still become very intense. As we encouraged him to relax, his tapping or self-stimulation (more commonly called 'stimming') reduced in intensity. I am sure that it was his rapidly improving understanding of us that helped him to relax around us. His tapping went from constant to frequent.

These stimming behaviours are very important and give a direct measure of how a non-verbal child is feeling. The level of stimming tells you how successful you have been and can also act as a guide to what situations the child finds difficult to handle.

Although autistics stim most of the time, normal people also stim but on a less noticeable scale, from a self-satisfied extra tap as you hammer in the last nail to the widespread use of worry beads in the Arab world. Personally I wiggle my toes when I'm sitting still and I have never been able to work out why that annoys other people.

In non-verbal children, stimming becomes another form of communication and shouldn't be ignored or suppressed. It should be acted upon if the stimming is causing the worry beads to keep breaking or causing calluses to form on the knuckles. To try to physically inhibit a stimming behaviour will only result in the stress manifesting in a different way. The only way to tackle excessive stimming behaviours is from the inside, removing the stresses and strains that caused the behaviours in the first place.

A lot of the time it is trial and error as the parents learn to read this communicative behaviour in its many different manifestations.

Our learning difficulties must be painful for the autistic child to behold.

Meanwhile, Ana had been battling on a different front. The physiotherapist had finally given in and made an appointment for Laurence to see an orthotist regarding his walking on tiptoe. Our constantly repeated command of 'feet down' worked for a just a couple of seconds before he rose back onto tiptoe again. As he had grown bigger we had become increasingly concerned about possible long-term harm. The orthotist agreed with us that something had to be done and arranged for some special shoes to be made for Laurence. They looked like a heavy pair of Doc Martens and they had a steel plate running through the length of the thick sole, forcing him to walk flat-footed. They worked until we took them off each evening and then he would rise back up onto his toes.

I could understand why he wanted to be on tiptoe. He led such a stressful life, always worrying about trivial things like what is going to happen next. He felt that he needed to be on tiptoe—that extra couple of inches in height and his quicker reactions could make all the difference between life and death out in the wild. We couldn't explain to him that a wild dog wasn't about to trot out of the bedroom.

Those heavy boots must have felt like we were deliberately handicapping him when we were out on the wild streets of Walthamstow.

Laurence soon discovered that his handicap was also a powerful weapon; even a gentle tap from his new bovver boots produced great displays of pain and anger. He was soon exploring all his old behaviours with his new understanding and depth of perception, but now it was with boots on as well.

He was becoming a real handful; his improved self-confidence made him more wilful and he was generating a wider range of strategies to get what he wanted. The progress that we had made in Florida had actually made it harder to control him. Now with boots on, he had to be controlled at arm's length. My Vulcan neck touch became very handy.

We wondered if these improvements were in fact progress at all.

Throughout our travels I maintained consistent strict discipline when we were out, no matter what the consequences. It was too dangerous to have misbehaviour on the streets. Laurence knew that misbehaviour meant going home and he never wanted to do that, but at home it was harder to impose sanctions. Time-outs were not an option; he loved being isolated, so he saw time-outs as more of a reward than a punishment.

I couldn't threaten him with 'No going out' because Ana wouldn't allow me to fulfil that sanction as she valued her time-outs from him. She expected me to punish him as her father had punished her brothers when they were young. They had all grown up to be well-behaved young men.

I am not against corporal punishment as a last-resort chastisement, but I felt it was needed a lot less often than she felt it was. All too often I could see how Ana could have avoided conflicts if she had bartered with him properly beforehand. Laurence understood barter-ing for good behaviour—the school regularly did it and rewarded him for doing so, and I did it as well. Ana didn't think that she should have to barter for basic decent behaviour, so Laurence logically gave her bad behaviour instead.

Like the experts, Ana couldn't see past the SLD label. She refused to accept that he was manipulating and controlling her behaviour. But he had found that he only got rewards from her when he behaved badly, and so he escalated the misbehaviour until she inevitably gave in and bought peace.

They were both becoming habituated to fighting.

I couldn't punish him for exploiting the weaknesses in Ana's logic; instead I tried to explain how she could have avoided the problems, but this was seen as being too soft and taking his side all the time.

There were, however, occasions when I felt that Laurence did need a smack. Florida was the first time, and now that he was becoming even harder to control, other situations arose.

I used a trick that I had learnt from my father when he was training our pet dog. He noticed my discomfort watching him smacking our new dog with a rolled-up newspaper so he came over to me and he whacked me with it too. Like the dog I jumped, but not from any pain—it was the swish and loud contact noise that had startled us both.

I soon found that raising my arm with the loosely rolled newspaper and coming down as hard as I could onto the palm of my hand made such a loud noise that no matter how loud he was screaming I got his immediate attention.

I felt that that sound was corporal punishment to Laurence's sensitivities. Inflicting physical pain on him with a smack was often not an option if he was inflicting pain on himself, which he often did when he was in full flow. Laurence would pull his hair while kicking himself, if there was nobody else for him to kick, and scream with pain and anger. It was a vicious circle.

The sound of the newspaper's whack seemed to send a painful shock through his body, but the eerie silence that followed allowed me to gain control by removing him and introducing distractions. I used it only as a last resort.

If I was caught outside without my weapon of choice, a newspaper, I found that a clap of my hands only worked to get his attention at the very beginning of an outburst. If I didn't catch it early enough and he became a danger to himself or other people, then it had to be a smack.

I felt it was important for him to see and be aware of everything that went on, so I performed a pantomime of an angry parent viciously smacking their child.

I exaggerated all my movements—raising my hand up high, the first two swipes would whip across his trousers so that he was well aware that he had just had a very close shave. If that didn't get his attention then my third swipe was intended to sting, but the exaggerated threat was usually enough. To complete the show I would shriek my disapproval with a wicked-stepsister voice; the high-pitched words were aimed at penetrating his thick red mist.

Hopefully bystanders thought that I was a parent out of control, wildly beating a naughty child, as that is what I wanted Laurence to think. It was as if my tantrum had to appear bigger than his; hence the pantomime and usually the first couple of warning shots across the bows were enough to get his attention without having to resort to that third painful swipe.

From the age of seven until he was eleven Laurence frequently suffered from these red-mist rages. I watched him transform. It was like a wave coming up from his body. It travelled up his face, his eyes glazed over from the bottom up and the mist exploded in his brain. He had no control from then on.

I probably hit him once or twice a year during these four years and most of those occasions were caused by me mistiming a warning shot against his wildly flailing legs. I know that the couple of bruises that I inflicted far outweighed the self-inflicted harm that I prevented.

He had to learn how to control these violent emotional outbursts before they started.

His teachers soon learnt that if Laurence said, 'Mustn't pull the hair,' it was a one-second warning that he was about to launch a vicious assault. They too had watched him closely and had seen him transform in seconds. They felt that 'Mustn't pull the hair' wasn't a warning to us, it was him attempting to control his rising tide of emotions.

Sometimes, whilst ducking, it was hard to see the progress made in enabling him to express his feelings by saying things like, 'Mustn't kick Daddy in the head.'

It was a long series of battles for Laurence, but over the years his attempts to control himself produced longer warnings, indicating that he was slowly winning the war. These longer warnings also meant that my pantomime distraction technique became more effective so there was less need to follow it up with a smack.

As Laurence struggled to control himself, I struggled to control him while he controlled Ana and Ana controlled me. These were the control years.

That summer we couldn't afford a holiday; I was working overtime to pay off the DHT bank loan. Instead we had odd days out to different places like Thorpe Park and London Zoo and it was always the case of Ana saying, 'You take them, I need a rest.'

As usual, Laurence wasn't interested in the animals in the zoo. They were behind bars and of no concern to him, but that year they had one species that he was interested in. He had seen them before buzzing around town and now he had an opportunity to examine one in detail. It was a brightly coloured police Land Rover. I think the police were there to encourage kids to consider a career in the force, but compared with the Miami police zoo venture, this was a feeble effort.

I felt that it was important for him to feel comfortable with the police. He was very apprehensive at first, but once he plucked up the courage to go in the Land Rover he got very excited. He was rocking in the seat, tapping the dashboard while opening and closing the door with his free hand. Laurence was very happy and I allowed him to play in his own way for as long as the policeman could maintain his painted smile.

As I led him away he gave the bodywork a final tap, and while the officer was considering if that was an act of vandalism I briskly marched Laurence towards the promised ice-cream van. He showed no interest in any of the other animals, other than the fish of course.

I suspected he wanted to eat them along with his ice cream.

*

The new term couldn't come soon enough for Ana. Laurence was winning all their battles but I was reduced to being an observer waiting for her to learn that she couldn't be a normal parent with him. I couldn't understand why it was taking her so long. With hindsight I suspect that as I was not used to young children I was better able to adjust to Laurence's bizarre behaviour than Ana, who'd been surrounded by normal young children throughout her life.

Laurence was in a new classroom. Nikki was still his teacher, Louise was still her full-time assistant, and she had two part-time assistants. There were five other children in the class, all boys. Laurence coped well with the changes. Now that he could understand our explanations of upcoming changes he was able to cope with them. The compic symbol timetables that we used at school and home allowed us to introduce changes even earlier, giving him more time to think them over and accept them. The autistic symptom of 'does not like change' was fading away.

Clearly it was Laurence's understanding of us that produced this change in his behaviour. The key to changing his behaviour was to improve his understanding, and that meant concentrating on his hearing and his speech.

I asked what provision of speech therapy there was for Laurence that term. The reply came back that he would be receiving speech therapy once per week from an assistant speech therapist.

Nobody had mentioned assistants to me before; I could have hired one to help Laurence instead of Lynette.

More to the point, why weren't the three classroom assistants, assistant speech therapists?

In a class where Laurence was now one of the more verbal children, all six of them could be described as having severe speech problems. Yet they were rationed to once a week from an assistant rather than five days per week from the classroom assistants, when they could have practised the programmes laid out by the speech therapist individually and in groups in a wide variety of lessons, in the playground and in the canteen.

If speech therapy is effective then its effects can be magnified at little extra cost. There is no evidence that once-a-week speech therapy is beneficial to our children; however, there is plenty of evidence to suggest that high doses of one-to-one speech therapy really can make a difference. Training the classroom assistants and the parents to follow a programme laid out by the speech therapist could make this difference relatively cheaply.

Instead, only those able to afford the private bills receive those rewards. Nowadays, the speech therapists' professional bodies have got their act together and you can pick up a good one for between fifty and a hundred pounds an hour. However, if you can afford meaningful quantities of speech therapy at these prices, then you would be better off investing in an appropriate ABA programme.

The other half of Laurence's understanding problems was his hearing, his reception. It was two and a half years since the AIT had made such a dramatic impact on his hearing. I was not expecting the same kind of impact this time. I saw this second course of AIT as a tidying-up exercise, to try to remove any last distortions or static to give him a level playing field with the rest of us. Although I found it difficult to practise it at home, I was confident that Laurence would be able to complete the audiogram this time, so that the modulation of the music could be targeted at his hearing difficulties.

For the treatment I turned to Tracey, who was the mother of an autistic boy. I first met them at the Hale Clinic. She had decided to change careers and trained under Aditi Silverstein to become one of the first AIT practitioners in this country. Tracey ran Communication Therapies Ltd from her home, which made it a more relaxing experience than the medical feel of the Hale Clinic.

It was remarkable how much Laurence had matured since the last AIT. He was no longer a frightened little puppy ready to leap out of the chair at the slightest distraction, and I no longer felt the need to sit at his feet to prevent that sort of thing. He was so much more self-assured and confident because he understood what was going on around him. He still didn't have the complete picture, but he appeared to have a working model that worked most of the time.

He understood that we went around town and had lunch between therapy sessions and then we went to a different park each day on the way home, so he was happy to comply with us by listening to the music. But he still couldn't understand what we wanted with the audiogram. Tracey explained that the results were too erratic, he wasn't giving the same answers to the same sounds often enough to give a meaningful result. This was a big disappointment.

I had imagined that his fine-tuning would require a proper audiogram result, even though the benefits of this were still unproven. We proceeded with a regular programme, and Laurence sat in the armchair listening to the music on the headphones while swinging his legs contentedly. His big, heavy boot heels thudded into the base of the chair, so I took them off and he was even more relaxed.

Most days it was just Laurence and me, as Ana was happy to have us out of the house for the whole of the half term. Occasionally I took Bianca along as well so that Ana could have a complete rest.

I liked having Bianca along, as when we went to the park without her I attracted quite a lot of attention sitting watching other people's children playing together normally. Out of the corner of my eye I monitored Laurence skipping along the perimeter fence on the other side of the park. He was happy, which was the purpose of going to a park, and he only moved towards me if he was concerned by the proximity of dogs.

He monitored what I was doing as well. When I stood up and waved he would come scampering across the grass, in his own time.

In response to my, 'Time to go home now,' he would whine and say, 'No go home, no.'

I could never force him to play on the equipment—he always preferred to run free—but when I said, 'Time to go home or play on the swings, which one?' he chose the equipment.

The swings were a mystery to him; he hated me pushing him but loved it when he was swinging through the air. He would push off with his feet, and then sit and wait expecting the swing to work. He used to get quite angry when it did not. I sat on the swing beside him demonstrating how to do it. I manipulated his legs but he couldn't get the rhythm, so instead he gradually learnt to tolerate my pushing him.

He fully understood the slide; to him this was high adventure. He would slowly climb the stairs, holding on with both hands and only letting go to tap a step before putting his weight on it. When he reached the top he liked to sit down and take stock; sometimes little five-year-olds would squeeze past and whizz down in front of him. I stood below, urging him to complete his adventure and stop blocking the slide. He carefully placed one leg at a time over the precipice and, holding on tightly with both hands, he lowered himself down the slope using his shoes as brakes. He went down even slower than he went up, but when he reached the ground he excitedly jumped up and ran around to do it again in exactly the same way.

On the roundabouts we had a couple of low-speed accidents, which he found very funny so I decided not to promote their use.

The seesaw was a toy for giving him the bumps, the harder the better. He had no idea that this was a turn-taking toy. It was completely one-sided to him.

He wasn't interested in climbing frames unless they were surrounded by sand. He liked to deliberately fall over and roll about on his back in the uneven sand like a dog with fleas.

Given the choice, he always preferred to be as far away from people as possible, which usually meant staying away from the play equipment unless I gave him no choice.

The time came for Laurence's second audiogram. I decided that it would be another waste of time, so I asked Tracey if Bianca could take the second audiogram and we would use the results of that on Laurence. Tracey had no objection; neither of us had any idea if it would be beneficial to him, but it certainly wouldn't do him any harm.

When Bianca was younger she used to cover her ears when we went on the Underground and when a motorcycle roared past, unlike other children that I observed on those occasions. With all the talk of a genetic element I had to consider the possibility that Ana and I had produced children with a hearing problem. Bianca was better able to learn and compensate for her sensitivities over the years, so that nowadays she didn't cover her ears any more.

Thinking like this also reminded me of a problem that I found with my hearing when I was a teenager attending discos. Although the music was deafening for everybody, it soon became clear that my friends could hear each other much better than I could. I tried focusing on their voices, watching their lips move and bending inwards to get my ears closer to their mouths, but I was still reduced to guessing what they said and laughing when the group laughed. Away from the disco my hearing was as good as the rest of my mates and I frequently tested it. The unsolved mystery was put to the back of my memory when I discovered more civilised methods of meeting potential mates.

Until now. Now I could understand. Like Bianca, I learned to compensate for the imbalances in my hearing when I was young so that my hearing seemed normal in all cases except in the extreme circumstances of going to a disco. There I was unable to filter out the voices from the loud music and compensate for my auditory imbalances. It seemed to be a good theory.

The result of Bianca's audiogram was a shock. Her hearing was all over the place. There were sharp peaks and troughs going right across the audio frequency spectrum. Her ears didn't match, and incredibly her hearing went down to minus ten decibels at certain frequencies. One decibel is defined as the lower limit of human hearing. Bianca's hearing was certainly odd and clearly very sensitive.

Bianca had other sensory issues as well. Remember her oversensitive feet on the Lanzarote beach? Also, she hated anything with even a hint of seasoning or spice. She never liked fizzy drinks because of the feel of the bubbles in her mouth. Despite these and possibly other undetected sensory issues, there was never any trace of autistic behaviour in her.

This indicated to me that it wasn't Laurence's sensory issues that caused his autism, although I'm sure they didn't help with his development. If multiple sensory dysfunctions caused autism then you would expect Bianca to display at least a hint of the symptoms of Asperger's syndrome, but she is socially fully functioning and to this day is as normal as a teenager can be. It seemed that normal children can overcome multiple sensory imbalances and create a normal reality, but in the confusing world of an autistic child, similar sensory imbalances can make the world an impossible place to understand.

None of us knew if using Bianca's audiogram had any effect on Laurence, and we also knew that if we saw any effect from this AIT, we wouldn't know if it was due to trying this.

It was all very unscientific, but it was worth a try.

Tracey compiled a thorough report and in it she noted some of our observations of changes in Laurence's behaviour. I said that Laurence seemed more aware of his environment and was more socially interactive. He seemed to listen more attentively and reacted by moving towards the person speaking.

I do believe that this second AIT did help to clear up Laurence's hearing a bit, but I feel that some of my comments were more about how Laurence was developing anyway. His greater understanding generally was also making him more socially interactive. To us it didn't matter what caused what, so long as we kept the developmental momentum moving, and the second dose of AIT did that.

Laurence knew that Christmas was coming, since he had spotted the first Christmas items in the supermarkets. It was a very long countdown. He repeated 'Christmas is coming' every time he spotted something to do with Christmas. I knew that all he was looking forward to was Christmas dinner and extra chocolates. Laurence had a very simple picture of Christmas.

It was to be a family Christmas and I wanted it to be as normal as possible. We had a big tree, lots of decorations all around the flat and I bought Laurence lots of little presents that were well wrapped as I understood that he was more interested in the wrapping than the present. To prevent Laurence from giving each parcel a token tear, this year I put a chocolate coin inside each present. At least now we had the illusion of a child having an interest in the contents of his presents. To him, it must have appeared a very strange way to wrap chocolates.

At Christmas time it was comparatively easy to not notice Laurence's isolation and differences, but each year when it came to Laurence's birthday two months after Christmas it was impossible not to see the reality of his life. He had no friends.

Laurence's classmates were the closest friends he had and they were spread across north London and the surrounding counties. We all understood the logistics of trying to get these children together, so, like the other parents, I asked the school if they would help to organise a birthday party for him with his friends. They were happy to help, as they were well aware of how much the children learnt from participating in such social situations.

We agreed on a venue and I went down to book us in and pay. Al's World in Fairlop Water was a large building, which had been converted into a soft-play jungle of ropes, slides, bridges and ball-pools. It was an ideal place for Laurence and his hyperactive mates to exhaust and then stuff themselves.

Bianca was the only girl who, along with the five other boys in his class plus another couple of boys who used to be in his class, attended his eighth birthday party.

When the children were eventually all rounded up to sit down and eat their meal they sat around the table, each one isolated in their own world. As the food was brought to the table on large trays it was wonderful to watch the children's faces transformed as a mountain of chips landed on the centre of the table, quickly followed by huge pyramids of chicken nuggets and fish fingers.

Each child was only thinking of himself and those piles of food. Nikki and her assistants worked hard to fill the gaps between the children by encouraging appropriate interactions and by separating children who were interacting inappropriately. I had to admire the teachers for all their hard work and tenacity. This was, after all, just another working day for them and a good opportunity to practise what they taught in the classroom.

At this time Ana had growing concerns for her frail father. She wanted to see him one last time and I couldn't argue with that. I wasn't concerned about whether she would come back, as she was really struggling to cope with Laurence. What I did object to was that she insisted on going for six weeks over Easter.

We tried to live together as peacefully as possible for the sake of the children but the reality of the situation was for me not to argue. I felt strongly that her family was being inconsiderate to expect Laurence to miss so much schooling, but when Ana got permission from both children's schools for them to miss school on compassionate grounds, I couldn't argue.

I could have taken two weeks off and looked after the kids while she went on her flight of compassion. That would also have been a lot cheaper, which was important at this time as Ana was expecting us to move soon.

I had my instructions for while they were away, I was to do everything that couldn't be done when Laurence was around, like repairing and repainting doors.

A week before Easter I drove them to the airport. Unable to stop them from going, I happily waved bye-bye, as I knew they would be back. The six weeks passed quickly. I took all the overtime I could get and I had an impossible list of chores to complete at home.

When they returned in May, we settled back into our usual routine. It was still my job to entertain the children from when I got home from work to their bedtime and on Sundays.

Bianca started taking dancing lessons on Sunday mornings in Walthamstow town centre. I used to take both of them down there and while Bianca had her lesson I took Laurence for a walk around the town. If the weather was bad we would sit on the railway platform watching the occasional train go by; he enjoyed that. Sunday afternoons were usually spent house-hunting.

I would have been happy moving to a larger place in the same area. There were seven schools within a ten-minute walk and although

Laurence always went to school on the school bus, his school was only a twenty-minute walk away. We were close to public transport and shops, and Whipps Cross Hospital was just a short bus trip away.

But Ana didn't like this area and wanted to move further out of London. Over the coming months, I scoured her desired areas but they were financially out of our reach and I gradually started looking further afield for affordability. I had to consider schools for both children and my ability to commute to work. As I was doing all this on Sunday afternoons with the kids in the back of the car, we also checked out the recreational facilities in each area. I had to keep them from getting bored, so progress was slow and as much fun as it could be.

At school Laurence was developing some new emotions. He now had a favourite adult, Louise, the classroom assistant. He hovered around her; he didn't know what he was supposed to do about his new feelings so he approached her and touched her, and pinched her and even kicked her. He was very confused. Despite these displays of aggression, she recognised that he was really just trying to be friendly.

About the same time Laurence started to cover his ears. It was eight months since the AIT so I didn't think it was anything to do with that. He put his hands over his ears more and more and it didn't seem to be related to the volume of the sounds around him. In fact, it seemed to correlate more with the levels of emotion around him. He seemed to be closing his eyes and covering his ears in an attempt to block out incoming emotions. It seemed crazy at first, but as I thought about it, it began to make sense. If I told Laurence off or praised him then my words produced emotions in him, so by blocking out my words he didn't have to deal with his emotions.

He didn't like emotions inside but he liked to watch other people's displays of emotion. Everything he did seemed purposefully intended to create a response from us. His answers to questions were based on what he thought would produce the biggest response. It was impossible to test him in conventional ways. If he thought an incorrect answer would produce more attention for him, then he gave it.

He was alert and attentive to all our responses—he even noticed our reactions to his comments when he was battling the red mist, so that now he would deliberately stand beside Bianca saying, 'Mustn't pull Bianca's hair,' trying to get a response from us.

While Ana continued to rise to his bait, a stern look was all he got from his teachers and me. He was playing with us and had reduced us to silent robots going about our business, giving him flashes of 'the stern look' whenever he went too far.

He was a charming child to engage with, but all too often he only wanted to engage with us in order to find new ways to provoke emotional outbursts. He was continually testing us.

As Laurence battled with his and our emotions his schoolwork seemed to be progressing well. Lynette had made a little progress with his handwriting, but it was always going to be difficult as breaking a pencil was a simple task-avoidance strategy.

'Put in bin,' he would kindly offer repeatedly. The trip to the rubbish bin would give him ample opportunity to provoke a response to his accidentally spilling or eating the shavings. He would love an angry outburst and a chase around the flat or classroom. Instead, he received a stern look aimed directly at him. Its effectiveness was remarkable, producing an immediate return to what he should be doing while he said, 'Must be a good boy now,' to let us know that it was over.

I was becoming aware that Laurence had many task avoidance strategies and reaction-producing strategies layered into all aspects of his life and therefore ours. He was playing chess with our lives, often thinking four to five moves ahead, and I began to grow concerned that, like Ana, I would get lost in his maze of mental strategies.

I spoke with Nikki. I was concerned about what would happen when the stern look lost its power. It seemed inevitable that one day he would reply to my stern look with an 'I don't care' giggle. She reassured me that something else always turns up, but I couldn't share her confidence.

She did share my concerns about his strategies in the classroom and the lengths to which he would go to manipulate situations. She was well aware that in Laurence's mind it was he who ran the school and that all around him were there for his convenience. I was very impressed by Nikki's understanding of Laurence and it was clear that there was a battle of wits between them—but who was winning? Laurence was happy at school and thought that he was in control, and yet Nikki thought that she was winning and thwarting Laurence at every turn.

I have nothing but praise for Nikki and her staff—they did an amazing job considering they had five other equally troublesome boys in their care—but I began to think that it was Laurence who was doing the driving.

I have reproduced his annual review in Appendix 5. In all subjects he had shown an interest and appeared to have learnt just enough to keep his teachers happy. They were happy with his progress and satisfied that their strategies were successful—a difficult child was learning and developing. But after all their efforts, he was still a lifetime from mainstream education. I realised that no matter how much my puppy learned to talk, he could never go to a proper school. He was happy learning a little bit at a time, reaping the rewards for each small step of progress that were heaped upon him, and he was convinced that his strategies were working as he was getting all the rewards.

If this lack of drive is a chink in the argument for special schools, then it is a chink created by the State.

It is the State that puts the drive into the system to push children through the special schools into the mainstream. But that drive costs money and it takes political willpower to follow it through. The drive to inclusion should have enlarged early-start special schools at the heart of the system, pumping out children capable of joining the mainstream. Instead, they are steadily starved of funds so that they are incapable of performing that function.

We know that the cost to the State for Laurence's class of six would be over £12 million if we failed to make them productive members of society, but we baulk at the cost of providing one speech therapist for that class and training for the parents. The system limps on, only able to push the top few pupils into mainstream education, while the rest swim along in the slow lane. However, I suspect that even with a fully financed special education system, Laurence would have been among the few that couldn't make the jump to mainstream.

Having said that, he clearly wasn't stupid. I believe that he found this weakness in his school. They didn't have the staffing levels to push him further, so he found that he could keep his teachers happy with a little bit of work and have a lot of fun while doing so. He was exploiting this weakness.

He was now untestable by conventional means, and Key Stage 1 was still a distant dream. He had learnt our language but we didn't know what else he had learnt. We were his toys and he was having fun playing with us. We had taught him to talk and now we were wary of talking to him. He exploited our language and manipulated our movements all for his own amusement. We were reduced to using facial expressions to cling onto control.

Ana thought Laurence was out of control.

I thought I was going to lose control soon if things got even more complicated.

Nikki thought that the teachers were still in control.

The speech therapists were lost.

But Laurence knew exactly who was in control, for it was he who was pulling our strings.

11

Home and Away

We were hoping to move the following spring, so for a cheap summer holiday before the children went back to school I decided to take up the offer of visiting an old friend who lived in Ireland. As the children were by now experienced flyers I decided to make the journey a bit more interesting—well, more interesting for Laurence.

Ana decided that a week without Laurence was more desirable than a week in Ireland with Laurence, so she stayed at home.

We travelled by train from Euston to Holyhead and Laurence loved every minute of the long, tedious journey. I had no concerns about him on the train, but I wondered what he would make of the ferry. He had never been on a big boat before and I was worried that I might have to spend the entire journey preventing him from trying to climb overboard to get closer to his beloved water.

I needn't have worried, as all he wanted to do was run-up and down the rolling deck. He found it funny, especially if he crashed, and Bianca was happy watching cartoons in the children's cinema.

My friend Mary lived in a small village north of Kilkenny. She owned the only takeaway in the village and lived above the shop. Laurence couldn't believe his luck; we had travelled all day just to visit a takeaway shop.

'Dinner downstairs' became a regular demand.

We spent the first couple of days visiting local places of interest, churches, castles and so forth, and then we headed over to the west coast, spending a couple of nights in B&Bs to give the children some seaside fun. However, the weather wasn't good and we ended up visiting even more ruins of churches and castles. We did have one bright afternoon and the children had fun splashing around in a large lake at a park.

Laurence was happy with the B&B lifestyle. If he had a busy day he didn't seem to mind where he slept, although we did have some arguments over which bed was whose. I always got first choice and Laurence accepted second choice, leaving Bianca with the third choice, which was quite often a camp bed. I knew that Laurence would have considered it very unfair if I made him take third choice. To him it would be a punishment and it could be used as such, but he was rarely any trouble when we were travelling.

Like father like son—Laurence loved a full English breakfast, although we never had one at home. I had his eggs and he had my sausages. This had to be done carefully as any spillage could get him upset very quickly. He also loved a cup of tea. Bianca and I didn't drink it so he usually had the whole pot to himself. He drank his cups of tea with his little finger sticking out, to Bianca's great amusement.

She couldn't contain herself and laughed openly. He would look at her over his cup of tea with a puzzled frown. He couldn't possibly understand what was amusing her, even when she tried to bend his little finger back in—it always popped out again the next time he picked up his cup.

I understood that in a more stressed situation he would have pulled her hair to stop her inexplicable emotional outbursts. It is not funny to laugh at people, and even though Laurence was often hilariously funny, she would have to learn when to be less open with her feelings. There were many times when I too struggled to hide my amusement and resorted to putting a menu or a handkerchief in front of my face.

As we travelled we had some good laughs—life is never dull with Laurence around.

Stripped of his safe school and home routines, he had no time for his clever strategies while we were on holiday. He had to concentrate on what was going on around him and you saw the real Laurence. A perpetual fish out of water, a clown who occasionally made me sad, but usually he filled me with pride, joy and laughter.

We spent the last night back at Mary's place. Mary wanted me to watch her partner Jack playing in a band at a local pub. She had two mums working in the takeaway that evening, so they would listen out for the children upstairs. They had our mobile numbers and the four pubs in this small village were all within 100 yards of the takeaway. The fresh country air seemed to be knocking the children out in the evenings anyway, so I had a night off.

213

The first pub was buzzing. I was surprised to find such an atmosphere in this sleepy village. I was also taken aback to find that this old pub was also an old-fashioned grocer's. It was a strange sight to see cornflakes, bread and other essentials behind one end of the bar. It was like a grocer's with a dance floor filled with people standing around drinking and smoking. We drank up quickly and moved on.

The second pub was more like I expected, with just a few old folks sitting around the tables. We got our drinks, sat down and Mary said, 'Now watch.'

As we sipped our drinks people started drifting in. Steadily the place filled up and, with everybody knowing everybody else, the air was soon filled with the buzz of countless conversations. There were now many people here who I had met in the previous bar.

The third pub also had its couple of old regulars sitting around and was ready for the arrival of the social wave as it headed towards the bar that would be selling afters that night. We had a drink and didn't wait to get socially swamped. Mary was in a hurry. She wanted to get a good seat for Jack's gig, which was in the fourth pub.

Jack and his two band members had little more than a soapbox in the corner to play on. During the week he had told me of much grander venues and opportunities that might have been. He had been one of those children that was playing music before he could read. Music was his life. The type of instrument didn't matter, as the music was in his blood.

When Jack first met Laurence, he tried to teach him to play the spoons. When Jack had an instrument in his hand he didn't need to talk to communicate. We marvelled at his natural rhythm as the spoons skipped across his body, but Laurence didn't seem interested in that—he just wanted to play, just like Jack.

Jack's band played all the traditional Irish songs. The drink flowed in harmony with the music, each song producing ever-greater applause as the band impressed this traditional gathering. Whether it was a whistle or a fiddle, the instrument was an extension of Jack's body and his body sang out. His body was incandescent. We loved it. We roared our approval.

This was what Jack lived for. He was feeding off us, and we were lapping it up, wanting more and more—and then the doors crashed open.

It was the Garda on an after-hours raid. They were having a clampdown as there had been some awful accidents recently involving drunk drivers, but there were no drivers here. We all claimed to be part of the band, which had been so true just a few seconds previously. They made a note of all our names and warned us that we could be in trouble if caught again, before allowing us to leave, with our full glasses.

A small group of us walked back to the takeaway, where Mary produced her speciality for these occasions — kebab baguettes. We ate, drank, talked and laughed, but I had to say my goodbyes early as we were travelling back to England in the morning. I fell upstairs into bed.

I didn't need an alarm clock as Laurence always woke me early. When I got up I was surprised to see Mary. She was still up and had been crying while watching the TV through the night. Princess Diana had died, and as she filled me in on the story I realised that she was in shock.

I felt bad about leaving her in such a state, but we had a boat to catch. Jack was asleep in the next room, but she didn't want to disturb him.

'I'm just being a silly woman,' she said, blowing her nose and she wished us a safe journey.

It was an uneventful journey home; it was quiet everywhere. On the boat people were crowded around the TVs, leaving the passage-ways clear for Laurence to run-up and down unimpeded. On the train he was more subdued. I'm sure he had a mental picture of each station along the route. One thing you can rely on in life is that one station always follows another, but Laurence had to check all the way back to Euston, just in case.

The death of Princess Diana was very sad, she had such tremendous potential and I hope that she falls into that select group of people that achieves more in death than they ever could in life.

Some stars shine too brightly, but at the end of the day it was simply the man wearing a seat belt who survived. We should be thankful that the speeding drink-fuelled driver lost control in the tunnel and not beside a Parisian promenade full of pedestrians.

She wouldn't have wanted that and she wouldn't have wanted me to lose a day's wages for her funeral. However I had to as it seemed everywhere was closing for the day. The country was in mourning. It was a collective sorrow that grew and grew. Ordinary people were communicating without words and everybody could feel it, with ever more people feeling compelled to travel to London to quietly pay their respects. For a while it seemed like ordinary people were communicating just like Laurence. People were beaming, but they were beaming their sorrow and we all felt it.

I found out that Legoland was planning to open on the afternoon of the funeral, so I decided to head there to try to make the most of my day off. Ana intended to watch the whole show on TV with a large box of tissues, so she was delighted to see the back of us.

We set off early as our route crossed the path of the coffin and we arrived in Windsor by mid-morning. Windsor was a ghost town; all the tourists were in London, while the locals had shut up shop and were glued to their TVs. Naturally the castle was closed, but we saw the sea of flowers at the entrance.

Bianca was particularly moved by seeing this and she stood and said a little prayer for the princess. There were quite a few of us funeral refugees in Legoland, but the park was nowhere near full. The children had a great time. There were no queues, so they could go on the rides as often as they wanted, which was great for Laurence, although if he was left alone he probably would have followed the model trains around all day.

I felt that Diana would have liked to see the children having such fun; it was a special day to remember.

I thought my luck had changed when later that month I won the National Lottery. It was a double rollover week and I had five numbers. I was one ball short of twenty million pounds and I picked up just thirteen hundred pounds. I was gutted. The saying 'so near yet so far' could be the story of my life.

Although it wasn't a life-changing sum, it did mean that we now had enough money behind us to move. It meant that I could start house hunting seriously on Sundays during the winter months. Having given up with London prices, I was exploring the M11 corridor.

The estate agents advised me to have the mortgage offer ready as properties were moving fast, and by December I had everything in place. All we needed was the right place.

Early in the new year I found a house that we could afford in a village called Takeley just off the M11. It was at the end of a row of houses that had been tagged onto the edge of the old village relatively recently. It was an ordinary-looking house but it had four bedrooms, which would allow us all to lead our separate lives, and it had the option to buy the field at the back of the house. That was the clincher. It was a useless bit of land to me, but it would be excellent for Laurence—it could be his space to get away from it all.

I felt trapped between a rock and a hard place. We had to move to have any chance of surviving as a family, but Ana had left me twice already. She seemed to have waited until after the Christmas festivities were over and then although we were supposed to be making an effort to live together peacefully, she picked on everything I did and didn't do.

I didn't tell her about the house and I stalled on signing the papers. I pleaded for peace but she wasn't interested and I wasn't interested in trying to buy a temporary peace with a £100,000 mortgage.

She felt that they could live happily in the flat without me and she wanted me out. Her attacks on me grew more frequent and she soon found my Achilles heel, the children. She was upsetting both of them, so she got her way.

Bianca was very tearful, as she could understand what Mummy was doing but not why. Laurence was also getting very upset, but what he made of all these new emotional outbursts I can only wonder, as I wasn't there to see his reactions.

I went to a local agency and found a one-bedroom flat, still in Walthamstow, so that the children wouldn't feel that I had gone far, but it was far enough away to prevent Ana harassing me on a whim.

For the first couple of weekends it was nice not having to go out, but we were soon going out again anyway to keep Laurence entertained.

It wasn't long before Bianca's little dance troupe combined with some others to put on a show. The hall was packed with proud parents. The children looked so cute as they strutted their stuff in their pretty costumes. We all loved it, except Bianca, who hated it. She did not enjoy the on-stage experience and didn't attend another lesson.

I felt it was important that she had out-of-school interests. She wanted to do gymnastics, but all the courses were oversubscribed. I tried to get her interested in judo as Laurence would always be bigger and stronger than her, but it didn't have the same appeal as gymnastics and after a few lessons she packed it in.

Ana made sure that the Child Support Agency was soon on my back again.

I was earning more now as I had been doing well at work; I had more responsibility, but I was even poorer now as I was paying the mortgage and the rent on my flat. Together, they equalled what I would have been paying for the new mortgage, so there really wasn't much left for the CSA. I also understood better how the system worked. I kept receipts for everything, and after months of arguing we agreed on six pounds a week, which they took directly from my wages.

I booked a summer holiday in Tenerife to use up my lottery winnings. Whenever I had a bit of extra cash I spent it on the kids (getting a receipt, of course) rather than leave it in my bank account for the CSA to scoop up.

Freed of our house-hunting duties, we returned to visiting places of interest around London during our weekends. Well, they were of interest to Bianca and me but Laurence only gave our destinations a cursory glance; he was only interested in the journey and his preferred form of transport was the train, but travel by car or bus was also acceptable to him.

There was one trip at this time that stuck in the memory and even Laurence still talks about it.

I drove to Trent Park in north London on the last day of a wet bank holiday weekend. I had heard that it was a nice park with lots of space to lose Laurence in and there was also a country show there over the long weekend.

We wandered around the sodden stalls, but the atmosphere had been washed out of the event and most stallholders appeared impatient to pack up, go home and have a warm bath. I noticed a tent where a children's magic show was about to start and we went inside. It was Uncle Purple and his Purple Puppets and, unsurprisingly, Laurence was bored within a couple of minutes. At nine years of age he was a few years older than the rest of the audience, so I told Bianca that I would be just outside when the show finished and I took him outside for a run-around.

He was happy skipping up and down waiting for the show to finish. We were close to the entrance/exit. They had to move it frequently over the weekend as the grass became trampled into a sea of mud. There was a steady stream of families leaving over the latest grass causeway. When a child slipped off the path into the mud his mother squawked and angrily pulled him up. Laurence saw it all and was very amused. He ran straight across and dived headfirst into the mud.

He was laughing as he stood up and accidentally slipped backwards. Sitting in the sea of mud he did look a funny sight, and he was hysterical as he got up and dived straight back down again. It was already too late to do anything, as he couldn't get any dirtier. It was his favourite TV programme but in real life, and he re-enacted every muddy fall.

People continued to file past his muddy show. Some were appalled, some were amused and some struggled to control their own children. I overheard a couple of ladies tut-tutting, 'Well I blame the parents. Where are the parents?'

I wasn't going to stop his enjoyment; I was busy doing nothing. I knew he was monitoring me amid the mayhem so I was giving signs of neither approval nor disapproval. That way I hoped he would continue as he was until I was ready for him. Bizarrely, I could genuinely claim that he was under my control.

Bianca came out of the tent to see her brother had been transformed into a giggling slime ball. I led Bianca to the exit, still giving Laurence no signals. When I felt we were at a safe distance I turned and gave a flick of my head for him to come and he scampered after us, leaving a muddy trail and the bemused onlookers behind him.

We didn't want him coming close to us, but to my surprise he recognised that and for the first time in his life, he chased us. He was still laughing too much to give serious chase and we were able to keep in front of him all the way back to the car. I had a blanket in the boot so I told him to take his clothes off and sat him in his underpants on the back seat with the blanket around his shoulders. He was still giggling.

I drove straight back to Ana, gave her the carrier bag of mud, explained that his clothes were somewhere inside it and made a hasty exit before she could see the smirk on my face. It was certainly another day to remember.

Laurence was very excited by the prospect of going to Tenerife. We had an evening flight from Gatwick, so Laurence had the whole day to run about and tire himself out, or so I hoped. The flight stretched his patience to the limit and I was proud of the way he contained himself, only managing to annoy the people directly in front of and behind him.

I had asked for a quiet family resort and we arrived at Los Gigantes in the early hours of the morning. It was a struggle to prevent him jumping straight into the pool, but I persuaded him that everybody was sleeping and he could go into the pool in the morning.

I awoke to hear a man shouting angrily. Our apartment was right beside the pool and the door was open. Laurence must have awoken, put on his trunks and jumped straight into the pool. Now that it was daylight I could see a big notice saying 'No swimming before 9.00 a.m.' and the pool cleaner was wildly gesticulating towards his watch. I called Laurence over to me and apologised to the cleaner.

He could not understand why the man was angry; he was, after all, just swimming in a swimming pool.

I distracted him with the idea of breakfast. As it was our first morning we didn't have any food, but Laurence was still happy when I explained that we would have to go to the shops first.

Our apartment block was set into the volcanic mountains surrounding the bay, but it was only a ten-minute downhill walk to the beach and shops. Ideas about shopping and breakfast disappeared when the children saw the beach. Fortunately I had the foresight to pack their costumes, towels and suntan lotion in my shoulder bag, so we went straight down onto the nearly deserted beach.

The tide was going out and there were only a few other families scattered around the beach, so I picked a spot in the centre of the bay close to the waterfront. The children were soon oiled up and splashing about in the sea.

Laurence preferred to run up and down kicking up spray as, just like in a swimming pool, the shallow end has to be thoroughly checked out first. Bianca was more adventurous and wanted to show off her swimming skills immediately. Her play skills were so much more varied than his. She liked to dig, she liked to build sandcastles and sea walls and she tried to bury her brother—not that he ever noticed, as he was having too much fun on his own.

Running back to me soaking wet, he flopped down beside me onto the black sand. He immediately noticed how 'dirty' he was and looked to me for my disapproval. When he got none he was falling about all over the place so that he looked like he had been playing down a coal mine. It was better than the mud because he could clean himself in the sea and get 'dirty' over and over again. He found it hilarious and never seemed to tire of the joke.

It was getting very hot. It was lunchtime and when I looked behind me I was surprised to see the beach had filled up with the sunbathing set. The beach had become a sea of towels and sunshades.

It was easy to lure the kids out of the sea, as we still hadn't had any breakfast. It wasn't so easy getting them reasonably free of sand and getting all our stuff sorted to go, all at the same time. However, we were eventually ready and started to cross the beach to the roadside. Immediately Bianca sat down, whimpering that the sand was burning her feet. I quickly realised that the black sand was absorbing the sun's heat unlike yellow sand, which reflects most of it.

Laurence was the first to solve this problem. Quick as a flash, with his feet beginning to burn, he raced off, leaping from beach towel to beach towel. He was like a gazelle as he made his way diagonally across the beach, grinding people's beach towels into the sand along the way. It didn't matter if the towel was occupied as he was nimble enough to avoid collisions, but he couldn't avoid spraying the sunbathers with black sand.

As I saw the bemused well-oiled bodies rising up from his trail of devastation I turned to Bianca and didn't have to say anything, as she knew what to do—we ran—in the opposite direction across the beach up to the road. I didn't look back, but I did keep Laurence in the corner of my eye and I knew that he would be keeping me in the corner of his. Our silent communication was useful, and we met up with Laurence again on the promenade behind the beach. He was exhausted. His diagonal run across the beach had been the shortest route to get off the beach, but it required several triple jumps along the way.

I could not think of a way to tell him off so we had a laugh and went for lunch a safe distance away from the beach.

After lunch we did some shopping and headed back to the swimming pool.

Bianca was soon splashing around in the large circular pool and it wasn't long before she had made some friends of her own age. Laurence remained aloof to the other children's advances and happily played alone. He would have been unhappy if I had tried to get him to join in.

He liked to jump in the water, so he jumped in beside the steps so that he could climb out quickly to jump straight back in again. Although he appeared to be oblivious to everybody else, I noticed that he carefully avoided jumping onto people.

Laurence noticed a man using the shower beside the pool. He was curious; he walked over and pulled the cord. He couldn't hide that the water was cold and his entire body shuddered. He ran away and jumped back in the pool. He then climbed out of the pool and went back to the shower. He looked like he was being electrocuted each time as the *brrrr* ran through his body. It was a funny sight and he clearly enjoyed the sensations as he did the dip and shower over and over again.

I became aware that other people around the pool were struggling to control their mirth, so I didn't constrain my amusement either. I knew that he would interpret my smiles as approval for his sensational new game.

Yet again I didn't know what to do for the best—should I encourage or discourage this bizarre behaviour? I decided that as it was only a week's holiday and he was having so much fun that I shouldn't stop him. I hoped that this self-inflicted cold-shower therapy might help to desensitise his skin, although there was no sign of that happening during the week.

I tried different-coloured sunglasses on Laurence during the holiday but he still showed no preference for any particular colour and he eventually settled on some circular dark blue John Lennon–style glasses. He looked so funny in them with his small white floppy hat.

Laurence was in heaven with our routine of playing on the beach in the mornings, shower therapy in the afternoons and eating out in the evenings. He didn't want to change anything until the arrival of a girl. She was in her late teens, and was on holiday with her mum; they both hung around the pool topless. Over the years he had poked and pinched more than his fair share of breasts, but this was the first time that he had seen what women kept under their clothes and he was fascinated. When she was in the pool his head was rarely more than a foot away and bobbing up and down in unison. His curiosity was shameless, but I felt so embarrassed.

I spoke to the girl's mum, explained the situation and expressed my fears that he might make a grab. She laughed; she had been watching his antics in the shower and reassured me that her daughter understood and told me not to worry.

The only bad day we had was the day before leaving. Laurence knew that we were going home the next day and ruined the day for himself by continually whining and moaning all day saying, 'No going home tomorrow.' However, on the last day he behaved well as we had time to go on the beach and play in the pool before catching the bus to the airport in the evening.

He sat quietly in his seat on the plane. He was sad and then his lips began to quiver and a tear trickled down his cheek. It was heartbreaking to watch, as his emotions were so real and coming from inside. He was silently mourning and I tried to comfort us all. It had been a wonderful holiday.

Laurence loved charging around an empty Gatwick Airport at five o'clock in the morning. By the time I dropped them off at Mummy's house he was his normal high-speed self. I suppose he had to check everything out for changes while he had been away as quickly as possible.

I had only signed a six-month contract on my flat, so I had to move again soon. The children were used to me living away now, so I could look further afield for a better place for them to visit at weekends. I went to look at a place in the countryside just off the M11. Surrounded by fields, it was an old stable that had been cleverly converted into a small block of flats. It would be a wonderful place for the children to visit, but mine was the tiniest of one-bedroom flats so it would not be good for them to stay. However, Ana had always insisted that I bring the children back to her every night so I decided to rent it anyway.

It had a communal garden, a large off-road car park and fields stretching into the distance. Linda, my new landlady, explained that the children could only go in a field when there were no animals in it. I assured her that I would always check personally.

Laurence was very wary of his new freedom and he wouldn't play outside without Bianca or me being there with him.

Bianca started bringing her homework home, so it would have been useful to get rid of him for a while, but I think he felt vulnerable and intimidated by the wide-open spaces all around.

'Going out now' was his way of saying, 'Come outside with me' but we deliberately took him literally and gave him every encouragement to go out alone.

'There's a good boy. Yeah! Bye-bye.' He got the message and clumped slowly down the stairs in his bovver boots saying, 'Bye, bye.' I heard the heavy door open and then slam shut followed by him rapidly clumping back up the stairs.

'Did you go outside?' I asked him.

'Yeah,' he replied as he settled down in a corner excitedly tapping something. Bianca laughed at her scaredy-cat brother but it was good that he was trying to be independent. It was still the case that most weekends we were out and about, but when we were at home it was a very relaxing atmosphere although a bit cramped.

There were no fireworks displays locally so we had a wider choice of organised displays across north London to visit. Some years, if the dates allowed, we visited a couple. It soon became clear which one was Laurence's favourite, although they were all times of high excitement for him.

Going to the Lord Mayor's firework display on the river Thames was a whole day out on public transport for him. I tried to combine seeing the fireworks with searching for potential Christmas presents in the capital's toyshops, but all he saw was the buses and trains on either side of the fireworks. He judged the different firework displays on the transport needed to get to them.

Typically, shortly after moving in to my tiny new flat, Ana relaxed her opposition to the children staying overnight. When the children chose to come to Dad's for Christmas I was overjoyed to have the problem of the logistics.

We had a special tiny Christmas tucked up in my cosy flat. We had a tiny tree and tiny decorations and when I tried to cook the tiny Christmas dinner Bianca had to keep flapping the tea towel underneath the tiny smoke detector. At night they topped-and-tailed in my bed and I curled up on the lounge floor as the settee was only a two-seater.

I judged my first solo attempt at Christmas to be a success as I managed not to poison the children and we had a few laughs along the way.

I had been trying to get Laurence interested in ball games for many years. Of course I desperately wanted to play football, but I would have settled for a simple game of catch. At long last he developed an interest in a soft beach ball. He could occasionally catch it but he mainly seemed interested in grabbing hold of it, and keeping hold of it with no interest in giving it back.

I saw this as an encouraging start.

He started to take it with him on his attempts to go outside alone. He then hit upon an idea. Standing in the doorway, he threw the ball outside. He then had to go and fetch it and they were his first nervous steps towards independence.

Around his tenth birthday I gave him several balls as I didn't want him becoming too attached to just one ball and I encouraged him to take different balls out with him on his adventures. His ball of choice became the basketball and its dull thud acted like a cowbell, alerting me to his every movement. One throw led him to the edge of the flats looking out to the garden and the open expanse of the fields beyond. He stood there bouncing his ball and it was a long time before he had the courage to throw the ball into the garden; I watched his progress from my bedroom window. If somebody came by he would dash back to the safety of the flat and he would follow their progress from the window. We always knew when he was hiding from somebody.

All this timidity was unusual for Laurence. When we were out together he would walk up to strangers (especially people in uniform) and demand, 'Where live?' With no big daddy around to protect him, he avoided other people at all costs.

He was confident beside me to the point of being unfazed by crowds of people or even high-excitement amusement-park rides, so that spring we took him to Alton Towers.

I drove up the M1 on the Saturday afternoon and we stayed in a hotel nearby so that we would be at the park early on the Sunday morning.

Laurence was thrilled by the train ride between the car park and the entrance of Alton Towers. Our first ride was the Log Flume. He said he liked it but he didn't want to go on it again. We walked around to the River Rapids and the Runaway Train and as it was still early and the queues were short we went on each one at least a couple of times. He definitely liked these two rides and would have stayed all day, but I moved us on.

The Haunted House didn't scare him but he took just one look at Nemesis and said repeatedly and forcefully, 'Not that one.'

What a sensible child, I thought. I was happy to miss out that and the Ripsaw ride, which he didn't like the look of either. We did go on the Blade, which made me feel sick and then we caught the Skyride cable car to another part of the park.

The children went on a couple of small rides but Laurence wanted to go on the Corkscrew roller coaster.

'Are you sure?' I said several times. When we joined the queue I made sure that he watched the people on the ride, but nothing would put him off. I realised that this was to be my first Corkscrew roller-coaster ride and I didn't fancy it, but I could not let him miss this experience if he wanted it. Unbelievably the children got the much-coveted front seats. I made sure that they were strapped in properly

225

and sat down behind them. When I was locked in I knew that he couldn't get out. Sitting behind him I couldn't see his face as the train slowly climbed to the top of the ride. Bianca said that he had a look of sheer terror but Laurence said nothing until we climbed off the train at the end, when he said, 'No that one, no that one.'

Despite my best efforts he still hadn't noticed the real nature of that ride before going on it.

I needed a rest so we had some lunch and went on a few quieter rides. For all his derring-do, Laurence still liked to go on the kiddies' roundabout rides. He sat like a man on a pony with his blank face staring out as he slowly circled round. We had to teach him that he was too big, but he didn't like being told this so sometimes we let him play on.

Mid-afternoon we arrived at Oblivion and some other awful-looking machines and I was very relieved to hear Laurence say, 'No this one' to all of them except the Black Hole. This ride is enclosed in what looks like a large gas tank, so none of us could know what to expect.

'Are you sure?' I asked sceptically, as the queue was over an hour long. He was adamant, so we joined the queue and to be fair he was very well behaved throughout the wait. I don't know what attracted Laurence to this ride. Maybe he liked the name. Maybe he thought there might be some mud in this black hole.

Just as we approached the head of the queue, Laurence screamed out, 'No this one, no this one.' I dropped down to the floor and cuddled him saying straight into his ear, 'No this one, is OK, no this one.'

One thing I did know was that I was not going to walk all the way back along the massive queue so I kept shuffling forward saying, 'No this one, yeah.' We reached the departure platform and I stepped aside to let others pass while I consoled him. He soon calmed down, as, with no worries for himself, he watched other people hurtling into the Black Hole. He trusted me. After a couple of minutes he started to see those same people climbing off the ride laughing at the other end of the platform. So they weren't hurtling to their doom after all.

He watched a couple more come out safely and then said firmly, 'This one.'

'Are you sure?' I really don't know why I kept saying that; after all, I doubt that he even knew what 'sure' meant, whereas his speech was very clear and unambiguous: 'This one.'

We assumed our normal positions: Bianca in front—we men aren't stupid—Laurence in the middle, and me at the rear keeping a close eye on him. As on all these rides, there is a photo somewhere on the way down and Daddy can clearly be seen gripping his chair with white knuckles. Bianca had a big 'yeah' of a grin across her face, but it was Laurence who was the star of the picture with a look of grim determination etched into his face.

I was full of praise for him when we got outside and he skipped around like a very proud puppy. In fact, I was very proud of him as he had behaved and spoken really well all day in a place that we had never visited before.

A couple more sedate rides and then, with the queues reducing at the end of a long day, we returned to his favourite rides, the Runaway Train and the River Rapids, until the rides closed down.

It was a long drive home and the children were exhausted. We stopped at a motorway service station for dinner and Laurence kept saying, 'Laurence went in the Black Hole.'

'Yes,' we replied, and we had the photo to prove it.

I felt that timid Laurence was making valuable progress, so I persevered in my tiny flat. Watching Bianca skipping through the field picking me a posy of wild grasses made all the inconveniences worthwhile. While Laurence was growing in confidence, he was also developing good ball control skills, but he still didn't want to pass his precious ball.

Linda had noticed him scurrying away whenever she approached. She watched him watching her and she developed a soft spot for him. She ran a farm with lots of stables and maybe she saw something in him that she saw in her beloved horses. Quiet unexpectedly, she had a vacancy in her only two-bedroom flat and she asked me if I was interested.

Of course I was interested, the children would be able to stay as often as they wanted, there was a huge garden and from Laurence's bedroom window he could see the horses in their stables and watch the general comings and goings of the farm. It seemed perfect for his development, so for the third time in fifteen months I was moving.

I tried to warn Laurence that I was moving but not very far. It didn't register. It was only when I drove into the driveway rather than the next turning along that he screamed out, 'No that one!' There was nothing I could say. I parked up quickly and bundled his distraught body into the new flat. I showed him his bedroom and took him out into the big garden with his ball and a cold drink. He calmed down quickly as he had time to consider that this place might not be so bad after all.

The children came to stay every weekend. It was a beautiful spring and summer. I felt like I was living in a holiday home. It was very relaxing when I came home after a hard day at work in central London. Bianca got to know a couple of young girls who owned some horses. This was dangerous for my wallet, but I think that learning about all the hard work that was involved in keeping horses prevented her from catching the horsey bug.

Laurence started playing just in the garden, but it wasn't long before he cautiously took his ball into the farmyard. There were always horse owners coming and going to muck out their stables or exercise their horses as well as other visitors and deliveries. There was an awful lot for Laurence to take in but there were many patterns to be observed in their movements and the twang of his bouncing basketball on the concreted farmyard area was a regular annoying sound.

Too regular, and it wasn't long before Linda told me that I would have to do something about that ball or she would. I switched him to a tennis ball without much complaint, as I wasn't stopping him from doing anything.

I was so proud of how he had learnt to control a basketball, so a tennis ball seemed a good way to continue his development. He would have to learn to control it quickly if he wanted to avoid close encounters with people when he was retrieving it.

Most of the owners were women and many had children of their own, although some horses were definitely child substitutes. All of them were very understanding of the silent ball boy. They didn't try to impose on him and they waited for him to approach them in his own time and way.

He didn't seem interested in the horses; in fact, he was very wary of them and had no qualms about holding his little sister between him and one of these enormous animals.

He started hovering around people; it was clear that he wanted to come closer, but any attempt to encourage him resulted in him running away. He made us laugh with his antics and his first attempts at independent communication were made as he ran past them bouncing his tennis ball. His 'Where live?' was fired at them, giving no chance to respond before he dashed off to a safe distance.

I realised that in all other situations he had a teacher, care worker or me to help and protect him. Now he was trying to interact unsupported and I felt that this was an important part of his development. If he was ever going to function independently in society he would have to overcome his anxieties, so I didn't interfere.

Instead I was indoors and ready for him when the excitement got too much. He would charge in, close the front door, take off his shoes and run-up to the safety of his bedroom, where he could watch from behind the curtain. Only then would I try to help him by talking it over.

'Did you see Heather?'

'Did you talk to Dave?'

'Did you ask Angela where she lives?' He usually answered my questions in terms of how he wished things had been rather than how things actually were. I hoped that by talking about his encounters he would feel less stressed about future meetings. It was clear that he wanted further social encounters from his habit of hovering around social groups, but first of all he needed to learn to control his instinctive tendencies to run away. Strangely, he didn't seem to be afraid of the people themselves—he seemed more frightened of the words that they might say and the emotions that they might unexpectedly produce.

Linda had a strong voice and was often barking out instructions across the farmyard, so when she walked by Laurence covered his ears before she could even speak. His antics were funny to watch, but I could also tell that at the same time he was capturing people's hearts.

Living in such a nice place, I did not feel inclined to go away for a summer holiday but Laurence expected it. It was now an important part of his annual calendar. We had already had two Spanish island holidays so I thought we would try a Greek island holiday instead and I eventually settled on Crete. The resort of Plakias was on the opposite side of the island to the airport. I knew that Laurence wouldn't object to the long bus journey across the island.

It doesn't matter to Laurence where in the world he goes on holiday so long as he gets to spend plenty of time in the water. We quickly settled into our regular routine of beach in the morning and pool in the afternoon, rounded off with a big dinner in the evening.

The beach at Plakias was long and natural and, with no sea walls, the waves could be quite large—as far as Laurence was concerned, the larger the waves, the better. He thoroughly enjoyed being chased by the waves and buffeted by the white surf. He seemed to be in tune with the turbulent sea and was at ease body surfing in the waves.

One morning it was overcast with a strong wind coming off the sea. The waves were over his head but he laughed even louder and it was well into the afternoon before he allowed me to lure him away for some lunch.

That afternoon, like all the other afternoons, we went to the pool. A rainstorm blew up and with no sign of thunder and lightning, I allowed the children to continue playing in the pool. Slowly the pool emptied as the palm trees bent double in the wind and the rain pounded down harder and harder until there was just Bianca and another little girl sheltering under the diving board, and Laurence. A couple of hardy people and I sheltered in the poolside bar and we watched him embracing the stinging rain and falling in the pool, laughing hysterically as if he was drunk.

I had seen it all before with the mud, the black sand and the shower therapy but this time it was with the hard rain and it was yet another sensational game.

The storm soon blew over and as we left the poolside a beautiful rainbow appeared. Back at the apartment before going out for dinner we all had a shower. The hot water was from tanks on the roof that were heated by the sun, so once the hot water was used up there was no chance of any more until the following evening. Laurence was always the last to have a shower, as he didn't mind the cold water.

It was in the evenings that Laurence struggled to cope because of all the cats wandering around the restaurants. His natural instinct to scoff his food meant there was rarely a reason for the cats to hang around his feet, but he resented the extra competition for our left-overs. We had to teach him to push the cats away gently as a swift kick from his heavy boots could do serious damage.

He insisted on reading the menu and making his own choice from it but I quickly learnt that the best menu was what was on other people's plates. After ordering, Laurence examined every plate that went past our table expecting it to be his. Too often he saw something that he wanted more than what he had ordered.

'That one, no burger, that one.' He would point frantically. It seemed that he wanted that one, the fish, but this wasn't the case. He loved coleslaw and raw onion salads and it was seeing that on the plate that made him suddenly want the fish. If it was too late to change our order I just had to make sure that his burger arrived with a similar salad to the fish dish.

It was all a matter of understanding. His improved speech had helped but it was all too often the words that he didn't say that mattered. When we were on holiday we led a simple existence which helped Laurence understand his interactions with the holiday world. In turn, we repeated the simple daily routines and began to understand what mattered to Laurence.

It didn't matter what the Greeks threw at us as we had the mutual understanding to adapt and enjoy ourselves. He was a joy to be on holiday with.

There was one thing, however that he couldn't adapt to—putting the toilet paper in the bin and not flushing it away in the toilet. He thought we were quite mad and used to sneak back to the toilet to flush the paper away later when we were not looking.

Sometimes we were impossible creatures to understand.

12

Totally Eclipsed

I was working six days a week and had the children every weekend. After throwing me out, Ana had set her legal team on me and put the matrimonial home up for sale. She wanted a divorce and they wanted a war. I saw no point in fighting; all I wanted was to be able to cover the bills from the divorce and sale of the flat and come out of this without incurring a debt. My offer wasn't good enough; they wanted everything, including the shirt on my back.

At the time it seemed like a foolish strategy, as they were forcing me to fight when I had already offered to surrender. However it became clear over the years that it was profits rather than ethics that directed their strategy. There is not much profit in a simple amicable surrender.

We got a good price for the flat—we would have had enough for the house deposit and some new furniture and a holiday as well, but that was not to be. Ana's solicitors held the balance in one of their accounts until all matters were resolved between us and then worked hard to ensure that as much of it as possible stayed in their account.

I had instructed my solicitor to keep costs to a minimum. I worked so I didn't qualify for any legal aid, but I had no money for a legal battle. They would have to win their fee and in the meantime I paid them each time we needed to write a letter. By contrast, Ana was on legal aid, her legal bill was assured and her legal team worked tirelessly to ensure that no opportunities were lost for further investigation or clarification, with each letter written adding to their profit margin.

Their procrastination ensured that the divorce took years and caused a lot of unnecessary stress for all parties.

When I read about the upcoming total solar eclipse on 11 August 1999 I decided to use it as an excuse to take a break from it all. I have always had a casual interest in astronomy. Having recently moved out of light-polluted London, I had started reacquainting myself with the stars and constellations.

The total solar eclipse was going to be visible from Cornwall, but having spent many hours trying to observe astronomical events such as meteor showers from the UK, I knew that it would be cloudy.

I looked further along the path of the moon's shadow. Syria and Iraq offered the best chances of a clear sky, but I wasn't that keen. Romania offered the longest duration of eclipse, but all flights were fully booked for that week so I took up a package deal to Hungary next door. According to NASA the chance of sunshine there was much greater than in Cornwall.

I flew into Budapest the day before the eclipse and spent the evening looking around some of the sights. The first thing I did the next morning was look out of the hotel window; it was cloudy and my heart sank.

We were a subdued bunch of eclipse chasers as we boarded the coach that would take us the 120 kilometres to Lake Balaton, where we had hoped to view the eclipse. It started to rain as we drove through the grey suburbs of Budapest. I felt that this adventure had been a complete waste of my time and effort, but we were heading to Lake Balaton anyway.

As we travelled down the motorway a chink of blue sky appeared in the distance and we felt a glimmer of hope. The patch of blue sky grew and the squeaking windscreen wipers stopped, so that by the time our coach pulled up outside our hotel we were underneath a clear blue sky.

The organisers of this eclipse-chaser excursion knew their stuff. We were on the top of a flat-topped hill on a peninsula in the lake. The presence of Hungarian TV cameras confirmed that we were at an excellent spot to view the eclipse.

There was a church and a park on top of the hill and our party mingled in with the scattering of fellow eclipse chasers and locals who were already gathered there. I found a patch of grass and waited in the glorious sunshine. I had eclipse glasses and watched the slow progress of the moon crossing the sun's disc. I was surprised that even with three-quarters of the sun's disc covered it was still a bright warm day. It was only when the sun was reduced to a thin crescent that it got noticeably darker and cooler. Across the lake along the horizon in the direction of England the sky turned red with the appearance of a sunset, which was confusing as the sun was still directly above me.

With less than a minute before totality things started to get really weird. The sky was dark blue, the slim slither of the crescent sun seemed unable to produce enough light and the air shimmered with grey bands of faint light. A gentle breeze blew across the lake; it was the eclipse wind created by the difference in the temperatures of the air under the moon's shadow and the air around it. Looking towards the wind, I saw the blackness of the moon's shadow racing across the lake towards us. I looked up to see the crescent of sunlight had disappeared and now there were just a couple of beads of sunlight due to the valleys and mountains along the rim of the moon. The beads were quickly extinguished one by one and we were in totality.

Totality hit like a silent clash of cymbals, it was sudden and startling. People, birds and animals alike fell silent and my spine tingled. I could understand why people in olden times fled in terror. I was surprised by my own natural feelings, as I understood exactly what was going on around me.

It was dark. Above us was a night sky; where the sun had been there was now a black disc. On the edge of the disc I could see a couple of small red smudges which were solar flares and all around the black disc was a strange white wispy cloud which was the sun's outer corona, normally invisible due to the brightness of the sun. The stars were out and I could see the planet Venus shining in reflected sunlight from the blacked-out sun.

In the distance, where I had seen a sunset sky only a couple of minutes, previously I could now see the yellow and orange of a sunrise sky. The trailing edge of the moon's shadow was rapidly approaching. As I looked up, the first bead of light broke through the moon's valleys; it looked like a diamond glistening in the sky. The shadow of the moon raced across the lake heading towards the Black Sea and the Middle East. Some more diamonds briefly sparkled and the sky brightened as a thin crescent of sun reappeared.

Totality lasted just over two minutes and it was over as suddenly as it had started. The partial eclipse lasted for some time after that but I had no interest in it. The sun was shining in a clear blue sky, the birds were singing again and I felt great.

Although I had fully understood everything that I had seen in the last five minutes, my subconscious had been completely fooled. I had witnessed a sunset, a night sky followed by a sunrise and my body was telling me that I had just got out of bed on a sunny morning in the middle of a park!

There was no time for a slow sleepy awakening, it was sunshine in your face wideawake. All the stresses of the morning bus journey and so on were yesterday and forgotten. I had had a night's rest since then and I felt refreshed, I felt invigorated, I felt high.

I had not read of this post-eclipse euphoria before, but I'll remember it for the rest of my life.

I was pleased that I had chosen not to take Laurence on this particular trip. I knew that I would not be able to explain to him what was going on so he would have been as frightened as an ancient caveman during an eclipse. It was an unnecessary experience for him but an enlightening experience for me.

What if every morning Laurence felt like I did after the eclipse? The slate wiped clean, refreshed and excited, every morning he would buzz around, verifying everything anew while we slowed him down with our more mundane demands like brushing his teeth. We weren't on his level but now I understood how little it took to completely throw our sense of reality. That perception of reality controls how we behave in the real world.

I floated among the trinket sellers and T-shirt vendors that appeared everywhere and I wanted to shop. In my normal reality, I would have tutted at the quality of the cheap tat being sold. I would have concerned myself with the reality of my not having checked into the hotel yet because I had wanted to make sure that I got to the top of the hill in good time for the eclipse. But in my altered reality, all of that was yesterday and history.

All I wanted to do was to enjoy the day and play.

I couldn't see Laurence's perception of our reality but I could see how he reacted to it and I watched and learned.

All he wanted to do was to enjoy each day. Every day he wanted to go to the shops and play in the park and simply enjoy the day because that is what days are for, in his reality.

While I watched and learnt, Ana remained stuck in her reality and Laurence was not fitting into it. She claimed to be getting on fine without me to mediate around the home, but occasionally I got a glimpse of the reality of their relationship.

I remember one weekend, it was raining, the children weren't ready for me so I sat in the lounge talking to Bianca while Ana got Laurence ready to go out. There was a bit of a commotion in another room and then Laurence came running into the lounge pursued by

Ana. She grabbed him, put her arm around his shoulders and tried to hold on to him while trying to put an asthma inhaler in his mouth.

Laurence knew how to play this game. It was a game that Mummy usually didn't like to play, but now she had started the game he was participating fully by wriggling and squealing as much as he could. He was enjoying all the attention he was getting, but I could tell that Ana was tiring and she was running out of patience.

'Stop!' I cried out above the commotion and I asked Ana what she was trying to achieve.

'As you are so clever,' she challenged, 'he has been wheezy and must have a puff on the inhaler before going out or he has to have his medicine and he doesn't like that either.'

I asked Ana for a spoonful of medicine so that I was holding the spoon in one hand and the inhaler in the other. I made sure I had his attention and asked, 'Which one, this one or that one?'

He smiled. It was a smile of recognition. He recognised that I had given him no choice, it was one or the other, he was trapped. But then he chuckled; he had thought of a way out of my trap. He grabbed my hand holding the inhaler and took a puff. He then quickly grabbed my other hand and rammed the spoon and medicine into his mouth as well.

He laughed as he ran away because he had thwarted my plan to impose one or the other on him.

Our humour and the ease with which I had completed her challenge infuriated Ana. It was all the proof she needed. I was just like him. I had Asperger's syndrome, she claimed.

It was Ana's answer to all her problems. It was why Laurence was autistic and it was why we had to divorce and I couldn't argue with her. She was being so irrational that my arguments became so logical that I felt like I was supporting her argument.

I had considered whether I was high-functioning Asperger's ever since I first found out about the possibility of a genetic cause to autism. I had studied my entire family and I had scoured my life for links to autism and I was surprised at what I found.

I remember when I was seven or eight years old there was a boy called Andrew in my class. He was a year or two older than I was because he had been held back as he wasn't very bright. I remember him because of his strange behaviour at the playtime. He would run-up and down whooping like a Red Indian, tapping his mouth. We thought he was playing cowboys and Indians and on a couple of occasions my friends and I tried to join in but he blanked us every time so we left him to himself and played our own games.

He was just like Laurence at that age, running around howling and stimulating his mouth by tapping, but the big difference between them was in the classroom. Fear of the ruler and the cane ensured Andrew kept himself and his hands in place during class time.

I wonder how far Andrew wandered through the education system before somebody helped him. I wasn't around to see as we moved. There was a new road called the M4 and we moved from suburban London to as far as this new road went—Reading. In fact, we moved to a small town seven miles outside Reading called Wokingham.

It was a shock for me, but although I was shy at first I settled in and developed a large group of friends. I liked to play football at the playtime; on the rainy days I learnt to play chess and occasionally I teased the girls. It all seemed so normal.

To my parent's surprise I passed my 11+ and I went to a grammar school. I adapted well and soon had several friends in my class as well as my chess team friends, my rugby teammates and my friends who I walked home with. I had a very active and interactive childhood; I liked to try everything. I even tried trainspotting with a school friend once, but I couldn't see the point of it.

There was a small group of children that I had little contact with. They supported whatever football team you supported, didn't listen to pop music and they weren't interested in girls.

Although they were normal kids there seemed to be little things wrong with their bodies that caused them to be useless at PE and team games. Usually they hid behind a string of sick notes, as their parents understood their sons' sensitivities. This was to the frustration of the PE instructors, who thought there was nothing wrong with them that a few strong doses of physical education wouldn't cure.

In those days they were more in danger of being bullied by the teachers than by the school bullies, who weren't considered hard if they picked on those wimps. They would prefer to catch a cheeky chap like me or one of my mates, as we didn't cower from them. We played together for protection and the bullies never caught me alone; after all, I was in the school cross-country team.

I didn't understand these nerdish wimps. If I had to sit next to one they insisted on talking incessantly about changes to the train time-table or about what they did in the computer room. I couldn't understand how they didn't understand that they were boring.

Our school was one of the first to get a computer. It filled two classrooms. You had to walk sideways between the floor-to-ceiling banks of delicate valves that filled the rooms. I was terrified of breaking something, but these kids spent all their spare time in there, hidden away from the bullies roaming the school corridors.

They would work away for weeks and months making adjustments and setting up the computer before proudly announcing that the computer had calculated a new prime number. Even then it was only the geeks who could read it as the computer printed the answer as dots on a ticker tape.

I confidently predicted that computers would never catch on and stayed away from the place.

I can see now that they had many traits of Asperger's syndrome and we didn't make it easy for them, but they were making it through the education system with no help at all. They were usually in the top ten in class while I was struggling to stay in the top half with teachers saying, 'Must try harder.'

They might not have found happiness in love later on in life but I'm sure they have earned more money than I ever will and they will probably never know that they have a syndrome.

How different to the situation in today's schools. In our one-size-fits-all comprehensive schools the bullies quickly find the children that are different and they make their lives hell. They don't attain their academic potential because of the constant disruptions in the classroom; they rebel, are labelled disruptive and eventually receive a diagnosis such as Asperger's syndrome or High Functioning Autistic.

It is not the children that have changed, it is the schools and the methods of teaching that have changed.

The Victorians didn't get education right, but they did ensure that as many children as possible got a good basic education. The children who thrived on routine in the classroom, sitting at their own desk in neat rows, chanting tables and having their spelling and grammar constantly corrected with strict discipline, went on to university and a career.

For the more artistic, questioning, social children this form of education was hell and totally unsuitable. We had the chance to rectify this with the introduction of secondary modern schools, but the concept was too blinkered by its limited objectives. Girls were trained for domesticity and the boys were trained to be tradesmen. It was assumed they had only limited intelligence and we consequently let down generations of intelligent children who learnt best by sitting in circles discussing and questioning things.

Secondary modern schools should have competed academically against the grammars, sending their pupils to university to study sociology and media studies and the like, while the grammars turned out the mathematicians, physicists and so on.

Two educational systems working side by side to get the best out of as many children as possible. It didn't happen. Those bright questioning kids had to endure the stuffy, strict grammar school education to get on their desired degree course. Over the last forty years they have gained an ever-increasing say on education in this country and they don't want their children to endure the same restrictive education that they had to endure. In fact, they don't want anybody's children to have that style of education, regardless of whether it suits them.

Gradually the boundaries imposed by the strict regimes have been demolished and the children are encouraged to express themselves. Sitting around in a circle under the enormous weight of all that eye contact, they interact inappropriately and a lifetime of trying to make them fit in with this new style of education begins.

Those with Asperger's and their like are tumbling out in increasing numbers and increasing numbers of psychologists are employed to study these children and give them a label as an excuse for their falling out of the educational system of the day.

This would appear to support the government's claim that the increasing incidence of ASD was largely due to improvements in diagnosing these conditions. But by accepting that claim, you have to ask why those children need to be diagnosed now.

We certainly didn't make it easy for the three or four pupils in my year of a hundred who showed some autistic features, but they stood a much better chance of getting through than they do nowadays.

Just a thought; if autism is in the genes, then are the perpetrators of this new educational system committing a form of genocide?

With just one education system we swing from one style of teaching to another and one day it will have to swing back again.

We are not all the same. Why can't we have two systems working for the maximum benefit of all the children all of the time?

I was surprised to find these undiagnosed children with autistic tendencies scattered through my schooldays and by comparison they confirmed for me that I had no autistic tendencies during my developmental years. I was very different from them. If Ana's claim was true, then I had to have developed those tendencies in later years, maybe even in response to Laurence.

To me that couldn't be a bad thing, but Ana didn't see it that way.

Rather than rely on Ana's opinion, I turned to the respected autism researcher, Professor Simon Baron-Cohen.

Freely available on the Internet is his Autism Quotient test. By answering a long series of questions, this AQ test is supposed to measure if you are autistic. A score of sixteen is normal and a score over thirty-two means you are autistic.

Before taking the test I figured that I should score somewhere in the twenties, as I do have a logical scientific mind with an attention to detail. I was surprised to get a score of sixteen so I tried it again and got a score of eighteen. The AQ test showed that I was normal, but I did wonder how good the AQ test was at measuring normality.

I have followed Simon Baron-Cohen's work for some time and have been intrigued by his work at the Autism Research Centre in Cambridge. He has been measuring the testosterone levels in the amniotic fluid of pregnant women.

Over the years they found that babies with higher foetal testosterone levels have a smaller vocabulary and make eye contact less often. Those babies are now young children and they have found that those that had higher foetal testosterone levels are now less socially developed.

Simon Baron-Cohen thinks that high foetal testosterone levels push brain development towards an improved ability to see patterns and analyse things. (These are tasks that men are usually better at, which explains why there are a lot more autistic boys than girls.)

This is precisely what I see in Laurence. He is always looking for patterns and I'm sure he notes a lot more than I ever notice. He was always analysing us, he was a natural scientist, but working without the basic ground rules.

I do believe that Simon Baron-Cohen's work is our best hope for helping future mothers-to-be to avoid autism.

Ana made sure that the children were ready for me when I came to pick them up from then on, so I got no further insights into how they were getting on. I certainly wasn't going to start pumping Bianca for information.

I suspected things were not going well at home when things began to go wrong in school and during my time with him. He no longer sheepishly left the kitchen when I walked in. He demanded a biscuit and he wouldn't take no for an answer. He threw temper tantrums before getting angrier and attacking with kicks or grabbing handfuls of hair.

I was sure that this behaviour was not coming from the school. I suspected that he had learnt that these tactics can work with Mum, who was giving in and not punishing him with sanctions after the event. She was not playing by the rules and all around her were now paying the price. Laurence was even putting on weight, which I suspected was down to Ana constantly bribing him, as I was not giving him extra food.

I pleaded that if she wouldn't listen to me then she should listen to the teachers, but she had fallen out with his teachers as well. She blamed the school for his bad behaviour. She believed that Laurence was copying this bad behaviour from other children whose behaviour was worse than his. This was feasible and the truth was probably a mix of both.

Ana wanted to change his school and asked me to look at a school that was much closer to where I now lived. It was a Catholic school called St John's, for children with moderate learning difficulties.

I was shown round the school by the deputy head. He was a pleasant man who had already met Laurence. I was impressed by the school and really wanted Laurence to go there, but it would be a big leap for him, as this school's structure was more like that of a normal school.

I was not sure if he could cope even though he had made such huge progress moving from the bottom to the top of his group. The deputy head agreed with me. We agreed that Laurence needed another year to prepare for this change; by next September he would still only be eleven and a half and he could be much better prepared for the upheaval.

Ana didn't agree. I explained that this school didn't take children with behaviour problems and Laurence had a behaviour problem. It was better to sort out the behaviour first rather than risk him being thrown out of the new school later.

I thought that was the end of the matter, but Ana was not so easily put off. She continued pushing for a change and she had other irons in the fire.

*

For the first time in this sorry tale some bright spark in social services thought it might be a good idea to talk to the father. Out of the blue I received a phone call at work. The man explained that he was from social services and he was working on organising a residential placement for Laurence. He wanted to know what I thought about that.

He was taken aback by my 'Over my dead body' response and invited me in for a chat. He clearly didn't know the Laurence that I knew and I explained that I would give up work to look after him if Ana persisted with this plan. That was the only excuse social services needed to back out and Ana was furious with me for interfering in her life again.

A couple of months later, on the first day of the new millennium, she triumphantly presented me with a letter. It was a simple letter stating that Laurence was to start a one-term trial in January at St John's.

She handed me his bags as he would have to live with me now. His behaviour on the bus in the mornings was so bad that the council was refusing to transport him to the new school, so I would have to take him to school before going to work.

She also handed me a behaviour report that she had withheld from the new school and me. I had read his school report; he was making steady progress in all areas, achieving his targets with new moderate targets set. I had every reason to feel happy with progress, but the behaviour report shed new light on his development (see Appendix 6).

I had a week to prepare him for the new school that did not accept children with behavioural problems.

I was furious with the way Ana had handled this, but I had to face up to the situation and calmness was the order of the week. I managed to establish that the problem with the school bus was confined to the mornings. There was no problem with the bus taking him home from school, so I could pick him up from Ana's house when I finished work.

In the mornings she had been giving him chocolate biscuits to behave. But Laurence soon found that he was only getting biscuits when he was naughty, so he was being naughty every day. This ridiculous situation was escalating and he was boarding the school bus in an increasingly agitated state, so the transport ban was imposed.

I would have eaten all the biscuits the night before. In the morning I would have shown him the empty packet and told him that I would buy some more only if he was a good boy on the bus. But I wasn't asked.

I should have been happy: Laurence was living with me now. But the way Ana had bulldozed this change through made it unnecessarily difficult for both of us, and I so much wanted him to succeed at St John's.

I was impressed by his knowledge of weeknight TV schedules. I puzzled over how he knew that it was time for, '3 please, Carnation Street,' or '1 please, Enders.' He had never shown any interest or understanding of clockfaces. Maybe he was counting programmes or maybe he had a damn fine internal clock or maybe he was sneaking a look at the clock hands, who knows?

I didn't mind him watching these programmes, but I soon became aware that he was following the storylines better than I had expected. He was able to anticipate the confrontational scenes and rocked on his belly with excitement. If blows were exchanged, which they often are, he screamed, 'Behave, behave,' whilst he rocked ferociously.

I was shocked at the impact these programme were having on him. He certainly didn't need this kind of stimulation and I changed channels, banishing soap operas forever. Laurence was a child who couldn't hide his feelings, but I wondered about the impact these programmes were having on normal children who can hide their feelings. If violent films make youngsters more violent, why can't soap operas be brainwashing youngsters into believing that soap opera storylines are the way normal people lead their lives?

'So that's what my mum does when I'm at school!'

I couldn't hope to change his behaviour problems in one week, but I worked on relieving the stresses that were causing them. Laurence welcomed listening to music instead of watching the TV and I started to work out his musical preferences. I spoke to him about the new school; I answered his questions over and over again. I didn't want him to be worrying; I wanted to keep him calm. I was lucky that he was looking forward to the new school, it was just a matter of him keeping his excitement under control.

I really can't remember where I heard about foot massages helping children who walked on tiptoe. I had been giving him foot massages for about a year at weekends and that week I gave him one every day. I used an odourless massage oil to avoid sensory distractions. His feet were so tense, but I could feel that tension ebb away as I worked on them and he liked that. If I had discovered this earlier I'm sure it could have shortened the time that he needed to wear those big steel-plated bovver boots.

The first day of school came round quickly, and I was sure that his character would grow on his new teacher. I was pinning my hopes on her seeing his good points above his difficulties before the term ended. I walked the last hundred yards to the school trying to keep him calm, rather than have him explode out of the car door at the gates.

He was in a reception class to prepare him for entry into one of the proper classes when he was ready. That was a relief, and Laurence was also blessed with a good teacher. Her name was Jo Nordan and I would classify her as a high-functioning teacher. She understood the children well and could deal with them on whatever level they presented.

She later told me that it was Laurence who organised their relationship. He quickly became close to her two assistants but he seemed to put her on a pedestal and he jumped when she spoke. She didn't mind playing it that way if that was what he felt he needed. She was aware of how difficult this transition was for Laurence and made many allowances.

I anxiously read the home schoolbook each evening. I soon realised that Jo was avoiding mentioning negative behaviours in the book. I popped in to see her frequently and I explained that I wanted to read about the good and the bad events so that I could talk to Laurence about them in the evenings.

They were experiencing 'physical outbursts' just as Whitefields had, but I hoped that given time he would calm down because he was much calmer in the evenings and mornings than he had been when he was living at Ana's.

We had set routines, which he accepted and followed. In the mornings I gently hustled him through the routine, giving him no time to think about being naughty in the shower or while getting dressed. I drove him to school playing music that he liked but I could do nothing about his excitement levels shooting up when we approached the school gates.

He would dash into the school pulling his coat over his head like a criminal. He was too excited to play in the playground and ran straight into the classroom while I turned to go to work with my fingers firmly crossed.

If only they knew how much he loved his new school.

It was at the end of January when I opened the home schoolbook to see that Jo had written a whole page and a half. My heart sank as I began to read it. They had a physical outburst in the morning followed by an attempt to bite a teacher in the gym at lunchtime. They had a play trip in the afternoon and Jo kept Laurence on the bus while the other children went to play.

She wrote that she wouldn't let him go to play until he listened to her and understood why she kept him behind. 'Okay was not good enough!' She then continued, 'I definitely feel I got through to Laurence today, he became bothered by what I said.'

I knew exactly what she meant as I had noticed that 'bothered' feeling before when I had pushed past his defensive sorrys and OKs. I knew that Jo had seen the real Laurence for the first time and we had won the first battle in the fight to keep Laurence in the school.

Less than a week later she described a couple of similar incidents and cut through his defences again to make sure that he understood the unacceptability of his actions. She wrote, 'Hopefully we're getting somewhere.'

She was. As we went through February the good days began to outnumber the bad days and the outbursts were getting less physical. Into March we experienced an inexplicable run of bad Tuesdays but by April it was clear that Laurence was to be accepted into the school.

It was a very happy Easter, we were very proud of Laurence. Jo had seen through the physical outbursts and found the frightened, insecure little boy inside. She did make it very clear that there was still a lot of work to be done before he could leave her reception class.

The pressure was still on but we were over the first hurdle.

Our next challenge was Bianca's First Holy Communion. Ana was adamant that Laurence shouldn't be there. This was Bianca's big day and she didn't want Laurence to mess it up and I was equally determined that Laurence should go. Eventually Ana gave in, saying that she would blame me if anything went wrong. That really wasn't much of a threat as she already blamed me for all that was wrong in her life.

I bought him a smart black blazer, a white shirt and a tie. I had to settle for elasticated black tracksuit trousers, as I couldn't find any trousers to fit him. He had put on so much weight. When we drove around to pick up Ana and Bianca for the church they were bowled over by his mature appearance, just as I was bowled over by Bianca in her flowing white gown. She looked angelic.

Laurence enjoyed the ceremony as much as everybody else did. He had been rehearsing for his own Holy Communion at school so he knew the songs and clapped and sang along to them with gusto—he didn't need the song sheet.

After the ceremony there were photographs and refreshments in the church hall. Laurence posed for photos and enjoyed the cakes. He was on his best behaviour and I allowed him to roam while keeping him in the corner of my eye. I was aware that he was keeping a close eye on me too so I could signal my displeasure from a distance without creating a fuss.

The trick with Laurence was to know when to leave. Watching him carefully I noticed the early warning tensions building. I said our goodbyes and moved in closer, encouraging him to come outside with me. Outside I was full of praise for him. We had got through the day without a hair pull or kick. We had proved Ana wrong. We went down to the corner shop to buy a lolly while we waited for Bianca and Ana to come out.

I had been practising these pre-emptive strikes to try to prevent his physical outbursts at home. I was having increasing success, although there were times when I picked up the tension around him too late and he responded to my distraction strategy with an 'Oh well, I was going to be naughty anyway' attitude and he would launch straight into a hair grab, dispensing with the tantrum preliminaries.

To an outsider and Ana it would have looked like an unprovoked attack, but I saw the missing manoeuvres that they couldn't see. I would just have to begin my pre-emptive strategies even earlier, but as I said, I was getting better at it and Laurence was learning that it could be to his advantage to control his violent urges.

In school during that summer term Jo was writing things like, 'Again he's been teetering on the verge of naughtiness; but he's done very well in controlling himself' or 'A small incident today, nothing too big, so he missed the first 10 minutes of swimming.' Ouch, that would have hurt Laurence, but there were also many good days recorded in his book.

As we battled to put the violence genie back in the bottle,

Laurence's challenges were still ever changing as he made new discoveries. He started to cut his own hair, he managed to take a snip in school once and at home once but he also had several snips at Ana's house. He was fast and devious, each time cutting a small bald patch on the side of his head. He found it very funny and liked to look at his handiwork in the mirror. It was all the more surprising considering he usually had to be bribed to get his hair cut.

Laurence also started running up to me for a hug. With his weight, these flying bear hugs could easily knock you over if you were unprepared. I was under no illusions, there was no affection in the hugs, but I did feel that he needed them. It felt like he was trying to squeeze some of his tensions onto me and I was happy to be there for him. I regularly received a big squeeze outside the school before he dashed inside.

He was so excited each morning. He had so many questions that he couldn't ask, so many worries that he couldn't express and so many emotions were swirling around the school playground that it would have been a surprise if he wasn't tense.

At first I loved these hugs, I wanted him to give me all his tensions, but all he gave me was a pain in the chest. He didn't rest his cheek on my chest while he squeezed, he chinned my chest looking straight up into my face as if searching for clues to the answers of his unasked questions. His chin hit the same spot every time and I soon had a very painful lump on that spot.

Unfortunately my attempts to divert his chin away from my chest put him off the hugs altogether. The pain slowly went away but the lump grew harder until it felt like an extra bone. I wished I could have some extra bony protection on my shins as well.

By the end of the summer term, it was mostly reports of good days in his home schoolbook. Despite this it was decided that Laurence should stay in Jo's reception class for the next school year. I was delighted with this. He needed stability and Jo had learnt how to 'bother' him on the inside. She was really getting through to him now, and with another year I felt we could make some really good progress.

That summer our holiday was another island holiday; this time it was Guernsey. Laurence loved going on the little plane and the short flight.

'No sleeping on Jersey European,' he told me. We hired a little car and explored the narrow lanes and quiet beaches around this picturesque little island. Undoubtedly the highlight of the holiday for Laurence was the small passenger ferry that we travelled on to get across to the tiny Herm Island. I made a note then about how much he enjoyed travelling by boat—he was so alert to everything, he was taking it all in.

We stayed for an entire day on Herm Island. There are no cars on this island so I could relax and allow Laurence to roam free while Bianca played happily on Shell Beach. It was a delightful little holiday and it got Laurence into a great frame of mind for the new school year.

Laurence was quick to settle back in the school routine. 'No more Whitefields, Laurence is a good boy now,' he told me. He really loved his new school. The reports in the schoolbook said, 'Laurence is doing very well,' and 'he's had a really good day,' and even, 'Laurence is proving to be a real asset to the class.'

His first annual review with this new school was in November, but by then Laurence was changing again. I noticed his legs were getting very prickly. The dreaded puberty had arrived at the ripe old age of eleven and three-quarters. His physical outbursts were changing; instead of writhing on the floor pulling his own hair and trying to kick himself, he was rearing up in the corner of a room hissing and spitting like a cornered wild cat, with boots on. It was tough on all of us as Laurence struggled to cope with the testosterone surging through his body.

Fortunately these pubescent behaviours arrived too late to be included in the review, which was comprehensive. Twenty-five pages in total. I have thinned it out and have reproduced just the main report and the music therapy report as Appendix 7.

I suspected Laurence of taking advantage of the change in school to lower his apparent abilities in some subjects to make life a bit easier for himself. I believed that he was clever enough to do this. I am sure that he learnt his alphabet and shapes while he was at his old school.

I was very impressed by the music therapy report. I hadn't met the music therapist before reading the report and I imagined a just-qualified young girl strumming and singing to Laurence while he dismantled xylophones and pulled her hair. I imagined a tremendous musical battle of wills and she was winning through. I felt that a new door into Laurence's mind had been opened and I had high hopes for the next year.

When I was introduced to the music therapist at the annual review meeting I was in for a shock. He was a little old man with patches on his sleeves and a battered old briefcase. I couldn't have been more wrong. I walked around the table and shook his hand, congratulating him on the wonderful job he was doing. It was unfortunate that I couldn't say the same to the speech therapist, whose report told me nothing new about Laurence as she continued to test and monitor him using different scales and schemes.

Christmas seemed to come early that year. Ana's legal team had been working hard to spend her legal aid and the files were now enormous. It appeared that after all this time they had forgotten my opening offer to surrender and out of the blue offered me what amounted to almost 50 per cent. My solicitor was shocked and couldn't believe it; she even started to allow me to run-up a bill.

I never planned on having any money left over from the divorce after all the bills were paid. This now gave me a new problem. I didn't want to tamely hand this windfall over to the CSA, but what could I spend it on?

It was the third Christmas in a row that the children had chosen to spend with me. Laurence loved my traditional Christmas dinners, in his eyes that was what Christmas was all about. He remained unmoved by the present-giving tradition, but he did like to help with the decorations and the tree.

On Boxing Day it started to snow and by the following morning there was a thick blanket. The children had never had so much snow to play in. Laurence laughed as he slipped and slid around while he threw snowballs at himself.

Bianca meanwhile struggled to build a snowman. She spent all morning building Snowy, who eventually was as big as she was. She pelted Laurence with snowballs if he came too close and neither of them felt the cold or grew tired. It was lovely to watch, from the warmth of the lounge.

I tentatively asked Laurence if he would like to see the dolphins again. He immediately said, 'No dolphins,' but I could tell that he was thinking carefully about it. He didn't protest and I could tell that his 'No dolphins' was more like, 'Not the dolphins.'

I spoke to him frequently about this and I was convinced that he wanted to go back to Florida but he was a bit apprehensive about the dolphin part. It was clear that we both had a feeling of unfinished business with regard to the dolphins. But would it work again?

I figured that he would be frightened at first but would settle down quicker second time around. I thought that there was a good chance that the shock might reorganise his mind again so that it settled down even more normally. It felt like we both wanted to do this, so I booked us in for another course of DHT in August.

Each spring the school competed in a swimming gala with other special schools. The previous year Laurence was still on trial and hadn't been chosen to go. He came home and told me that he didn't go to the swimming gala because he was a naughty boy. I must confess that I didn't correct his misunderstanding and allowed him to think that was the case. At that time it was so important that he behaved well that I was prepared to use whatever weapon came to hand.

This year he was invited to the swimming gala and he was so happy. He definitely remembered the disappointment of the previous year and was determined not to miss out this time. He even went to sleep clutching his swimming trunks so that he wouldn't lose them.

I suspect that the reality of the swimming gala and all the waiting around between races didn't quite live up to Laurence's expectations of what a swimming gala was but he still returned happy and clutching a medal. We were so proud of him and I believe he was pleased with his medal as well.

It was several weeks later when I discovered the truth. Laurence had come last but all the children got medals. When his race started Laurence carefully climbed into the pool and cautiously explored the pool. Only then was he ready to start the race, but the organisers were waiting to start the next race.

It was so predictable. Whenever he came across a new pool he always checked it out carefully before jumping in. Unfortunately there was no time for warm-ups at the swimming gala.

At home he was generally calmer. In the evenings we often listened to Bob Dylan, as he was Laurence's favourite. I became sick of Bob Dylan and encouraged him to listen to other artists without success. The TV remained heavily censored. If I was flicking through the channels he could spot a soap in a flash but he didn't object to my refusal. He seemed to readily accept my censorship.

Another example of the strong influence the TV was having on him was the Channel 4 news. I liked to watch this programme but I soon noticed that no matter what Laurence was doing he sprinted out of the room just before the theme music started and only returned when the music had stopped. He seemed to be terrified of the music and with all the ad breaks it was a stressful hour for him. It was another reminder of how important music had become for Laurence.

As the evenings grew lighter I allowed him to spend more time on the farm. He had started to befriend one of the horses. His name was Stafford; he was a magnificent black-and-white Shire horse who towered above him. At first Laurence was very nervous, preferring to hug his rear end rather than go to the sharp end with the teeth. I noticed him inhaling while he hugged and wondered what he learnt from that.

Stafford had a wonderfully gentle nature and tolerated Laurence's repetitive behaviours with an air of understanding. He could knock Laurence away with a simple flick of his head if he chose, but he never lost his patience.

As their relationship developed it was lovely to see them standing together on either side of the stable door. Stafford would stand with his head bowed, cheek to cheek with Laurence, quietly watching the world go by. They both seemed very relaxed and the best of friends at these times. Each night Laurence went out to say goodnight to Stafford before going to bed and he could see Stafford's stable from his bedroom window.

We still regularly went out somewhere on Sundays. Sometimes it was a cheap walk in the local woods, where I tried to show him the seasons, and other times we travelled further afield. We named animals in the zoo, got lost in the Hampton Court maze and I showed him where naughty boys go in the Tower of London. We also did another overnight stop to Alton Towers, where Bianca was horrified to find that her big brother had turned into a wimp. He didn't want to go on the Corkscrew roller coaster, the Black Hole or even the Log Plume.

All of these events were just sideshows counting down to the year's main event—Florida.

Laurence asked the same questions over and over again as we

counted down the months. From his questions I gathered that he was apprehensive about the dolphins but he was very keen about going to Florida and staying in the same hotel and visiting the same places again. He loved to look through the photos of our previous visit and I dug out his old dolphin video for him to wind back and forth.

I was surprised at how well Laurence coped with the protracted countdown, but eventually it was time to finish our unfinished business.

We flew from Gatwick on an American Transair flight to a small airport in Newfoundland, Canada, which takes between three and a half and four hours to cross the Atlantic, depending on the strength of the wind in the jetstream.

We had to disembark there while they refuelled the plane and this gave Laurence time to run-up and down the small terminal bouncing his tennis ball and burning off his pent-up energy. I made sure he kept his ball in his pocket when we crossed the tarmac to reboard the plane via stairs at the tail of the plane.

Laurence loved boarding and I momentarily held him back at the top of the stairs so he had time to take in the bleak scenery. The jet engines were screaming, the wind was blowing in our faces and Laurence gasped with wonder before we ducked through the door and went back to our seats.

The second flight was of equal duration as we flew down the east coast of America to Sanford Airport near Orlando in Florida. It was another small airport and a lot more civilised than the hectic Miami International Airport, which we had used last time.

Using Sanford meant that we had a much longer drive to the Florida Keys, but we had two days to get there before the therapy started.

I succumbed to the sales patter of the car-hire clerk who, for a few dollars more, offered me a convertible. It seemed like a good idea at the time. It was nearly midnight when we left the air-conditioned terminal and walked into the oppressive heat of a Floridian August night.

We spent the night at a local motel and the next day there was only one place to go. We drove into downtown Orlando and decided to spend our day at the Wet 'n' Wild theme park. Neither of the children had ever been to such a place and even though there were plenty of wild rides that Laurence didn't want to go on, there was plenty that he did like. He loved the swimming pool with waves, but his favourite was the lazy river, which he wandered round for hours on end.

It was a cloudy day so I didn't have to worry too much about sunburn, but mid-afternoon storm clouds gathered and suddenly whistles were blowing all round the park. There was the possibility of lightning strikes and children were flying out of the water all around me. Mine were somewhere on the lazy river and I didn't know how Laurence would react to all this mayhem around him.

I frantically ran around the lazy river looking for them, only to find them calmly waiting for me back at our base. Bianca told me that he had been a good boy and jumped out of the water with everybody else. Fortunately the storm soon passed and they had a couple more hours playing before we headed off to our next motel.

I had decided to take the scenic route to the Keys, going via Tampa, down the west coast of Florida and through the Everglades. Unfortunately as we got to the Everglades we hit the tail of a tropical storm. I had never seen such rain. The sound of the rain hammering on our soft-top was deafening and there was a grey wall of water in front of me. I had to stop as I couldn't even see the bonnet of the car and I dreaded a thump in the rear, but it didn't come.

The deluge didn't last long, but the roads were now waterlogged with huge puddles everywhere. Our little convertible was very light and I had to drive very carefully through the puddles. It was a nightmare journey and I was relieved to arrive safely at the Holiday Inn in Key Largo. The children, on the other hand, enjoyed it; Bianca thought the journey was exciting.

At 9.00 a.m. the next day, we were at the new home of Dolphin Human Therapy. This new site was a lot bigger and more open, with much improved facilities. We were introduced to Ric, who was the speech pathologist who would be working with Laurence. Ric had already read Laurence's file and had a few follow-up questions. He then asked me what I wanted. This time I was ready for that question and swiftly retorted that I wanted 'why'.

'You don't ask for much,' he chuckled. I knew it was a big wish but they did do miracles after all. We agreed that he would do other work while working towards an understanding of the 'why' question.

He asked me if I had any other questions and I couldn't resist asking him what the difference was between a speech therapist and a speech pathologist.

'In the old days,' he explained, 'we called ourselves speech therapists but we didn't really have much of an idea. Nowadays we think we have figured out a few things, so we call ourselves speech pathologists to differentiate.'

I laughed. I couldn't believe my ears. The speech therapists' wall of secrecy tumbled down. They didn't have any secret therapies after all; their secret was that they had no therapies. It all made sense now.

Genie had retired but I was told that she still popped in occasionally. Instead, the dolphin that would be working with Laurence was her son Alfonz who was the baby we saw on our first trip. I explained to Ric that Laurence would scream a lot for the first couple of days, but I was sure that he would quickly calm down.

They went down onto the pontoon and began work. Laurence knew what was expected of him and worked well. He soon earned rewards and Ric invited him into the water. He was apprehensive and whined in protest, but he soon slipped into Ric's waiting arms. There was no crying or screaming; he was breathing hard and Ric gave him lots of encouragement. He was coping really well and when Alfonz came by Ric put Laurence's hand on the dorsal fin and let them swim around in a circle. Laurence liked that, he was giggling and I was flabbergasted. It was so emotional, I was so proud of him. He was coping so much better than I could ever have dreamed of, on his first day.

They did some more work on the pontoon and Laurence went back into the water a couple more times, getting more comfortable each time. He was so excited when they finished; he obviously liked Ric and Alfonz too. Ric was very happy with the session and predicted that they would get through a lot of good work in the next two weeks.

I was shocked by Laurence's demonstration of control and I wondered how effective the DHT could be without the shock and trauma of the first couple of days. Only time would tell.

On subsequent days Laurence maintained his control and did some excellent work. After the morning therapy sessions we revisited old haunts and visited some new ones, or we just chilled around the hotel pools. It was very, very hot for the entire time we were on the Keys. It was too hot to drive around with the roof down for any length of time; we preferred to be in the shade with the roof up and the air conditioning on. No wonder they were virtually giving convertibles away at this time of year.

The highlight of this holiday was an incident at the therapy. As usual Laurence had been working well and he went into the water with Ric. Laurence took hold of Alfonz's dorsal fin and started to go around in a circle when suddenly another dolphin pushed between Laurence and Ric. Laurence looked around, saw Genie beside him, and grabbed her dorsal fin with his spare hand. With a dolphin in each hand the threesome happily sped off into the sunset.

Well, not quite—they could dive under the fencing into the sea, but they couldn't take Laurence so they took him to the end of the lagoon, turned around, and returned a giggling Laurence to Ric, who was asking the dolphin trainer what was going on. It was the trainer who told us that it was Genie who had uncharacteristically interrupted the lesson.

It was a beautiful event and the tears flowed down my cheeks. Mother and son had independently decided to give Laurence the ride of his life. I cannot know if Genie recognised Laurence after five years, but I like to think that she did, especially as Ric assured me that it was unheard of for Genie to misbehave like that.

Who knows what communications were wafted between the three of them as they frolicked around the pen that morning.

Laurence benefited greatly from his two weeks of working with Ric and Alfonz. He was even answering some why questions, but it was clear that the concept of why was still very vague in his mind. They had done a lot of work on sequences of events and consequences. Ric also recognised Laurence's problems with understanding and expressing emotions and feelings. He had his assistant make some laminated cards with line-drawing pictures of faces with different expressions and gave them to us to continue working with them when we got home.

It was Laurence's self-control from day one that amazed me. His determination to control his fears of bottomless water and dolphins with big teeth swimming silently around his legs probably deprived us of a third awakening, but I was still very happy with the progress we had made.

I wondered how he had managed it and I thought about his relationship with Stafford. The timings matched. In his memory those dolphins were huge and he started trying to befriend Stafford, the biggest horse on the farm, at the same time as we started to talk about going to see the dolphins again. Was he training himself, preparing to finish his unfinished business months before our departure?

If this was true, then I realised that we had received the benefit of the DHT before we even left England. He had made good progress with the speech pathologist but the biggest benefit of the DHT was undoubtedly his newfound self-control.

I realised that my clever plans for his third awakening had been foiled and totally eclipsed by Laurence's own intelligent and premeditated plans.

13

Puberty at Five

After the last session of DHT I had a 400-mile drive to catch our evening flight from Sanford Airport. We arrived in Canada in the middle of the night and the children insisted on having an ice cream in the terminal just like they had going the other way. To this day if you ask Laurence what he did in Canada he will tell you, 'Eat the ice cream.' Thankfully they slept well on the flight back to England.

I took the children straight round to see Ana when we got back to London. They only had one day with Mum before she flew off to Colombia. The DHT had been booked well in advance, so I was very unhappy with Ana's arrangements. I felt her plans caused unnecessary anxiety for both of the children. They hadn't seen their mum for two weeks and now they had just one day before saying goodbye to her again for another month. Both children were upset when I picked them up the next day.

However, they got over it as kids do and we settled down to family life. Having Bianca stay for more than one night meant a major upheaval to our normal routines, but it was great to be living together again.

I tried to give Laurence every opportunity to use the emotion flash cards that Ric gave us to help him express his feelings through this turbulent emotional spell.

I spread the cards out in front of him, saying, 'Which one?'

He always replied by handing me two cards and saying, 'Which one?' He wasn't asking me to choose; he was asking me to ask him.

'Which one, happy or sad?' I would ask. The reply was always the same, 'Sad.'

He could easily have said that he was sad outright, so it seemed like he was going through this long-winded procedure for my benefit. Did he think that I needed these aids to understand him? Did I really appear to be so stupid in his eyes?

The sad answer to these questions is yes. It was me who needed the cards to establish the answer to what was a blindingly obvious question. Of course he was sad; he had just returned from a wonderful two-week holiday with the dolphins and now Mummy was away for a further month.

When Laurence returned to school he was very well behaved, although for a short period we did have a few incidents of urinating in inappropriate places. On one occasion he stood up in class, turned around and urinated on his chair. He also left little messages in the playground and the gym, but not at home. We didn't have any messages at home as he knew that I didn't approve and he soon learnt that the teachers didn't approve either. The teachers put his unusual behaviour down to Mum being away, whereas I knew that he was just trying to communicate.

Ana was due back on September 13, 2001, and two days before her arrival Laurence saw the TV news pictures.

'Mummy's plane no crash,' he told me, without any outward trace of emotion. However, he had to be concerned otherwise he wouldn't have said it. As they kept repeating the pictures I kept reassuring them both that Mummy's plane wouldn't crash.

In the days and weeks after Ana's return Laurence was visibly more relaxed. Jo was writing glowing reports about his excellent behaviour and we were recording incident-free weeks. Laurence was very happy in school and Jo explained why.

During the previous year, she had noticed that increasingly Laurence was sitting next to a girl called Rhiannon. She was autistic and they seemed well matched. Neither gave any outward indication of emotional interest—they just happened to be together most of the time.

At the start of the new term, there were some new pupils in the class. One of them was Jenny. She was a pretty little girl with long blonde hair and she wasn't autistic at all. We had already noticed that Laurence had an attraction to blonde teachers and blonde family friends, but this time he was besotted. On Jenny's first day Laurence stood up from his seat beside Rhiannon, walked round the class and sat down next to Jenny. He had no shame, but Rhiannon was furious at being so openly dumped. She had no words to express her feelings so she unleashed what Jo called 'the autistic eye'.

When she got eye contact with Laurence he was left in no doubt how she felt and he hated it. The communicative intent of the autistic eye was clear for all to see and Laurence reeled away in terror. He would grab a book and tear a page with a frightened look of 'If you don't stop I'll tear some more.'

He had no idea how to handle her 'autistic eye' and she wielded it with the full fury of a woman scorned. How he suffered, and Jo said that she had to distract Rhiannon when it got too much, but he had to learn this very important lesson.

How teachers handle these lessons can make all the difference to a child's education. At 12 years old, Laurence and Rhiannon were just beginning to learn how to interact socially. Normal children would have been learning these social skills throughout their childhood. I believed that Jo handled these lessons very well—a fact proved by Laurence's social temperament today.

Jo told us that Laurence was becoming obsessed with Jenny. One day in class he spontaneously serenaded her with his best rendition of 'Baa baa black sheep'. I shudder to think how this primitive display of love would have gone down in a mainstream secondary school. We all have to learn to socialise with the people around us, and for those who fail to learn these skills naturally, they need special lessons.

Rhiannon and Laurence were on Lesson One; it was as if they had never noticed other people's interactions. To them we were the robots. They didn't pick up any of our social skills so unsurprisingly they thought we had no understanding of their feelings.

I described Jo as a high-functioning teacher because of the inventive ways she incorporated these social lessons into the curriculum. Unfortunately teachers are not judged by these higher functions any more; instead they are judged on how well they administer the National Curriculum. No thought is given to what lessons are best for these children. Lessons on the Second World War, the ancient Romans and understanding a Kenyan village are considered more important than teaching these children the skills to survive in our urban jungles.

Just as the primary school system had failed these children before the start of their education, so the secondary school system seemed set up to deliberately fail them as well. In the twenty-first century it is ridiculous that we are tied to the simple mantra, 'All children should have access to the National Curriculum'.

How could any Ofsted inspector expect to know what is best for my child's education? The teachers try to weave life's lessons amongst the National Curriculum subjects to keep the school inspectors happy.

It is such a waste of effort when we should be fine-tuning an Autistic Curriculum to give these children a fair chance.

By the time an autistic child reaches secondary education many reports and extensive statements of the child's needs are written, and yet we say they cannot have a specific curriculum appropriate to their needs.

This is yet another example of the State condemning these children to a life of being handicapped in social skills and in the understanding of our plastic artificial world. By the age of eleven, the Statement of Educational Needs should state the curriculum necessary to give each child the best chance to fit into our complex society.

Each autistic child is given an Individual Education Plan, but these IEPs are usually just a list of attainable targets for the teacher to achieve over the coming year.

Freed from the curricular and financial restraints that plague special schools, the right approaches could be found to motivate these children to learn much quicker.

Alongside the IEP, there should be an IAP, an Individual Autism Plan designed to help each child with its type of autism and its many phases. It could cover such things as dietary plans, behaviour modification plans, therapies and coping with sensory issues.

This is where the psychologists have failed the parents, teachers and children. They are so busy determining the least amount of support to give a child, that they have no time for IAPs to help the child through life.

At first Jenny appeared to like all the attention she was getting from Laurence, but it was a romance that was always doomed. Poor Laurence, Jenny wasn't autistic and had no patience for his obsessive behaviours. He should have stuck with Rhiannon, but he was a sucker for a blonde and he would soon be unable to face either of them.

Life was just beginning to get complicated for Laurence and I felt it was my fault. I had opened him out to all these new emotions and I sometimes worried if he really was better off with his hard-coated autistic shell removed. We couldn't put it back.

Laurence adopted a pragmatic attitude to life's lessons. He learnt to pick up his undying love and place it in front of another pretty blonde; after Jenny it was a blonde teacher in another class—age didn't seem to matter.

This transfer process was graphically demonstrated when his buddy Stafford became ill and had to be quarantined for a month. Normally Laurence visited Stafford every day even if it was only to say goodnight, so we expected him to be upset at being kept away. However, by the next day, he was the best of friends with another horse on the other side of the yard. Cheyenne was smaller than Stafford but he had a very similar black-and-white coat.

It seemed that Laurence fancied blonde women and black-and-white horses. Laurence and Cheyenne spent many happy days standing either side of the stable door, cheek to cheek and chewing straw, with Laurence repeatedly moaning Cheyenne's name like the lovelorn child that he was.

When the quarantine was over he wasn't interested in going back to Stafford. Poor Stafford missed the attention from his old buddy. He even neighed when Laurence came outside, only to see him scurrying away in the other direction, towards Cheyenne. Stafford only got a look in when Cheyenne went out for the day; only then did Laurence seem to remember his old buddy. He had used his friendship with Stafford to gain some self-control, but now Stafford was reduced to being a reserve to fill in during Cheyenne's absences.

Laurence was compartmentalising all his relationships to put some order into his emotional world. He liked to play, 'Who do you like the most?'

I would ask him, 'Who do you like, Cheyenne or Stafford?'

'Cheyenne,' he would reply.

'Who do you like, Rhiannon or Jenny?'

'Jenny.'

'Who do you like, Jenny or Cheyenne?'

'Cheyenne.'

'Who do you like, Daddy or Cheyenne?'

'Cheyenne,' would come the immediate reply.

Cheyenne was Top of the Pops for some time.

It was interesting observing Laurence work out that it could be to his advantage to put Daddy above the horse sometimes. He learnt surprisingly quickly, but it was clear that he didn't have a clue to begin with.

He appeared to have learnt nothing about the emotional side of us from his early years.

I knew that Laurence's hearing was switched on by the AIT seven years previously, his first awakening. He had the comprehension of a seven-year-old now; it was just his speech that hadn't been able to keep up with his understanding.

I wondered what had switched on his emotional receptors. I suspected it was the shock and upheaval of that first bout of DHT five years ago, his second awakening.

In that case, Laurence was now going through puberty with the understanding of a seven-year-old and with the emotions of a five-year-old.

Strangely that seemed about right; it was a fair description of his inept, innocent blundering behaviour.

Laurence's annual review and report that winter were again thorough and extensive. The teachers had had nearly two years to get to know Laurence and understand him, so their comments were valid. Last year I was wowed by the music therapy report; this time it was the Information and Communication Technology (ICT) teacher who got me excited.

Somehow she had broken through his understanding barrier. He had learnt that pressing buttons and controlling the mouse could influence what appeared on the computer screen. She reported that he had made a vast improvement, showing a degree of spontaneity and becoming naturally curious in response to some programs. I hoped that we had opened another doorway into his mind.

I haven't reproduced the entire report, just the summary of progress in Appendix 8.

Yet again I have not included the speech therapist's report. She hadn't learnt much. We had a meeting. I revealed that I knew that she didn't have any therapies for autism. She was taken aback and blustered, but I didn't pursue the point. I didn't see any benefit in dwelling over her profession's betrayal. I wanted Laurence to get some benefit from his time spent with this woman. I suggested that she should treat Laurence with the therapies that she used on children with a stammer. She confirmed that she did have some therapies for such children and I explained why.

Laurence would often run-up to me saying, 'Daddy . . . Daddy' and then after a pause, 'No trains in Italy.' I knew that wasn't what he had wanted to tell me. All too often he would resort to uttering a pre-recorded statement or question because he couldn't spit out the words he wanted to say. He was taking the words in but something was blocking the words from coming out. So, in the absence of any speech therapies for autism, I told her to treat Laurence as if he had a massive stammer.

I was serious about the severe stammer and would direct people to Temple Grandin's opinions on this subject in *An Inside View of Autism*.

The speech therapist was a sweet lady and she smiled considerately before moving on to tell me that Laurence was making good progress. He was sequencing photos of the tea-making process while he was making cups of tea. It was clear that he had her drinking out of his hand. She wasn't listening to me so there was no hope for any real progress and it was our last meaningful conversation. We were on different planets.

Laurence was approaching his thirteenth birthday. I had hoped that his birthday presents would be based on accessories for the Scalextric set that I had bought him for Christmas. However, during the months after Christmas it was difficult to get him excited by the Scalextric. At first he showed no interest in learning to control the car; it was only after he noticed the faint electric smell in the handset that he began to experiment to get more.

It was another strange case of Laurence being motivated by smell rather than via audio or visual stimulation. Seeing his car racing around the track didn't motivate him; he was motivated to get more of the smell by controlling the car carefully around the track.

Smell and touch were more important to Laurence than sights and sounds. He seemed programmed to learn through these senses and yet audio and visual channels dominate our world.

Modern schools teach with no touch and utilise bright visual aids. Most of what is taught is through the auditory channel, which is assumed to be working properly, with no consideration or explanation given to all the confusing smells in today's classrooms.

In the olden days, all children smelled pretty much the same through the week. With so many cleaning brands on the market today, couldn't the school uniform include a school smell?

Classrooms were more drab with less visual stimulation and you could hear a pin drop while the teacher was talking. With so little sensory stimulation there was no excuse for not paying attention, but if your mind did wander the teachers were not afraid to employ the sense of touch. There was a little stinger in each classroom with an even bigger stinger in the headmaster's office.

I am not advocating a return to Victorian schooling; we live in the twenty-first century and can do a lot better than that, but let's not forget the lessons of the past. When you look at the sensory state of our modern schools and the numbers of sensitive children falling out of them, then it is clear that we can still learn a lot from their old-fashioned methods.

I found that violence was not necessary. The threat was usually enough and a near miss was just as effective as a direct hit, but the threat had to be credible or it would inevitably become ineffective.

Smells became more important to Laurence, especially his own. He monitored his armpits throughout the day. He regularly put his finger in his armpit, sniffed and then tasted his finger. I saw this as similar behaviour to his regular water sampling in the sea. It puts a completely new slant on the idea of talking to oneself.

I wondered what he learnt.

He became interested in Mummy's perfumes and deodorants. The supermarket aisle packed with smellies became one of his favourite places. I could leave him furtively inhaling while I did the rest of the shopping. He understood that he mustn't open the packets, but he was happy because he could still take the smells.

We let him choose what he liked. At first it seemed that all he liked was overpowering intoxication. I would have expected him to be susceptible to subtle scents, but he seemed more interested in being able to block them all out with one overpowering pong.

He called them odourants and I couldn't argue with that description. He preferred the sprays to the roll-on types, so that he could cover his entire body with the smell.

Maybe he didn't like giving away his inner secrets and he was covering up, just like everybody else does. His olfactory inspired behaviours were falling into line with our normal but artificial behaviour.

His senses were running amok at this time. A shocked stable girl who was working in the yard early one morning told me the following tale.

It was a bitterly cold but bright winter's dawn, the yard looked beautiful in a thick white carpet of frost; it was −3 degrees at least.

She was surprised to see my front door open and Laurence step outside, stark naked. He ran outside towards the stables but he only got half a dozen strides before reality hit him. It was freezing and he froze before turning around and running straight back inside.

We had to laugh, it conjured up such a funny picture and I would love to have seen the expression on his face. I considered myself lucky that he had chosen such a cold morning to cavort naked outside, as he was unlikely to repeat the experience, which he didn't. If he had chosen a bright summer's morning he might have wanted to try it again. You have to take your luck wherever you can get it.

I kept taking Laurence out during these unstable times. It was more important than ever as Ana had given up taking him out because of 'what if', and social services had suspended taking him out because he had kicked a passenger on the train for no apparent reason.

I was not going to lock Laurence away—I decided that I would tackle the 'what ifs' when they happened—and they happened. There were many 'what ifs' that could have turned out differently. Maybe I was lucky—we left a trail of bewildered members of the public behind us, but no lasting harm was done.

I remember a routine trip to the supermarket. I had just parked up and Laurence was naughty again, he had pulled Bianca's hair. I told him that was it, no shopping and began to drive away. He flew into a rage, screaming and kicking the car roof. I pulled over and jumped out. He was a ball of fury so I checked that there was no traffic and I let him out of the car.

He tried to kick me as he fell out of the car but I anticipated that. He ran straight across the road without looking, which I had also anticipated. He was screaming at the top of his voice and kept running in a straight line across the wide pavement, through some open doors into a large office. There was a momentary silence and then I heard Laurence screaming again as he ran out of the building into my waiting arms on the pavement. I hugged him tight and his screaming turned to crying. A man approached and asked me if this was my child and he was silenced when I replied simply, 'Yes.'

A startled lady came out of the offices.

'Is he all right? What's his problem?' she asked.

I explained that he was autistic and having a bad day. She told me that she understood as her sister had one. The man seemed reassured by this and withdrew. I cuddled him some more and I could feel the tension leaving his body. We could go shopping another day.

A more worrying situation occurred on a trip to Greenwich. It was a sunny Sunday in the spring. I had popped into work in the morning and then parked up near the foot tunnel going below the Thames to Greenwich. Laurence was keen to go to the other side of the river. He behaved well in the tunnel and we had a very pleasant afternoon exploring Greenwich Park.

At the end of the afternoon we were walking back through the tunnel to the car. Ahead of us were some young lads kicking a football about. The inevitable happened, the ball skidded off the tunnel wall smacking into Bianca's calf. It stung and Bianca cried out. Laurence flew into a rage and charged towards the group of young lads who were all twice the size of him.

Momentarily instinct pulled me towards Bianca's distress before I pulled myself away to chase after Laurence. I was too late; my initial indecision meant that he had already got in two blows before I pulled him away. I pinned him against the wall trying to prevent him from kicking out at the group of youths ominously gathering around us.

I apologised to them and explained that he was only defending his little sister who was struck by their ball. Their mood changed immediately. One thirteen-year-old against a dozen eighteen-year-olds and he had got stuck straight in; they admired his bravado.

'All right!' said one. 'Defending his little sister, heh?'

'Spunky little fella, ain't he,' said another.

My fearless little fellow had earned their admiration and they went on their way laughing and joking amongst themselves about 'Kids these days!'

For her own safety I kept Laurence pinned until Bianca had regained her composure and we then calmly made our way back to the car. It was a close shave, but you could have close shaves in the safety of the home as well.

One Sunday dinnertime Laurence suddenly lost his temper. I had no time to examine what had happened previously. He lashed out, throwing the knife in his hand straight at me. He was a good shot; my glasses deflected the blade onto my eyebrow. Blood poured out onto my plate and Laurence was mortified.

He screamed and ran out of the room and up the stairs to his bedroom. I followed him out. There was no real pain, I was calm and I was determined that he would see and understand what he had done. Poor Laurence, I milked the scene for all it was worth. Between washing the wound, I kept returning to his room to show him what he had done.

I kept 'bothering' him with my 'pain'. I made sure that he wouldn't want to go through that again, without having to lift a finger against him. I had a much better weapon—his discomfort at seeing my feelings.

Every morning I showed him my scar and I told him that it still hurt. He was grounded until Daddy didn't hurt any more. He knew what I meant and he accepted the punishment.

It was always difficult to remain cross with him for any length of time. He tried so hard to be good and he was learning all the time.

He was learning more acceptable ways to express himself. When he started to get distressed he would stand up and throw a plate on the floor. It seemed somehow to relieve the stress. Some thought that he liked the sound of the plate smashing, but I suspected that he liked the smashing silence that followed it.

He would also slowly pour milk or water on the floor. That was strange because he had always disliked a mess, but he was now using our dislike of these messes to get our attention. These minor outbursts were treated with the minimum of fuss to give him no reward, but they were also valuable warnings of his rising stress levels.

These incidents were isolated thanks to his improved self-control and throughout the spring and summer terms the school reports remained generally good. The bad points were noted, but usually Jo was writing things like:

'An excellent day.'

'A trouble-free week.'

'A bubbly day but no bursts.'

'Very high today but he kept control. Well done Laurence.'

He was thoroughly enjoying the school experience.

He was also learning about himself. He was very amused by his inability to fall over backwards. For weeks he could be seen in the playground and in my garden trying to fall over backwards in between fits of laughter when his body failed to do what he wanted.

He wasn't so pleased when his voice failed to do what he wanted. He whined and got cross with himself as he tried to make his squeaky voice work properly.

For a child with such an interest in tactile sensations it was no surprise that he quickly learnt what he could do with his hands. He had no shame. Jo told me that she was always telling the boys in class, 'Hands on the table please.'

I decided that I was never going to stop him from playing so I set out to restrict his activities to the bedroom. He seemed to get the message quickly and he responded well to 'No touching' commands, if I noticed him become distracted while we were out.

Like many normal teenagers he developed a liking for his own bedroom and spent hours alone up there. The lounge became quite peaceful and I started to miss him. I practised luring him downstairs without resorting to using food. Listening to Bob Dylan was sometimes successful, but on some occasions when he was quietly doing a jigsaw or reading a map in his bedroom I left him in peace.

But all was not well in the bedroom. Every night I kissed him goodnight and every morning the sheets were off the bed, the duvet was out of its cover and the pillow was out of its case. Sometimes the bed linen disappeared completely as he threw it out of his window. On a windy morning, you could see his sheets flapping in the trees, or on a rainy morning, they would lie in a sodden heap under the window.

Some phases of behaviour were short-lived, but this one lasted over a year. I am no psychologist; I couldn't hope to understand the meaning of this frequent and very annoying behaviour. He also threw out favoured books and toys, so the practice had to stop. After all, his favourite book was a tome called *Eighty Years of Civil Aviation*, and it would have done serious damage if it landed on somebody.

I started putting some of his liberated items in the rubbish; he didn't like that, so I concluded that he wasn't trying to get rid of things. Gradually I managed to reduce the number of 'throwing out the window' incidents but I couldn't stop him sleeping on the bare mattress.

His mattress was getting into a terrible state. I suspected that he picked away at the mattress while he slept. He had picked around the edges and there were rips across the middle. The stuffing was coming out, but I didn't want to get a new mattress until I had stopped him from picking.

That battle centred on keeping the sheets on the bed all night. I tried different materials and different ways of fastening the sheets to the mattress, but it was a battle that I was finding hard to win. When the springs started to appear I caved in on safety grounds and bought a new one. When it was delivered, they collected the old one. I was so ashamed. It was worse than a dog's mattress; it looked like a tiger had been sleeping on it.

I renewed my efforts to keep the sheets on the bed with little effect. He still slept on the mattress, but once he had established that this one had the same stuffing inside it he stopped the picking.

I wondered if he was trying to make his bed more like that of his mate Cheyenne—a bed of straw. They had remained best friends. Sometimes Cheyenne lay on his bed and other times he stood at the stable door while Laurence talked to him. The conversation appeared to centre on Laurence repeating Cheyenne's name over and over again but in slightly different ways.

I wondered if he was trying to find a way to express himself. Cheyenne was a horse with a character all of his own and he had a very expressive face. If somebody had said to me that one of the horses spoke I would make Cheyenne my first guess. Even I felt like I could understand him sometimes, especially when he looked at me after enduring a couple of hours of Laurence's serenading.

Next to Cheyenne's stable were two stables joined together by a tack room, making a little three-room block. The two stables were empty and Linda decided to clean them up and repaint them before new tenants moved in. Laurence took a great interest in the work and when they finished, he started to hang around the empty stables.

One day he took me by the hand into the stables and tentatively pleaded, 'Laurence's house.'

With its freshly painted walls, clean floors, little windows and low ceilings I could see how he saw it as an ideal home. It wouldn't worry him that there was no heating or plumbing. My big puppy had grown into a young man searching for his own little place in the world. I talked about the advantages of living inside the house; fortunately the stables were not empty for long and he gave up on the idea.

However, his idea did get me thinking. During the summer he would have been happy living in a stable with a bed of straw. He seemed suited to living as a horse or even a dog. He liked a rough bed, he could tell what not to eat and his big brown eyes could beg as well as any dog sitting beside the dining table.

It occurred to me that if there was a terrible holocaust and the breakdown of civilised society, Laurence would be better able to survive than I could. I have relied on supermarket food for my entire life; I've never had to kill for my dinner or to scavenge. If somebody taught him to kill for food then I'm sure that he would have no qualms about doing it and he was an excellent scavenger already. Admittedly he had only had to scavenge around people's kitchens and houses, but he could find food wherever it was hidden.

I had read about feral children and how they exhibited some autistic features and Laurence was definitely exhibiting some feral features. Is this a chicken-and-egg situation? It seems strange behaviour for parents to abandon or lock up their offspring, but this behaviour could be understandable if the child was autistic in the first place.

In his early years I can see that in different circumstances, in a less supportive society, I might have been tempted to allow Laurence to live with the animals in the stable. By doing so I would have been protecting the rest of my family and I would have made him happier too. He could have led a feral life and grown up understanding the animals better than he understood humans.

Increasingly I was finding it difficult to see his autism as an illness or disablement, he was just different. His autism seemed natural, but if he was naturally autistic then there should be evidence of autistic behaviours throughout history.

Evidence of Asperger's syndrome over the last 500 years is easy to find. Einstein and Newton are noted for their quirky behaviours, and history is littered with autistic behaviours in the scientific community.

An excellent example is Henry Cavendish, who lived in the eighteenth century, inherited a fortune and never had to worry about making a living. He was probably this country's finest mind, but he was so reclusive that little of his work was published. Sadly, when his papers were eventually edited a century later, many of his discoveries had already been accredited to others.

His biographer described him as suffering from shyness to a 'degree bordering on a disease'. All human contact was extremely uncomfortable—even his housekeeper communicated with him by letter.

If this man had had to interact with society he would have undoubtedly ended up in an asylum, labelled mad. His vast inherited wealth meant that he rarely left his house/laboratory. When he did venture out to a scientific meeting, other guests were told on no account to talk to or even look at him.

There must have been many people with Asperger's born into less comfortable circumstances. Their scientific studies would have been confined to surviving in a cruel society.

Not having to fend for himself, Laurence has also been able to continue his scientific research into the communicative contents of seawater and his study of the changing tastes of his body odours throughout the day.

For many, autism must have been fatal, but some got through, doing mundane repetitive jobs around the family farm or business to earn their keep. Learning through repetition with an attention to detail, some would have become great craftsmen in their own right.

This ability to hone skills with sharp observation would have helped people with autistic tendencies to survive throughout the ages of human development. An individual with the ability to repeatedly make good quality axe heads would be held in high esteem in caveman society.

So why has Mother Nature kept on churning out these genetically 'defective' specimens throughout our evolution? Why haven't they died out through natural selection?

I suspect that Mother Nature keeps producing genetically autistic people for a reason, and she doesn't let them die out in the same way that she doesn't let genetically gay people die out, no matter how much these groups are discriminated against.

I read about a theory that Neanderthal man was autistic and that interbreeding with Homo sapiens before the former died out resulted in cases of autism today. I didn't waste much time reading this simplistic theory, as it seemed to ignore the fact that we see autistic behaviours in many different species.

Temple Grandin's book *Animals in Translation* gives many examples of this.

Neanderthal man may well have been autistic, but it is just as likely that all-conquering Homo sapiens had Asperger's and soon overran Neanderthal man with better-flighted spears and other superior technology. I see no point in blaming Neanderthals for autism, but I will show that there is good reason to believe that autistic behaviours could have been the norm in the past.

As we begin to piece together our distant past we learn that our ancestors were not social creatures. Living in small family groups, their interactions with the neighbours were limited to raping and pillaging. Progress was slow over millions of years with just the fine-

271

tuning of the making and use of basic tools. Natural selection, survival of the fittest, dominated the evolution of our species.

Big, strong males alert to potential dangers were the most likely to survive long enough to father and protect plenty of offspring. The fight, fright, flight trilogy for survival was just what I saw in Laurence. He had grown up big and strong and on his toes, ready to react to the slightest unexpected danger. He is finely tuned for survival and totally out of tune with our modern-day laid-back society. He could be a massive genetic throwback to our distant past. Who knows?

Incidentally, if Laurence was a massive genetic throwback, his body could be designed for a diet of meat, fruit, nuts and roots. He would struggle to cope with a diet dominated by wheat, dairy produce and other new products that were not around at that time. In addition, his LAD might not have been well developed.

Somewhere in our past, sexual rather than natural selection took over the evolution of our species and our development accelerated. Patriarchal and matriarchal societies flourished, but over the last 10,000 years, it was the patriarchal-structured societies that dominated.

For thousands of years males have been selecting their mates based on whether they look healthy and whether they are likely to stay faithful and obey him. The women in these societies compete to fit into this patriarchal agenda.

In a matriarchal society, the females are selecting their mates based on whether they are likely to accumulate wealth and be around long enough to provide for and protect them and their children. For a long time both societies had the same ideal male—big, strong and smart enough to survive long enough to look after his family.

This began to change with improved verbal communication and the consequent growth in size and complexity of communities. Males that mastered speech found that they could amass wealth through trading with the neighbours rather than the more traditional raping and pillaging. Their communication skills also meant that they were better able to woo the women while the alpha males were away accumulating their wealth.

As villages grew into cities, empires and kingdoms, the rule of law followed to protect these weaker but essential citizens. Words were the new wealth makers and no civilisation could survive and thrive without these wordsmiths in their many guises. Women were not slow to latch onto the security that these new professions offered their offspring.

The testosterone-charged males still thrived while following their traditional pursuits in the army that was needed to protect the vast wealth that the wordsmiths accumulated.

The army controlled our own empire and it was built on trade and run by accountants, lawyers and the church, all excellent wordsmiths. On top of that, they were entertained and inspired by the wonderfully over-elaborate eloquence of William Shakespeare and his like.

With increased stability, family sizes could grow and over the generations, stereotypes of the children have formed. Usually the first son is just like his dad, a chip off the old block and happy to follow in his father's footsteps. The second son is more unstable and unsettled; a mix of Mum and Dad, he is more likely to join the army or seek his fortune elsewhere. The third son might be more artistic or creative or like his mum in some way. The fourth son could be less social but clever. He might go to university or be a mute village idiot. He might stay at home doing mundane repetitive jobs in the family business for the first born while the second son was off seeking his fortune and the third-born joined the circus.

They are only basic stereotypes and there are many exceptions, like Laurence, who is my first-born, but they do represent the four main types of fish swimming in our society. They don't look different, they just think differently. Give them a problem to solve and they will tackle it in different ways.

Mother Nature has kept producing these four main groups throughout our evolution. In our modern society we have found places even for those on the fringes of the first three groups. For those on the fringes of the fourth group, like Laurence, we are struggling to find their place in our society. The mix of Mum and Dad's genes that makes up the fourth group produces academics and scientists. These kids have open, enquiring minds with few preconceptions. Laurence had no preconceptions—remember he was equally open to everyone and everything. He was the ultimate scientist. He would have happily crawled off with a troop of monkeys. He would have been happier with them as he would have understood them easier than us.

There seems to be ever increasing numbers on the fringes of the fourth group.

Why is Mother Nature doing this now?

We have evolved in a patriarchal society for thousands of years, but over the last hundred years our society has moved on. Equality for women and effective contraception means that it is no longer the family or the male that chooses a mate. In our modern western society it is only the female who decides who the father of her children will be.

I've got no problem with that—it seems very reasonable. But there is a problem. Although we now have the procreation selection practices of a matriarchal society, we are still living in what is basically a patriarchal society.

Not long ago men begrudgingly conceded equality, but they do not look likely to concede further ground. Equality means that women have to compete against men in the workplace. They are putting off having children to fit in with their career.

In reality a society that puts its women to work before allowing them to have a family must be a society under stress. In a truly matriarchal society these young women would be cosseted and nurtured to produce their best offspring.

In a time of prosperity, we are bizarrely producing children as if in wartime, with the women having to pull their weight alongside the men.

These and other factors are having unseen effects.

It is well known that stressed-out males experience a lowering of testosterone levels, but psychological and physiological stress have the opposite effect on women. Older mothers also tend to have higher testosterone levels than younger mothers. These effects bring us back to Professor Simon Baron-Cohen's research into foetal testosterone levels and autism.

There is another problem being generated by exclusively female sexual selection practices. In our multicultural society the need to select a mate with specific traits within a culture has disappeared. Women can now choose a procreation partner using whatever criteria they choose.

They still want a partner capable of providing security for their brood, but the picture of an ideal male is diversifying rapidly. As women look beyond the tall, dark and handsome stereotype, a wider variety of males is being presented with procreation opportunities. Older men and the more socially inept are chosen if they can offer security and stability in our society.

In nature we see that all species are affected by natural selection. Sexual selection is evident in many species and has been responsible for rapid evolutionary growth in those species like peacocks. Cultural selection, however, hasn't yet been observed in other species; maybe we are the first. We don't know and we can't know how cultural selection will affect the evolution of our species. However, I think that it would be fair to assume that the evolutionary effects of cultural selection will be even faster than sexual selection.

I cannot believe that we are travelling in the wrong direction— female selection has to be the best and fairest way—but we seem to be lacking the understanding that comes with our enlightenment. We object to scientists wanting to conduct experiments into human genetic engineering, but the real experiments are going on all around us as women choose mates with their own idiosyncratic images of an ideal male.

Most women are still attracted to the fit, strong male ideal, but what if the macho posturing that goes with it started turning women increasingly towards more academic stereotypes for mates? Who knows how long it would be before we were producing weak-limbed eggheads? I suspect that it could be frighteningly fast. Just look at the diversity of dogs.

Recent research has shown that evolutionary change isn't necessarily a slow process taking thousands of years, it can occur within decades. The rapid observable changes wrought by dog and livestock breeders were thought to be a special case, but we all know now that plants and insects can rapidly evolve to be resistant to pesticides.

Because of generations of fishermen adopting the policy of letting the little ones escape, fish are becoming smaller. Modern fishing policy favours fish that take longer to grow to a smaller size. We should be throwing the big ones back to make it an evolutionary race to grow big enough to escape.

The same is being seen on land, where the hunting of animals for their tusks or horns is favouring animals that grow them more slowly.

Likewise, our own species is evolving too. These changes would have only been subtle as our bodies adapted to living in a comfortable urban environment, but if the worst effects of global warming predictions come to pass then billions would die and only those able to adapt to their new environment would survive to evolve. These days our young are evolving thumbs that can text quicker. Rapid evolutionary change is a reality.

Female equality must wait until after child rearing; before that, women should have the benefit of a matriarchal-structured society around them. I suspect that if our society hadn't spent billions of pounds pursuing patriarchal agendas we may well have spent that money gaining a better understanding of the development of our own species.

We have ignored the warnings of long-established religions that oppress women, subjugating them to male sexual selection agendas. Now we are faced with a knowledge gap that we cannot hope to fill before the results of successive generations of female, sexual and cultural selection start pouring in.

It is this 'knowledge gap' that is so important here. I had been facing a knowledge gap since first meeting Laurence. I was convinced that I knew it all, but over the years I have been forced to slowly change my perspective to see that in fact I knew very little indeed. It was my knowledge gap, not his. I couldn't sense its presence until he showed me that there were other ways to see, hear, feel and interact with our environment.

Whilst we have spent a lot of time and resources studying and manipulating our environment, little has been spent on studying human genetics. We are undoubtedly a very clever species, but are we clever enough to recognise the knowledge gap in front of us now?

It would be easy to dismiss Laurence and his like as throwbacks to a distant time, irrelevant to our modern times, or simply as a genetic mistake that needs to be labelled and thrown into the bin with the other unfortunates who need to be cared for.

In fact, evolution is all about propelling species forwards, not back. Therefore, if our autistic children are for the benefit of our future, then they have fallen into our knowledge gap.

We certainly don't have a clue what to do with them for now.

Maybe these naturally autistic children, finely tuned for survival, are the natural offspring of a struggling society that is forced to put its young women to work beside the men.

This would be an incredibly clever trick by Mother Nature to pre-empt a cataclysmic future and give the species a chance to continue to survive after the society collapses. Professor Simon Baron-Cohen's research into testosterone levels indicates that Mother Nature has the tools to perform this trick.

However, maybe it is not all doom and gloom for our species. Maybe the glut of autistic kids is here for another reason. Bright people with mild autism or Asperger's syndrome are in high demand in modern technologies. Technological developments are now happening so fast that it may be time to move on to exploit the insights and understandings of the more autistically minded.

The idea that increasing amounts of autism leads to higher intelligence, as in Asperger's, but that too much autism makes the individual thick, has always struck me as odd. It would be more logical to assume that the profoundly autistic have the potential to be even more intelligent than those with Asperger's and more intelligent than we can comprehend.

Scientists have been trying to create an artificial intelligence cleverer than us for many years. Consider what will happen when they succeed. To our simple minds, the AI will keep producing wrong answers, and they will say it is broken. Isn't that exactly what is happening with Laurence? To our simple minds he was coming to all the wrong conclusions so he was labelled as having SLD.

As a parent, I don't know if Laurence should be in a special school learning how to use a tin opener or whether he should be outside learning how to skin and cook a rabbit. I know which he would prefer, but either way I could be selling him short. Perhaps he should be studying in a special research facility looking into things that I cannot begin to imagine. With the right handling, he would like that too.

Could the next Einstein be profoundly autistic, communicating through some unknown language? We just don't know, as we are already lost in the knowledge gap. Unable to communicate properly with these children, we are forced to make them learn our primitive and yet complex verbal communication. Their unique insights are lost as we drag them down to our level.

The American military's quest for inter-species communication in order to be ready for ET might have an interesting spin-off. If they learn to communicate with dolphins then a dolphin might be able to translate for a profoundly autistic Einstein. With humans mastering the universal language, other species in the galaxy might start communicating with us, leading to the solution of all our problems. Ha!

A flight of fantasy, but it would make a good film, especially set against the backdrop of our polluted planet's plight. I can't help feeling that we are in a race. It's the human race versus Mother Nature and evolution. So far we have managed to keep our heads in front, avoiding epidemics and disasters, but we now seem to be lagging behind. We need a leap forward to get our heads back in front.

Win or lose, the future may well be autistic, and Mother Nature knows that.

Depending on who you believe, the number of plant, insect and animal extinctions is somewhere between ten and a thousand per week. In reality we have no idea. Whoever is right, in geological time this era will be seen as a mass extinction event. If we are to be one of the few species to survive this mass extinction event, then the future is in our own hands.

We are producing children who are finely tuned to survive ferally after the collapse of our civilisation or to give us scientific insights into the reality of our environment. They are children blessed with the potential to make our world a better place to live in, but they are born into a polluted world without the appropriate culture to nurture the gifts that come with their neurological conditions.

They are born into our dog-eat-dog patriarchal culture and we try to force these square pegs into the neatly rounded slots in our education system. We know they won't fit but we keep trying because they have to fit in with our society. We can only see their disability as they fail to fit into the round slots; we are not looking at how we can exploit their sharp edges.

So far we have found that the best way to deal with these sharp edges is to wear them down with comprehensive and intensive ABA programmes. There are plenty of different types of ABA in this country nowadays. If you find the right style of ABA for your child, then the child will have a great chance of fitting in with our society.

But are these children attaining their full potential? I would suggest that a dog on an ABA programme could learn some things quicker than an autistic child. We know that our children are more intelligent than dogs, so we also know that the ABA teaching styles are still not right.

While we work to our agenda, hammering these children into our society, we only learn how to hammer in better ways. If we are to learn anything of value we must start working to their agenda. I don't profess to know what that is, but we do know where to start.

Shortly after birth, autistic babies' brains seem to grow much faster than those of normal children. With all those extra synapses craving stimulation, parents are hopelessly unprepared for their demands and needs. Bizarrely, the experts view this spurt of brain growth as damage.

As we no longer measure the growth of babies' heads, a money-saving measure, we no longer have the means to recognise these children early and so we fail to stimulate their enlarged brains. It should come as no surprise that this underused part of the brain fails to work properly.

In Laurence's case the start line was before six months when Ana was struggling to cope with his non-stop demands. A second mum trained in autism was needed to relieve the strain and stimulate his rapidly growing brain. By eighteen months, a second dad was needed as I started to fail Laurence as well. It wasn't because we were inadequate, it was simply because Laurence had us labelled as his cook, cleaner, dresser, chauffeur and armchair playstation.

He needed much more.

Born into a matriarchal social structure or even a large extended family, we might have been able to plug the gaps with aunts and uncles, but sooner or later he would have needed professional guidance. We had nobody else to turn to so we turned to social services. They procrastinated for over a year while he slipped into the black hole of autistic behaviours if only to prove that autism equals bad behaviour.

I would suggest that when we start dealing with autistics properly their need to express themselves with bad behaviour will disappear.

When he was finally introduced to the professionals, he quickly established their function and purpose and interacted well.

He responded to the teachers as the teachers expected—namely, like a child with SLD. The teachers are compelled to follow the National Curriculum while educating the children to fit into our society. Their efforts are aimed at helping the disabilities, which is fine, but there is no time for exploring savant gifts and special senses are trampled underfoot in the rush towards the National Curriculum and normality.

The knowledge gap yawns in front of us but, sadly, we are learning nothing.

14

Toxins

All through Laurence's childhood, we were indoctrinated with the idea that because he was developing differently he was damaged or disabled. Yet as Laurence reached his teens I could see plenty of differences but no sign of any damage.

However, it is clear that there are many autistic children who have been damaged. It should not come as a surprise that these finely tuned children are the first to suffer from modern pollutants. These children have senses tuned to a degree that we can only imagine, and they might even be in contact with senses that we cannot begin to imagine.

It would appear that finely tuned and apparently normal children are also susceptible to these pollutants, which are as diverse as vaccinations, foodstuffs and fluorescent lighting. Their intoxicating effects produce similar behaviours to Laurence's sensory inspired behaviours. They are called autistic behaviours so all the children are labelled autistic, even though we know that their behaviours are caused by a wide range of environmental, dietary and sensory factors.

A label of regressive autism does no favours for these children. It gives the authorities an excuse to do nothing, as autism is incurable despite all the evidence suggesting that some of these 'autistic' children respond very favourably to some interventions.

Shamefully, it is left to the parents to haphazardly explore interventions and discover if they are among the lucky ones to find a 'cure' or more often an alleviation of symptoms.

We had done just that.

Looking for clues to Laurence's condition, I had explored the case against these toxins. We had seen magic bullets everywhere but they were all for other people's children. That's life.

I consider myself blessed to have two healthy children, even though Laurence is sometimes a bit too healthy. I cannot begin to understand what it would be like to have Laurence with a debilitating illness to cope with as well. However, having followed the story of the poisoned autistics, I couldn't resist having my say on the subject.

I followed the MMR story from a curious and impartial perspective, as it had not harmed my kids. The controversy had rumbled on over the last decade, but it appeared that matters would soon be resolved. Dr Andrew Wakefield had claimed that he had found the first evidence for a possible connection between autism and the MMR vaccine and now the Prime Minister Tony Blair had refused to state whether his own son Leo had received his MMR jab. I thought that at last there would be the political will to sort this mess out.

Parents across the country were now forced to think about the safety of vaccinations. To give their healthy child a vaccination for the greater good of the entire population requires an act of faith that the government and the manufacturer have ensured that the risks to their child are minimal. People's faith had been severely tested with recent government assurances like 'Mad cow disease does not pose a threat to human health' still fresh in the memory.

As each side in the MMR debate rubbished the other side's research, people didn't know whom to believe, but they did know that there were a lot more autistic children around now than when they were young. People were so confused they even asked me for advice, presumably because I have an autistic child.

I have always been pro-vaccination and I feel that we have a moral obligation to behave responsibly for the greater good. I have always emphasised that the risks of anything going wrong are remote despite all the publicity. I also explained that there were still risks of autism with single vaccines or through a natural infection of measles. In other words, it's a lottery.

At the same time, it can't hurt to be cautious about possible causes for concern, so I encouraged people to consider all aspects of their own lives while deciding what path to follow.

It is known that older parents are more likely to have a child with autistic tendencies and there are strong indications of a genetic link so I'd suggest they look closely and honestly at their own families and circumstances for signs of prior autism.

A colleague at work had expressed concerns about his own son. The boy had been very ill and he had spent several sleepless nights watching over him in hospital. It was a serious infection but they pumped him full of antibiotics and he got over it. However, less than a week after his son had left the hospital he received notification that his son's MMR was due. His GP had assured him there was nothing to worry about, but my friend wasn't so sure.

I felt it was important that he followed his natural instincts on this matter. He knew his son better than his GP ever could and his instinctive desire to delay the MMR to give his son's young body a chance to recover from the recent onslaught of antibiotics seemed eminently more sensible than the GP's message of 'carry on regardless'.

The GP was only following the rules, but the needs of the individual are often ignored these days because of the need to fulfil GPs' quotas. When parents can't trust their GP's advice they begin to lose their faith in the system.

Now if Tony Blair had come to me for advice I would have had to agree with their choice of path. They are ageing parents and already have an established family. They should have no financial worries, so Mum's body might have been tempted to experiment with an evolutionary special child.

Tony Blair did what was right for his family and he deserves applause for sticking to the task, as the pressure on him to endorse the MMR jab must have been enormous.

It was what he did afterwards that was such a kick in the teeth for many parents across the country.

He did nothing.

He hid behind his son's privacy, which was a tenuous argument considering every child is supposed to have one, so it could only be a matter of privacy if he didn't have the triple jab. I suppose it was all you could expect from a solicitor, but as the Prime Minister, he had the power to do something about it. He had the power to launch an inquiry with terms of reference that were acceptable to both sides in the argument so that all parents would know what was best for their children.

Instead he spent even more of the taxpayers' money campaigning that the MMR was safe. The parents lost another chunk of faith in their government, as they perceived it as not keeping its end of the bargain to ensure that risks were being kept to a minimum. Immunisation rates continued to fall.

In a sensible society both my colleague and the Blair family should have been able to go to their GP to receive the single vaccines as soon as possible to alleviate their specific worries and to ensure that the children were protected as quickly as possible.

By depriving parents of this opportunity for peace of mind, the State encourages parents to delay having this vaccination—to delay until they can afford to go private or to delay until they go on holiday to France or just to delay and then not bother at all.

If immunisation rates continue to fall then soon children will be killed and severely disabled through outbreaks of measles. The government will say, 'I told you so' and then roll out another 'independent' study that proves the MMR really is safe.

It is not the government's job to prove that the MMR is safe. That is the job of the drug companies who should be spending their profits proving to us that their product is safe. It is the government's job to find out what is happening to these damaged children who now number in their thousands.

It is outrageous that this government says it's not the MMR that damaged them so therefore we are not looking any further. If it's not the MMR then what is it? This government should be just as keen to find the underlying cause of this mystery as the parents, but the Prime Minister shamefully did nothing.

What was causing these apparently normal toddlers who were sailing past their developmental milestones to suddenly deteriorate and regress? The parents generally noticed a change in their normally bright children during the weeks after the vaccination. Parents spoke of losing their children as they lost their vocabulary and withdrew into their own world. They were not autistic like Laurence. They were normal children and now they were sick. Parents commonly reported the onset of chronic bowel disorders and epilepsy. Their children were in pain. Many parents reported constant screaming, crying and terror in the eyes of their innocents as the effects of the toxins hit their brains. Is it any wonder that they withdraw from their new painful, frightening world and they commonly develop autistic behaviours as a result?

Can these children really be expected to behave normally?

These conditions are complex and the confused parents have to travel to many different experts before they eventually receive any answers. After years of searching, a diagnosis of regressive autism with other medical complications does not answer the parents' questions.

The studies that the government is keen to quote from all monitor adverse reactions for up to only three weeks after the vaccination, so they do not pick up on these delayed neurological reactions and consequently the vaccine gets a clean bill of health.

Originally it was just a parental guess that the MMR was involved—call it parental instinct. These parents found that there were many other parents who had the same instinctive feelings.

One mother's search for help with her autistic son's bowel problems led her to Dr Wakefield's office. Dr Wakefield was a distinguished gastroenterologist who had built his reputation working on inflammatory bowel diseases like Crohn's disease. His research was already pointing at the measles virus as prime suspect in his inflammatory bowel disease patients. At that time he had no interest in autism and no interest in vaccinations.

He and his team looked at the boy solely because of his bowel problems and their initial examination found what looked like Crohn's disease. They also found traces of measles protein in his gut. They put the child on an experimental diet that was being designed for Crohn's patients and the results were startling.

Dr Wakefield and his team found that by treating his bowel problems they also appeared to be improving his autistic behaviours. His mother joyfully reported that he had smiled and even giggled for the first time in months.

When you consider the effects that alcohol and drugs going into the stomach have on the brain, it is reasonable to suggest that a leaky gut disease could end up poisoning the brain and therefore creating the autistic behaviours.

You didn't have to be a world-class gastroenterologist to discover this. Some parents had already discovered that by adjusting their child's diet they could alleviate some of the bowel problems and some of the autistic behaviours. These dietary interventions were circulated by word of mouth at first and then they achieved mass circulation through the Internet. Improved communications meant more parents heard of the successes and failures.

It was kitchen science; parents had to learn their E numbers and new words like gluten and casein, but it was a lot more helpful to the parents then the advice offered by the health professionals.

A diagnosis of autism doesn't help these children at all. The experts don't want to encourage false hopes for a condition that is considered incurable. But they are not autistic; they just show the symptoms of autism. They show the same frustrated behaviours as the naturally autistic children do in their confused world.

These children were poisoned by an unknown substance, around the time of their MMR injection, which gave them assorted painful bowel disorders, which in turn led to the obsessive routines and destructive and hyperactive behaviours that we associate with autism.

If only it were as simple as a gluten-free or casein-free diet equals an antidote to the poison. All children are different, so parents have to mix and match different diets and supplements to find what works best for their child.

Although a few parents report a cure from using these diets, most parents need professional help to fetch their children back. Unless you can afford to pay, that help can be hard to find and yet it would seem eminently sensible to try to return these children to their parents as quickly as possible. The less time they spend lost on the autistic spectrum the better, with possibly less long-term damage.

As soon as one of these children appears they should be put on a food-allergy testing programme and the parents given professional advice on the best diet for their child. Trying all the possible interventions at this time is much more important than ensuring that the child has had all its vaccinations. However, the State's efforts are solely directed at proving that it wasn't the MMR that poisoned this child.

Perhaps these poisoned autistics and the natural autistics do have something in common after all. Both sets of families have to get on with it, despite the worst efforts of the State with its offers of a lifetime of disability, no answers and no hope.

Wherever you find the measles virus there will be a small number of children who will die or develop serious disabilities like autism and brain damage. There is no escape.

Even the Victorians observed that a small number of children developed Heller's syndrome shortly after an infection of measles. Heller's syndrome is now called childhood disintegrative disorder. Typically these children develop normally until about the age of two, when they start regressing and develop behaviours indistinguishable from classic autism.

They sound very similar to our modern-day poisoned autistics, but how could the measles virus have poisoned our children after being vaccinated against the disease? The experts will have to slug out the answer to this as they slowly uncover the truth, but nobody seems in a hurry to do so. In the meantime, what should a good parent do?

In the sixties, seventies and eighties, the single measles vaccine also had a small number of parents complaining of bowel, development and behavioural problems arising after the vaccination.

JABS (Justice Awareness and Basic Support) told me that since the introduction of the MMR in the late eighties the number of parents complaining of adverse reactions had gone up a hundredfold compared with the numbers who were complaining about the single vaccine reactions.

So how safe is this MMR? No vaccine is 100 per cent safe. The drug companies acknowledge that there can be mild reactions to the jab and on occasion there are more serious adverse reactions that can give rise to life-threatening conditions. The government says the MMR is the safest option and cites the millions of doses being dispensed in an ever-increasing number of countries around the world as proof of its safety.

However, the government refuses to give out any figures on the claims settled by the Vaccine Damage Payment Unit (VDPU) for the MMR vaccination. It does seem suspicious that the official number of MMR damaged children is an official secret. (The VDPU was set up in 1979 after hundreds of children were left brain-damaged from an early whooping cough vaccine.)

Clearly there is a massive difference of opinion between JABS and the government over the safety of this vaccine. Maybe we should look to America, a country that puts a price on everything, for a more objective evaluation.

In the USA, vaccine manufacturers pay a tax on each jab. The rate of tax on each vaccine is determined by a sliding scale of risk. The higher the risk of a damages claim, the higher the tax rate. The MMR vaccination attracts a tax of $4.44 per jab compared with the polio vaccination, which attracts a tax of just 29 cents per jab.

It would seem that the obvious option is to return to the single vaccine as soon as possible, but the Japanese experience is cited as the reason for not going down that path. Japan started giving its children the MMR in 1989, one year after the UK. Like the UK they also had the original dodgy version of the MMR and like us they didn't stop until 1992 after many children were made seriously ill. Unlike the UK, the Japanese decided not to take the new improved MMR mark two.

They went back to the single measles jab, but confidence in the vaccination programme had plummeted. Outbreaks of measles followed and the subsequent fatalities were running about one per month over the next five years. The situation has improved since then; vaccination rates have risen, but a few children are still dying.

Japan should be a warning to all parents wanting to rush back to single vaccines, but it should also be a warning to our government about the perils of declining confidence in the vaccination programme.

It should be noted that Japan is still experiencing an increase in autism rates, but it does seem to be lower than the increases being experienced in the West.

Is this the ultimate trade-off—the single vaccines with outbreaks of measles and the inevitable small number of fatalities versus the triple vaccine and the large numbers of bowel disease and autistic features?

I can't believe that somebody hasn't done these sums already. Faceless experts weighing up the number of permanent disabilities and fatalities inflicted by measles compared with the severity of the disabilities inflicted by the MMR. At the end of the day autism isn't considered to be fatal, at least not in the civilised world, so the MMR wins the vote.

The MMR is the safest.

But autism does destroy lives and it can also destroy the families around them.

I think I could just about live with this if I was convinced that the people doing the sums were fully independent and not in any way involved with the vaccine manufacturers. But we cannot know that, as they are faceless people doing sums that don't officially exist.

The statistical case against the MMR does appear flimsy. Autism was on the increase before the MMR came along. If the MMR was responsible for an increase in autism, then after nationwide coverage of the MMR we would expect the number of autism cases to level off, but the graph continues upward to this day. At the same time, I cannot believe that thousands of parents are wrong. At least some of them must be right, so there must be some unidentified third factor.

All of the government's 'proofs' are based on studies comparing general populations with and without the MMR. They all show that there is no appreciable difference, but they cannot show whether the MMR is having a disproportionate effect on a small minority of the population. This is what the parents claim.

For example, if a drug manufacturer conducted a lot of surveys into the effects of a tablet on the general population it may well show that the medicine was safe. However, the evidence provided by our own eyes would soon alert us if this tablet adversely affected just the West Indian part of the population. In the case of autism, we cannot easily see which part of our young population is being disproportionately affected.

Maybe the MMR is picking on the most sensitive finely tuned part of the population. In which case it is picking on the Henry Cavendishes of the future, and we are depriving future generations of their finest minds. Unless we start applying our finest minds to the problem of identifying these persecuted children, soon there may well be no super minds around to sort it out in the future.

The MMR seems to have been unfortunate in that other causes of autism have been on the increase at the same time. The public has therefore seen an explosion of autism around them while listening to the only debate in town, the debate on MMR. They have created their own opinion because they no longer have faith in what the government experts are saying to them.

It may not be the increasing autism rates that finally force out the truth about the MMR. Maybe it will be the likes of Dr Wakefield, who, with no interest in vaccines or autism, is simply trying to find an explanation for the massive increase in the incidence of inflammatory bowel disease. In the 1930s, it was one per 100,000. In the 1980s it was one per 10,000 and it is now a frightening three per 1,000. They are also seeing these bowel diseases in very young children for the first time.

These figures alone were enough to alarm Dr Wakefield and his fellow researchers. He had no proof that the MMR was in any way connected with this, but he was concerned by the direction his research was taking. He felt a moral duty to alert the government to his suspicions and the possible consequences.

Of course, nobody wanted Dr Wakefield to be right but the character assassination that followed did not bode well for rational argument. It was a classic case of shooting the messenger; Dr Wakefield was professionally ostracised and forced to continue his research in America. The only beneficiaries of this are the American children now receiving treatment in his new clinic.

The government's position is clear—it will defend the MMR until it is forced to say otherwise. Any future attack on the MMR will have to come with firm proof or it will be pilloried, rejected and ignored. Some might say I am being cynical, but that is precisely what our government has just done in another matter concerning a different vaccine.

The MMR only came second in the American table of tax rates for vaccinations. Top of the risk table was the three-in-one DTP, which protects children against diphtheria, tetanus and whooping cough. This vaccination is given at two months, at three months and again at four months. The vaccine contains thimerosal, which has been used for over fifty years to prevent vaccines from spoiling. Thimerosal contains small amounts of mercury.

It is well known that mercury poisoning mimics the symptoms of autism and can cause learning difficulties and even brain damage in children and adults. However, the quantity involved was so small that all agreed that there was no risk to the children.

Over the years the number of vaccinations given to our children has increased dramatically and the age at which we start to vaccinate children has fallen too. It used to be common practice not to vaccinate babies less than six months old.

Eventually somebody (not the drug manufacturers) remembered those tiny amounts of mercury and they added up all the doses that today's children receive. The combined total of mercury now became a worry and the Americans ditched the DTP in 1999 without waiting for conclusive proof. Canada, Japan and most of the countries in western Europe also stopped using these vaccines, but the UK steadfastly refused to change.

In March 2004, in response to the latest research showing that children given the DTP were up to six times more likely to receive a diagnosis of autism than those given mercury-free jabs, a Department of Health spokesman stated, 'Vaccine manufacturers are actively developing research programmes to replace or reduce the levels of thimerosal.'

Clearly he was under the delusion that most of the developed world, having banned DTP already, was currently unprotected against these diseases.

He went on to state that other (older) studies had shown thimerosal to be safe.

Then, five months after stating it was safe and five years after the USA ditched it, in August 2004 the government announced that the DTP was to be withdrawn in a couple of months' time, to be replaced by a mercury-free five-in-one jab. Although it was long overdue it still had to be great news that we were finally getting rid of a totally unnecessary toxin.

The government insisted that this change was because of the new polio vaccine not because the DTP was unsafe. The government's position was clear: it defended the DTP until it was convenient for the drug manufacturers to change and it ignored the mounting evidence that the rest of the world was seeing.

When the health spokesman continued by extolling the virtues of the super new five-in-one jab with improved polio, people couldn't be blamed for lacking faith. But it would be criminal incompetence if a government failed to convince the public that this new jab was better than the potentially poisonous DTP.

Although the MMR contains no mercury, it might also benefit from the withdrawal of DTP and restore some of its tarnished image. Many parents and some researchers believe that some children with a genetic predisposition to autism are affected by the MMR because the mercury in the DTP damaged them somehow. It could be that mercury is the mysterious third factor.

After all, while the MMR vaccination rates were falling, the rates for other vaccines, including the DTP, were going up, and at the same time the rate of autism went up as well.

There is some research that has shown some autistic children do not have the same levels of mercury in their hair as normal children. They appear unable to excrete the toxic heavy metals safely away into their hair like normal people. The inference is that these heavy metals are therefore accumulating elsewhere and poisoning the children's bodies and minds.

If you cannot afford to pay, pay, pay then it's a very long battle to get help for these children. The trek from specialist to specialist stretches into years as appointments are awaited. All too often it is left to the parents and their kitchen science to try to help their children.

Detoxification plans can be found on the Internet for parents who are convinced their children are suffering from mercury poisoning or some other heavy-metal poisoning. These plans range from foods with detoxifying properties and special teas to more technical plans like chelation therapy that shouldn't be attempted without proper medical advice.

The Department of Health seems unwilling to help these children.

Society must accept that most of the time it is the parents who have done their homework and they are the experts regarding their own children.

There is another group of young children showing signs of poisoning. They are diagnosed as having ADHD, attention deficit and hyperactivity disorder. Many parents have found their ADHD children are being poisoned by chemicals with E numbers or through a food intolerance or from a deficiency in some vitamins and nutrients.

Our grandparents swore by a daily dose of cod liver oil and now several recent studies have shown that fish oil supplements can produce an improvement in attention span and behaviour.

The medical profession scoffs at these old wives' tales and follows the drug companies' advice. They offer chemical coshes like Ritalin or Risperadol in an attempt to modify the sick child's behaviour rather than expensive tests to identify the cause of the disorder. The use of Ritalin and other similar drugs has doubled in the last four years. If one of these coshes works then the drug companies have a customer for life.

We have already seen how much guesswork is involved with prescribing these drugs and even less is known about the long-term effects these drugs have on children's brains. Developing brains are profoundly different from the mature brains that a lot of these drugs are tested on. There are increasing concerns about how drugs might alter the structure and chemistry of these young developing brains and how they possibly trade one mental illness for a more serious one in later life.

Researchers studying young rats on Ritalin described a state of 'learned helplessness' on reaching adulthood. Is this what we want for these children, a lifetime of dependency?

Just like with the other forms of poisoning, the ADHD children do not respond all in the same way. Some respond to the different dietary interventions, but some of them do not respond to any.

The big question is what to do with the children who do not respond. Should they be given Ritalin as a last resort? The idea fills me with horror.

These children who struggle to sit still in class, let alone pay attention to the teacher, are being fed a drug which is pharmacologically very similar to cocaine so that they don't disrupt the class. Are these the same few children who have appeared in all generations and who have required the threat or use of the cane for them to sit still and pay attention in class?

Although I have occasionally smacked Laurence I am against corporal punishment and I have never smacked Bianca. However, I have often found the threat of punishment valuable and as Laurence's understanding improved, the punishments could become subtler. Laurence learnt acceptable boundaries to his behaviour, but what does a child learn under a chemical cosh?

Like Bianca, the vast majority of children do not require the threat of violence to behave normally, but what about the rights of the children who do? Are they being coshed so that the majority of the children can continue to be educated without the threat of violence in the school's disciplinary procedure?

How did we get into this mess?

The use of drugs can never be considered a positive intervention in controlling autistic behaviour in children. The use of drugs on children is an admission of failure. Their brains must be allowed to develop naturally so they can achieve their maximum potential while we find positive ways to help them cope.

Autistic adults with mature brains may well benefit from the use of some drugs, but the decision to use them should be based on a childhood of trying to find the cause of the problem behaviours first.

We cannot blame the drug companies for pushing their drugs and vaccines. They have a business to run which is driven by the need to make profits. They are continuously looking for new applications and markets for their existing and new products.

With increasing numbers of poisoned autistic people around, the potential market for drugs is becoming more valuable. No doubt the industry is searching for improved behaviour-controlling drugs to help these people, as that is their business. They are definitely not searching for natural remedies, which are unpatentable and therefore unprofitable.

This story is depressingly familiar. The Department of Health and the Department of Education have the same motto: Autism requires comprehensive specialist assessment. All parties know that this can take years, inevitably causing great frustration for the parents who instinctively know that, in fact, autism requires intensive positive early intervention. Whether that intervention is an educational resource or a detoxification plan, it needs to be delivered early to be effective.

The blame for this inertia lies squarely on the shoulders of governments on both sides of the Atlantic who are swimming in the profits of the pharmaceutical industry. Their negligence in allowing biased under-reporting of research data is criminal. The feeble acquiescence of governments and the medical profession to the pharmaceutical industry has shattered the faith of the public in these matters.

Tony Blair had an opportunity to sort out this mess but he did nothing.

The experts are learning nothing.

The parents must fight on alone, following their instincts as they look for the next piece in the poison puzzle.

15

Happy Days and Bad Days

The summer of 2002 was a very busy time for me at work, covering other people's holidays and illnesses. There were no gaps left for me to take a holiday, so I booked a holiday for the half-term break in October to make it up to the children.

The start of the new school year presented its own problems. Laurence was leaving the reception class and starting in a new, larger class. He had a new teacher but he knew most of the children from when they passed through the reception class. Although he had had many practice sessions during the previous term it was still a big leap for him. He was happy with his new class, so I could only hope that he could cope with all the extra excitement.

Bianca was also starting in a new class, in a new school. She seemed too young to be starting secondary education. It was the beginning of the end of her childhood. With Laurence requiring constant attention, it was often difficult to give her the attention she deserved.

We had the normal battle to get her a place in a good school. Ana's top priority was that Bianca should have a Catholic education and I had no problem with that. Unfortunately the Catholic school in their parish was miles away.

Ana was free to take Bianca to school in the mornings but she wouldn't be able to pick her up, as she had to stay in and wait for the arrival of Laurence's school bus in the afternoons.

Bianca's new school wasn't far from the area in which I worked. I juggled my hours at work so that I finished a bit earlier on a couple of days a week and shared the after-school run with a friend of Ana's who also had a daughter in the school. It was tough; the hours would have to be made up somehow and I couldn't possibly start work earlier because I still had to take Laurence into school in the mornings. I had become a fully fledged school-run parent.

294

Laurence's school entrance was in a quiet residential road. There were not many cars delivering their children like me, as most of the children arrived by minibus. Although the small road was often blocked for a short while by all the minibuses waiting to pull in and offload, it was well organised and very safe.

I was in for a shock when I picked up Bianca and her friend from their new school. It didn't help matters that the school entrance was on a busy main road and there was another school right next door disgorging its pupils at the same time. The free-for-all melee and blatant disregard for child safety was shocking.

There were yellow zigzag lines with 'no parking' clearly painted on the road outside the schools. Those instructions were obeyed for most of the day, but half an hour before the excited children leave school the no-parking zone fills with four by fours and people carriers waiting to pick up their children.

As the children poured out of the school some inevitably wanted to cross the road. They poked their heads out from between the vehicles to spot a gap in the traffic to run to the central reservation while the parked vehicles were also manoeuvring to join the traffic.

It was a recipe for a tragedy. I couldn't look, and that was the trouble—nobody was looking. The council had painted the yellow lines and the school had sent letters warning the parents of the dangers so they had done their bit and covered their backs. Not once during that winter did I see a traffic warden outside the school and, come to think about it, I didn't see a policeman walk by either, although they did occasionally flash past in their cars with sirens blaring.

No wonder we are one of the worst countries in Europe for road accidents involving child pedestrians. In 2002 the toll was 79 children dead and 2,800 seriously injured.

I used to park in a side turning beside the school. There was always plenty of space there and it did the children no harm to walk for a couple of minutes, no matter how hard the exertions of the school day had been.

Looking back, I am so pleased that I managed to make this time for Bianca. We would drop off her friend and then park up around the corner from Ana's house and chat. We didn't park outside Ana's house in case Laurence's bus was delayed. He would have become distressed if he saw us before he went into Mummy's house. He would have worried that his routine was going to be disrupted.

After a hard day at school he liked to take a refreshing bath while Mum prepared his dinner. While we discussed Bianca's day and homework we often saw Laurence's bus go by and we watched him dash from the bus into Ana's house. It was clear that he didn't like these transitions. He would dash into school in the mornings and he would dash into my place as well.

Whilst driving him home I tried to get information out of him regarding his school day, with little success. He didn't like to mix his school world with Daddy's world or Mummy's world. I had a copy of his timetable so I knew what subjects he had each day, but it was impossible to find out what he had done in the lessons. Like all teenagers he had learnt how to be evasive.

I would ask him what he had done in geography today and he would reply, 'Hard work.' I couldn't get past the 'hard work' barrier without upsetting him. To him it was enough that I should know that he had done 'hard work' and that he had been 'a good boy' while doing it. His new teacher was writing good reports in his home schoolbook so I believed them.

During the summer months Laurence spent most of his time after school outdoors in the garden or on the farm. He liked to help some of the horse owners, although communication was still strictly on his terms and he often ran away if they spoke to him. He liked to help mucking out the stables. He could use a pitchfork to pick up the mucky straw and he could tip it into the wheelbarrow, but he insisted on meticulously picking off any bits of muck that got stuck to the pitchfork.

He liked to wheel the barrow around to the dung heap but he couldn't understand the difference between running into a wall and a parked car. To him both required going back and trying again. Two angry car owners and two hundred pounds later I banned him from pushing a wheelbarrow.

Sometimes he liked to sit on the garden step like a gnome, watching and trying to understand this microcosm of life going about their daily business. From his strange perspective the movements of the humans and the horses would have been of equal significance and they would have been equally perplexing for him.

Wherever he went he took his tennis ball with him. It was still his reason to go somewhere, but his ball control skills had improved dramatically as a result. He had a tennis racquet and had developed excellent fine motor control of the ball. I noticed him trying to hit cracks in the concrete to make the ball bounce erratically. He was a good shot.

His PE teacher also commented on Laurence's ball-control skills. One day she watched Laurence walk up a flight of stairs while bouncing two basketballs simultaneously. You should try it.

We all wanted to capitalise on Laurence's ball skills but it seemed impossible. His PE teacher tried to encourage him to shoot baskets in the gym. Laurence would happily throw the basketball against a wall as it would bounce straight back to him, and he could dribble the length of the court at speed, but he didn't like shooting a basket as the ball could bounce anywhere off the hoop. He didn't like to give away possession of his ball. Likewise, he wouldn't hit a tennis ball to somebody else. He could skilfully hit a line on the tennis court with the tennis ball but he had no understanding of the ball being in or out.

As the winter evenings drew in Laurence still liked to play outside with his ball and, weather permitting, I allowed him to. I watched him throw the ball high up into the black sky and then catch it as it fell out of the gloom. There was no street lighting, so he relied on the lights from the farmhouse windows and the stables. There was definitely nothing wrong with his night vision.

When there was nothing to watch on TV we listened to music. He was still only interested in listening to Bob Dylan. Originally I only had a Bob Dylan greatest hits CD but my collection of his music had grown as I tried to vary what we listened to. I watched him as we listened, hoping to discover why he liked Bob Dylan so much. He did seem to get excited by some of the mouth organ pieces but overall I think it was Bob Dylan's voice that fascinated him. The rhyming tempo of his clear lyrics seemed to strike a chord inside Laurence. I had to agree with him, there was nobody quite like Bob Dylan.

When we listened to the radio his musical preferences were clear as he would say, 'Music up' whenever a song he liked came on. For a while Bianca and Laurence shared the same musical taste, liking the Spice Girls and S Club 7, but while her taste developed he remained unashamedly stuck on bubblegum pop. His favourite radio station was Magic, with its soft-pop mixture of old and new songs.

Like most kids of his age he chose to spend more and more time alone in his bedroom. I often heard him holding one-sided conversations in there. He was practising and he spoke much better when he was alone than when other people were around. He yearned for the flowing conversations he heard other people having. When he was amongst people there was too much information coming in for him to concentrate on getting the correct words out. The result of this was Laurence spewing out pre-recorded phrases and questions that had no relevance to the situation or to what he originally wanted to say.

It broke my heart when he ran towards me excitedly saying, 'Daddy, Daddy, Daddy,' and then after a painful pause he would blurt out something like, 'Qantas goes to Australia.' I knew that wasn't what he was running to tell me, that wasn't news. I pleaded with him, 'Tell Daddy,' and gave him every encouragement, but his original words were lost in his mind. I knew those words and ideas were in there somewhere, I would just have to get better at catching them when they bubbled towards the surface.

On the occasions when I did interrupt him in his room I found him playing with a jigsaw or tapping his way through one of his coffee-table books on transport. I felt guilty for disturbing his peace, as I understood how much he needed this quiet time. It certainly wasn't wasted time.

All through his schooldays I didn't try to continue his schoolwork in the home. There was always a lot to learn and talk about around the home so we tended not to talk about schoolwork. That suited Laurence, but now he had to step up a gear in his new class—he had homework.

Depressingly, the handwriting exercises given for homework were the same old exercises that he had been doing for years. His new teacher had correctly identified his weakness in this area and now the problem was in my lap.

Laurence was happy to trade a few handwriting exercises in return for listening to Bob Dylan. He was very good at writing when he had a trail of dots to follow, but on a blank page he was hopeless. Despite the years of private tuition and the best efforts of all his excellent schoolteachers we totally failed to understand Laurence's problems with handwriting. He was physically capable; he could hold a pencil properly and had the manual dexterity to do all the exercises. But when he was presented with a sea of blank paper he froze. It seemed to me that he was frightened of something, but I have been unable to find out what it is.

Our battle to give Laurence an alternative means of communication to talking, that we could understand, had been long and hard.

Our best hope of success appeared to be with computers. Over the last year Laurence had made a quantum leap in his understanding in this area. He now understood the purpose of the mouse, keyboard and printer. He could type with one finger and he knows how to print out his words. So far he is only interested in writing the same words that he liked to talk about anyway, but he is still young and only just beginning to learn in this area. It seemed much more likely that he would be able to communicate through typing rather than writing.

Overall these were happy evenings and even more importantly they were calm evenings. We coexisted with a good understanding of what we expected of each other. I didn't expect of him things that he couldn't do, so he didn't seem disabled to me, he was just different.

Finishing work early to pick up Bianca meant that I had longer evenings with Laurence, but I had to catch up on the hours by working on Sunday mornings. This resulted in me taking the children on a tour of the shops each Sunday morning before going out somewhere in the afternoon. After that, we had time for a meal in a restaurant with the other divorced dads and their kids before taking Bianca back to her mum and Laurence back to my place ready for school in the morning. My weeks were bursting.

Although I had tried to avoid working on Sundays as much as possible, the children were no strangers to 'Daddy's workshops'. The staff had watched the children growing up through the years and Laurence knew them all.

Laurence loved going on these tours. He liked to climb all over and romp with the young lads who worked for the company. They didn't mind obliging him when he was younger, but he didn't under-stand how heavy he had become, so he still pestered them for horsey rides even though he was a solid thirteen-year-old.

At the onset of puberty Laurence developed a crush on a fifty-year-old cashier with blonde hair. He was besotted, but now he felt embarrassed about his feelings and he couldn't face her. Lil was a lovely lady who understood Laurence well and he knew that she always had a treat for him. He wrestled with the dilemma of how to get the treats without falling into her clutches, while Lil insisted on a kiss or a hug in return for her goodies. After a few months of this uneven battle Laurence decided that the price was too high and he opted to remain in the car when we visited Lil's shop.

Laurence knew that there was a fridge in the staff area in all the shops. These fridges often contained people's lunches so he was banned from them. But Laurence was an expert urban scavenger, so he volunteered to make everybody a cup of tea. They thought it was sweet of him to offer but it gave him an excuse for going to the fridge twice. He thoroughly cased the contents of the fridge when he took the milk out and he returned the milk when he thought nobody was looking.

The girls in one of the shops liked to make a fuss of their customers' dogs. They kept a packet of dog biscuits behind the counter. It didn't take long for Laurence to discover them. He liked dog biscuits; his favourite brand was Markies. He liked to gnaw away at the hard exterior to get at the dark bit inside. I knew it wouldn't do him any harm, and while my puppy sat quietly living up to his stereotype I was able to get my work done.

The half-term holiday came round quickly. We went to Puerto Rico on the island of Gran Canaria for our belated summer holiday. Our coach finally drove through a tunnel into a steep high-sided valley with hotels covering the hillsides at one o'clock in the morning.

'Imagine staying in a hotel right up there,' I said to Bianca, pointing up to the illuminated hotels right at the top of the mountain-side. As we dropped off small groups of holidaymakers at their hotels around the town, it became increasingly clear that that was exactly where we were staying.

I had hoped that the children would be exhausted and sleep late but there was no chance of that. It was a cloudy first day and we were in the clouds so we could see nothing from our lofty balcony.

The apartments were in rows and stuck to the side of the mountain. There were lots of these rows going down the mountainside. The outdoor swimming pool was down ten flights of stairs at the bottom of the hotel.

Standing beside the pool, we were now below the clouds and we could see the entire valley and bay below us for the first time. I grabbed the fence as my stomach turned queasy as the panorama spread out below us. It was a solid fence so I had no worries about safety. Not that Laurence was interested in the views—he only had eyes for the pool. It was a fair sized rectangular pool with a shower at each end. It was ideal for Laurence as he continued from where he left off in Tenerife.

He swam a length, had a shower, swam another length, and had another shower. Over the holiday he spent many happy hours swimming and hopping between the two showers. There was also a bar and covered area there so I was happy to watch over him while Bianca made some new friends.

I was relieved to find that we didn't have to go down into the valley for everything. There was a large commercial centre with shops, bars, restaurants and amusements on the top of our hill.

We decided to try Laurence on the crazy golf course.

He was so funny. He understood that he had to get the ball into the hole but he couldn't leave his ball alone. He played like he was playing hockey, running behind his ball tap tap tapping it towards the hole. Bianca was keeping the scores so she ran along behind him counting all the hits.

'Right, that is a score of twenty-three for Laurence on this hole,' she would proudly announce as she returned to the tee. He then had to stand around impatiently bouncing his golf ball waiting for us as we played this game more sedately. Bianca played very well—competitive Dad only just managed to beat her. That evening I got Bianca to add up Laurence's score. It was good practice for her maths skills.

We had beautiful sunny weather for the rest of the week. From our apartment balcony we could see a water park at the far end of the valley and that was where the children wanted to go.

It was smaller than Wet 'n' Wild in Florida, it didn't have a lazy river or wave pool, but it did have lots of slides. Laurence had been too scared to go on the slides in Florida so I was a bit surprised when he wanted to go to the top of the slides with Bianca. I gave her strict instructions not to try to force him to have a go.

There were about six lanes on this particular slide. Bianca sat down at the top and Laurence sat down in the lane beside her. He started examining the slide, carefully tapping the plastic around him. The other lanes filled up; the lifeguard blew his whistle and the kids jumped off. It was purely a reflex response from Laurence, who had no intention of jumping at that time, and he regretted it immediately. He desperately clawed at the slippery wet plastic to climb back up but gravity was too strong for him. To be fair, he quickly realised that he couldn't win and he set about trying to slow his descent with his hands and feet. He arrived at the bottom about thirty seconds after the other kids had splashed down.

He loved it. 'Go again,' he demanded immediately after clambering out of the water. They walked back to the top and this time he was ready for the whistle. It was still a controlled descent but he splashed into the water only about ten seconds behind the other kids.

He didn't want to stop and went round again and again. It wasn't long before he was splashing down a fraction of a second behind the other kids. Bianca went off to try some other slides while Laurence insisted on using the same lane of the same slide every time.

As he walked round and round I thought that his legs were going to ache the next day. I didn't mind as I always tried to give the children plenty of exercise while we were on holiday.

That afternoon Laurence seemed indefatigable. I lay on a sunbed watching him go round and round. Then suddenly he stopped half way up the hill. He lay down in the middle of the path, curled up and had a rest. He must have been exhausted. People had to step around and over him, but fortunately I could see that Bianca and a couple of her new friends were only a few yards behind him. They couldn't miss him. They pulled him up, put his arms around their necks and together they carried and pushed his bulk to the top of the hill. He slid straight back down and I was waiting with a towel. He didn't want to know—he wanted to go round again. I let him but decided that it was becoming an obsession and next time around I lured him away with the promise of a hot dog. He was happy to go in search of Bianca and the hot dog stall. After our snack, there was only an hour until closing time, so I let him ride on the slide again and again until it ran dry.

The children were not impressed with the local artificial beaches. They soon became bored, as there were no big waves like those they enjoyed in Crete. They wanted to go back to the water park, so we did. As this holiday was developing a water-park theme I booked us on a coach excursion to the island's largest water park.

The coach visited an allegedly authentic traditional market in the morning before taking us to the water park. As we pulled into the coach park we could see the waterslides snaking up into the hills. Part of this excursion was a visit to the pearl centre next door to the waterpark. A lady from the pearl centre stepped on board to give us an informative little chat on the local pearl industry. We all listened politely until Laurence's patience snapped.

'Time to go on the big slide now,' he said so that the entire coach could hear.

The astonished woman turned to Laurence. 'Have you heard a word I've said?' she asked.

Of course he hadn't and he didn't answer her either so she wisely chose to finish off her talk quickly. She ended her speech with a question for the kids. Bianca's hand shot up. I felt sorry for her, as I thought she had no chance of being picked sitting next to Laurence. Perhaps the woman wanted to teach Laurence a lesson, I don't know, but she did pick Bianca.

She got the answer right and won a lucky dip from a tank of oysters. They opened it up, cleaned it and presented her with the black pearl that was inside. It was a nice memento of the holiday for her.

To get to the rides in the park we had to filter through a darkened hut. They slipped a parrot on your shoulder, took a photo and whipped it off before you realised what was happening. It was a slick operation but not quick enough to catch Laurence. He ducked around and hid behind me as we went through so I only had to pay for two photos at the end of the day.

We wanted to go on the big slides but Laurence didn't want to, so Bianca went off to explore the hills while I watched Laurence switch between the lazy river and the wave pool.

It was another lovely day.

Each evening after getting cleaned up, we would go out to different restaurants for dinner. One evening we noticed some ice creams with sparklers being served at another table. Both the children wanted one of those and I told them they could, if they ate all their dinner, which they duly did. When our waiter served the ice creams with the sparklers lit, Laurence and his chair flew backwards.

The waiter instinctively pulled back, alarmed by Laurence's over-reaction. I had to calm the waiter and reassure him that it was OK to put the sparkling ice creams on the table. Laurence had learnt a lot about self-control over the last couple of years, but even though he knew what was coming he was unable to control his instinctive flight response on this occasion. Bianca laughed while Laurence slowly returned to the table as the sparklers fizzled out.

'Fireworks in the ice cream,' he informed us as I removed the spent sparklers before he could put one in his mouth. Laurence was special, he could make a meal memorable, he could make a dull day delightful and he made a holiday very special indeed.

We had a night flight home. Laurence was sad but he had lots of happy memories. He kept reminding us that he went 'on the white slide'. When we got home we found that he had worn a hole in the seat of his swimming trunks doing just that.

I realised that our holidays were autistic-friendly experiences. The routine of the journey was always the same, only the airline changed. Our daily routines were based around playing with water and eating food, which was easily understood and it suited Laurence to a tee. He relaxed. If travel broadens the mind then surely autistic children need travel more than most.

Laurence's teachers often commented on how well behaved he was when they were out and how well he learnt during hands-on situations. This is not uncommon with children like Laurence. Clearly current classroom environments are not suitable for teaching these children. Experienced teachers who understand this are always on the lookout for opportunities to get these children out of the classrooms and into more learning-friendly environments.

I suspect that during two weeks in a holiday environment with his teachers Laurence could learn more than in six months of working in the classroom.

A couple of weeks after the children returned to school it was the parents' evening at Laurence's school. I was looking forward to having a decent chat with his new teacher. We had exchanged a few words on a couple of mornings, but it was never a good time as she was always in a rush.

She was an experienced teacher of children with moderate learning difficulties. She was very pleasant, the sort of person that you couldn't help liking. However, I didn't like to hear what she had to say. There had been some behaviour problems.

I squirmed as she told me that the physical outbursts had returned. I was annoyed, as she hadn't mentioned any of this in the home schoolbook. She apologised and explained that she didn't want to worry me unnecessarily. She was confident that after further consultations with his old teacher and the headmaster they had a plan that would see him moving positively into the new year.

That night I spoke to Laurence. I threatened him with a return to his old class. He didn't like that idea. He liked his new class. He was proud of being in this big class with children of his own age. He assured me that he was a good boy in the classroom. I was convinced that he was trying to be good and I felt that, through his eyes, he thought he was.

The children had decided to spend Christmas with me again. My Christmas dinners were getting pretty good by now. Bianca told me so, she said that my cooking had improved a lot! Bless her, she never complained during those early culinary experiments.

I cooked the turkey slowly overnight so that the children awoke to its tantalising aroma. This wasn't the only torture that Laurence endured during Christmas time. The glittering chocolates on the Christmas tree teased him to eat them. I often caught him mesmerised like a cat watching goldfish swimming around in a bowl. He knew that I watched these chocolates as well. I knew that he escaped with a few as I found the silver foil casually thrown behind the toilet. He didn't have much of an idea regarding the disposal of evidence.

Another source of Yuletide torture for Laurence was nuts, or more precisely, nutcrackers. He loved cracking nuts and eking out the small rewards. Although he never seriously hurt his fingers, his strained expressions as he squeezed caused my hair to turn grey. I had searched for a safe way to crack nuts to no avail until a good friend came to the rescue.

The new nutcracker was a bit bigger than an eggcup and made of wood. There was a large wooden screw in the side which, when turned, crushed the nut in the cup with supposedly no mess but, much more importantly, it was safe and effective. This simple device transformed the nut-cracking experience for all of us, but it had been incredibly hard to find.

That Christmas Lil gave Laurence a present securely wrapped in a Christmas carrier bag. Knowing Lil, I had a fair idea of what the bag contained and I was also sure that Laurence knew what was inside as well, so I made him wait until Christmas Day before opening it.

It was the first present that he opened. It was packed with the sweets and crisps that Lil had noticed he liked during the year. Laurence was in heaven and saw no reason to open the other presents. This was what Christmas was all about for him: eating the contents of the Christmas stocking and presents in the morning, followed by eating the Christmas dinner and then Christmas tree chocolates and nuts, to see him through to eating the Christmas cake.

Left to his own devices he would have gorged the lot; it was my job to ration him over the length of the holiday so that he could enjoy it all. I think he understands that but that didn't stop him trying all his tricks continuously testing me to see if it was time for another tree chocolate or another satsuma. It was always time for another satsuma.

It was important to remember through all this that he wasn't always hungry; he just liked the oral stimulation that eating provided. Oral stimulation had always been important to Laurence. As a young child he continually munched on Lego bricks, books and his clothes. Over the years we have stopped him chewing these harmless items and he has turned to eating things like dog biscuits, cooking apples, lemons, curries and chilli sauces to satisfy his craving for more and more oral stimulation.

I always tried to tantalise his taste buds at Christmas time. This year Lil had done just that with her Christmas bag of goodies.

The new year and the new school term were filled with hope. Laurence was behaving well at home and the notes in the home schoolbook did not report any violent outbursts. There were reports of him struggling to stay on task or concentrate, but there were also plenty of reports that he had quite good days as well. He told me that he was a very good boy in class so I had reason to be hopeful that Laurence was finally settling into his new moderate-learning-difficulty environment.

That spring it became clear that the company I worked for was to be sold to a large multi-national company. My job was safe as I was being sold along with the rest of the staff, but I now had to fit in with my new employer's rota.

I could not continue to pick up Bianca after school, but I had seen her safely through the first dangerous winter and she had matured a lot in that time. However, I could continue to take Laurence to school as my new employer put me in a shop close to his school. It certainly made my life less stressful and I was keen to learn how to operate my new employer's modern computerised systems.

This was a difficult time for me, so I could be excused for taking my eye off the ball, but with the clarity of hindsight I should have questioned why I was receiving such mixed messages from Laurence and his teacher. Laurence thought that he was a saint and yet his teacher saw him as a sinner perpetually teetering on the edge of being naughty.

Laurence was behaving strangely, even by his eccentric standards. He was walking around with his eyes closed, he was walking backwards, and even more amusingly, he was walking sideways while looking up in the air in the opposite direction. He was doing this at home and at school in the classroom and the playground. His teacher was thoroughly perplexed by this behaviour so I offered her my opinion.

I felt this behaviour was puberty related. He still didn't understand that we didn't know what was on his mind. These days those thoughts were very embarrassing for him. I had seen him walking around me crablike and with his head in the air when he didn't want me to see his thoughts.

As I've explained before, he often covered his ears to block out words and therefore block out basic emotions. He still does it when he expects to be told off. With the onset of puberty he was finding it even harder to block out his new emotions, so he was resorting to covering his eyes as well.

Somebody once said that the eyes are the windows to the soul and I would add that autistics don't like people looking through those windows, especially at his age!

I suggested that she look in the opposite direction to him to see whose gaze he was avoiding. In my experience, it was usually a blonde female like Lil or an authority figure like me that he was avoiding.

The next parents' evening was a couple of weeks away and I was determined that this time I would talk about his academic work rather than his behaviour, but I didn't get the chance.

I got a phone call from the headmaster asking me to come in as soon as possible as there had been a serious incident. This wasn't the first time that I had been called in to see the head, but I realised that this time it was much worse.

He told me that in mid-lesson Laurence had jumped up and flown into a rage, dashing across the classroom sending desks and chairs flying before viciously assaulting a defenceless little girl by violently pulling her hair. I was horrified to hear how it took the combined might of the teaching assistants to subdue him and rescue the poor girl. She was shaken but not seriously hurt.

While the headmaster told me this, a subdued Laurence sat outside his office. It was school policy not to tell me who the victim was, but

I suspected that the parents knew who attacked their daughter. He did tell me what he was going to do and then he summoned Laurence into the room.

He was upset and nervous. The head knew Laurence well and he knew how to make his words penetrate and bother him. I watched Laurence squirm under the bombardment. I didn't say anything; I made sure that Laurence knew exactly how I felt through my devastated facial expression.

Laurence couldn't return to his class; he was temporarily placed in a class with older children and more robust teaching staff. They would be ready for him if he misbehaved again. He was to stay in that class while they investigated the incident. The facts seemed clear—it was a totally unprovoked attack, and there could be no justification for his actions. They were the actions of a vicious bully and the school was not going to accept such behaviour.

When the letter arrived it didn't actually say that Laurence was to be expelled but it was the only way that it could be read. It was full of regret that we had arrived at this situation. I was to meet the headmaster after the parents' evening to discuss their decision regarding the incident.

I decided that I would defend him to the best of my abilities even though his actions seemed indefensible. I understood that if the school decided that he had to go then no amount of arguments would prevail.

At home I couldn't get any information from Laurence. He would run away covering his ears saying, 'No, no, no. Laurence is a good boy now,' whenever I asked him about it. He was clearly full of remorse and he was also frightened by what had happened since. Laurence loved his school and all the people who went there to play with him every day, which made this time all the harder for both of us. He was desperately trying to ingratiate himself back into people's good books; he was on his best behaviour, as he didn't have the words to express his remorse in the normal way.

I wrote in the home schoolbook at this time, 'Laurence is very subdued at the moment. He fully understands that he is in the doghouse but what he doesn't understand is that he cannot get out of it.'

It seemed so very unfair.

On the night of the parents' evening, I had a plan and I also resolved to try to find out who was Laurence's victim. I visited his form teacher first. She was genuinely upset that it had worked out this way but explained that Laurence was just too strong for them.

She was absolutely right, there was no way that Laurence could return to this class and I was not going to try to defend him here. I looked at the pictures of the children on the wall and wondered which one was Laurence's victim, as she wasn't going to tell me.

I politely thanked her for all her efforts over the last couple of terms and did a tour of the building visiting his specialist teachers who taught him subjects like science, cookery, PE and French. I queried why they were trying to teach him French when he clearly struggled to learn English. They explained that children like Laurence who learn English as if it were a second language sometimes learnt a second language like a normal child learning a second language.

He liked his French lessons and I was getting good reports from all of the specialist teachers. They reported that he had his moments, but overall he was a good student. This was all ammunition for my meeting with the head later.

During these informal chats one of them let slip a first name. I didn't recognise the name so I went back to his classroom to look at the pictures again. The pain of recognition made me understand why the school hadn't told me. Now that I had a face I could see the assault all too clearly in my mind. To make matters worse, we regularly said hello in passing to this little girl and her mum while going into school in the mornings. She was a lovely girl who always had a smile on her face. She had such a sweet nature that she couldn't harm a fly. I felt my eyes well up as I wondered why he had attacked such an innocent child.

I reeled out of the classroom straight into that child's mother. We said our polite hellos and I wondered if she really did know. She had had plenty of opportunities to say something over the last couple of weeks but she had said nothing. I couldn't bring myself to talk further as I was too upset. I felt like Laurence, I just wanted to block my eyes and ears and reel away out into the fresh air.

I was in no fit state to fence with the headmaster, but I had to stick up for Laurence. The head was waiting for me and we went into his office. I opened with how pleased I was on hearing the good reports from the specialist teachers that evening. The head was a pleasant and shrewd man. I suspect that he saw the direction I was taking and told me that he had also heard these reports. He also had a report from Laurence's temporary form teacher who stated that he had settled into the new class very well with no further physical outbursts.

In fact Laurence had been an exemplary pupil and in the light of this transformation he had earned himself a temporary reprieve. They would reconsider Laurence's position in a couple of weeks. If he continued in this vein and his new teacher felt he could meet Laurence's needs then they would allow him to stay in his new class next September.

That was all we wanted, a chance to earn a reprieve. I knew that Laurence had been trying so hard to get back into everybody's good books. The school had recognised that as well and they saw the opportunity to capitalise educationally through Laurence's enthusiasm. Expulsion clearly wasn't in his best interest, as Laurence dearly loved his school and his new class of big boys.

That, however, was now a potential problem, the head explained. Every effort had been made to demonstrate to Laurence that his placement in the new class was a punishment for his disgraceful behaviour in his old class, but it wasn't working.

This was now all a matter of perceptions.

When Laurence arrived at this school at the ripe old age of ten he considered himself an old hand in school matters and in his eyes his teacher, Jo, was new. She told me how Laurence had set up the classroom with her on the disciplinarian's pedestal while he got friendly with her assistants. Now his new teacher was stepping into the disciplinarian's shoes to emphasise the punishment nature of his new class, but Laurence was lapping it up.

He loved his new class among the big boys with all its strict boundaries.

The headmaster was right, as usual. It was now imperative that Laurence didn't perceive this class change as a reward for his bad behaviour, but bizarrely it was becoming difficult for us to make it appear any other way.

I threatened him with 'No more St John's' if he was in any way naughty again, but he didn't want to hear it, he was too happy in his new class, just as he had been happy in Jo's class.

Over the past year I had received mixed messages from Laurence and his new teacher regarding his behaviour. I certainly don't blame the teacher, who had a wonderful caring way with her pupils, but she didn't have a bark. My puppy was therefore receiving mixed messages and becoming more confused and unhappy. I blame myself and the head for not recognising the signs and taking steps to avoid what was an inevitable meltdown.

Over the next couple of weeks Laurence continued to work hard so the head announced that Laurence could stay. At the end of the day there was only one person responsible for the school's change of mind and that was Laurence. We could only hope that he didn't perceive his new class as a reward.

There was one other factor in this sorry affair that I became aware of when I discovered the identity of Laurence's victim. In no way do I bring up this matter as an attempt to justify his unjustifiable behaviour, but I mention it in attempt to find out why he picked on that innocent little girl.

She had a glass eye and with all the difficulties that Laurence was experiencing at this time with these 'windows to the soul', I have to wonder if she was unwittingly frightening him.

This could have been happening for some time—with Laurence unable to verbalise his feelings, nobody noticed his fears. I could understand that, but Laurence would have to learn to respond in a more socially acceptable manner.

Laurence had another upheaval to deal with, this time at home. His best mate Cheyenne had been sold and was moving to a new stable. We all decided to tell Laurence that Cheyenne had gone on holiday to give him time to get used to Cheyenne's absence. By colluding with this ploy I was breaking my golden rule of never lying to him, which had served me well throughout his childhood. He was too smart to lie to. I knew that I would have to tell him the truth eventually so I saw it as breaking the news in stages.

True to form, Laurence was soon downloading his love onto another black-and-white horse called Billie. Billie is a lovely gentle-natured horse who lived just one stable away from Laurence's old friend Stafford. Poor old Stafford could only stand and watch as Laurence ignored him while pouring his new love over Billie. He only had eyes for Billie.

Meanwhile Laurence hadn't forgotten Cheyenne; far from it, he kept asking, 'Where's Cheyenne?' as only an autistic child can.

I responded every time with, 'He's gone on holiday.'

I relied on his inability to progress the conversation. This was a technique I often used. I knew exactly what answer he wanted, but it was down to him to find a better question to get the answer out of me. I could be as autistic as he was when it came to repetitive conversations.

It took a few days of hard thinking for him to come up with a solution to the problem of furthering the conversation.

'Where's Cheyenne?'

'He is on holiday,' I replied for the millionth time.

'Daddy look at the map, yeah?'

Of course Laurence was capable of saying, 'Where's the holiday?' but after days of thought he came up with this clever but convoluted solution instead. This and other similar situations taught me more about the nature of Laurence's speech impediments than a decade of speech therapists' reports.

The half-an-hour-per-week sessions of speech therapy were nowhere near long enough to begin to probe into his way of thinking. Remember Laurence was desperate to find out where Cheyenne had gone. I wonder how many times the speech therapists had reproduced that kind of desperation for an answer during their sessions.

Laurence is a good-natured kid who was happy to answer the questions and do the exercises that the therapists set for him. He also liked to get through these exercises as quickly as possible, so his answers were always quick and superficial. They had no time to probe any deeper and they had no time to listen to the silly ideas of the one person who did have time—me.

It was time to finish the Cheyenne saga but I was still able to keep one step in front of him. I told him that Cheyenne was being very naughty because he didn't want to come back from the holiday. I knew that Laurence could relate to those feelings. By introducing the naughty element I was playing on his concept of naughty equals funny. This was an idea that I generally discouraged as it produces a lot of silly behaviours, but in this instance I was using it to introduce a feel-good factor into the equation.

Laurence giggled—he was happy that his mate was being naughty.

I had won, I had buried the Cheyenne saga with Cheyenne naughtily not coming back. And Laurence; well, he was happily in love with Billie by this time anyway.

I had learnt a lot over the years and I began to feel comfortable describing myself as living in harmony with my autistic son.

I look back and see that I made many mistakes through Laurence's childhood. I just didn't know any better and was totally unprepared for my robotic alien puppy.

If only I knew when Laurence was born what I know now. With my current understanding, I could have done a much better job.

I could have understood his behaviours and been more aware of his perceptions of our world. I might even have understood when he was trying to teach me something. It was only when he made his wishes obvious by leading me by the hand to where I should go, that I even understood that there was a lesson going on.

I am sure he still has me labelled as an SLD parent but at least it is an improvement on being an SLD alien, which was his perception when he was under five. There was nobody to help him teach me and there was nobody to help me teach him to adjust to our world.

Before the age of five, the 'experts' did not want to commit themselves and after five there was nobody who knew him better than me. Before the age of five, the 'experts' were happy to listen to me but after five they didn't want to know about my hunches.

Over the years I have formed my opinions about autism just as many parents of autistic children have done before me. We all have valid theories about our child's autism; we all have some amazing and sometimes horrendous tales to tell, so why should anybody take note of mine?

Firstly, I came to realise that Laurence had had a remarkable run of good fortune that resulted in him getting what he needed when he needed it. From the very beginning when we were forced to move back to Walthamstow and hence into the Whitefield School catchment area, his savant stunt that led to him getting into school a year early, the chance reading of relevant newspaper articles and even the family break-up seemed to benefit Laurence by money becoming available for therapies at the right time.

Laurence's long run of good fortune put some strange ideas into my head. Perhaps Luz Maria, who died on the day he was born, was looking out for him and guiding my hunches.

Who knows? I had learnt so much, that now anything was possible.

Secondly, I realised that my quest to understand my son had led me to an exceptional understanding of autism that needed to be passed on to the next generation of parents of autistic children.

Finally, something spooky happened that made our story unique and convinced me that it had to be told.

So the next tale is what inspired me to pour out my observations and theories. Therefore, what you have read so far is simply the introduction, A Naturally Autistic Tale, and what you are about to read is truly Weird, Wild and Wonderful.

16

On The Road . . .

About a year previously I had booked some time off for a holiday at this time. With everything that was going on around me I was tempted to skip it, but my new employers were obliged to honour it and I felt that I needed a break to clear my head.

I had chosen the end of May because there was another solar eclipse. This one was not a total eclipse—it was called an annular eclipse. The distance between the moon and the earth varies and at the time of this eclipse the moon was further away than usual. This meant that the disc of the moon was not big enough to fully cover the sun's disc, leaving a ring of fire hanging in the sky.

The best place to view this spectacular phenomenon was Iceland, but it could also be seen from the far north of Scotland just after sunrise. People in other parts of the British Isles would see the remarkable sight of a crescent sun rising above the horizon, if they could be bothered to get up early enough.

I realised that viewing from Iceland the sun would be higher in the sky and would therefore require viewing through special filters. But viewing from Scotland the sun would be lower and therefore appear bigger, while if the early morning cloud cover was thin the eclipse might even be a naked-eye event. I decided to risk the weather and headed for Cape Wrath on the northwestern tip of Scotland.

I had seen pictures of the area. It looked bleak, with towering sheer cliffs and no safety barriers at the edges. I decided that it wasn't a good place to take Laurence so I left the children at home. For company I did take a friend along who was intrigued by my quest for a highland ring of fire.

The train took us as far as Inverness, where we hired a car. We took a leisurely two-day drive along the scenic route to the Cape. The scenery was simple and yet serenely stunning. The small roads were empty, it was all so peaceful, but occasionally the serenity was shattered when the sky screamed as a Harrier Jump Jet passed by. The Cape Wrath area and nearby islands are RAF live-ammunition bombing ranges.

We decided to avoid the Cape Wrath area and any possibly awkward late-night encounters with military policemen. Instead we headed to a nearby uninhabited peninsula called Faraid Head. We had an evening meal in Durness, the nearest village. There was a campsite in the village that was bursting, probably for the first time in its existence, but I had no plans to stay there.

There was no road on the peninsula so I parked as close as I could get and we continued on foot. The scenery surprised me as we walked along a mile-long gently sloping sandy beach.

The sun was setting over the tranquil blue sea. It was beautiful, more like the Caribbean than the Scottish Highlands. Beside the beach there were grass-topped sand dunes as high as a house. The children would have loved this, I thought.

At the end of the beach we climbed a small hill and there below us was another pristine sandy beach glistening in the warm setting sunlight. To see the sunrise, however, we had to climb across the sand dunes to the other side of the peninsula. That was a tough trek, carrying our camping equipment at the end of a long day.

On the far side we were still in sand dunes but on top of some rocky cliffs. This side of the peninsula took the full brunt of the North Atlantic waves. The sea was crashing into the base of the cliffs and the huge rocks that were scattered about in the sea. There were no warming rays here; this was the bleak harsh Scottish coast that I had expected.

We pitched tent and waited for dawn. The tide was going out, being pulled by the gravity of the sun and moon as they raced towards each other. It was impossible to sleep. The sound of the waves crashing into the rocks and the rustle of small stones bashing into each other was rhythmical and relaxing but much too loud to allow sleep. There was no volume control.

The shades of sea and sky grew steadily darker but it never got really dark. The red glow from below the horizon slowly moved around to our side of the peninsula. A couple of hundred miles further north and we would have been in the midnight-sun zone.

As dawn approached, the red and orange glow along the cloud-covered horizon grew brighter. The sky grew lighter, with only a few scattered white clouds to be seen, but there was no sighting of the sun because of a narrow strip of dense cloud along the horizon.

As the time for the annular eclipse came and went you could feel the collective groan coming from the silhouetted small groups of people that were huddled together along the clifftops. My gamble on the low Scottish cloud had failed. I should have gone to Iceland, I mused.

The annular eclipse was due to last just two minutes, so we had failed to see the ring of fire, but we hung around for a while hoping to catch a glimpse of the less spectacular partial eclipse that followed.

It was a beautiful sunrise, the sky turned yellow and the clouds glowed orange, but there was still no sign of the partially eclipsed sun. Some people had already left and we dejectedly started to pack up our tent when suddenly our neighbours some thirty yards away started shouting wildly and pointing out to sea.

I turned to look and couldn't believe my eyes, it was impossible. The top half of the sun had pierced the clouds, miraculously just as the annular eclipse was taking place. A thin golden arc hugged the moon's black disc and shone through the shimmering clouds.

There was no time to wonder how, I grabbed my camera and snapped away. By now the small huddled groups all along the cliffs were all shouting and leaping around and my joy overflowed as well. We were suddenly catapulted from a sense of dejected failure to a wonderfully warm feeling of unmitigated success. There wasn't much time to view the ring of fire before the sun and moon started to drift apart. As the ring turned into a crescent sun, it became too bright to view with the naked eye so we sat and basked in the eclipsed sunlight reflecting off the becalmed sea from our cliff-top vantage point. Dawn on Faraid Head felt like a beautiful place to be, for a while.

Another quest beckoned; we finished packing away our equipment, trekked back to the car and set off in search of a hot breakfast. I realised that somebody responsible for converting NASA's Universal Time into BST had made an awful mistake when publicising the times of the eclipse. It was the only possible explanation of why the eclipse had appeared exactly an hour after everybody had expected it.

This must have been one of the biggest events in the history of Durness and the few shops around were open even at five in the morning. However, we had to drive beyond the village before finding a café without a long queue outside.

As we basked in the warm glow of the hot food and our caffeine fixes a couple of well-dressed rather agitated young men walked in talking loudly on their mobile phones. We couldn't help overhearing their conversations and it became clear that they were journalists talking to other journalists who were covering the eclipse at other locations.

We struck up a conversation and they confirmed that they were from the Press Association. They told us that in Iceland they had seen nothing, as it was too cloudy. Between phone calls they told us a similar tale for other locations—even the people in the campsite at the village just a couple of miles from our site had unbelievably seen nothing. My head was swelling as I smugly realised that I had found the perfect viewing spots for the last two eclipses.

'Did you see the eclipse?' I asked them.

They were further along on the same peninsula as we were. One of them explained that they also had the wrong times so he had already packed away his tripod and special lenses and was walking around the crowd taking some human-interest shots with his general purpose camera when the clouds parted. He snapped away but the photos wouldn't be of a good enough quality to get into the papers. He was gutted; he had missed out on a good payday, considering the lack of pictures from other locations.

We followed the coastal road as it wound around the cliff tops admiring the stunning views. We stopped in a clifftop lay-by to take in one last look at the sea before heading south. The cliffs here were made of red rock so the beach was red as well. The warmth of the morning sun amplified the colours. The big waves were back, there were a couple of tents on the beach and a few brave lads were surfing on the incoming tide. Not for the first time my mind returned to the kids as I realised how much Laurence would have enjoyed joining in with them.

A couple of days later I was facing up to the realities of work. I had a 'cards on the table' meeting with my new boss. It became clear that they had not wanted me included in the sale, they had no interest in me and would not be offering me a job commensurate with my salary, which they were obliged to pay. I could start at the bottom and work my way up as my natural skills shone through. Well, that was the theory, but the reality would be very different.

I would be up against career-minded youngsters with inherently better keyboard skills than me. In reality I would be running just to stand still. My line manager would love to make a saving in his budgets by getting rid of my inflated salary, so there would be no prospect of the pressure ever easing off.

He went on to tentatively suggest that if by any chance I should consider leaving then they would be able to come up with a redundancy package to ease the way. He was at pains to stress that he wasn't trying to induce me, he was just informing me that the option was available.

Although I could have risen to the challenge I couldn't reconcile myself to spending the last twenty years of my working life in a backwater shop being henpecked by a kid half my age trying to make a name for himself.

I told him to do the sums while I considered all my options.

The long school summer holiday was approaching. With the children now 14 and 12 years old, this might be my last chance to spend an entire summer with them. That was a tempting idea, which wouldn't go away. I decided that I would forever regret it if I didn't take this opportunity. I didn't have a clue what I would do when the children went back to school, but if it was worse than what was on offer now, then so be it. I handed in my notice.

Before worrying about what I would do in the winter, I had to plan what we would do for the summer. I didn't want to go on a two-week package holiday even if it was to a luxurious destination. I wanted us to take full advantage of all this time off. The idea of cheaply touring around appealed to me, but I realised that it could be a real challenge for Laurence.

Our previous package holidays had fitted into autistic-friendly routines, which allowed him to relax and enjoy himself. Travelling around, continually changing accommodation, and not knowing what tomorrow might bring would be a real test for Laurence. I realised that this could be a beneficial exercise, but I knew that I could also be forced to return in less than a week with my tail between my legs if it all went wrong.

The summer of 2003 was turning into a scorcher; everybody was going to the seaside. Touring the south of England during August would be uncomfortably hot and crowded. If it were a few degrees cooler up north it would still be very pleasant. Scotland was calling me; I'd had a taster and now destiny seemed to be pulling me back to those golden beaches and rugged mountains.

318

All the signs pointed north, so I got my maps out and started planning possible routes. Bianca had a few social functions to fulfil at the start of the school holidays, which gave me time to make sure that I hadn't forgotten anything. We would be going to some remote areas with nothing pre-booked, so we had to be prepared to rough it when necessary.

A Saab has a large boot and it was packed full with two large cases of clothes, a tent and sleeping bags, a gas stove with some food, plastic cups, plates and so on, and a small fridge that plugged into the car's cigarette lighter. We were prepared for anything; well, I hoped we were.

I had this strange feeling that had been steadily growing inside me. It was the sort of feeling that I would normally have scoffed at. I had a sense of inevitability about this expedition.

If I hadn't gone to Hungary and been bedazzled by the total eclipse then I certainly wouldn't have bothered trying to see the annular eclipse.

If I hadn't gone to Scotland and been bedazzled by the beauty of the beaches I would never have considered taking the children to the remote Highlands.

If the business hadn't been sold at that time I would not have been in a position to consider this type of long holiday.

If it hadn't been such a hot summer that year I might well have chosen not to travel so far north.

All these ifs had steadily narrowed the options that were now in front of me. I was happy to explore this path and find what was at the end of it, as I didn't believe in destiny—I just had that destiny feeling.

For now our path was up the M1. This was a road that Laurence knew well, as Grandad lives at Milton Keynes, and Alton Towers was further up the M1 as well. I explained to Laurence that today we were going a long way past Alton Towers. He was happy. I had no particular destination in mind for our first night as the M1 is very unpredictable, but it was in a good mood that day and we made good progress.

I am fortunate to have two children who are good travellers. If Bianca got bored she would simply fall asleep and Laurence never got bored watching the world go by his window.

After a couple of much-needed breaks at the service stations I was able to get around Newcastle before the afternoon rush hour began. We continued heading north, and Laurence noticed that the road had changed from M1 to A1. We had a long chat about that.

Over the years I have travelled extensively around the British Isles but I never had reason to travel this far north on the eastern side of the country. It is, after all, the long way around to Scotland, so our first destination was the remote Northumbrian coastline. There were a lot of large beaches to explore and I wanted to visit Holy Island.

As teatime approached I pulled into a pretty market town called Alnwick and it was bedecked in bunting. I couldn't believe my luck; we had arrived in the middle of the 'world famous' Alnwick music festival.

This was probably the one week of the year when there was no room for us.

I decided to continue heading northeast in the general direction of the coast to look for a seaside B&B. It appeared that we were heading towards a fire. I thought that it must be a farmer burning his fields, but as we got closer I realised that it was a sea fog. We arrived at a village called Seahouses, which I thought must be beside the sea but we couldn't see it.

We drove around in ever-increasing circles but there were no 'Vacancy' signs to be seen. While we were driving around we came across four campsites and they were all full as well. I was tired and the children were hungry, so I drove back into the village for some dinner.

This was turning into a disaster. After dinner I drove back to a long-stay car park which already had a couple of camper vans parked up in it. Laurence was thrilled when I announced that we would have to sleep in the car. We each had a blanket, and Bianca stretched out on the back seat while Laurence and I had the reclining front seats.

I sat outside while they settled down. We were parked outside Bamburgh castle, which was now lit up in the night sky. I disapprove of such wasteful light displays polluting the night sky, but I have to admit that for the few people who do see this castle at night, it is a stunning sight.

Bianca slept well but Laurence didn't settle all night.

Unlike me, he seemed unaffected by the lack of a good night's sleep. I found some 24-hour toilets and then drove us back to the car park for an 'in-car breakfast' as it was much too early for the cafés to be open. It was a dull, cloudy morning.

Our top priority was to find a place to stay in this surprisingly popular area, as I didn't want to spend a second night in the car. The vacancy signs started to go up and I booked us into a guesthouse on the seafront for the next two nights. With that worry out of the way, we decided to explore the village, buy some things for a picnic lunch and then go down to the seaside for the afternoon.

Seahouses is a small seaside village with a few basic shops, some large cafés, a couple of amusement arcades, crazy golf, bouncy castle and a house of horrors. We wisely chose not to visit the house of horrors and months later we saw it on a TV programme about this country's ten worst holiday attractions.

While we were looking around, the lifeboat alarm sounded so I whisked the children round the corner to the quay to watch the lifeboat launch. To my surprise, we got there before the lifeboat.

There was a tremendous clattering and clanking as the lifeboat slowly appeared, being pushed by a tractor along the road. The lifeboat was on a trailer with metal caterpillar tracks. The tractor slowly pushed the clanking trailer down the ramp into the sea where they could float off the lifeboat. I'm sure the lifeboat men performed this manoeuvre with maximum efficiency, but it was still a painfully slow process. In this instance another boat brought the casualty in before the lifeboat got out of the harbour.

I decided not to go on one of the many boat trips to the Farne Islands that were just offshore. If this was all fate then I wasn't going to tempt it.

We had our picnic in the sand dunes and spent the afternoon exploring the wide, expansive beach. The weather didn't get any better but Laurence seemed to relish the wide-open spaces. He scampered around, splashing in the shallow pools scattered around the beach. It wasn't long before he wanted his swimming trunks on so that he could go in the sea.

There was no stopping him. Bianca went in as well, but she soon returned to me shivering. I called him in but he didn't want to come. He was having too much fun splashing around on the sandbanks. Eventually I used the lure of dinnertime to bring him in. I asked him if he was cold, to which he robustly replied, 'No' and then he added, 'Come here tomorrow, yeah.'

As I quickly dried him off and dressed him his skin felt as cold as ice. I marched him across the sand dunes and into the warm car as the sea fog started to roll in again. I was just wondering what to do next when Laurence's teeth started chattering.

It was a new sensation for Laurence and he was confused. Bianca found this very funny and couldn't conceal it, even though I expressed my concern that Laurence would get cross with her. I needn't have worried, as he seemed more annoyed with himself than with her.

Within five minutes we were back at the guesthouse and he was de-icing under a warm shower. I allowed him an extended play in the shower because I felt guilty for allowing him to stay in the sea for too long.

While Laurence played, Bianca and I watched the kids' programmes on TV. *Blue Peter* came on and they showed a thermometer in the Blue Peter Garden. It was 36 degrees and kids were splashing around in a paddling pool. I remembered the thermometer in my car had showed 16 degrees. It was an unbelievable temperature difference; we had to be in the coldest part of the country.

The guesthouse did do evening meals but they had pretensions beyond our needs. At over twenty pounds per head for one course, we opted for freshly caught fish and chips in the village instead. Laurence lapped it up and ate what we couldn't eat as well. He was happy and showed no signs of ill effects after his big chill.

The next morning brought even more low grey cloud. I decided to visit Bamburgh castle in order to keep Laurence out of the sea for as long as possible. He was on a promise of 'later' if he was a good boy.

As we approached the castle, its cloud-covered battlements and turrets reminded Bianca of a Scooby Doo castle. That made me Shaggy and Laurence could only be Scooby Doo, so I pushed Thelma inside first, in case there were any ghosts lurking around.

Bamburgh is a well-maintained castle. The interior was more like visiting a stately home with delicate crockery on the tables and eighteenth-century chairs that really shouldn't be sat upon. I had to keep Laurence under close control inside, so we couldn't hang around to learn much about the history of the castle. We spent more time exploring the grounds and parapets outside.

The castle stood on a rock surrounded by a sea of grass-covered sand dunes. Beyond them was a wide strip of flat sand, and the grey sea merged into the grey sky obscuring the Farne Islands that the guidebook said could be seen in the distance.

When Laurence's patience started to wear thin we went back to the car to pick up our picnic lunch and crossed the dunes to the beach. He loved playing in the dunes. He ran down them, deliberately stumbling and tumbling into a sandy heap at the bottom.

Bianca dug a big-brother trap while Laurence was playing. She tricked him into falling in and bundled in with him. A pile of sand fell on top of them and they were a giggling mess of arms, legs and sand. When he did manage to pull himself out he stood in the same spot and asked Bianca to do it again. She was happy to oblige.

We couldn't keep him out of the sea all afternoon, but he went in knowing that it was only for a little while. With no time to waste he sprinted off towards the sea. Having learnt the day before how cold the North Sea can be, Bianca chose to keep her clothes on and made sandcastles instead. There was nobody else in the water, just a couple of families sheltering in the dunes and a few people walking their dogs along the expansive beach.

Although Laurence was up to a hundred metres away I could see that he was monitoring my movements and also the movements of any dogs that strayed within his long-range radar. I noticed that as a dog started to approach him he would start to drift towards me.

While I watched I realised that I had seen this type of behaviour before in the time warp, but this was on a different scale. Just as I had observed Laurence constantly reassessing his chances of pinching a grape from me and behaving accordingly, so now he was monitoring the trajectories of the dogs on the beach and behaving according to the perceived risk of an encounter.

If he noticed that the dog often ran into the sea then Laurence would drift towards me, but if the dog was just a beach sniffer he retired deeper into the water. As each danger passed he gravitated back to his favoured play area.

With just the odd intrusion on his radar his behaviour was easy to understand. It was also easy to understand that as the intrusions increased in more 'normal' situations his behaviour would become more difficult to understand.

In a normal situation like walking down the high street his behaviour would be the sum of his responses to all the intrusions occurring around him. I had learnt to subconsciously add and subtract the intrusions while accompanying him so I always had a rough idea of his stress levels. If a dog came by he would drift towards me and if a baby suddenly cried at the same time I would move towards him as the intrusions increased. If a police car with siren blazing suddenly appeared on the scene I would already be in place to grab his arm as the potential for an overload escalated. Any one on its own would not be cause for concern, it was the sum of all the factors that affected his behaviour, including things like the purpose of the journey, the number of people around us and his overall mood.

It is important to realise that his 'sum total behaviour' would often be different from the 'normal' behaviour that we expected of him at any given time. Arrogantly we say that he displays inappropriate behaviour, when it is we who have the blinkers.

We only behave in response to what we perceive to be most important. If somebody trips on the kerb and falls over we behave appropriately. We temporarily forget our mission while we show concern for the stranger. To Laurence running on 'sum total behaviour', the incident might have had a humorous aspect but it had no real bearing on the whole picture and he would see no reason for interrupting the mission.

Laurence's behaviour was appropriate to the overall picture.

He had taught himself how to control his responses to most normal situations. Only exceptional circumstances like I described above or a person with a glass eye unnerved him these days. I could never hope to be as observant as Laurence, so inevitably there were times when I was left scratching my head wondering what had triggered that. Over the years those occasions had steadily become rarer.

Although Laurence was clearly enjoying the expansive sands I was fed up with the dismal weather so the next morning we headed north in search of some sunlight. First stop was Holy Island, the reason for us coming to this cloud-covered corner of the country in the first place.

Access to the castle and monastery on Holy Island was via a tidal causeway. I had seen the place on TV but I don't know what I expected from the visit. I was unimpressed and would say that Bamburgh castle was a more interesting place to visit, so we had a quick look round, took some photos and returned to the mainland before the tide came in.

I continued heading north on the A1 and turned off just before Berwick-upon-Tweed, where I started following a trail of hand-painted signs directing us to a B&B. It was a long trail winding left and right through the lanes, leading to an old isolated ivy-covered cliff-top house.

I knocked on the doors, front and back, but apart from a very excited dog there appeared to be nobody at home. Just as I wondered where to look next a voice behind me made me turn to face a man of about my age with a shock of red hair. As we exchanged pleasantries

I wondered how this strange man had crept up on me wearing his waist-high waders.

The house was stranger still. The hall and stairwell were cluttered with antiques and bric-a-brac. I think the encounter with the Scooby Doo castle had set Bianca's imagination racing as she found it very creepy. Clinging to me she whispered, 'Daddy, why are there dead animals stuck on the walls?'

Our host showed us into a huge first-floor bedroom with two single beds and no dead animals. I decided to keep us all together in one room, as there was plenty of space to put a camp bed on the floor. I paid for just one night.

As he showed me around it became clear that the facilities were basic. If you couldn't live without a power shower then this place wasn't for you, as the shower was just a trickle, fed by water from a natural spring.

He led us round to the back of the house to show us a rough path down the cliff to their private beach, which really did stretch the Trade Descriptions Act. The tide was out and there were rocks and rock pools stretching in either direction. He had been down there picking shellfish when we had arrived, which explained how he had managed to pop up behind me. He told me that there was a sandy beach just a hundred yards along the lane, or we could walk across the rocks around the headland to the beach.

He was a likeable chap and we talked for some time. He dabbled in antiques and other things and clearly he didn't like throwing things away. There were wind breaks, deck chairs and other clutter around, the children soon found a couple of bikes and he had no problem with them cycling down the drive and around the garden.

He told me that he used to be the landlord of the pub on Holy Island and pointed out the castle further along the coast; beyond that, Bamburgh castle could be seen when the clouds on the horizon lifted. He was full of tales from his youth of how this remote part of the country and its folk had been dragged into the twentieth century. In the warm evening sunshine, with the children giggling on the bikes, gloomy Seahouses seemed a world away. Coincidentally, this house was called Sea House. Warily we were warming to this rustic old place and we ended up spending a delightful week of our holiday there.

We could have walked to Cocklawburn Beach in two minutes along the lane, but Laurence insisted that we went down the cliff and crossed the rocks along the shore to the beach each morning. That could take him a couple of hours. Laurence found the rocks a challenging, fun-filled playground. The gently sloping strata of the rocks jutting out of the sand made relatively easy walking, but we often looked back to see him clambering over the rocks on all fours. His laboured progress gave Bianca and me plenty of time to collect the abundant pretty little stones found amongst the gritty sand around the rock pools.

As the week went by he gained more agility over the irregular surfaces and I noticed Bianca leading Laurence over more difficult terrain. I suspected that she was trying to get him to fall into the deeper rock pools, and of course he was happy to oblige and jump. I accused her of trying to get her big brother bitten by a crab. She couldn't suppress her giggles as she tried to deny it.

We saw our landlord and his son collecting shellfish among the rocks at low tide. I realised that this was their allotment, which they tended throughout the year. I also realised that Laurence would love to do that job.

The penny finally dropped—I was a bad dad for him to have. My work involved working with the general public, customer services and public relations. Even though he often came to work with me, there was no way he would ever be able to do this sort of people-based work. If our landlord had been Laurence's dad then they could have worked together during his teen years training for the time when dad was too old to go out with him.

Here, Laurence could have led a happy semi-independent and productive life.

My mind turned back to the recent tragedy involving the cockle pickers in Morecambe Bay. Laurence would like that job too, and there must be others like him that would love to work at the seaside, but it's a jungle out there. With the explosion in autism and other similar conditions we must start schemes now that can evolve into communities offering people who need it a simpler way of life.

Initially experts could pass on skills to the parents, like in farming, for example. A parent would work alongside their child on the farm passing their skills on over the years. That parent would then teach another younger parent and the four of them could work and learn together. A farm could support several of these working groups and these communities could therefore offer sustainable stability in the

326

workplace, degrees of independence in a caring society and, above all else, peace of mind. That is what all parents seek, the contentment in knowing that their offspring will be able to carry on when they are gone.

The parents do need to be at the heart of these communities whether they are based on a farm, in a factory, or fishing or gardening. As we have seen many times before, the parents understand the abilities and limitations of our widely differing children. Although working at the seaside would be his favourite, Laurence could learn about plants and lawns or finding items in a warehouse if he had time to gain confidence and learn it working alongside somebody who understood him.

Throughout their childhood we try to hammer these square kids into our rounded schools. As they reach maturity, can we please give in gracefully and give them what they really need rather than what we think they should have? The alternative is a very expensive lifetime in care with occasional day trips to the seaside and meaningless work experience schemes like licking envelopes in an 'understanding' office.

As our education system labels increasing numbers of children as dysfunctional in some way, the cost to society of setting up these small, simple communities would be a saving of millions of pounds in care costs for each autistic adult involved. It would be important to introduce the autistic individuals to this type of community during the learning years so that it becomes a natural progression. With proper jobs, even severely autistic people can contribute to society and to the cost of themed autistic retirement homes. If they are given a chance.

I was hoping to see other jobs that Laurence might like to do while we were on our travels, but while the weather stayed sunny we remained at the Sea House as the children were having a great time.

Bianca painted a glass vase for Mummy at a local craft centre and she also went horse riding. Laurence wasn't allowed to go riding—the riding school used a popular excuse for withholding facilities from the disabled—they had no insurance for children like him. With so much emphasis on access for the physically disabled these days, this kind of excuse shouldn't be allowed.

After clambering over the rocks in the mornings the children spent many happy afternoons playing on Cocklawburn Beach. Bianca was happy exploring the rock pools and digging while Laurence splashed about in the chilly North Sea. Mid-afternoon I would call him in, dry him off and send them both off to the solitary ice-cream van parked up on the headland at the far end of the beach. It was a long walk for them, giving Laurence plenty of time to warm up. By the time they returned there was no sign of the ice creams except for the stains down Laurence's T-shirt.

This place reminded me of my childhood trips to the seaside before everywhere became so commercialised.

We spent our evenings exploring the history of Berwick-upon-Tweed and had our evening meals there.

With rain forecast for the next day, we had our last evening meal with our host. There could only be one thing on the menu—fish. The first course was smoked salmon, smoked in his own smokehouse. Our host explained, 'Not like that fish you get in the supermarkets these days with the taste painted on.' Laurence was unimpressed with this offering of thinly sliced fish and salad.

'Chips,' he implored. I knew that 'chips' was just his way of saying, 'I'm hungry, this isn't enough.'

'Later,' I quickly replied to head off any further protests, but I really wanted to hide under the table as I realised what our host would say about that 'city kid' when he was out of earshot.

The second course was freshly caught sea trout, boiled potatoes and fresh veg. There were no more requests for chips and it was probably the best meal of the holiday so far.

The next morning we said a sad farewell to our friendly hosts. We could have spent the rest of the holidays here, but I felt that our destiny was elsewhere.

16A

... to Serenity ...

I continued heading north up the A1. My plan was to travel inland from the east coast of England, and go under Edinburgh and over Glasgow towards the west coast of Scotland. We got past these major conurbations without delay and stopped at a town called Callander for lunch.

As we walked down the high street looking for a place to eat, we wandered into a couple of gift shops for our first taste of the Highland theme. It didn't take Laurence long to find the pretty girls walking around these stores offering free samples of fudge. He liked these girls and I noticed him beaming at one trying to get more out of her.

I was really proud of how well Laurence was coping with this travelling holiday.

We spent the afternoon admiring the scenery, driving between lochs and mountains as the road followed the railway line as it squeezed through the passes and alongside the lochs to Oban on the west coast. We were to spend the weekend in Oban before setting sail on the next leg of our journey. It was early evening when we pulled into Oban, there were a lot of 'No Vacancy' signs, so I took the first place that could fit us in. It was very basic.

Oban is a small town waking up to its tourism potential and we found the area full of pleasant surprises. It was a good base for all sorts of holidays on land and water, but we were just passing through. I found a better B&B in the hills behind Oban for our second night.

It was a modern house with a couple of spare bedrooms. Everything was brand new, our room was immaculate in stylish pink and grey and it had an en-suite bathroom. Our first hot bath in over a week was made even more sumptuous as the shelves in the bathroom were full of free samples. Our landlady had a sideline selling a wide range of beauty and skin care products. It was simply sensational.

There was a large pub and restaurant next door, so when we were all cleaned up we stuffed ourselves silly with a three-course dinner and had a long, comfortable night's sleep in the new beds.

At breakfast time, family and guests ate around the same table and we discussed our plans for the day. It was a very pleasant atmosphere and the family was a font of local knowledge. It was here that Laurence had his first taste of haggis. Bianca watched with a look of disgust as he scoffed his haggis and the black pudding. Our landlady was delighted with his healthy appetite and offered him more; he wasn't going to refuse.

I drove back to Oban and parked near the town centre. My phone started bleeping madly; I had five messages, all from Ana. The first call was a relaxed 'please call me back' but with each call the messages became more frantic. By the fifth message she was hysterical, demanding to know what I had done with her children. I couldn't help laughing, as Ana always liked a good drama.

I called her straight back and explained that we must have been in a 'no signal' area last night and passed the phone over to Bianca to reassure her that the children were safe and well.

The weather had changed and we realised we had lost the children's coats. We couldn't remember seeing the coats since Bamburgh castle; there could be no going back, so we went shopping. Laurence chose a loud yellow and blue waterproof while Bianca chose a more subdued grey number.

The proximity of the Inner Hebrides ensured that the waters around Oban were generally calm. The seafront was awash with seagulls and ducks competing for people's leftovers. An armada of boats large and small cruising along the waterways created the gentle waves lapping the seafront. There were yachts and all kinds of pleasure boats offering fishing, diving, bird-watching and sightseeing excursions.

And then there are the huge car ferries run by Caledonian MacBrayne. It was their website, *www.calmac.co.uk*, that convinced me that our route was feasible. They offered Hopscotch tickets for touring the islands that did not require pre-booking and saved a lot on individual ticket prices. There were regular ferries to the local islands, but there was only one ferry each day that went to the Outer Hebrides, and that left at ten to three every afternoon. It was the return leg of the ferry's daily journey, which meant that we would arrive at South Uist at half past nine at night, in the dark.

I had tried to book a night's accommodation at the tourist information office, but the islanders are deeply religious folk who do not answer their phones or even watch television on Sundays. I had to accept that we might have to spend our first night on the islands in the car.

I checked in and parked on the quayside to wait our turn to board. There were many large lorries, coaches and caravans as well as cars waiting to board. I couldn't see how we could all fit in until we drove onboard and I saw that there were two vehicle decks.

The crew were on deck 3 and the passenger decks were on decks 4 and 5. We had a quick look around and found our way outside to say farewell to the mainland.

McCaig's Tower, which looks like the Coliseum, sat like a crown on the hills above Oban. It was a grey day and Oban was soon just a grey smudge on the horizon. For the first hour or so, the ship chugged smoothly along the Sound of Mull, but we could see little of the landscape passing by on either side. The grey-green hills merged into the grey sky. A few sailing boats skipped across the white-tipped blue-grey waves.

Laurence's bright coat shone out in the gloom. He was very happy and excited. When I held his hand, I could feel the tension inside him and I suspected that he wanted to flap. Over the years he had learnt how to control these physical urges, but the feelings were still buried inside.

With the wind blowing in his face I thought I could see the trace of a smile. It was so unusual that I couldn't be sure that it wasn't a trick of the wind. Laurence could beam, which was an endearing look, and he could laugh in many ways, but he couldn't smile. Bianca would roll about laughing at his weird facial contortions when she told him to smile and many family photos were ruined by the words, 'Smile please'.

As we left the shelter of the Sound, the sea grew choppier and a fine mist fell from the low clouds. I was freezing and I lured Laurence indoors with the promise of some dinner. The restaurant was up on deck 5. Laurence chose the chicken curry without hesitation. Bianca reluctantly chose a shrivelled piece of fish and some dry-looking chips. Faced with such a choice, I opted for the curry.

The decks were no longer rolling; our ship was beginning to lurch back and forth in the mounting waves. When Bianca asked, 'Where shall we sit?' I replied, 'At the nearest table.' I felt like I was on *It's a Knockout* as I staggered about carrying our tray to the table.

I don't know how Laurence managed to eat as he kept laughing at his plate sliding across the table. While we were eating the waves were crashing against the large windows around the restaurant, and we were on the fifth floor! I was beginning to feel like I was on a roller coaster while Laurence finished off Bianca's chips. We retired to the comfortable seats in one of the TV lounges to ride out this squall.

Minutes after sitting down to watch TV Laurence told me he felt sick. He was a good boy; he kept it in until we reached the toilets. He had a strong stomach, he needed it to cope with all the rubbish that ended up in his mouth, but when his stomach did turn, he retched and vomited at full volume. His loud retching echoed around the toilets and made my stomach heave. Although he made it to the bowl, he still managed to splatter the entire cubicle. I cleaned him up and sent him back to Bianca while I cleaned up.

It was my turn now.

I returned to the children feeling much better. I told Bianca that Laurence had been sick.

'I know,' she hissed, 'the whole boat heard.' She pointed, 'Look there, there and there.' I could see that the crew had been busy with the sand buckets. I didn't know if Laurence's vociferous vomiting had started a chain reaction, as Bianca suspected, or whether there were just a lot of people feeling seasick at the same time.

Bianca said that she was feeling fine so I left her watching TV while I took Laurence outside for a breath of fresh air. I had to push hard against the wind to open the metal door. We staggered outside, clinging to the handrails. The wind was whipping up so much spray it was impossible to tell if the low grey clouds were producing rain. Our ship was being tossed about in the foaming sea and the spray was washing all over us so that we had to hold on really tight.

My mind turned to the large lorries and coaches beside my car in the bottom of the ship. What if, I wondered? I had a vision of a heap of tangled metal, but I took consolation in that we were close to the lifeboats. I made Laurence hold the handrail with both hands while I took a firm grip of his coat with my spare hand.

In this hellish environment as we clung to life, there could be no doubt about it, he was smiling. It wasn't just a smile it was a broad grin. My mind went back to birthdays, holidays, Christmas presents, horse riding and roller coasters, for all of my efforts none had made him smile like this. I clung to that smile, it was so precious.

Occasionally a person staggered outside, but the wind made it impossible to vomit overboard and they soon returned, vomit splattered, to the warmth of indoors. The sea spray soon washed the deck clean. Amid this maelstrom of turbulent water he was smiling such a warm smile that I couldn't ask him to come indoors. This was a once-in-a-lifetime situation and we were in it together, to the end.

The elemental forces trying to prevent us reaching the islands eventually tired, the sea calmed down and his grin faded to a smile. The grey clouds lifted and we could see land ahoy. We went inside to join up with Bianca, but we were soon outside again taking in the magnificent view.

Barra is a small island at the southern end of the Outer Hebrides chain. The harbour was very picturesque, with a small castle built on rocks in the middle of the bay to protect the quaint village. It was half past seven and the setting sun was beginning to break through the clouds behind the island.

I regret that I had decided to skip Barra and go on to South Uist but I thought we would have a better chance of finding some last-minute accommodation on the larger island. We watched the passengers disembark and their undamaged cars disappeared into the hills. The ferry chugged out of the harbour and followed the coastline north.

Two hours later, we approached the village port of Lochboisdale on the island of South Uist. I searched the hillside for clues as to where to look first for a room as the last daylight faded away. There were only a few buildings and even fewer dim lights as the huge ferry pulled into the tiny harbour. The lights on a tourist information office flickered into life, piercing the gathering gloom. That would be my first stop.

Unfortunately we had to wait our turn before driving off the ferry, so by the time we got to the tourist office it was packed. I left the children in the car while I tried to glean some information. I couldn't get through the door, but as I stood in the doorway I heard one of the assistants, on the other side of the heaving throng, say that there was a hotel a couple of miles down the road.

That was all the information I needed. I jumped back into the car and pulled away fast, aware of the pack close behind me. There was only one road. It was an unlit single-track road with passing points every couple of hundred yards for vehicles coming in the opposite direction, but there were none.

We could see nothing of the landscape around us; just the road ahead illuminated by my headlights. With everywhere so dark it was impossible to miss the hotel. I left the children in the car while I checked to see if they had any vacancies as the first of the chasing cars pulled into the car park. They did and I booked us in for two nights, remembering not to stand too close to the receptionist in case my breath still smelled of vomit.

It was a nice warm modern hotel and after such a day we appreciated the comfort it offered. The children had bunk beds, which was a novelty for them.

As my stress levels lowered, I realised that Laurence was the least stressed of us all. He was coping so well with whatever was thrown at him. There had been no trace of naughty behaviour on this holiday. It was as if he was too busy dealing with all the new things going on around him to think about misbehaving. We all slept well that night.

The next morning brought another grey sky. There were some low hills in the distance but the landscape around us was flat, natural grassland littered with small black lakes and white rocks. Blending in with the rocks were grazing sheep scattered in all directions.

After a hearty breakfast where Laurence renewed his love affair with haggis, we set off. We visited the island of Eriskay in the morning where the old black-and-white film *Whiskey Galore* was made. Eriskay was joined to South Uist by a causeway and there was a small car ferry from Eriskay to Barra. I wished we had taken that route, as it would have meant an extra boat journey for Laurence.

After a picnic lunch sheltering in the sand dunes, we explored part of South Uist's twenty miles of sandy beaches. It was a windy day; the grey clouds were racing across the overcast sky, producing frequent light showers. Bianca and I agreed that it didn't matter which direction we were walking in, the rain was always in our faces.

The sea was angry and the waves were pounding the beach with such ferocity that they left a trail of foam fizzing along the shoreline. Laurence embraced the sea, he loved its magnificent fury and he wanted to play with it. I was equally determined that he wasn't going in. We had a long autistic-style debate on the subject. He played on the fact that he had been a good boy, I couldn't argue with his logic and he couldn't comprehend the potential dangers.

Eventually I came up with a compromise that we could both agree on. I allowed him to wear his swimming trunks and paddle along the waterline, but he had to wear his jumper and coat. They would remind him that he was not allowed to swim and they would help to retain his body heat in this squally weather.

While Laurence skipped gaily through the foam kicking spray into his own face, Bianca and I skipped along the shoreline trying to keep close to him while keeping our feet dry. He was so happy and relaxed. In fact, this environment was so simple that there was absolutely nothing for him to worry about.

The sky seemed huge in this empty landscape. To our left was the mighty North Atlantic stretching for thousands of miles, orchestrating the impressive soundtrack to these islands. To our right the sand drifted into grass-topped dunes and the grasslands stretched into the distant hills on the other side of the island. This simple environment was littered with rocks and in places the rocks were huddled together in the shape of houses. The construction of these houses and their thatched roofs hasn't changed over thousands of years.

In fact we stumbled upon some unmarked Stone Age ruins among the dunes. They looked like they had recently been partially excavated and left for later study. This was a good classroom; it would have been simple to start reconstructing the walls with the rocks scattered along the beach.

Laurence was learning some basic facts of life, simple things that we take for granted. He could make sense of this simple environment and he could see his place within it.

I wished Laurence could have experienced the natural peace and inner tranquillity that this simple lifestyle offered at an earlier age. The understanding that he could have gained here would have helped him cope so much better during those wild early years in our over-crowded, artificial and totally confusing city.

He had spent years trying to puzzle out our unreliable world of falsehoods. He had built his understanding on the one thing that he could rely on, the transport system. One station always followed another, the 48 bus always went to London Bridge and the 38 bus always went to Victoria. Building out from this was difficult for him. People never parked their cars in the same place in the street outside. Their garden gates were a mess and it was impossible to tell the reason or motive of all the people and animals interacting with his world. It all made no sense in those early days.

Here were the basic building blocks for his understanding of our world. The principle of breaking everything down into simple chunks, like in the TEACCH programme, was naturally in use here, helping him to make sense of this simple society and consequently helping him to understand that he had a place in our society.

It was the middle of August, but we saw just a solitary cyclist that morning riding through the wet sand along the shoreline. We followed her tracks as she rapidly disappeared around the next headland. Laurence was freed from all the worries regarding what other people were going to do or say. He could truly relax.

The best our society could offer him was the noisy psychedelic environment of a suburban special needs classroom. This was not an easy arena for him to make sense of our world. Here, devoid of distractions and with sensational rewards in the sea on offer, I wondered what could have been achieved with appropriate one-to-one teaching in this environment.

I suspect that we would all be staggered by what all of us could learn. A year spent in a pre-school here would give these over-stressed children a chance to calm down. The teachers would have a chance to understand these children and identify their sensitivities and susceptibilities. They could make informed recommendations for the style of future education and therapies needed, while the children would gain a template on which to base their reintegration back into our more complex society.

Despite his years, Laurence was also benefiting from this simple therapy. He was relaxed and skipping through life, while I felt more connected to him than ever before. I think this was due to an increased desire in him to engage in conversation with us. His conversational abilities didn't improve, but he was relaxed enough to try to initiate communication.

That afternoon the weather did improve a bit. We even had shadows for a while as the sun tried to break through the thinning cloud. It was still windy, but we were in a beautiful sheltered bay where the tamed waves were running up the gently sloping beach. There were a lot of jellyfish on the beach stranded by the receding tide so I made Laurence wear his sandals as he splashed through the water.

At the end of the bay was a grassy hill rising out of the sea. At high tide it was an island, so the current low tide beckoned me to climb it. Laurence wanted to come, but Bianca was uncharacteristically fed up with all this walking and chose to stay on the beach.

I couldn't see a path so we walked straight up. It was bigger than it looked and we had to stop a couple of times to give him a breather. The view from the top was breathtaking. To my right was the wide white arc of the bay we had walked across and to my left was another identical sandy bay. The symmetry made me feel like I was at the centre of the world. I felt that there should have been a castle built here, but I couldn't see any ruins.

The view was my reward for climbing the hill, but Laurence's motive only became clear when we started to descend. He wanted to roll down. He rolled a bit, stopped, rolled some more and then sat in the long grass clutching his knees. His face turned white and I could see his head was spinning inside.

Cruelly I egged him on, telling him there was still a long way to go. 'No,' was all he could tersely reply.

His colour slowly returned and he got up and held my hand as we walked down. He did a couple of token rolls on the way down but he had learnt his lesson: you can have too much of a good thing.

We returned to our hotel and ate a hearty dinner in the bar. The fresh air and walking knocked us all out early.

The grey clouds were still there the next morning and there was no respite from the wind. After breakfast we continued heading north through the island chain. Causeways link the islands of South Uist, Benbecula and North Uist. I could find no reason to stop, so we drove straight through Benbecula on to North Uist.

The road on North Uist circles the island. It didn't matter whether we went left or right. The maps told me that there was nothing except stunning scenery in either direction. Although Laurence was happy roaming this empty landscape, Bianca needed a bit more than spectacular views. In desperation I followed the signs to a bird sanctuary.

None of us had any interest in birds, but I hoped to see some puffins, though it was the wrong time of year. The sanctuary consisted of some toilets—hooray—an honesty box in a hut and a long walk.

We probably made too much noise for serious bird watching but we did manage to disturb a pair of herons sitting quietly on one of the small black lakes. I felt a bit guilty as they flapped majestically into the air.

I gave Bianca the job of following the small red-tipped posts marking the route. While Laurence purred and lapped up the serene solitude, Bianca was suffering. In this simple reality, it was Bianca who was the disabled one. To her, holidays were about meeting and making new friends, electronic games, exhilarating rides and lovely weather.

She couldn't appreciate the exhilarating scenery. However, with a big brother like Laurence, she had to grow up tough and she struggled on. Today we were rewarded when the trail led us to an almost circular lagoon with just a small gap for the sea to get in. A family of seals were playing in the becalmed water near the shore. A couple of them were floating on their backs chewing on some seaweed, and even lumbering Laurence couldn't disturb them.

We got back to the car without getting lost and we continued on our journey. Before long I had crossed the causeway onto the tiny island of Berneray. We had lunch in the café and I looked at the map for something interesting to visit on the island.

The beach on Berneray was difficult to find but it was well worth the trouble. In fact, I would say that it was the best beach we visited on the islands. The wind had built sand dunes as big as houses and the smooth beach arced into the distance. The gathering dark clouds only added character to the magnificent panorama.

The dunes were soon ringing with the children's laughter. Laurence was chasing Bianca and she was making it as difficult as she could for him on the dunes. At one point he was stuck, sliding down as fast as he could climb upwards. Bianca climbed down, grabbed his hand and pulled him up, landing in a giggling heap at the top. Laurence spent no time reflecting at the top. He tumbled down and started climbing up again and again.

We spent a couple of hours here but we had no reason to stay on this island, so I drove across the island to catch the last ferry from Berneray to Harris. This was a much smaller car ferry with no restaurants and bars. There was just an indoor lounge for shelter and some vending machines for the one-hour crossing. We spent the entire journey outside taking in the views that on a clear day would have been spectacular.

The Sound of Harris is littered with small islands and rocky outcrops. These must have been very dangerous waters in the olden days as many of the rocks lay just below the surface. The ferry zigzagged around the hazards, keeping within the narrow deep channels. Laurence was wearing his smile again and we had a lovely ride.

We arrived on the Isle of Harris at half past six. A couple of miles along the road I found a B&B nestling on the hillside. There was a sheep dog on a long tether in the garden. It was a clever dog and wasted no time identifying Bianca as the soft touch. It ran up to her and dropped a ball at her feet. She was hooked and they played together for hours while Laurence and I got cleaned up.

The view from our bedroom window was superb. Below us was a golf course and beyond that there was a beach arcing round to the base of a cloud-topped grassy hill. The bright yellow sand seemed to glow in the encroaching evening gloom.

The wind howled all that night but it did not manage to shift the grey clouds hanging over the hill on the other side of the bay. I wanted to explore this area but the weather was uninviting so I continued north. The Isle of Harris was more mountainous than the previous islands and some of the views were the most spectacular yet.

A few miles down the road I stopped at an unmanned tourist information point. There was information about the local wildlife and about the Golden Road. It got its name from the local press because of the enormous amount of money spent on building a road that nobody wanted and that went nowhere. It went for miles but ended up just a hundred yards from where it started.

I had to explore this folly and I would recommend it to anybody who likes driving. Of course the scenery was stunning, but it was the road that was the star. It was a single-track tarmac lane with passing points on all the blind corners and humps. It snaked over and round hills and wound around lakes and rocks like a natural roller coaster. From the top of the hills the road could be seen winding through the green landscape like a crazy stretch of Scalextric.

On our way around we stopped for a walk and got lost for a while. While I worried about finding the car again, the children were having great fun picking their way through the boggy ground between the hills and around the lakes. Between the rain showers I took a picture of them beside some raging rapids and Laurence was smiling again.

He was so happy in this environment and his smile was infectious. The strange thing was that when Bianca asked him to smile he still contorted his face into painful-looking expressions. It seemed that he could smile and was smiling naturally but he didn't know how to smile. Very strange!

The Golden Road is an awful blight on some gorgeous scenery but it was great fun to drive along. When Daddy finally finished playing on this road, we continued heading north.

We arrived in Tarbert, the capital of Harris, at lunchtime. It was a picturesque little village and the closest we had been to civilisation since we left the mainland. Scattered around the village were some old-fashioned shops still stuck in the time warp that makes these islands so enchanting.

In contrast we sheltered from the rain in a trendy café that made a big fuss over its organic food. That must have seemed very odd to the islanders. After lunch it was still raining. It was not like the showers that we had encountered throughout these islands; it was heavy, continuous rain.

I had planned to spend some time here. It looked like a good base for exploring the area and I hoped to find something to spice up the holiday for Bianca, like pony trekking or even canoeing. In the torrential rain there were no signs of any activities and the tourist information office was closed for the afternoon. We retreated to the warmth of the car to reconsider my plans.

The children were not interested in hanging around on the off-chance that the weather might improve and we would find something to do. It made sense to drive through this rainy spell but I now had the strange feeling that we were being driven onward by the weather. The same force that had tried to stop us reaching these islands was now pushing us onward to the Isle of Lewis, the northernmost island in this chain.

Was I starting to see autistic patterns or was I simply going a bit mad, in which case the madness started when I was planning this adventure. While I was making my plans I searched the Internet for places of interest to visit on our tour. I didn't have much success, but I did find the standing stones of Callanish.

Some people call Callanish the Stonehenge of the North; it dates back to 3000 BC. Over the millennia, the site was buried by peat, leaving only the tallest stones showing. This meant that the site remained intact until modern times, when locals started cutting the peat away just a couple of hundred years ago.

The odd shapes of the stones intrigued me. Some were like large headstones and others were tall and thin. Some were triangular, while some had a sort of diamond shape, which led to myths of giants being turned to stone. All the stones were quarried locally and erected skilfully. It seemed reasonable to assume that the different shapes were chosen for a reason.

While I was looking at some aerial photographs of Callanish on the Internet, I had the strange idea that I needed to visit this site twice. I wanted to view the stones in different lights as I thought that their shadows might have some relevance. Well, that was how I justified my rather odd idea at that time to visit this site twice.

Now, sheltering from the rain in the car, that odd idea seemed to fit in neatly with our situation. We could drive across to the Isle of Lewis visiting Callanish late in the afternoon, find a local B&B and visit the site again next morning before continuing our journey. Hopefully the weather would improve by the time we got there. It seemed like a good plan.

I do wish we could have spent more time on Harris, as what we did see of it was stunning. With better weather, we may well have become side-tracked there.

I had that funny fateful feeling again.

16B

. . . and Enlightenment

Laurence was in a good mood as I tested the car's suspension along the undulating but straight road approaching Callanish. I was enjoying driving along these empty roads. Mid-afternoon we pulled into the nearly full car park. The car park along with a gift shop and café had only recently been built due to the increasing popularity of this place.

The weather had improved but it was still very windy. The clouds were racing over the wide-open landscape, allowing flashes of sunlight to flicker in and out. We decided to go straight in and hit the café later.

A grassy rocky mound stands between the visitor centre and the stones. The path goes around the mound to the stones on the other side. This mound must have had some significance to the stones.

Unlike Stonehenge, at Callanish you can roam around the stones without restriction and there were several people photographing and connecting with the stones when we arrived.

There are about fifty stones in total. The tallest, at sixteen feet tall, stands in the centre beside a small cairn. Thirteen different-shaped stones, between eight and twelve feet high, surround it, forming a near circle. Radiating out from this circle were rows of stones pointing south, east and west. Pointing north were two much longer parallel lines of stones. It looked a bit like a Celtic cross, but this place predates the Celts.

Walking among the stones they are much more impressive than in the photographs. I had walked through the centre circle into the avenue of stones pointing north when I instinctively turned to see Laurence flying towards me.

His eyes had glazed over and his face was full of fury. The red mist had returned. Taken completely by surprise, I reacted too slowly. Simultaneously his boot collided with my shin and he grabbed two handfuls of my hair. His momentum pushed me backward onto the

342

grass and we rolled about as I tried to free my head from his grip. When I did manage to prise us apart he was left holding a handful of my hair. He saw that and screamed. He jumped up and ran out of the nearest exit from the field, the east gate. He ran screaming down the lane for about fifty yards before diving onto the grass verge crying loudly.

There was no traffic so he was quite safe. I dusted myself off and turned to Bianca. 'What set that off?' I asked her. She was as confused as I was; he was happy and then he inexplicably turned crazy. I was not going after him, he could stay there until he had calmed down and then he could come to me.

Of course I kept a watchful eye on him from afar as he lay there sobbing and eventually he did calm down. He walked back along the lane still whimpering. I had not seen this behaviour since those early testosterone surges during the onset of puberty, although the attack on the defenceless little girl at school was probably also from a similar blind rage. On each occasion he was always full of remorse for what he had done, so I opened my arms to welcome and comfort him.

He was within a couple of yards when I saw his eyes glaze over again and the rage returned. I dodged his boot and ducked from one hand but he still managed to grab my hair with other. I tried to roll him down to the floor to maximise my slim weight advantage, but he wriggled from my grasp and the next thing I saw was the sole of his boot.

I remember thinking that I must stay conscious as my body recoiled from the impact. Fortunately I landed in soft grass, I did not bang my head on a stone and his boot caught me squarely on the cheek and did not do any real damage. At the same time Laurence recoiled in horror and ran out of the nearest gate again; this time it was on the west side. He ran down the footpath screaming his head off and slumped onto the grass verge crying, about fifty yards away again.

'What on earth is going on?' I panted as I struggled to my feet. I had seen for myself, he had been sobbing gently and then spontaneously combusted into an uncontrollable rage. This was no longer like previous attacks—he was always full of remorse after an attack, and when we went through the same routine for a third time I knew that something very strange indeed was going on.

What I didn't know was what to do about it. I had to rely on instinct and that told me to stand firm. I felt that we had to treat this like all the other hurdles that he had had to overcome in his life. I didn't know what this particular lesson was but I felt that he had to learn how to cope with it, regardless of how painful learning that lesson was to me.

It was time for that true grit.

The attacks continued and followed the same pattern. Each time I welcomed him back and he attacked until he fell into my open arms, sobbing.

He was exhausted and distraught and we both consoled him. I couldn't get any sense out of him; he answered all my questions with, 'Mustn't hurt Daddy.' He could not know what caused it. I asked him how many times he hurt Daddy. 'Five,' he replied morosely and I had no reason to doubt him.

I had switched off from the daggers I was receiving from the other visitors to the site. Now as he sobbed in my arms, I realised that we had emptied the site completely with our antics. I decided not to rush away, so we hung around a while to see if there was any more rage hidden amongst these stones. We took some rather wooden photos as the atmosphere was still tense but he remained calm. He had regained his control.

Visiting Callanish had been thirsty work so we retired to the café for refreshments. It was full but fortunately several tables became available as soon as we walked in.

Our next objective was to find a bed for the night. There were several B&Bs in the village but they were all full. Whilst driving around I noticed a hand-painted sign for a Callanish Exhibition, so I pulled over. It had been a long day and Bianca was not interested, while Laurence was unsurprisingly subdued sitting in the back seat. It couldn't be very big, so I told them I would have a quick look around and be back in a couple of minutes.

I was right, the exhibition was in a large garden shed with chickens running around in the garden. My eyes slowly adjusted to the gloom inside the shed. The walls were covered in maps with lines drawn across them and there were lots of photos of the surrounding hills. The tables were full of displays of how the stones were laid out and erected. It was clear that the person who had compiled this exhibition had spent a lot of time studying the stones.

From a quick scan of the walls I could see that the alignments found were all lunar and the site builders seemed particularly interested in the periods of the lunar cycle when the moon skimmed along the hills on the horizon. My ideas about the sun and shadows were clearly nonsense, so thankfully there was no reason for us to come back to this strange place tomorrow.

I put some money in the honesty box, took a booklet called *New Light on the Stones of Callanish* as a souvenir of our visit and left the shed. As I turned blinking into the daylight, I was surprised to see a frail-looking woman with long white hair. She looked like a white witch and was very friendly, insisting on personally showing me around the exhibition. I could not resist her charm and followed her back into the shed.

The light switch was hidden around a corner and she switched it on; that helped. Her name was Margaret Curtis and she had spent most of her working life studying Callanish. The exhibition was the result of her work so far and she was the author of the booklet that I had just paid for.

Showing me the maps, she explained that there were twenty other Callanishes scattered around the area and probably many more still to be found buried in the peat. So far they were all smaller and less complete than the main site. She was currently looking for lunar alignments between the sites, hence all the lines on the maps.

I told her the shape of the stones intrigued me and she asked if I had noticed the small notches on some of the stones. I had not and she explained that some of these notches formed alignments with moonrise and moonset at specific times in a lunar cycle of 18.61 years. She must have spent years of nights measuring the stones in the fickle weather.

She asked if I had noticed the Earth Mother and yet again I had not, plus I had to admit that I did not know what an Earth Mother was. She showed me some photos of distant hills and pointed out the profile of a sleeping woman. Locally she is unflatteringly called Cailleach Na Mointeach (the old woman of the moors). I am normally quite good at seeing shapes in clouds, but I could not see her.

Callanish is built on a special latitude for the moon. Every eighteen and a half years the moon does not rise into the sky; it rises and skims along the distant hills before setting below the horizon again. The moon appears to visit the Earth Mother. Five thousand years ago the locals were interested in recording these events with the aid of the stones.

I could have chatted all evening but I made my excuses to leave because of the children in the car. She told me to bring them in as they could play with the models of how the stones were erected.

345

Normally I would have, but I was still a bit wary about Laurence. I started to tell her that we simply had a difficult day but I ended up telling her of our experience with the stones.

She knew nothing of autism but she said that we must come back tomorrow. I explained that I had originally planned to come back tomorrow but after our experience today I had no intention of returning.

'No, no, you must come back tomorrow,' she urged. 'If you come back tomorrow everything will be all right. Trust me,' she smiled. This strange tale was becoming a bit spooky and I asked her to explain how she could possibly know this.

She explained that to make ends meet she did some individual and group guided tours of the sites in the area. She met many people in the course of these tours. Among them a few claimed to be psychic mediums. Some of these reported that they were unable to go into the site. It was as if some strange force was preventing them from entering, but bizarrely when they returned the next day they had no problem entering the site and walking around the stones.

The idea of Laurence being an autistic psychic amused me but I have never been impressed by the claims of clairvoyants and their like. I didn't believe Ana when she claimed Laurence was psychic when he was a baby, and in time we found the sensory reasons for her beliefs.

I believe that these psychics pick up similar sensory signals to autistics like Laurence. The only difference is that the psychics are not autistic and they choose to interpret their heightened sensory inputs as somehow being mystical. It is not that difficult to make somebody think you are psychic with the clever interpretation of acutely perceptive vision.

I was not convinced, but Margaret's next example did persuade me that we would have to return.

One day a trainer with two trained-for-TV dogs visited Callanish. The trainer was astonished when both of the dogs refused to go onto the site. These usually obedient dogs steadfastly stayed outside, but when they returned the next day they ran onto the site without hesitation.

If the dogs felt it then I could believe that it was real and I asked her what she thought it was. She didn't know but pointed out that the stones are made of local Lewisian gneiss and have a high crystalline content. Some people think the crystals are causing this effect, she told me, but stressed that she didn't necessarily agree with any of this. She was just passing on what she had seen and heard over the years.

I thanked her profusely for her insights as I limped back through her garden. Unfortunately she was giving a private tour in the morning so she would not be able to talk to us then, so I promised to write.

I needn't have worried about the children; I think they were too tired to be naughty. We had exhausted the B&Bs in the area so I decided to drive across the island to Stornoway, the capital of Lewis and only real town on these islands. We could be sure to find a hotel there and it was only a half-hour drive.

Laurence liked our hotel as it had a lift and Bianca liked it as she had her own double bed in her own room. I had several aches and bruises so I appreciated the hot bath and soft bed. I lay in bed reading the booklet about Callanish from cover to cover. I wanted to be better informed before we went back.

People have speculated about the original purpose of the Callanish stones for as long as they have been known. From the earliest tales of giants turned to stone, alternative theories have flourished and have got even crazier. In 1973 Tom Lethbridge suggested that wild dancing around the ring charged the stones with 'bio-electrical potential' which flying saucers could detect!

Greek gods, Norse gods, Druids and other religions have all been associated with this site at some time or another. Nowadays astrono- mer-priests are in vogue. Complex computer programs calculate the positions of astronomical bodies five thousand years ago. Modern accurate surveying techniques allow archaeoastronomers to claim that there are too many alignments for them to be mere chance.

This tells us that the builders were clever people, but that is all. We cannot get into their heads to find out why they went to such an effort to build these sites. I wondered where Laurence fitted in to all this.

If Laurence had visited Callanish five thousand years ago he would have been 'afflicted by some sort of strange madness' and fled the scene, probably never wanting to return. It wouldn't have been difficult to persuade him to stay away and keep the demons that lurk there happy with regular peace offerings.

Laurence, like most children, would have returned to work along- side his father in the fields or making pottery or axes. Like the majority of the population, it would be a simple, honest life learning and perfecting the skills passed down through the generations from father to son. That would suit Laurence then and now.

Occasionally a child would pass through the ordeal of the stones without being afflicted by the madness and would be taken in by the elders. Capable of learning the ways of the elders, they learnt how to control the 'herd'. As good communicators, they controlled the trade that produced the wealth of the society that built the sites.

Maybe we would call these children normal or say they have Asperger's, but it is not difficult to imagine a time in human development when such children might have been at a premium—a time when man started to live together in larger groups than families and some men, with better communication and social skills, learnt how to control and manipulate these larger societies. They had thousands of years to practise their skills; they prospered so much that nowadays we are all infected with their genes. This explains why the vast majority of visitors to Callanish these days are unaffected by the stones but nature still produces the old models just in case the new strain of humans fails.

My theory felt just as plausible as any of the others that I had read. My head was full of strange ideas that night. One thing I did know was that whatever the white witch foretold, I should be prepared for another battering in the morning.

After a full Scottish breakfast we set out for round two. I told Laurence where we were going and he seemed relaxed about it. I wanted him to be as relaxed as possible just like he was yesterday when we approached Callanish. I wanted him to run free and not to feel under my thumb, so I didn't put any pressure on him to behave.

The car park was nearly empty when we arrived. We decided to get this over and done with and went straight in. Laurence seemed relaxed ambling along behind us. As we walked around the mound I noticed Laurence climbing up the mound. That was unusual. Laurence would follow me up there but left to his own devices he always chose the easiest route. Maybe that was the correct way in. We met up on the other side and entered the field of stones together.

As before I walked through the centre of the site and this time I turned to see Laurence rolling on the floor scratching his back in the long grass. He was giggling and totally transformed from yesterday. The wind still whistled around the stones but the atmosphere felt altogether lighter. We took some happier photos and I tried to point out the Earth Mother to Bianca. She couldn't see her either and looked at me as if yesterday's blows might have affected Daddy's head.

With this success under my belt, I decided to push my luck and visit Callanish II and Callanish III as they were only a mile down the road. Access to these stone circles is along a footpath through some very boggy sheep-filled fields. The children enjoyed jumping from one dry patch to another but inevitably we all ended up with dirty wet feet.

We reached Callanish III first. There were sixteen stones in a circle with four inner stones. Callanish II was smaller, with just five stones still standing. At each site the same haunting stone shapes stood fast against the relentless wind. It was impossible to imagine the warmer, drier and wooded landscape that surrounded these stones when they were erected.

Laurence had no problems at both sites and was in fact positively enjoying our trek across this boggy terrain. It was time to leave the Callanish stones and leave the mystery of their shapes behind us. I was utterly confused and wondered what the lesson from our second visit was.

I have decided that I would like my ashes spread over Callanish when the time comes. The journey would be fun for my friends and it would ensure that Laurence gets another chance to enjoy the serenity of these islands, while I could look for the 'old woman of the moors' in my own time.

I took my time following the road along the west coast of the island. After a picnic lunch we arrived at the Blackhouse Museum. I wouldn't have chosen this place to visit, but in the absence of anything else we had a look around.

It was another excellent classroom for Laurence. Made from readily available stone and thatch, on the outside blackhouses have not changed over thousands of years. As we went between houses the evolution of the interiors unfurled. Animals sheltered in one end of the long thin houses and the family lived at the other end, with the middle used for storage.

These houses were lived in until the 1950s, and one house was preserved as it was when the last occupants left. The roaring peat fire made it feel snug and the fittings reminded me of my earliest memories of my grandmother's house. With table and chairs, beds and sideboard it was a home that Laurence could recognise as well. It would have been a smelly house but that would be an environment that he could understand.

In some ways, apart from the odd diversion around the world, here was the entire history of human development right up to the fifties, when the people moved into artificial houses with electricity, running water and sanitation. Maybe this was the end of the road for natural autism. Was this the last place where Laurence could have led a normal life? In this simple environment, he would have understood what was required of him and he would have understood the needs of his smelly livestock better than any veterinarian. He would have been useful in this society; he could have fitted in normally.

One of the blackhouses was converted into a youth hostel. It would have been fun to stay for a night but it was full. We ended up staying in the same hotel back in Stornoway.

That night we decided that it would be our last on the Hebrides. The next morning I booked us onto the afternoon crossing to Ullapool on the mainland. That gave us plenty of time to explore Stornoway and do some shopping. We bought new socks and some souvenirs before queuing up to board the ferry.

My gamble on the southern heatwave having a knock-on effect to the weather up here had failed. We had been battered for a week by the Atlantic winds and I was ready to head straight home. Laurence was happy to be going on a boat again, but his joy was tinged with sadness as we were saying goodbye to his beloved Hebredeez.

Apart from that mad couple of hours in Callanish he had loved every minute of our tour. From the roller-coaster ride of the sea crossing, to climbing over rocks and up hills and falling down the dunes, the Hebrides had been an amusement park and classroom built for Laurence. From walking across the empty peat bogs in the interior to walking beside the huge crashing waves along the wide-open deserted beaches, he was able to truly relax and take in all that this simple landscape had to offer.

He could understand this life.

The ferry left at two in the afternoon and takes three hours to make the crossing. We watched Stornoway shrink into the gloom of another cloudy day and turned our attention to the opposite horizon where we could see Scottish mountains in the distance and some blue sky. It was not long before we were basking in sunshine, while behind us a bank of grey cloud hung over the Outer Hebrides on the horizon.

As we sailed through the Summer Isles and between the mountains into Loch Broom, our ferry felt more like a cruise ship. Ullapool is a beautiful village port sitting beside the loch and surrounded by mountains. I had visited this place before on my way to see the eclipse.

We found a guesthouse on the hillside overlooking the loch and walked back to the village for some dinner. The pub facing the ferry does some excellent seafood and I can heartily recommend it. After dinner we went down to the shingle beach. Bianca and I skipped stones on the smooth water of the loch as the evening sun made the surrounding hills glow orange.

Laurence liked the sound of the pebbles plopping into the water but he was not content with that. Typically he had to do it to excess and he scooped up and hurled handfuls of pebbles into the air in quick succession. Many did plop into the water while many others clattered back onto the shingle and several fell on him, but he did not seem to mind that. We stood back and watched while he excavated part of the beach. He was laughing as he conducted his own seaside symphony and we had to laugh with him.

It is amazing how a bit of sunshine had transformed our outlook. For the first time in over a week, not only could we take our coats off but we could also take off our jumpers. Life felt so much better in a T-shirt. That night we decided not to go home just yet. The next couple of days were forecast to be scorchers so we decided to head for the seaside.

On the map I could see a few small beaches nearby but I could not be sure what we would find there. A two-hour drive north would take us to Durness, where I knew the children would enjoy the beaches.

We pulled into the car park beside the beach in Durness just before lunchtime. It was a beautiful day with just a few wispy white clouds floating high up in the sky.

As I got out of the car Laurence burst out of the car behind me and ran across the car park towards the beach clutching his towel. Partly because of a shortage of clean clothes I had dressed him in his swimming shorts that morning so he was all ready and waiting for no one. Bianca and I stood by the car laughing as we followed his progress down onto the beach.

As he ran across the beach, he kicked of his sandals and tossed aside his towel and T-shirt without stopping. He did not stop until he collided head on with the thundering waves. After a week of only being allowed to paddle in the sea he must have been bursting

There was a sign in the car park pointing to various global destinations. London was 886 kilometres in one direction and in the opposite direction there was 3,500 kilometres of water and ice between the North Pole and us. The water must have been freezing but it did not bother Laurence.

Bianca and I packed some items for a picnic on the beach and followed his trail, picking up his discarded articles along the way. I allowed him to play for a while before having lunch and I made sure that he warmed up thoroughly before allowing him to return to the sea later in the afternoon. Bianca wisely chose not to go in the sea, so she built sandcastles and explored the rocky stacks on the beach.

Later that afternoon we booked into the half-empty campsite on top of the cliffs behind the beach. We had hauled around all our camping equipment but the weather had discouraged me from using it. Now seemed like a good time to try it. With an evening breeze picking up, Bianca and I struggled to get the tent up and pegged down. Laurence was no help; he was too excited by the prospect of camping and skipped happily around our wreck.

Eventually it was up and Laurence wanted to sleep in it straight away. I did have a camping stove for emergencies, but we chose to eat out that night instead. We had a good pub dinner and the children slept well.

Next morning the children were up early and we soon discovered that we had no milk for breakfast. Bianca volunteered to go to the village shop, which was a couple of hundred yards along the road. Not wanting to be left out, Laurence wanted to go as well. Normally I wouldn't dream of imposing such a responsibility on Bianca and I would have gone with them. But here and now his behaviour was not a concern and he could have gone on his own if it was not for his problem with handling money.

I realised that if we lived in such a small community, people would get to know him and with a tab he could easily go shopping for me. They were longer than I expected and I was beginning to get worried. When they did return Bianca explained that they had to wait for the shop to open. Laurence was a good boy throughout.

We ate our breakfast sitting in the morning sunshine and then went to explore Smoo Cave, which was nearby. Well, it kept Laurence off the beach for a while. Access to the cavernous mouth of the cave was via a footpath down the steep side of a narrow valley. Laurence got quite excited as we made our way down, but we reached the cave safely.

After the excitement of the descent the cave was a bit of a disappointment. The cave mouth was huge but we could not walk far inside the cave as an underground lake blocked the way. In the gloom we could not see the other side of the lake. For two pounds per head a guide would row us across the lake to see more of the cave.

I asked Laurence if he wanted to go on the boat. 'No thank you,' he quickly replied and ran off as if to emphasise that there was no way that he was going into that black hole. I was happy with his choice and we left the cave. The steep grassy sides of the valley were covered in people's names made from rocks found in the cave mouth. Bianca wanted to put her name there.

She soon found out that it was no picnic as she climbed to an empty space with a jumper full of rocks. While she toiled Laurence was skipping in and out of the cave. I suspected that he was experimenting with the acoustics so I left him alone while I supervised Bianca's work. The B alone took two jumper loads and it didn't help that rocks frequently rolled down the hill of their own accord. When she had nearly finished Laurence ran up to me and said, 'Go in the boat now.'

I checked that he really did want to go in that boat and then promised him that we would when Bianca finished her work. He was happy with that and skipped off again. I realised that he had been watching other visitors go on the boat and return unscathed and happy. I have no doubt that he counted them all out and he counted them all back again. Satisfied that people were not coming to some gruesome end in this black hole, he decided that it was safe for him to go in as well just like he did at the Black Hole ride at Alton Towers.

My mind went back to all those times in his early childhood when I dragged him into places kicking and screaming for no apparent reason. He was unable to express himself in any other way. I was unable to understand his fears and I was unable to reassure him in a way that he could comprehend.

'Autism experts' reassured me that this was normal autistic behaviour and unavoidable, while in reality our modern high-speed world meant that we rarely had the time or inclination to indulge his idiosyncrasies. Normally we never had the time to wait outside buildings until he felt confident enough to enter, but on holiday we were in no hurry to go anywhere.

Bianca completed her name and posed beside her masterpiece for a photograph. I told her to be thankful that I didn't name her Charlotte or an even longer name. I explained that Laurence now claimed that he wanted to go on the boat and we returned to the cave, rather sceptical as to how far he would go.

I paid for the tour and the guide issued us with hard hats. The first obstacle was a tricky descent down a ladder to board the inflatable rowing boat. I could tell that Laurence was very excited but he was equally determined and he followed his sister onto the boat, while I followed behind. Another family joined us with four children whose ages ranged from younger than Bianca to older than Laurence.

Our guide rowed us across the smooth black lake. We disembarked and our guide led us along a narrow slippery cave. Laurence was finding this very exciting and he gripped my hand firmly. We hadn't gone far when the cave abruptly ended. We gathered around a water-filled hole in the ground at the end of the cave while the guide tried to string out the tour by giving us a talk on the nature of the rock and how the caves were formed.

He also explained that the water-filled hole at our feet was shaped like the U-bend in a toilet. They had squirted a dye into this and it came out several hundred yards away, but all their attempts to find a passage through had failed. He turned to the youngest child in the other family and claimed that they had been waiting for somebody small enough to turn up and go down there to find a way out.

'Not for Laurence,' gasped Laurence loudly.

My first priority was to calm and reassure him, but I was amazed that he had followed the gist of the talk. It was so typical, he had simply failed to see the joke and realise that it wasn't aimed at him.

Fortunately it was the end of the talk and Laurence calmed down as we returned through the cave. He was the first off the boat and skipped away into the sunshine very pleased with himself indeed.

We spent a lot of time on the beach. Bianca spent an entire afternoon playing with another collie dog. She seemed to wear an invisible sign which dogs read as, 'Play with me'. It was such a shame that Laurence could not read this sign or maybe he could but he just

354

did not understand it. She always had to play with him; he never initiated playing with her.

While I monitored and rationed the time Laurence spent playing in the icy waves I had plenty of time to reflect on our Highland adventure.

Foremost in my mind was the Callanish experience and I had to consider that I probably handled it all wrong. First, I felt guilty because I suspected that I had inadvertently tricked him. Over the previous couple of weeks he had relaxed, and he trotted into Callanish beside me with his guard down. I should have given him more time at the entrance to give him a chance to detect the danger and decline entry just like the dogs did.

Second, when we were inside the site I think I should have left after the first or second attack. With us both out of the site he could have had the opportunity to re-enter the site if he chose. By standing my ground all I did was give him no alternative to returning to the stones time after time.

I have lost track of the number of times that I have been wrong while I have tried to unravel his autism over the years. It is a testament to his wonderful character that he always forgave me for my mistakes. I do believe that he forgave me for the same reason that I forgave him for his indiscretions. I saw him as autistic with SLD and he saw me as a simple creature unable to communicate with him. After all, it was he who had to learn our language. It was he who had to learn how to behave in our society because we were unable to comprehend his.

Despite my mistakes at Callanish I am convinced that there was no lasting effect, beneficial or otherwise, at this place but it was an interesting effect and deserves further research. What is the force that some psychics, autistics and animals detect but we cannot?

However, this holiday undoubtedly did have a big effect on Laurence. To check if it wasn't just me, I asked Bianca if she had noticed any difference in him.

'Have I?' She sighed. 'He doesn't stop talking.' She was right.

Of course his vocabulary hadn't magically expanded, but he was using his existing language much more often. It was tedious for Bianca, but for me it was wonderful that he appeared more willing to communicate.

It is important to remember that I set out on this holiday to test

Laurence and to deliberately make it difficult for him. By constantly moving around I wanted to remove all routines and by doing so I inadvertently created a heavenly holiday for him and a hellish holiday for Bianca, although she did warm to it when the sun came out back on the mainland.

Over the last three weeks he had totally relaxed and his need for routines had vanished. He had probably not been so relaxed since he was in the womb and he hadn't wanted to come out of there. In this simple environment he had relaxed, so he felt comfortable and his confidence to communicate grew.

His desire to communicate was a symptom of his growing confidence, as was his increased competitiveness with Bianca. Whatever she did he wanted to do it as well. He followed her up towering sand dunes, crossed over a river on a fallen tree and clambered after her over slippery rocks; it was all so normal.

Again I wished I had brought him here when he was younger. I think the optimum time for Laurence would have been some time after the first auditory training sessions but before the first session with the dolphins. I wonder what might have been if I had been able to give him one month on the islands that summer. By the time we blundered up here he was relatively acclimatised to our world, but in those wild early years this opportunity for thorough relaxation could have given him the chance to form a simple template to aid his comprehension of our more complex society.

This newfound confidence in Laurence felt like a third and totally unexpected 'awakening'.

All too soon we awoke one morning to a cloudy sky and cool breeze. It was time to go home.

September was approaching. We packed up the tent and I told Bianca to ring Mummy and let her know that we would be home in three days. I was not going to rush home.

That morning we stopped to watch a herd of deer and at lunchtime we arrived at Mohamed Al Fayed's place just outside Lairg. I was unimpressed with the mini Harrods that he built there but it sits beside the Falls of Shin. Here you can watch salmon trying to leap upstream. I was not sure whether they would still be trying this late in the summer, so we watched and waited.

Laurence wandered off and Bianca was getting bored when suddenly a salmon leapt out of the water right in front of us. It balanced precariously on the cusp of the waterfall with its tail flapping wildly in the air as it tried to wiggle that extra inch to safety. Its efforts were in vain and it fell back into the pool at the bottom of the waterfall to try again. Bianca was hooked.

Laurence did not go far, he sat on a boulder beside the raging river. I could not make out if he was watching the fish or listening to the soothing sound of the torrent racing beside him. Either way, he looked at ease—in fact, he looked like a large bear studying the river while waiting for lunch to arrive.

It seemed symbolic: he chose to sit naturally on the boulder while we stood on the man-made concrete viewing platform with safety railings.

As it was the end of the holiday we splashed out on lunch in the Harrods restaurant and then continued heading south. We spent that night in a hotel that was just south of Inverness and well placed for a day of driving round the big tourist attractions of Scotland as we continued our journey home.

The next morning we started with Loch Ness and Urquhart Castle, followed by Fort William and Ben Nevis. We had lunch in the awesome Glen Coe and spent a few hours in the afternoon relaxing in a picturesque village on the banks of Loch Lomond. It was a beautiful day.

The children were very well behaved during all this driving. It is true that they were well behaved on the way up, but that was in near total silence. Now Laurence wanted to interact, so Bianca teased and played with him while he lapped up the attention. He always wanted more and their laughter and giggles filled the car. It all felt so natural and yet it was still not normal. He was still autistic and the playing was still one way. The illusion of normality only lasted for as long as Bianca could continue to initiate play, as he still could not reciprocate.

We lingered by Loch Lomond, not wishing to leave. From here on it was all dual carriageways and motorways. My plan was that that evening we would drive around Glasgow onto the M6, crossing the border into England, leaving me with a straightforward journey home the following day.

We could already feel the shadow of the encroaching modern world. There were crowds of tourists, cars and coaches, powerboats and jet skis all along the shore of Loch Lomond. Laurence started to walk around with his head in the air again. I understood that he was being forced to take in too much visual information again.

Observing the sudden return of this autistic behaviour made me realise that my naturally autistic puppy was being poisoned. His poison was people.

I had read autistic adults' accounts of this type of behaviour on the Internet. They described it like a picture in vision facility on a TV set. By taking just a small part of their field of vision and placing it in a corner, they could concentrate on that while ignoring the rest of the overwhelming visual clutter.

He had started experimenting with this technique, clumsily bumping into people and tripping over things before we came on holiday. We had removed the need for this in the wide-open sparsely inhabited landscape of the Outer Hebrides. Now, as the number of people and other visual clutter around us increased, he returned to looking with one eye in the sky. He was getting more adept at doing this but it all had to be self-taught.

Why can't we, with all our cleverness, teach young autistic children to do this so that they can sit and concentrate on what is written on the blackboard by looking up at the ceiling and ignoring all the other visual distractions around the classroom?

Laurence, with his 'SLD', had to teach himself. It took him most of his childhood to find a way to reduce his overwhelming optical input. I think the marvellous best-selling book *The Curious Incident of the Dog in the Night-Time* describes the debilitating effects of a visual overdose much better than I ever could.

It's too late for Laurence, he cannot return to primary school to restart his education at his age. His path is clear; his teen years should be spent teaching him how to become a productive member of society. It will take years of training, trying different jobs and utilising all that we have learnt about each other so far.

I am in no doubt that some overpaid expert will insist that Laurence continue studying the 'sacred' National Curriculum. So much time will be wasted on this while they pay lip service to the notion of transition into the workplace by simplifying work to suit his disabilities rather than focusing on his abilities.

As the quest for a proper education fades into insignificance, the future battle for a meaningful career for him now comes into focus. I am in no doubt that it will be another tough journey and the experts will make it as difficult as they can, but Laurence is still learning. Like a sponge, he absorbs our mad world with its deceitful and illogical ways. We cannot know how much he soaks up and we can only guess at his interpretations of our odd behaviours.

The expert's perception of him had not changed over the years but my perception of my robotic alien puppy has matured. This was my 'awakening' too.

These days I see Laurence as a poorly programmed super-computer trying to calculate and predict the vagaries of the weather. In years to come, who knows how good he will get at predicting our unpredictable actions? However, I suspect that he will never know exactly which way the wind is blowing.

APPENDIXES

Appendix 1

Epsom Road Under 5s' Centre

Laurence aged 3 years 6 months

Report of child's attainment:

I first met Laurence on a home visit. Then he came to nursery and had a settling-in period with his mum for one week. He was very attached to me for the first few weeks and then he gradually formed relationships with another two members of staff in the room. Laurence would interact with the other children occasionally. He would notice a child near to him, observe what they were doing and join in with the play for a few seconds, i.e. build together or pass each other toys.

The other children would welcome Laurence in the morning and tried to include him in the day's activities. Laurence's reply to this would be a smile or high squeaks and then observe the children at play. His favourite activities were the Duplo Bricks, Stickle Bricks, painting, water play, cars and playing outside. When outside he would run around repeatedly or play on a push-along toy, also he enjoyed being chased and caught.

At meal times when Laurence first arrived he would eat only white-coloured foods using his fingers to feed himself and be very unsettled. By the end of his time at Epsom Road he was more calm at dinnertime and ate foods of different colours, using a spoon to feed himself.

Laurence was still in nappies when he left Epsom Road and needed to be supervised in the bathroom when washing his hands.

After Laurence had settled he would separate from his mother well and run to greet her in the afternoon and always kiss his sister.

The staff saw definite improvements in Laurence by the end of his time at Epsom Road.

He will be missed by staff and children.

Appendix 2

Special Education Advice Conference

Held on 29 March 1993.

Laurence aged 4 years, 1 month

Section A

I *Physical state and functioning*

No cause has been found for Laurence's difficulties. His general health is good.

Vision: Mildly long-sighted with astigmatism.
Hearing: Normal.

(Addendum—Father queried Laurence's hearing—he should be referred for further tests.)

II *Behaviour*

a. *Strengths*
   1. Laurence is generally a contented child.
   2. Laurence is not destructive.
   3. Laurence shows pleasure and displeasure.
   4. Laurence generally responds to firm, consistent handling.
   5. Laurence is able to self occupy using a variety of materials.
   6. Laurence can be cooperative to adult demands, though on his own terms. He is able to show an unwillingness to carry out a specific activity.
   7. Laurence responds to adult initiated games, i.e. will sustain eye contact, turn-take, on his own terms.

b. *Difficulties*
   1. Laurence does not readily accept changes in familiar routines.

2. Laurence sometimes becomes very distressed if separated from his classmates.
3. Cooperation to most adult-directed activities is on Laurence's terms. Laurence displays a number of stereotypical rituals, e.g. continuously banging his knuckles on pieces of equipment/repeatedly removing and replacing objects (e.g. pieces of puzzle).
5. Laurence shows restricted facial expression.
6. Laurence shows obsessive interest in certain toys and objects i.e. vehicles—particularly trains.
7. Laurence interacts inappropriately and sometimes obsessively with some of his peers, he may touch or smell their hair or hold them tightly round the neck.
8. Laurence has displayed an obsessive, slightly aggressive approach to one classmate in particular; this continued for a sustained period, but has almost ceased.
9. Laurence does not enjoy close physical contact with adults and resists being held.
10. Laurence is very easily distracted by slight noises or movements, he continually 'checks' what his classmates are doing by turning or moving away from an adult working with him.
11. Laurence sometimes finds it difficult to 'settle down' and will run from one part of the room to another.

III *Attitudes and approaches to learning*

a. *Strengths*
  1. Laurence has shown that in a 1:1 situation, with a series of tasks presented by a familiar adult, he can concentrate for periods of up to 25 minutes.
  2. Although Laurence can be encouraged to work for edible rewards, this is on his own terms.
  3. Laurence is just beginning to be aware of verbal and physical praise.
  4. When carrying out familiar or preferred tasks, Laurence is able to work on an individual or group basis (e.g. jigsaw puzzles).

b. *Difficulties*
  1. Laurence's cooperation to adult-directed activities is generally on his terms.
  2. Laurence's stereotypical rituals (e.g. tapping) increase when Laurence is under pressure.

3. Laurence is very easily distracted from tasks.
4. Laurence appears to use task-avoidance strategies, e.g. will make deliberate mistakes, in order to stop an adult working on a particular activity with him.
5. Laurence's attention span is short.

IV *Cognitive functioning*

This section has been written in conjunction with the Assessment Teacher.

Laurence was formally tested on 2 of the scales of the Griffiths Mental Development scales, namely Performance and Eye–Hand Coordination. On the former, Laurence was found to perform as a child with a mild delay. However, the results are likely to be depressed by his behaviour, e.g. although Laurence is able to complete, using visual discrimination, an eleven-hole board, he is unable to do this within the prescribed time because of the rituals which he performs between each part of a task (tapping the shape with his knuckles or removing it from the inset).

On the Eye–Hand Coordination scale Laurence was found to have a moderate delay.

a. *Strengths*
1. Laurence is able to complete formboards at a high level; he can differentiate between very similar shapes, e.g. a circle and pentagon, using visual discrimination.
2. Laurence can post complicated shapes in a post box.
3. Laurence is able to match objects and pictures and match identical pictures given an array.
4. Laurence is able to match words to words and pictures and is beginning to recognise some very familiar, motivating words when printed, e.g. car/sweets.
5. Laurence is able to sort 3D and 2D materials by colour into four categories, when the categories are determined for him and only a small amount of materials.
6. Laurence is able to sort by shape when no other criterion (e.g. colour) is involved.
7. Laurence is beginning to show an interest in and ability to complete simple jigsaw puzzles, taking into account shape and orientation.

8. Laurence operates simple touch screen computer programs in cause and effect activities.

b. *Difficulties*
1. Laurence does not copy 3D models using bricks.
2. Although he is beginning to show some problem-solving abilities, Laurence does not readily learn from experience or demonstration by an adult.
3. Using sequencing beakers, Laurence is unable to nest more than three inside one another unless by accident.
4. Laurence does not show any understanding of amount or one-to-one correspondence.

V *Communication skills*

Laurence's communication skills are at about the single-word stage, with expressive language presenting at a slightly higher level than receptive language.

Receptive

a. *Strengths*
1. Laurence generally responds to his name.
2. Laurence responds to very simple contextual commands, e.g. get your coat, sit down, etc.
3. Laurence shows awareness of adult disapproval.
4. Laurence responds to adult's tone of voice.
5. Laurence is able to match objects to photographs and recognises familiar people in photographs.

b. *Difficulties*
1. Laurence's attention can be difficult to gain and maintain.
2. Laurence is not yet able to demonstrate comprehension of single nouns or performative on request (i.e. hand an object from an array).
3. Laurence does not demonstrate understanding of Makaton signs.

Expressive

a. *Strengths*
1. Laurence has a vocabulary of 30+ words; he is using single contextual words spontaneously to label and comment.
2. Laurence uses some performative appropriately, e.g. broom, broom, choo, choo, etc.
3. Laurence is showing consistent use of one sign (drink).
4. Laurence will wave goodbye, in response to adult waving, as he leaves the room.
5. Laurence will respond vocally in interactive activities with a familiar adult, he will maintain eye contact and shows some anticipation of play activities, e.g. peek-a-boo.

b. *Difficulties*
1. Some of Laurence's verbalisations appear to be used automatically with automatic associations, e.g. 'bus, train', 'bus bye bye'.
2. Laurence resists adult manipulation to use Makaton signs.

VI *Motor ability*

Gross motor

a. *Strengths*
1. Laurence walks and runs, negotiating obstacles in his path.
2. Laurence can walk up and down a sloping bench and along a horizontal raised bench.
3. Laurence can jump from a height of 2′ onto a safety mat.
4. Laurence uses P.E. apparatus appropriately.
5. Laurence can catch a large ball when he is sitting down and the ball is thrown from a short distance.
6. Laurence explores and uses the adventure playground and soft play equipment appropriately and with enjoyment.
7. Laurence understands and anticipates his turn at movement activities, e.g. being swung in a blanket.
8. Laurence will sit on wheeled toys and push himself along with his feet.
9. Laurence now allows himself to be held by a familiar adult in the swimming pool and moved through the water.

10. Laurence is more amenable to joining in physical games, e.g. seesaw with another child or adult now.

b. *Difficulties*
   1. Laurence needs direction to follow a sequence of activities on a circuit of P.E. apparatus.
   2. Laurence often runs on tiptoe.
   3. Laurence requires physical prompting to imitate even simple body movements, e.g. clapping hands, stamping.

Fine motor

a. *Strengths*
   1. Laurence is able to build a tower using bricks of various sizes.
   2. Laurence is able to thread beads onto a lace.
   3. Laurence can unscrew the lid of a jar to retrieve an edible, e.g. a crisp.
   4. Laurence is aware of the purpose of scissors and attempts to cut by holding them in two hands although he is, as yet, unsuccessful.
   5. Laurence will use a variety of pens, crayons etc. to make marks, he is able to make circular scribble and has on occasion drawn lines on paper and around his hand.

b. *Difficulties*
   1. Cooperation to adult-directed fine motor activities is inconsistent and on Laurence's terms.
   2. Laurence is not interested in drawing activities and often resists joining in by repeatedly putting down his pencil/crayon, etc.
   3. Laurence tends to use materials repeatedly in the same ways.

VII *Self help skills*

a. *Strengths*
   1. Laurence is an independent little boy who tries to do things for himself.
   2. Laurence can take off and hang up his coat on his peg on request.
   3. Laurence recognises his own clothes; he can pull off most articles of clothing and put on socks, pants, trousers and coat unaided.
   4. Laurence has recently begun to verbalise when he needs the toilet and has started to stand to urinate in a potty.
   5. Laurence is able to feed himself using a spoon and fork.

6. Laurence eats a wide array of foods at school, he has definite likes and dislikes and will refuse a snack he does not like, he is able to indicate when he wants more.
7. Laurence will walk short distances in school holding hands with one of his classmates.

b. *Difficulties*
1. Laurence needs adult manipulation through hand washing and teeth cleaning routines.
2. Toilet training is not well established yet and Laurence often wets himself. He wears a nappy on journeys to and from school.
3. Laurence does not attempt to do up any fastenings.
4. Laurence needs to be firmly held by the hand on outings out of school, as he is unaware of the dangers of traffic, etc.
7. Laurence may refuse to use the potty for certain adults; however, it can be any one of the adults in his room that he is difficult with, on different days.

VIII *Personal interests/level of play*

Laurence is able to keep himself occupied in the classroom, he will generally choose to play with vehicles in preference to other toys and particularly likes to play with the train-set; using this, he will play alongside up to five other children, sharing the pieces and pushing trains around the track, under bridges, etc.

Laurence prefers to play without adult supervision and may move away from a chosen activity if an adult attempts to join in.

Laurence shows interest in what his classmates are doing, but can be persistent in approaching them inappropriately, apparently gaining pleasure from their responses.

Laurence shows some doll play, he will place a doll in a bed and give it a drink, he also uses objects on himself in play, e.g. will brush his own hair. Laurence has overcome his earlier fear of 'messy' play and will now prod dough, move his hands around in paint or corn flour mixtures and make marks with a loaded paintbrush.

Laurence enjoys tactile play with sand, although he uses this inappropriately, throwing it on the floor or over other children unless directed. He tends to eat other tactile materials (e.g. lentils) unless closely watched.

Laurence is able to pour water from one container to another, but in group water play he likes to drink the water or pour it on the floor or over a classmate.

Laurence shows amusement when another child misbehaves or is being reprimanded, by laughing infectiously.

Laurence will sit for the duration of most group activities, e.g. greeting circle, and is most interested in activities with a visual element, e.g. puppets.

Laurence needs adult help to join in musical activities, but is able to use simple percussion instruments. He has had a series of sessions with the music therapist and is always happy to leave the classroom with her.

IX *Factors in the child's environment which lessen or contribute to special educational needs*

(Due to an extended family holiday and some illness, Laurence has been absent on 41 out of a possible 93 days during his assessment period. This has affected the amount of input he has had and progress on his educational programme set at his initial conference).

The parental advisor has visited the home when the family has been there to give advice and information. The mother has attended parents' groups at school and both parents have been into the classroom. Laurence comes from a supportive home background and his parents are very involved in his activities. He presents a very similar picture at home to that at school.

Laurence becomes frustrated because of the lack of a garden and he therefore requires to be taken for walks on a very regular basis.

X *Summary of special educational needs*

1. Laurence has severe receptive and expressive communication difficulties.
2. Laurence has attention difficulties.
3. Laurence has mild delay in non-verbal cognitive skills and learning difficulties associated with 1.
4. Laurence has hand–eye coordination difficulties.

Section B

Aims of provision

1. *General curricular aims*

   Laurence requires a curriculum modified for a child with severe communication difficulties and associated learning difficulties. At present a nursery curriculum is appropriate. When he is 5 years, Laurence should have access to the National Curriculum at the appropriate level.

2. *Specific techniques or approaches*

   Laurence requires individual teaching of new skills. Tasks should be demonstrated initially, but presented in small steps; new skills to be generalised to a variety of situations with a variety of familiar adults.

3. *Programmes to meet stated needs*

   a. A programme to develop receptive and expressive communication skills.

   b. A programme to develop attention skills.

   c. A programme to develop cognitive abilities.

   d. A programme to develop hand–eye coordination.

4. *School environment*

   Laurence requires a structured environment in which routines and expected behaviors are clearly defined. Staff should be experienced in working with children with severe communication and associated learning difficulties.

Appendix 3

Behaviour Report 14/06/94

Laurence aged 5 years 4 months

Laurence has adapted well to the change in class since January. He participates well in most of the weekly activities and is aware of parts of the daily routine. He will often predict the next activity by removing and reading the correct timetable Compic symbol, e.g. drink/playtime/toast/dinner/home. However, he does not appear to be overly dependent on the routine and accepts changes to it.

Laurence continues to enjoy working with the adult in a 1:1 setting and sits for up to 30 minutes choosing what tasks he wants to do from his basket. His attention to tasks can be fleeting, particularly if there are other distractions in the class. He needs lots of encouragement to keep on task. He may try and task avoid by hugging the adult but will return to the task if looked at sternly.

Laurence has shown tendencies to become obsessed with particular objects or toys, e.g. particular chairs, a page in a book and shoes. He can become anxious if these objects are taken away. However, if he is distracted with a song or a tickling game while the object is removed he is happy. Although Laurence may still tap objects and tasks he has completed, these incidents have reduced.

Laurence seems to have become more confident and independent. He appears to be less dependent on gaining adult confirmation and approval when carrying out tasks at snack-time as reported in his last conference.

He continues to contribute verbally to class life by joining in with favourite songs and activities, choosing what to play with, repeating words and naming peers and objects in books and the classroom. Although he makes a range of non-specific vocalisations (particularly when undirected), Laurence's language has become more spontaneous and appropriate and less obsessive. He now rarely refers to big red buses and trains.

Laurence has recently developed a 'naughty' streak by carrying out particular actions in order to gain a reaction from the adult, e.g. climbing on the tables, running around the classroom and pulling down children's trousers. If the adult responds, he will laugh and continue to do it. He has become aware of the unacceptability of his actions and responds to the adult's disapproving facial expressions by saying 'no' to himself and stopping. Observations have shown that he tends to hug and kiss the hair of children who react most strongly to his approaches, although these incidents have decreased.

Self Occupation

Laurence will often sit and self occupy for periods of up to 20 minutes with favoured toys although he may sometimes get up and run around the classroom tapping his hand over his mouth and making vocalisations. He likes to rub textured materials over his mouth for sensation but will generally stop and return to his chair with a gestural prompt.

Play and Relationships

Laurence will sit alongside a peer at a table but has become more assertive, often refusing to share the equipment. He needs encouragement and direction to use different equipment, preferring toys he likes.

He has become increasingly aware of his surroundings and the people in it. He will now accept more physical contact on the adult's terms and will often initiate contact in the playground. With adult direction, Laurence will 'play' with children more appropriately in the playground, e.g. holding hands and going down the slide.

Recommendations

1. *Gaining attention/task avoidance tactics during work sessions*
   That the adult should remove all equipment from the table and tell Laurence quietly, but firmly, to sit down, before recommencing task.
2. *Obsessions with objects/mouthing objects*
   The adult should continue to distract him with a song or a game before taking the object away and directing him towards a more appropriate activity. When in the classroom, Laurence to place objects he mouths in appropriate place, e.g. bin or correct basket.

3. Laurence to continue to take part in cooperative activities with different children and contribute more verbally to class life.
4. To be encouraged to use a variety of play equipment appropriately, independently and share it with another child.

Appendix 4

Educational Psychologist's Report, dated 30/06/94

Laurence aged 5 years 4 months

This report is based on notes from Laurence's file, and an observation of Laurence in his classroom together with a discussion with his class teacher, which was held on 23.6.94.

Laurence's current learning environment
Laurence is in a group of 5 children all of whom have communication difficulties. His programme is demanding and highly structured, and he is required to be active and responsive for each part of the day with a carefully developed and stimulating developmental programme.

Laurence's strengths and difficulties
I observed Laurence in his group for 1 hour. When I arrived, they were having outside playtime, followed by a group activity where the children acknowledged each other, sang a song, passed a hat from one to the other, and chose the next partner. The other children then left to go on a bus trip, and Laurence was kept behind with another boy so that his teacher could show me what work she was doing with him. In this part of his day he had a social interaction game with the other boy, did some matching of letters, some work on comparisons, some colouring in, and then the two children had some toast.

The group now is using both Makaton signing, and also has clearly diagrammatic pictures to denote objects in the classroom, and activities during the day. His teacher says that the pictures have greatly aided the children's understanding of the routines of the day, as well as help their naming skills. Laurence is clearly happy to be in the group, and his teacher says there is a noticeable change in the way in which he responds to other children. He is now able to note when other children are displeased, although he is not always aware of when they are showing pleasant or happy expressions. A brief account of his various areas of functioning is as follows:

Personal/social:
Laurence knows the names and acknowledges all the different people in his group. He tends to have an obsession about one particular person, currently it is a non-teaching assistant in the group and prior to his entry to Whitefield, reports suggest that he has always been affectionate and cuddly with both his parents, and this is continued and he has now increased his repertoire of emotions with other people. During the session I watched, he was able to say which child had not yet had a turn. He appeared to be watching and noticing what was going on in the group for all the time I was there. He enjoyed a one to one game with another boy, but it appears that he doesn't yet have one particular friend within his group. Laurence is becoming more adaptable now to changes in routine, within his known environment. He does require advance warning and preparation for change, if transition is to be smooth.

I did not make enquiries about his independence skills in dressing and so on.

Language:
He uses signing, and refers to the pictorial cues, which are around the classroom to understand what is happening during the day. He uses single words, which he says in a quiet voice. He is able to match pictures, and can do exercises where he matches letters, to go underneath a picture, and can then say the name of the picture. He is just beginning to do work on comparison (at present big/little). His signing has lessened since the verbal communication has developed. Since he is still in a signing environment due to the nature of the group, he is able to use and develop signing as his own choice.

Gross Motor Functioning:
He is climbing and running and riding tricycles and is physically active. He enjoys physical movement. During play, he is rather unfocused, tending to flit from one thing to another.

Fine Motor:
This is his area of less development, according to my observation. He does have an ability to scribble, but is not yet drawing any recognisable

picture, and his scribble is not within defined boundaries. He can, however, draw upon request a straight line between two points. He is cutting with a pincer grip but is not yet using scissors.

The aims of his programme as I see it at present are:

1. To increase and develop his interactive skills with children.
2. To develop signing and verbal communication.
3. To develop his formal learning skills in a practical activity based setting.

Laurence is already making pleasing progress in his group. He is interacting more readily with other children, and is a watchful and observant boy of what is going on in the classroom. He is able to take turns, to choose, and to acknowledge other children in the group. He is at the single word utterances stage yet, and still dependent upon pictorial cues and the use of Makaton signing. Close liaison with teachers and speech therapist will help to extend his verbal communication. The highly organised nature of his present class group seems to be a big element in increasing his participation in the group and harnessing his high activity level. He prefers practical activities in the class, but loses concentration on more passive ones.

It may well be worth considering if possible now placing Laurence in a group of children who are more socially interactive, and who have more highly developed language skills. This should not be done, however, in my opinion at the cost of giving him a less stimulating or structured group than he is in at present.

His placement at Whitefield is an appropriate one, and he is in my view, making good progress and his current needs are being met.

Educational Psychologist.

Appendix 5

Laurence aged 8 years 3 months

Laurence enters the classroom happily and engages cooperatively with most classroom activities. He requires less adult supervision to remain seated during interactive group activities, e.g. drama, parachute games and story time. He continues to show increased interest in his surroundings and the people in it, often commenting if anyone if absent and the possible reason for it, e.g. 'Louise is sick. Louise gone hospital.' Although he relies on situational and gestural cues, he responds more consistently to a variety of adult instructions in functional settings. He continues to make clear choices of who he wants to interact with and is wary of some children inside and outside the classroom, often needing encouragement to interact with them. He is very amused if he or another child does something he knows they shouldn't!!

Although he can often be distracted if a child is upset, he generally shows less distress and will now often move away from threatening situations. If hurt by another child he may become anxious and hit out at others or cling to adults for comfort. If this happens he has been encouraged to talk simply about his and others emotions, e.g. '_____ is crying. _____ is sad.' 'It's finished.'

Laurence remains particularly fond of one child in the class, having transferred most of his attention from adults onto him. He will gain attention and show affection by touching him, hugging him excessively/ smelling his hair. Laurence will often initiate rough and tumble activities with him in the playground and soft play area but when undirected the play often escalates into lying on the floor, kicking and pulling hair. Both children enjoy these activities but have been encouraged to participate in more appropriate interactions, e.g. building towers in soft play, shaking hands to greet each other and holding hands to walk around school. He has also been encouraged to say 'sorry' if he kicks or hurts people, although minimal adult attention is often given for inappropriate behaviours. Laurence shows awareness of his actions and will comment on the adults' disapproving facial expression, e.g. 'No pulling _____ hair. It's naughty.' 'It's finished.' Laurence follows the daily timetable, turning over symbols of completed activities and showing and naming the symbol of the next activity to his class mates with adult direction. He has been encouraged to name the days of the week and develop a concept of the future, 'Tomorrow we are going to do _ it's Tuesday.' He responds to a structured learning environment, noticing the way the classroom has been set out and sitting in the correct area often spontaneously.

In 1:1 work sessions Laurence has been encouraged to complete all work tasks placed on the left and place finished tasks in a basket on the right. He knows he has finished when there is nothing on the left. He responds to the instruction 'hands down' if he engages in distracting behaviours, e.g. mouthing objects/tapping the table.

He finds working in groups of more than 2 difficult and often requires adult direction to remain on task as well as symbolic timetable to highlight the sequence of events.

His level of participation in pair work activities has increased, particularly if distractions are minimised by working in the 1:1 room. Again, compic symbol schedules add structure and anticipation to the sessions.

During undirected time Laurence may still engage in different behaviours to provide sensory experience, e.g. vocalising, running, mouthing/tapping objects.

He will generally respond to an adult redirecting him to another activity. The structured TEACCH method has helped Laurence to develop more productive ways of self-occupying. He is now able to complete a variety of activities following a 3-part compic symbol schedule every morning with minimal direction and has been working on completing up to 5 tasks set out in numbered baskets following a numbered schedule from 1–5. He will also sit for brief periods colouring over pictures, listening to music tapes and completing puzzles.

Behaviour strategies written at the Annual Review in 1996 have proved to be effective and will continue to be implemented as necessary with a few changes.

Change to Behaviour Strategy
1. Excessive hugging/smelling/holding hair.
- If appropriate time, adult to encourage Laurence to make

appropriate contact with child, e.g. say 'hello' and shake hands. Adult to say, 'It's finished' and redirect him towards another activity.

- If inappropriate time, adult to say nothing but redirect Laurence towards another activity.
- Adult to establish times to encourage Laurence to interact appropriately, e.g. morning circle, goodbye circle, soft play sessions, adventure playground.

2. *Incidents of distress.*

- When a child is distressed adult to comment on child's emotion explaining simply why they are 'sad' and reassure Laurence that they will be fine. Then engage him in an activity. If necessary withdraw Laurence from the situation to calm.
- When Laurence is hurt by another child adult to comment on Laurence's emotion, explaining simply why he is upset and comfort and reassure him that 'it's finished'. Then engage him in an activity or withdraw from the situation to calm and encourage him to express his feelings.

3. *Hitting/attempting to hit adults and children.*

- If Laurence is excessively rough with a child he should be withdrawn from the situation and looked at sternly by the adult. Before returning to activity Laurence to count to 10 then be encouraged to interact appropriately with the child and say 'sorry'.

Work Strategy

1. Laurence to continue to have set tasks handed out in bags on the left of the table. As each task is completed Laurence to place the task in his basket on the right. Laurence knows he has finished when there is nothing on the left.
2. If he distracts himself all materials should be removed and Laurence told 'hands down'.
3. When he has finished his work Laurence to be allowed a choice of activity and a smiley face.

Annual Review of Progress

GENERAL PROFILE

Laurence continues to be happy in school and remains an active member of the group. He responds well to a structured learning environment, generally sitting in designated areas for particular activities spontaneously. He shows increased interest in the environment and the people within it, often commenting if someone he likes is absent. He is particularly fond of one child, often initiating rough and tumble games with him. He continues to show affection by hugging or touching people and remains wary of some children. He has been encouraged to talk about his and others' emotions and withdraw himself from stressful situations.

COMMENTS ON ACHIEVEMENT OVER PREVIOUS YEAR AND GOALS FOR THE COMING YEAR

The Levels Of Achievement Have Not Been Confirmed By Statutory Procedures

Personal and Social Development

Laurence has a positive relationship with the adults and most children in the class. He can be excessively rough when playing with favoured children and has been encouraged to use more appropriate ways of interacting.

Laurence remains seated at snack and dinnertime and has been encouraged to eat more slowly and count to 10 before leaving the table. He has worked on 'giving' plates to children at snack time and then putting equipment in the sink afterwards. He is now able to respond to adult instructions to fetch named snack items from next door and has worked on asking other staff for equipment while directed by an adult, 'Books please, Louise.'

With the use of symbols Laurence is more focused and independent when dressing and undressing and makes a good attempt at undoing fastenings and putting clothes on the right way round. He now attempts to imitate an adult while brushing his teeth but prefers to suck off the toothpaste!

On shopping trips he can read up to 3 items on a shopping list then been encouraged to relay the information back to the adult.

Laurence has worked on developing more productive self-occupation skills and will now complete up to 4 tasks following a schedule with minimal direction.

Goals

• To continue asking for equipment from other classes.

- To extend the range of activities when completing self-occupation schedules.
- To practise doing up a range of fastenings.

Learning Skills

Laurence continues to enjoy work and although he may be distracted by materials or activities in the classroom he will still sit for up to 30 minutes at a time. He participates much better in a 1:1 setting or in pairs than in larger group, where he loses concentration more easily.

He continues to be motivated by praise on an activity of his choice and the smiley face reward system.

ENGLISH, INCLUDING ALL FORMS OF COMMUNICATION

Although Laurence still depends on situational and/or symbolic/ written cues to minimise distraction and aid his understanding and expression Laurence has made steady progress in work and functional situations. He remains very vocal and often accurately reproduces a range of familiar sounds, e.g. dogs, tube, trains. He is using longer phrases to comment on likes and dislikes, e.g. 'Don't like Nikki's car. Go shopping in Louise's car.' He has been encouraged to comment on what people are doing/wearing in photos. He recognises cross, happy and sad expressions and has been working on 'who/why' questions to explain people's emotions in pictures. With help he will often use 1–2 word answers. His understanding is improving and is able to tune into key words and identify the correct picture from a choice when given a short description. In pair work activities he has continued to work on his listening skills and now recognises more sounds during sound Lotto games/listening/feeling objects in a bag. Activities to extend his sight vocabulary have included word/sentence to picture matching using first 100 words vocabulary and forming 3 part sentences under photos using a variety of nouns, objects and verbs. Laurence remains motivated by pencil skill activities. He has been made to use his index finger to complete tasks before using a pencil to prevent him from rushing. He is more focused during tracking, tracing and overwriting activities but still presses too hard and needs more practice in these areas.

Goals

- To sequence photos of up to 4 parts to form a story.

- To identify 'What's wrong' looking at different photos.
- To extend sight vocabulary and complete sentences for meaning.
- To continue pre-writing skills.
- To be encouraged to transfer information from one place to another via home/school symbol diary.

MATHS

Laurence has made some progress in this area. He is now able to name and sequence numbers from 1–10 and will point and count amounts up to 5 with an adult when laid out from left to right. He will place up to 5 objects onto the correct cued numeral and has been working on counting amounts up to 5 into the adult's hand when shown a numeral. He has been working on overwriting numbers 1–5 using the correct starting point. Although he is inconsistent at recognising all colours he is able to match colour-coded words to corresponding colour pictures and has used a coloured dice to play a simple board game performing the action shown on the back of the corresponding coloured card.

With gestural and symbolic cues, Laurence is able to identify big/small objects.

Goals

- To work a number concept using numbers 1–10 and overwriting/copying.
- To work on the concept of simple addition using the concept of 1 more for numbers up to 10 in a work and functional setting.
- To identify the 'odd one out' in a series of shapes, colours, numbers.
- To name and use 2D shapes to construct simple pictures of objects and overdraw/undercopy 2D shapes.

SCIENCE

In our topic on the Environment Laurence helped to collect, name and sort objects found in the forest and explored the different textures and colours. In our topic on food he experienced and made preferences of different tastes and recorded his likes and dislikes on a sticker chart with adult help. He observed materials changing when heated and cooled by helping to make vegetable soup then experiencing the difference in appearance and taste of raw and cooked vegetables. He also took part in making ice-lollies, experiencing the texture and taste of unfrozen and frozen liquid.

Goal

• To observe the effect water has on a variety of materials in our current topic.

TECHNOLOGY

Laurence has used the 'Podd' computer programme to activate a character to perform various actions on the screen by pressing a variety of words on a concept keyboard overlay. He has also begun to choose and copy known verbs onto the screen using the QWERTY keyboard with adult help. During our food topic Laurence took part in a variety of food-making activities, being encouraged to follow simple written/symbolic recipes. He also used a range of kitchen equipment for different tasks. Laurence was often tempted to eat the ingredients during the preparation stage!

Goals

• To continue to have access to the computer to develop word recognition and formation.
• To use a variety of building equipment to copy simple structures.

CREATIVE

Laurence continues to show an interest in art activities and although he tends to rush ahead he is more aware of gluing/sticking within boundaries. He likes to use crayons to colour bold pictures and has been encouraged to use a variety of colours and stay within outlines, pressing more gently. In our food topic he enjoyed choosing and printing with fruit and vegetables. During singing sessions Laurence will make choices given symbolic/pictorial cues. He is able to sing parts of songs independently and his voice has become louder and clearer. In our food topic he made a shaker with help by filling an empty pot with dried beans and lentils and then used it to take part in some musical songs.

Goals

• To copy colour pictures of up to 3 parts.
• To use scissors to cut accurately along a variety of bold lines.

- To take part in weekly group music sessions with the music therapist.

PHYSICAL EDUCATION

Laurence takes an active part in all physical activities and generally waits his turn well. During apparatus sessions he will travel over equipment using different parts of his body following adult instructions and/or a model. During simple team games Laurence can become over-excited and often needs direction to keep him on task. He will make a good attempt at hitting a large ball with a bat up to 2 metres away and throwing ball underarm into a large container. Laurence has gained some confidence in the water but is still afraid of being out of his depth. Adults have been working on gradually extending the distance he swims back to the shallow end.

Goals

- To work on ball skills particularly with another child.
- To swim 1 length independently.

HUMANITIES

Laurence was encouraged to explore and observe the school, forest and shops in the vicinity in our topic on the environment. He has shown a great interest in photos displayed from the topic. He continues to follow the compic symbol timetable and has been working on naming and sequencing the days of the week and identifying particular activities done on certain days. At the end of each day he has been encouraged to talk about the activities 'he has done' and what he will do 'tomorrow'.

He recognises that some days are school days and some he stays at home.

Goals

- To look at and comment on photos of himself and other children taking part in activities in a specially compiled album.
- To visit the pond and seaside, looking at, collecting and displaying objec
ts and pictures related to days out in our water topic.

Appendix 6

Whitefield Schools and Centre

Behaviour Report — June 1999

Laurence aged 10 years 4 months

Laurence moved into a new class group in September 1998 with five members of his peer group and new members of staff. He did not appear to find this change difficult and quickly adapted to new routines. In February 1999, Laurence experienced another minor change in class groups and moved into the classroom next door with three familiar pupils and two members of staff whom he knows but has not worked with. Laurence found this change more difficult to tolerate and began to verbally protest at home about coming to school. He continued to work well in school but gradually began to show an increase in agitated, upset or over-excitable behaviour.

STAR charts monitoring Laurence's behaviour from January to March 1999 have identified four possible reasons for aggressive behaviour:

- Another child upset (29 incidents)
- Change in routine (39 incidents)
- Inappropriate contact — chinning, pulling hair, etc. (29 incidents)
- Wanting/not wanting an activity (9 incidents).

There have also been 39 incidents when the reason is not obvious to classroom staff.

In the period since the last Annual Review there has been an increase in aggressive behaviour and the incidents have also increased in length and severity as Laurence has become bigger and stronger.

387

Occasionally two adults have had to physically intervene to prevent Laurence hurting them or to enable him to calm down.

There has also been an increase in anxious and upset moods which sometimes Laurence is able to articulate by talking about his own behaviour, e.g. 'mustn't hit ... Laurence is very naughty ... is very cross with you', etc. However, sometimes this continuous talk continues the upset mood and adults find it difficult to redirect him to another topic. Occasionally adults have not been able to identify a reason for his upset.

Laurence has shown more difficulty tolerating a change of routine, prompting repeated questioning of adults and attempts to seek reassurance from adults. This is particularly in relation to his attendance at an after-school club and the form of transport home.

Laurence continues to seek out and constantly chin another pupil, he finds it very difficult to inhibit this behaviour and may require an adult to physically intervene.

Laurence is still greatly affected by other pupils' upset or excitable behaviour. Laurence himself becomes very excited and may attempt to hit or pull their hair. Sometimes he has difficulty understanding that he is not upset and requires an adult to indicate to him 'that it is not you'.

Laurence continues to respond well to 1:1 work and follows an independent work schedule with minimum adult direction. He prefers activities to be divided by a short time away from the classroom, e.g. in the playground outside the classroom, and will often request these breaks. He has limited self-occupation skills but will attempt to use equipment appropriately with adult direction. He has responded well to the concept of 'first ... then' in the classroom environment.

Behaviour recommendations
Generally:
- Adults continue to encourage Laurence to talk about and recognise positive aspects of his own behaviour by appropriate rewards, telling other adults, etc.
- Adults to minimise constant questioning by referring Laurence to written or symbolic list—tell Laurence talk about it one more time and then it's finished.
- Adults to continue to be vigilant when other pupils upset—continue to emphasise that it is not Laurence—explain it is an appropriate reason for upset.

- Adults to give Laurence choices, e.g. of activity to calm over-excited behaviour or opportunity to spend some time alone.
- Adults to continue to encourage Laurence to articulate what he wants if he initiates inappropriate contact with adults.

Specifically:
It was agreed at the conference not to give verbal attention to negative aspects of Laurence's behaviour. Tell him what he should be doing if necessary, e.g. hands down rather than don't pull hair, etc.

Appendix 7

St. John's R.C. School

Annual Review

Date of review: 28 November 2000
Laurence aged 11 years 9 months

Laurence joined St. John's School in Spring 2000. Laurence is currently in a class with six other children. It is staffed by one teacher and three classroom assistants. In addition Laurence receives input from other teaching staff working in the specialist areas. This enables Laurence to gain regular opportunities of 1:1 support.

English
Speaking and Listening
Laurence receives speech therapy on a weekly basis. He has worked well this year and he enjoys these lessons. His attention and listening skills have shown improvement through a variety of tasks, and he is generally more cooperative, having become more familiar with the structure of the sessions and his teacher.

Laurence needs frequent prompting to listen during group lessons. When he is being questioned, he looks very intently at the adult's mouth for a verbal prompt to help him give the correct response. Laurence is too quick to try and guess an answer rather than listen to, think and recall the information. Consequently, it becomes difficult to ascertain and assess how much he understands.

Laurence has taken part in many different activities to improve his listening skills. He tries hard when playing 'Round games' (e.g. 'I went shopping and I bought . . .', each child offering an item as well as listing suggestions made by the other children in the class). These turn-taking activities have been effective and Laurence has listened to his classmates and remembered up to 5 items in the correct order. However, he is not consistent in this task and he generally needs frequent reminders to focus and listen when the other children are speaking.

On a weekly basis Laurence relates his weekend events. Laurence's father has been supportive and he generally gives a written account of his experiences. Laurence recalls this information with encouragement and prompts. He is more forthcoming with the information, however he still tends to omit the majority of pertinent events. Instead he will talk about his usual routine (e.g. 'I went to Daddy's house'). Laurence needs encouragement to listen to his classmates in this situation.

Reading

Laurence has begun to follow the Oxford Reading Tree (ORT) programme. Laurence seems quite enthusiastic about reading these books, and he is currently on Stage 2 reading the supplementary books at this level, having completed the first 6 books ('Trunk Stories'). Laurence has been encouraged to gain a sight vocabulary of the key words and he is able to consistently recognise most of the key characters' names. In addition Laurence consolidates his understanding of the text by working on accompanying workbooks.

Laurence enjoys looking at books and he tends to choose this activity during any free time in the classroom. He likes to have another piece of equipment in his hands (usually some play plastic hangers) which he uses to tap each page as he looks through the book. Generally Laurence is good at returning the book to the shelf when it is time to move onto a different activity.

Laurence is working on letter recognition. He has gained some success in this skill and he can name some lower case letters (b, o, a, p, r, s, t and w). However, he is inconsistent when naming all other letters and he needs further practice. Once again Laurence is too quick to try and guess the answer rather than look at, think and recall its name (when he is guessing, Laurence usually says the letter 't').

Handwriting

Laurence has worked hard on his handwriting and he is becoming a lot more accurate when tracing over an adult's example. He needs reminders to keep on the lines and not to rush his work. He also needs prompts to use the correct starting points and follow the directional flow. Laurence continues to need practice tracing letters since he needs this guidance to ensure that he forms the letters properly.

Spelling and Creative Writing
On a weekly basis Laurence records his weekend news. He tends to describe his weekend events using one or two words. When recording his news he needs encouragement to place these key words into a sentence; however, he has recently shown improvement in this area. With adult assistance he will type it on the computer and read back what he has written using the 'Words With Symbols' programme. However, over the past term, Laurence has learnt a general patter to complete this task and he has been encouraged to exclude some of the more mundane routines occurring during the weekend and instead write about significant events. He continues to need prompting to offer this information.

Mathematics
Number:
Laurence is able to identify, read and order numbers up to 15. He has completed this task up to 20; however, he is inconsistent when completing a number line above 15 and he needs further practice to consolidate his understanding. With adult help he is encouraged to complete the task up to 30.

Laurence uses counters to add two numbers together up to 10. With help he counts out the correct number of counters for each number and then he combines them and recounts. He has also used a calculator to check his answers.

Shape, space and measure:
Laurence can consistently name triangle, square and circle. He usually names a rectangle as a square and he needs encouragement to note 2 longer and 2 shorter sides. He can also name a star and with verbal prompts a kite and oval. Laurence has recently begun work matching 3D shapes and will continue during the next year.

Laurence has completed work on biggest/smallest and longest/shortest. He can compare two objects with minimal prompts, and he needs further work to help him transfer this knowledge when comparing three objects. He has used Information Technology programmes, e.g. Tizzy, to help consolidate his understanding of these concepts.

Time:

Laurence has a good awareness of the daily timetable and he has been encouraged to note the symbols on our day board. He can name all the days in the week in order and the months of the year with occasional prompting. He has difficulties naming the months that key events take place (e.g. his birthday, Christmas, Bonfire Night, Easter).

Using and applying:

Laurence uses and applies mathematics in a variety of ways. He has had weekly practical experiences dealing with money. He is able to give lps to pay for an item up to 10p, although he needs to be reminded to stop at the given price. Laurence has been given a mixture of lps and 2ps and he has not yet realised the difference in the value of the coins. He continues to need further practice in this skill. Laurence is consistent when naming all coins to 20p and he needs more experiences to gain the same success with 50p and £1.

Science

Laurence has completed work on 'Sound' and he has shown an understanding that there are many different kinds of sounds from many sources, and that sounds are heard when they enter the ear. Laurence explored that sounds are made when objects vibrate and he observed the movement of a guitar string and felt the tremor on a cymbal. He was also encouraged to note through practical experiments that the pitch and loudness of sounds produced by some vibrating objects can be changed.

Laurence achieved most of the targets set for him whilst working on 'Electricity'. He showed a good understanding that many everyday appliances use electricity. He has constructed simple circuits involving batteries, wires, bulbs and buzzers. He appears to know that electrical devices will not work if there is a break in the circuit, and that a complete circuit including a battery or power supply is needed to make electrical devices work. He has observed the uses of switches and he has demonstrated how they can be used to control electrical devices.

During the Summer (2000) Laurence was working on Living processes and Living things. With help Laurence has sorted food into different categories (e.g. food from animals; food from plants; fruit and vegetables; cereals; milk and dairy products). He has been encouraged to note that eating the right types and amount of food will help to keep healthy. Laurence has also experienced the effects of exercise (e.g. warming of the body; increase of the heart rate). He has been encouraged to understand that exercise has an important role in healthy living.

Laurence worked well when making a picture of a skeleton. He pointed to the head, ribs, hand and foot bones without prompts.

Geography

'People at Work' was one of the topics covered in the Spring term (2000). It enabled Laurence to familiarise himself with staff in the school, since the first activities involved identifying the people who help us daily. Laurence was introduced to the people who work in the school (teachers and classroom assistants who help the children in classes and subject areas), and also those who help indirectly (e.g. the secretary). With some prompting Laurence could identify the emergency services and the jobs they perform. He also helped to identify most of the jobs of the people in the local village and using pictures, he identified people at work and the job in progress. Laurence has also taken part in drama activities, acting out role plays for some occupations.

Laurence also completed work on the other topic covered in the Spring Term—'The Street'. Laurence was able to identify many human features (e.g. traffic lights, post box, bus stops, etc.), and he was encouraged to use geographical terms to describe his surroundings (e.g. road, shops, stations, river, bridge, etc.). Laurence has also been encouraged to become more aware of road safety and he is prompted to identify safe places to cross busy roads. He needs practice and further experiences to increase his awareness of the dangers on the roads.

Laurence enjoyed 'The Seaside' topic and he has looked at maps to help him understand that the seaside is found in coastal areas and the colouring on a map is yellow. He listened to stories about the seaside and he showed an interest in the variety of photos shown depicting summer holiday scenes, including some of his own, which he allowed his classmates to look at too. He helped to conduct a survey to identify where pupils and staff went on their last holiday and with support he presented it in graphical form. To consolidate his understanding of the environment, Laurence went on a trip to South-end with his class. He enjoyed his day out and he was very well behaved.

History

During our 'Shops and Shopping' topic, Laurence has been encouraged to note how shopping areas and chores have changed through time. He has looked at the key features of a shop built a long time ago and with support he has made comparisons with modern shops, identifying the similarities and differences between physical features, stock, services and delivery methods. Laurence has also looked at old coins, and with help, he has completed work sheets to observe the changes of money from 1900 through to 2000. He has also looked at other street furniture and he has been encouraged to note how they have changed in the last 100 years.

As previously mentioned, Laurence enjoyed 'The Seaside' topic and this was also evident in his History work. He has been encouraged to find out about holidays in the past from a variety of sources, including photos, written accounts and by asking questions of an adult. He has been prompted to recognise that some things change and others stay the same and with help he identified activities which have been experienced throughout the last century (e.g. building, sandcastles, swimming). Laurence also enjoyed experiencing seaside-related activities from two different times (watching a Punch and Judy show and visiting a seaside location).

Self Help Skills

Laurence is capable of doing many tasks independently. He needs little supervision at lunch times (occasional reminders not to drink too much water and not to eat food directly from the serving dishes) and he will help at snack times. He can dress and toilet himself without any help. However, he does require help with shoelaces and he is currently working on crossing the laces to form the first knot.

Approximately one day a week Laurence becomes the 'helper of the day' in which he will carry out tasks for the teacher (e.g. taking the register to the office, asking for the keys for the Art room, getting a drink prepared for snack time etc.). These tasks vary; however, Laurence seems to enjoy this post of responsibility and he is usually eager to please.

Music

Laurence has music once a week. During the last year he has covered the musical elements of duration, dynamics and tempo.

Laurence participates with encouragement in music. He enjoys playing the percussion instruments. He has an excellent sense of rhythm and can accompany songs and music with a steady beat. He listens carefully when we are singing and sometimes will join in. He also seems to enjoy listening to a variety of music.

RE

Laurence tries very hard in RE. With adult reminders he is able to stay on task for short periods of time and with this help the work produced can be quite presentable.

Laurence enjoys his time in the Prayer Room awaiting his turn to receive the 'message' from the Holy Book. His smile at this time is reward enough. Hopefully as Laurence matures a little more he can begin preparation for the Sacrament of Holy Communion.

Information and Communication Technology

The emphasis has been to make the keyboard and mouse familiar to Laurence and to try and provide him with enjoyable experiences, so that it will stimulate his interest and naturally extend his skills.

Laurence did struggle to interact or respond appropriately to a variety of software, but gradually improvements are being made. Laurence's targets for the following year are to build on Laurence's skills.

Design and Technology

Laurence has been given the opportunity to develop his Design and Technology capability, while working through practical projects within a modified National Curriculum. These projects titles will include Mechanisms, Structures, Energy, Mouldable Materials and Electricity. Using various materials and equipment, including Plastic, Wood and Construction kits.

Laurence is working towards Level 1 in Design and Technology resistant materials using Key Stage 1 programme of study.

With encouragement and one to one instruction Laurence has had the opportunity to:

- Take part within a group discussion.
- Select materials to complete a task.

- Select tools to complete a task.
- Assemble parts of a construction kit.
- Applied finishing techniques to project.
- Evaluate finished project within a group discussion.
- Followed safety instructions in the workshop.

Laurence is able to reach the shorter term objectives which are set for him.

PE
Laurence has made good progress in many areas of this curriculum. He has developed in terms of commitment to activities and his relationships with his peers and adults. His gross motor movements are steadily progressing, being able to run, jump, twist, turn, change direction and speed, all with good control and quality of those movements.

He can roll, slide, climb and balance well. He has well-coordinated ball skills. He can bounce and catch medium-sized balls with both hands, also being able to use both hands simultaneously and/or alternately when bouncing his preferred activity ball, a basketball. His control here is very good, adapting well in each given situation. He is developing his ability to cope better with changes to his environment and with changes to personal relationships within his learning group dynamics.

Behaviour, Social and Emotional Development
Initially, Laurence experienced difficulties settling into his new school environment. He regularly (3–4 times a week) displayed many inappropriate behaviours, including hair pulling, kicking, hitting and spitting directed towards both staff and other children. During these times Laurence was removed from the situation and given time to calm down. When he returned to the classroom he was very aware of any harm that had been done and he was encouraged to apologise. Although there appeared no obvious triggers, Laurence was generally very tense during his first term. He would often comment before he acted (e.g. 'mustn't pull hair'), and consequently when he did verbalise in this way, he was quickly engaged in an activity to try and distract his attention.

Steadily there has been an improvement in Laurence's behaviour. Although he continues to display aggressive behaviour, these incidents are occurring a lot less frequently (1–2 times a fortnight). He tries hard to control his outbursts and he is praised and rewarded for his efforts. Laurence seems more relaxed in the classroom, although he still has days when he is agitated or upset. Laurence can be quite excitable at times and he needs reminders to 'calm down'.

Laurence benefits from a smaller class and high staff-to-pupil ratio. He has shown some progression in all areas of the curriculum, and this is due to his willingness to partake in lessons and the improvement in his general behaviour. Laurence is a well-liked member of the class who is a pleasure to teach.

Music Therapy Report

Music therapy is a recognised intervention for children with ASD. As a non-verbal means of communication, it is valuable for those whose verbal language is impaired and inadequate to express moods and feelings. It has the potential to make contact and build relationships with children who avoid other modes of communication, for several distinct reasons.

Music therapy is non-confrontational, allowing sounds to be exchanged without the need to observe the conventions of verbal conversation. On the other hand, once a relationship has been established, musical activities can be specifically chosen to motivate the development of these conversational skills, either in musical or verbal terms, and to offer structures for shared activities, which can increase understanding.

Music can reflect and contain difficult feelings such as anger and anxiety so that they do not disrupt the relationship, or more stable and calming music can be offered, in order to focus attention and encourage relaxation. Finally, the 'play' aspect of music therapy can circumvent resistance to more didactic approaches, and foster the development of imagination and creativity, which may be limited or absent in autistic children.

Laurence's music therapy sessions started in January. He does not display the full range of difficulties mentioned above. His verbal skills are developing, and the instances of echolalia are usually context-relevant, for example 'proxy' remarks reproducing those he has received from adults. He has from the start been able to receive information, verbal or musical, from the therapist, though only inter-mittently and has developed a degree of trust based on growing familiarity with the therapy situation and activities.

There have been no emotional difficulties beyond an initial and understandable caution and need to withdraw at times, and calming music has been used, not to discourage such withdrawal, but to acknowledge it as a reasonable coping strategy, provided it is not too persistent.

Developing music from Laurence's 'singing'
The word has been put in quotes because although his dreamy vocalisations are sweet and musically suggestive this may well not be their main intention. At first they coincided with his periodic withdrawal from playing and interacting with me, so it seemed more appropriate to support them than to try to develop a dialogue with them.

In two sessions in May the 'singing' occurred while playing with an instrument rather than while avoiding instruments, and also seemed to be more related in pitch to my supportive accompaniment. The next week it alternated and contrasted with complaining spoken remarks, and in June when it seemed once more to be a form of retreat I accompanied with quiet calming music. In July his singing seemed to increase if I echoed it, and he seemed to be aware and content that I was doing so, although he would not allow me to develop a turn-taking dialogue. On our return in September, prolonged singing felt once more like avoidance, and after first going along with it, I decided to override and ignore it when necessary. Since then it has diminished, mainly because of the increase in other activities to be described.

Exploring ways to develop our relationship through improvised playing
Laurence at first played instruments mostly in random rather quick succession without regard to me, but did briefly give eye-contact during cymbal playing and was able to accept a limited amount of guidance and prompting. As his early displeasure at being with me and away from his class fluctuated, this was reflected both in an alternation between steady rhythmic playing and a-rhythmic fiddling and between intelligible speech and 'grizzling'. By February he was looking at me to see my reaction to his cymbal playing, and was able to play steadily for longer with suitable musical support, and to accept suggestions to play different instruments.

At this point a lengthy period of mildly 'difficult' behaviour started, consisting of inappropriate touching of my hair and inappropriate treatment of instruments. I was sometimes able to divert the touching into more appropriate forms, such as the clapping game Laurence had already introduced and shown me he liked, and when he suddenly sat on my lap I treated this dramatically, first acknowledging his 'baby' self and needs by rocking him and singing a lullaby, then singing 'but now you're a big boy', whereupon he stood up.

It is an interesting question how far I should use music to distract Laurence from a socially undesirable activity and how far I should instead try to give the activity a musical/dramatic context in which deeper meanings (if any) can be explored by us both. Laurence showed what he understood to be my expectations when he rushed through playing two instruments to placate me before asking to leave. In reality, I intend that he and not I should choose what to say musically, and how.

In May Laurence seemed calmed by being allowed to sit or lie on the cupboard to a soothing accompaniment, and shortly afterwards we were able to have some lively interactions on drum and keyboard. The following week I tried to make him aware that my music mirrored his state by playing quietly for his lying down and louder as he started to explore an instrument. In that session he progressed to initiating a glissando (slide) on two pitched percussion and then a sustained drum improvisation. It was becoming clear that it is important to allow his musical advances to occur in their own time.

Dismantling a xylophone was dealt with by helping him to reassemble it (twice), but having had this 'protest' neutralised he pleaded headache—I responded by singing a sympathetic song about his headache. At all times it felt important that I avoided being drawn into any sort of confrontation which Laurence might find either rewarding or possibly distressing.

In June, although he was allowed to lead in the sense of choosing and changing instruments, moving the action round the room, etc., he was more prepared to follow musically in the sense of imitating my pitches while face to face sharing a xylophone and my rhythms when sharing a drum. There was a general increase in music making by this time, only occasionally interrupted by the urge to keep changing instruments or to abuse them, and it became easier to play with him.

After the Summer break some of the developing organisation seemed at first to have gone from his playing, and I decided he might benefit from greater use of a more structured and directive approach (see next section). At times I could only interact effectively by sharing the instruments he chose, which was difficult in the case of the automatic keyboard effects. Singing about his drum and xylophone playing helped to sustain it, and resisting his attempts to take over the whole of the shared keyboard led to a partial acceptance of turn-taking.

Repertoire for more structured activities and interactions
In Laurence's first session it was encouraging that phrase endings in my (unfamiliar) song were met by clearer beating on his part, suggesting some awareness of musical structure. He sang along with the (familiar) 'Rainbow' song and showed his understanding of the (unfamiliar) goodbye song by quietening expectantly, and eventually by asking for the song when he wanted to go, usually at the appropriate time, and once by accompanying it in time on instruments. Once in July, he greeted the familiar tune with the question, 'stay here?' — not wishing to leave after a session he had enjoyed.

I devised several new, repetitive songs to try and support playing activities, which I did not find suitable opportunities to follow up. In March one such repeating song led to accurate imitation of my cymbal beating and another to quiet vocal contributions. In May I used a repeating song while we re-assembled the xylophone, contrasting with chaotic music as Laurence dismantled it.

A turn-taking song with a single tambourine was first treated with caution, but gradually welcomed, although at first he preferred to be the person actually holding the instrument. By May he could execute it even if I moved the tambourine around in the air between each phrase. He remained erratic about the starting points of phases, but precise about finishing on time, which is clearly supported by the accompanying song.

He welcomed this activity on his return in September, giving good eye-contact, and filled in odd words if I omitted them. Similarly a song-supported march across the room to bash the cymbal was first watched, but since March readily imitated, and still enjoyed. Eventually he sang along with it, and even introduced the song himself, presumably to request the activity. The clapping game (probably originally a song) which he himself introduced may have lost its appeal when I tried to reintroduce it because it was already too familiar.

The key to further development of our relationship and Laurence's understanding of different forms of interaction seems likely to be balancing familiar musical structures, capable of flexibility, with encouraging freer improvisation, relaxation and listening, always being guided by his mood.

J. Strange SRAsT (M)
Music therapist

Appendix 8

Summary of Progress

Laurence aged 12 years 10 months

Behaviour, Social and Emotional Development
Laurence has made a great effort to improve his behaviour within the school environment. Episodes of hair pulling, kicking, hitting and spitting are diminishing and during this term, Laurence has shown a greater maturity and improved self-control. He continues to verbalise undesirable behaviour (e.g. 'pull hair'); however, these threats are rarely acted upon, and with verbal encouragement he will 'calm down'.

Although Laurence is working hard eradicating inappropriate behaviours, he has developed new behaviours, which he displays mainly in specialist areas. These take the form of tearing paper, books and urinating in inappropriate places (playground and gym).

Laurence appears to tear paper at times of heightened anxiety (e.g. when another child's behaviour is being addressed). Recently Laurence has been given a verbal reminder before entering a lesson and, so far, these incidences are not as frequent. Laurence has urinated in the gym and on the playground on four different occasions. Through questioning, Laurence appears to know that he should not do this and he names the 'toilet' an appropriate place to urinate. Most of these incidences occurred early on this term and there has not been a repeated performance for approximately six weeks.

Laurence can be quite an emotional boy. He finds certain situations difficult to cope with (another child being corrected, changes in the timetable). During these times Laurence's behaviour can deteriorate; however, he is finding greater self-control with verbal reminders and reassurance. He continues to have days when he is agitated, tense or upset, although his general demeanour is a lot calmer and relaxed. Since July 2001 Laurence's classmates and some staff have changed. He is aware of these changes and has adapted well to his new situation.

Laurence has made a significant improvement in his interaction skills. He continues to follow a programme of work in the soft room and he has begun to initiate interaction with select members of the class. Once again, Laurence appears comfortable with the routine of the session and he works well in this environment. Laurence has also transferred these skills into the classroom and he has approached other children and initiated conversation. However, this does need careful supervision, since Laurence appears to struggle to act appropriately to express his feelings for his friends.

In the classroom Laurence is generally well behaved and compliant to adults' requests. He experiences difficulties coping when working with 1:1 support for English and Maths and he will often verbally object. However, he does complete his work once the initial objection has been noted, and with lots of encouragement and praise works towards his targets. Laurence has been on many class outings where he has been exceptionally good. He is a pleasure to take out on these occasions.

Self Help Skills

Laurence continues to assist the teacher when he is 'helper of the day'. He carries out tasks for the teacher (e.g. taking the register to the office, asking for keys for the mini buses, getting a drink prepared for snack time, etc.) and he completes those tasks with minimum of fuss or help from an adult.

Laurence is an independent young man who enjoys doing things for himself. He still needs some supervision at lunch times to give occasional reminders not to eat food from other people's plates; however, these incidents are less frequent.

Laurence has practised hard tying his shoelaces and he is gaining success forming the first knot without any physical prompts. He also is much more aware of putting his socks on correctly and before he attempts to complete this task he will say, 'Heel goes to the back.' Once he is verbally reassured he puts on his socks without any further help.